CONTENTS

CW01457706

	Page
Who's Who in Scotland's Gardens	2
Message from Scotland's Gardens President	3
List of Sponsors	4
Message from Scotland's Gardens Chairman	5
Message from Guidebook Sponsor	7
What Happens to the Money Raised?	8

Beneficiaries

Maggie's Cancer Caring Centres	9
The Queen's Nursing Institute Scotland	10
The Gardens Fund of the National Trust for Scotland	11
Perennial	12

Scotland's Gardens/Brightwater Holiday Tours	13
Fife Diamond Garden Festival	14 - 15
Duntreath Garden Show	16 - 17
Ardmaddy	18 - 19
New Gardens for 2012	20 - 23
Snowdrop Openings	49

Gardens Open: on a Specific Date	**50 - 62**
Gardens Open: on a Regular Basis	**63 - 65**
Gardens Open: by Arrangement	**66 - 68**
Plant Sales	**69**

Map of Districts	70
General Information and Guide to Symbols	71

Garden Listings by District A-Z	**72 - 271**

Index to Gardens	272 - 275
Index to Advertisers	276
Order Form for "Gardens of Scotland" 2013	277
Opening Your Garden' Form	279

Printed by J Thomson Colour Printers   Maps by The XYZ Digital Map Company

WHO'S WHO IN SCOTLAND'S GARDENS

PRESIDENT
HRH The Duchess of Rothesay

VICE PRESIDENTS
Mrs R Hunt   The Hon Mrs Macnab of Macnab DL
Mrs M Maxwell Stuart

EXECUTIVE COMMITTEE
Chairman   Mrs Tricia Kennedy*
Deputy Chairman   Mr Mark Hedderwick*
Honorary Treasurer Mr Peter Yellowlees*

Mrs Sarah Barron   Lady Mary Callander
Mr Simon Edington*   Lady Erskine
Mrs Sarah Landale   Lady Lister-Kaye
Mr David Mitchell   The Hon Mrs R Noel-Paton
Mrs Minette Struthers*   Mr James Wardrop OBE DL
Mrs Tinkie Welwood

*Also a member of the Finance Committee

Co-opted members of the Finance Committee
Mr Richard Burns   Mr Nigel Pollock
Mr Max Ward

DIRECTOR
Mr Paddy Scott

ADMINISTRATORS
Mr Ray Browne
Ms Hazel Reid
Mrs Fiona Sloane

42a North Castle Street,
Edinburgh EH2 3BN
T: 0131 226 3714
E: info@scotlandsgardens.org
W: www.scotlandsgardens.org

BANKERS
Adam & Company plc, 22 Charlotte Square, Edinburgh EH2 4DF

SOLICITORS
Turcan Connell, Princes Exchange, Earl Grey Street, Edinburgh EH3 9EE

AUDITORS
Douglas Home & Co, 47-49 The Square, Kelso TD5 7HW

ISSN   0967-831X
ISBN   978-0-901549-26-6

SCOTTISH
CHARITY NO
SC011337

As the proud President of Scotland's Gardens, I am delighted to welcome you to the 81st edition of its Guidebook. Over the past 80 years, Scotland's Gardens has become an excellent means of raising funds for countless worthy charities, whilst giving huge pleasure to so many garden enthusiasts. The past three years have seen record sums being raised, thanks to the magnificent efforts of the growing band of private garden owners, ably supported by their dedicated volunteers and members of the public who return year after year.

It is wonderful that so many diverse gardens now open for Scotland's Gardens (including several in Shetland), and it is particularly encouraging that the small gardens and village openings are so very popular. I feel sure that 2012 will be another record year for Scotland's Gardens, and that more visitors than ever will be able to enjoy the delights of these remarkable gardens.

Camilla

SPONSORS

We would like to acknowledge and thank the following organisations that will be sponsoring Scotland's Gardens in 2012. Their support is invaluable and enables us to maximise the funds we give to our beneficiary charities.

Investec Wealth & Investment

Corney & Barrow

D C Thomson & Co

Lycett, Browne Swinburn Douglas Ltd

Johnstons

Savills (L&P) Ltd

The Edinburgh International Conference Centre

Maxxium UK

Escrivo Internet Consulting

In addition we would like to say how grateful we are to the many private donors who have given us their support.

CHAIRMAN'S MESSAGE

How time goes, already I am almost at the end of my term as Chairman. Much has happened over this time – a new information database and the ability to put garden information straight into it, how did we ever survive without it? A new website, already in the process of being updated again; splendid information packs for new garden owners; substantial sponsorship and to cap it all a new look that I hope and believe will bring us to the attention of a wider audience.

Last winter was another difficult time with long periods of deep frost and deep snow which saw the demise of our Barn Owls at the farm and of a great number of shrubs in the garden -countered by delight at the astonishing vigour of some supposedly borderline hardy herbaceous which performed as never before. After a hot April we spent most of the next four months feeling as though we had got stuck in March. Fear not, the famously redoubtable garden owners and garden visitors of Scotland may have cursed a little, but busily have produced some very good totals. As I write now, in October, having had three record years in a row, our 2011 figures look hopeful for a matching of last year's splendid result.

It has always been a pleasure visiting your gardens and I plan to continue to do so, still so many to see! In March 2012 I will hand over the mantle of Chairman to Mark Hedderwick, presently Deputy Chairman. I can do no better than to wish him as happy a time as I have enjoyed being involved with Scotland's Gardens, especially the last five years as your Chairman.

Trish Kennedy

Mrs Trish Kennedy
Chairman

⊕ Investec
Wealth & Investment

Tending to your future

Talk with an Investec Wealth & Investment Manager about making the most of your assets and savings, and you could soon see your family's financial future begin to take shape.
Our specialist teams manage over £12.7 billion* on behalf of our clients, seeking the best and most tax-efficient returns on their capital. And with a network of 11 offices across the UK, we are well placed to offer insight and expert advice on your investments, pensions or other financial matters. We believe great relationships start with a conversation, so why not give us a call?

For further information, please contact:

Fenella Maclean   **0131 226 5000**
fenella.maclean@investecwin.co.uk

Stuart Light   **0141 333 9323**
stuart.light@investecwin.co.uk

investecwin.co.uk

Out of the Ordinary™

The value of your investments may go down as well as up and you might not get back the money you've put in.

Individuals • International • Charities • Financial Advisers • Court of Protection

*as at 31 March 2011. Member firm of the London Stock Exchange. Member of NYSE Liffe. Authorised and regulated by the Financial Services Authority. Investec Wealth & Investment Limited is registered in England. Registered No. 2122340. Registered Office: 2 Gresham Street, London EC2V 7QP. Offices at: Belfast Cheltenham Edinburgh Glasgow Guildford Leeds Liverpool London Manchester Reigate Sheffield

Welcome to your Scotland's Gardens Guide for 2012

Investec Wealth & Investment, until recently known as Rensburg Sheppards, has a long and proud association with the Scotland's Gardens Guide and, as a principal sponsor, we wish you many pleasant garden visits with this detailed and handy guide at your disposal.

This book's pages are a testament to the extraordinary work and organisational skills of around 200 volunteers who liaise with garden owners across 27 districts to ensure the success, and smooth running, of Scotland's Gardens.

Then of course there is the large number, more than 200 in fact, of charities that directly benefit from proceeds generated by the organisation. Funds raised are distributed to the charities supported by Scotland's Gardens, ranging from The Queen's Nursing Institute Scotland and The Gardens Fund of The National Trust of Scotland, to Maggie's Cancer Caring Centres.

There is obviously a tremendous amount of effort and good work going on behind the scenes and we hope that your knowing this serves to add even more enjoyment to your tours of the gardens.

Should you like to know more about us, and the expertise we offer, please visit **www.investecwin.co.uk**

Jonathan Wragg
Chief Executive
Investec Wealth & Investment

Out of the Ordinary™

Investec
Wealth & Investment

WHAT HAPPENS TO THE MONEY RAISED?

All garden owners who participate in the Scotland's Gardens programme are able to nominate a charity of their choice to receive 40% of the funds raised at their openings. 224 different worthy charities will be supported in this manner in 2012 and these vary from small local ones to several large well known organisations. Examples include:

- Highland Hospice
- Leuchie House
- Red Squirrel Survival Trust
- The Stroke Association
- Erskine Hospital
- Camphill Village Trust
- Appin Village Hall
- St. Columba's Hospice
- Arran Youth Foundation

- Children 1st
- Coulter Library Trust
- World Wildlife Trust
- Cancer Research Scotland
- Macmillan Cancer Support
- Motor Neurone Disease Scotland
- Dogs for the Blind
- Combat Stress
- British Heart Foundation

60%, net of expenses, of the funds raised at each garden is given to Scotland's Gardens beneficiaries:

- Maggie's Cancer Caring Centres
- The Queen's Nursing Institute Scotland
- The Gardens Fund of the National Trust for Scotland
- Perennial

Information on these organisations is provided on the following pages.

Several garden owners who open their garden on a regular basis and generously support Scotland's Gardens give a donation and the net sum is split between Scotland's Gardens beneficiaries.

In this book details of the charities nominated by the Garden Owners are provided and those gardens giving a donation are also indicated.

BENEFICIARY MESSAGES

maggie's

You can't miss Maggie's centres, beautifully designed and conveniently located on hospital grounds across Scotland. There's no entrance policy - anyone affected by cancer can come in. But what happens when you come along? Complementing NHS cancer centres across the country, Maggie's provides a unique approach to cancer that, at its simplest, can be described by 'calmness, clarity and a cup of tea.'

Calmness comes from the relaxing atmosphere at our centres. They're warm, friendly, informal places, full of light and open spaces, and with a big kitchen at their heart on the inside. And outside, the inspirational design of our gardens provide a soothing, calming refuge from the stress of dealing with hospitals, waiting rooms, and sometimes even the overbearing concern of friends and family.

The experts who work at Maggie's give our visitors some clarity. We'll listen to your questions and your concerns and provide useful, practical information. We'll help you take a big deal like cancer and break it down into smaller, more digestible chunks.

And a cup of tea. Because Maggie's is a place where you can feel at home along with other people who are experiencing cancer or who have experience of cancer. People who are happy to chat if you want, or leave you alone if you want. Come in, put the kettle on and spend some time reading or thinking or sitting with others who know what you're going through.

Picture: Maggie's newest centre at Gartnavel General Hospital, Glasgow.

So calmness, clarity and a cup of tea – that's what we do. That's the Maggie's approach to cancer, an approach that we want to continue to improve and grow to make the biggest difference personally at a scale that can make the biggest difference nationally.

Thank you for your help in bringing our unique approach to cancer to as many people across Scotland and the rest of the UK as possible.

Please call 0300 123 1801 or visit **www.maggiescentres.org** for more information.

THE QUEEN'S NURSING INSTITUTE SCOTLAND
Patron: Her Majesty The Queen
31 Castle Terrace, Edinburgh EH1 2EL
Tel: 0131 229 2333 Fax: 0131 228 9066
Registered Scottish Charity No: SC005751

The QNIS is a registered independent charity. The main aim is to promote excellence in Community Nursing in Scotland. QNIS has a long relationship with Scotland's Gardens and is enormously grateful for the financial support it receives from SG, enabling nurse-led projects to be undertaken throughout Scotland. The Projects Co-ordinator provides practical support for nurses to develop project proposals and ultimately to disseminate learning and good practice from projects.

QNIS works closely with the NHS and the professional bodies involved in the support, training and further education of Community Nurses. The NHS has ever-increasing demands and regardless of how worthy the cause cannot meet every demand.

QNIS is a Charity governed by Council. The day to day business is managed by the Nurse Director with the help of a small dedicated administrative team. As a non-political organisation QNIS is uniquely placed to listen to and support nurses working at grass roots level.

The work of QNIS can be summarised as follows:

- Raises awareness to influence policy and decision-making at local and national level

- Supports the professional development of nurses by providing a QNIS Fellowship programme, education grants and research fellowships

- Organises conferences and workshops on current Community Nursing issues throughout Scotland

- Addresses the welfare needs of retired Queen's Nurses (pensions, special grants, holidays, newsletters, annual gatherings)

- Funds innovative Community Nurse-led projects to improve patient care

Recent examples of projects awarded funding include:

Pilot: Health Promoting Residential Unit in Renfrew
This project is working with staff and young people to encourage a health-promoting environment for this vulnerable group of people.

Enhancing Community Nursing Research Capacity
A research fellow completed training in Australia to become an accredited trainer for the Joanna Briggs Institute and will be encouraging Community Nurses to expand the evidence base for Community Nursing.

Developing and testing a dignity-conserving intervention delivered by Community Nurses for people with advanced cancer at the end of life.
A Community Nurse in Oban is working with Dundee University to develop and test the effectiveness of a tool that aims to improve care for patients at the end of life.

The contribution of perceived stress in stroke.
This research project aims to build on emerging evidence around the role of perceived stress in stroke, to develop a screening tool for Community Nurses.

A VERY BIG THANK YOU – to Scotland's Gardens, the organisers, garden owners and the visiting public. QNIS is extremely grateful for your support in enabling enthusiastic nurses to lead innovative projects and share new knowledge to improve patient care.

the National Trust for Scotland
a place for everyone

On behalf of the teams and volunteers looking after the National Trust for Scotland's gardens, I would like to thank all associated with Scotland's Gardens for their ongoing support to the Trust in general and its gardens in particular. We are grateful not only for your financial support, which enables us to take forward many exciting garden projects and developments, but also for the help you provide us with in so many other ways.

At times of great change in the world, the challenging economic situation and the vagaries of the Scottish weather, including an exceptionally cool and wet 2011, we are heartened by the high numbers of visitors going to gardens and the encouragement they give to our respective organisations.

During 2011, 25 Trust gardens were opened on 37 occasions in support of the Scotland's Gardens with events such as guided walks, tours, demonstrations and workshops.

In 2012, we plan to host a special evening talk on roses at Drum Castle in addition to its open day; at Fyvie Castle there will be a tour of the garden of Scottish fruits followed by a meal. At Brodie Castle there will be tours of the national daffodil collection in mid April; in June, Crathes Castle garden will celebrate its 60th anniversary in Trust care and this will be marked by special garden events, and; Broughton House will celebrate artist E.A. Hornel's birthday on 17 August with a garden open day.

Our School of Heritage Gardening, in part supported by Scotland's Gardens, provides a high quality framework for training across the Trust's gardens with student placements at Threave Garden, Kellie Castle, Inverewe and Geilston House Garden. It is anticipated that additional student placements will be established at other Trust gardens in the coming year.

In spite of relatively difficult times, our gardens have continued to flourish as our staff and volunteers work hard to uphold the high standards of maintenance and presentation. They are invaluably assisted by your generous financial donation in doing so.

Kate Mavor
Chief Executive

PERENNIAL
GARDENERS' ROYAL BENEVOLENT SOCIETY
Helping Horticulturists In Need Since 1839

PERENNIAL TO THE RESCUE!

The positive effect of plants and green spaces is now widely recognised, but the role horticulturists play in providing our beautiful gardens and parks is often overlooked. Low pay, a high incidence of injury and few support networks for the many self-employed people in the gardening trades are just some of the problems horticulturists encounter.

That's why Perennial's work is so important – and why we're committed to offering practical, hands-on help whenever it's needed. This begins with a personal visit from one of caseworkers to see how we can best respond to whatever difficulties a client is facing. Our support can mean anything from providing a grant to helping with benefit forms and appeals, advising on home and residential care and liaising with social services where necessary, and we also provide a comprehensive debt advice service.

Perennial receives no statutory funding, so the donation we receive through Scotland's Gardens is an important source of income for Perennial. We would like to thank Scotland's Gardens, the garden owners and visitors for their kind support. You can find out more about Perennial's work or make a donation by visiting www.perennial.org.uk or calling 0845 230 1839.

Maureen McKellar
Fundraising Development Manager (Scotland)
e: mmckellar@perennial.org.uk
m: 07960 589038

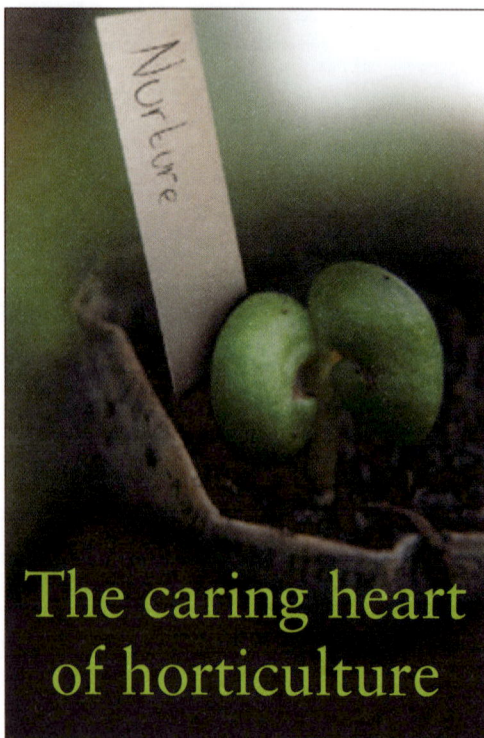

Nurture

The caring heart of horticulture

PERENNIAL
GARDENERS' ROYAL BENEVOLENT SOCIETY
Helping Horticulturists In Need Since 1839

Perennial provides help, advice and support for anyone working in the gardening trades who is facing need or crisis.

In these uncertain times the demand for our services is growing and the contribution Perennial receives from the SGS is all the more appreciated.

You can discover more about our services and how you can support Perennial's vital work by visiting our website or calling 0845 230 1839.

www.perennial.org.uk

A charity registered in Scotland no SC040180

SINCE 1931
SCOTLAND'S
GARDENS
GROWING AND GIVING

Blair Castle

Two wonderful Private Garden Tours for 2012

Private Gardens of Galloway and Northern Ireland
9-13 June 2012
Five days' half board from
£525.00pp

What's included

- Visits to the gardens of Portrack, Corsock House, Castle Kennedy, Glenwhan, Logan Botanical Gardens and Cally Gardens; Mount Stewart and selected private gardens in the Ulster Gardens Scheme

- Ferry crossings between Stranraer and Belfast

- An evening presentation by Scotland's Gardens

- Based at the North West Castle Hotel, Stranraer and the Dunadry Hotel, Co Antrim

Private Gardens of Badenoch and Speyside
21-23 July 2012
Three days' half board from
£245.00pp

What's included

- Visits to the gardens of Aberarder, Ardverikie (both Loch Laggan), Craigmore Mill (Nethybridge), Glenkyllachy (Tomatin), Blair Castle, Easter Meikle Fardle (Meikleour) and Parkhead House (Perth)

- An evening presentation by Scotland's Gardens

- Based at the Balavil Hotel, Newtonmore

Pick up points for both tours
Glasgow, Edinburgh, Perth, Kinross, Dunfermline, Dundee

For full details on both tours contact:

01334 657155

brightwater
holidays

Brightwater Holidays Ltd
Eden Park House,
Cupar, Fife KY15 4HS
info@brightwaterholidays.com
www.brightwaterholidays.com

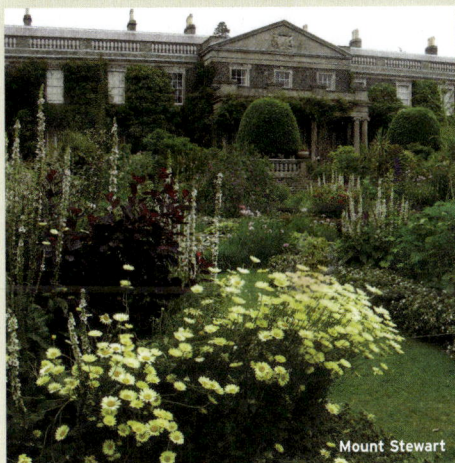
Mount Stewart

FIFE DIAMOND GARDEN FESTIVAL

Her Majesty Queen Elizabeth II celebrates her Diamond Jubilee in early June 2012, and in honour of this event Scotland's Gardens Fife District is holding a garden festival, the Fife Diamond Garden Festival, over the weekend of 18 - 20 May 2012. Do join us!

We have a magnificent mix of gardens for your enjoyment, stretching from the Forth to the Tay. Some are grand, some informal, some are centuries old and full of history, some newly hewn from the barren ground, some in exposed locations with magnificent views, others hidden from sight behind busy town streets. Each one is individual, and a garden gem in its own way. Several have never been open to the public before, making this a particularly exciting opportunity. Between them they contain a delightful mix of beautiful plants, shrubs, trees and creative whimsy.

The official opening of the Garden Festival will take place at Cambo House, Kingsbarns, on Friday 18 May 2012, with a walkabout in the Cambo Walled Garden from 1.00pm - 5.00pm. On Saturday 19 and Sunday 20 May the remaining eleven gardens will be open from 11:00am to 5:00pm each day. For a full list of open gardens see the Fife Diamond Garden Festival entry on page 166. Directions are given in the brochure that will be sent with tickets.

Homemade teas will be available in St Andrews, at 46 South Street on Saturday 18 May, and in St Leonard's School grounds on Sunday 19 May.

There will be a mega plant sale at Barham Bow of Fife with a wide selection of interesting and unusual plants, grown locally and sourced from private gardens.

Cambo Gardens

46 South Street

Teases

Micklegarth

Newton Mains

Admission: £20.00 for all gardens
(Tickets are limited and must be purchased in advance.)

For credit card payment go to: **www.scotlandsgardens.org**

For payment by cheque send to S. Lorimore, Willowhill, Forgan DD6 8RA, making cheque payable to Scotland's Gardens.

60% of the proceeds from the festival will go to Scotland's Gardens beneficiaries, the remaining 40% going to the Association for International Cancer Research (AICR). AICR supports best basic cancer research worldwide and is a Fife charity, based at Madras Lodge in St Andrews.

Newton Barns

Rosewells

Glassmount Garden

Barham

The Murrel

Strathmore Cottage

St Leonards Headmaster's Garden

Duntreath Castle Garden Show

DUNTREATH CASTLE, BLANEFIELD, GLASGOW G63 9AJ

FRIDAY 15 JUNE 2012
Gala Evening 6.00pm - 9.00pm

Tickets: Min. £15 donation to the Show's charities. Wine & Canapés in the garden and a private preview of Show. The Band of the Royal Marines. Sponsored by Brewin Dolphin, Glasgow.

For an invitation contact the Show Office (nigel@garden-shows.com) or Scotland's Gardens.

SATURDAY 16 & SUNDAY 17 JUNE 2012
10.00am - 6.00pm

Come to the Show and visit the Duntreath Castle garden.

Gardening Talks by experts incl. Steve Brookes, BBC Gardening Presenter & Author • Cooking Talks & Demonstrations • Floral Art Show & Demonstrations • Gardening Competitions • Children's Entertainments • Hot & Cold Food • Famous Afternoon Tea Garden

SUPPORTING: Scotland's Gardens, Canine Partners, Erskine Hospital, Artlink Central, S.A.F.A.S. Rotary, Camphill Village Trust and others.

FOR FULL DETAILS VISIT WWW.DUNTREATHGARDENSHOW.CO.UK

ARDMADDY –
'THE HEIGHT OF THE WOLVES'

Ardmaddy – 'The Height of the Wolves' – originally a MacDougall stronghold, became a Campbell property in the 1600s. It was bought by my parents-in-law just before the Second World War during which time much use was made of the Walled Garden for growing vegetables which were sent as far afield as Glasgow.

We took on the garden, along with the rest of the estate in 1976, at a time when our children were very small; we were in the middle of removing the larger Victorian part of the Castle; restoring the older part; as well as trying to create a sustainable home through holiday cottages, sheep farming and pheasant shoots.

The walls today are dwarfed by huge rhododendrons most of which date back to the 1960s and early 1970s and are the product of a tenant Bill Davidson, an Edinburgh solicitor, who was a keen hybridiser of rhododendrons. On leaving, his larger plants remained.

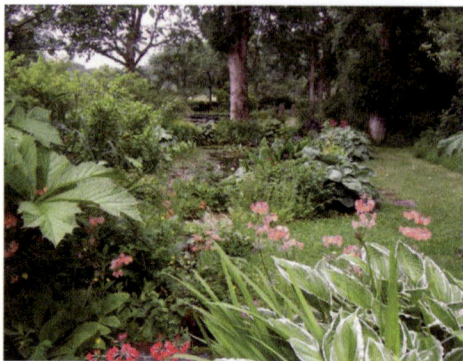

These rhododendrons and azaleas offered a riot of colour in the spring but there was little else. My priority therefore was to create a garden for all seasons. This was much hampered by lack of cash – we were stretched enough rebuilding the Castle and if I had so much as asked for even £50 for plants – no chance! So with an almost empty Walled Garden (incredible to think that today!!), we started. The formal Victorian dwarf box hedging made 6 plots – the first 4 surrounding a roundabout, with 5 and

6 stretching across from one side to the other as the walls narrowed to accommodate the burn on the outside. First came the grass lawn in plot 5 so that the boys could ride their bikes and the dogs chase a ball, then I took over the first 3 plots for vegetables, most of which were sold locally. Plot 4 became the permanent veg/fruit site. Finally at the far end, I slowly and gradually filled plot 6 with any plant or shrub that I managed to propagate or layer or was given by kindly friends. Now 30 plus years on I am having to clear out or reduce in size all those early plants to make way for a fresh start and more interesting material!

As the years went on I experimented with growing unusual and tender plants, especially climbers planted under and through the canopy of rhododendrons – Billardiera longiflora, Berberidopsis corallina, montana Clematis – rubens and Wilsonii both of which have taken themselves some 40 feet into a laurel and holly outside the walls. Most spectacular of all is the Hydrangea petiolaris now some 60 ft up through and along the branches of an old Sycamore tree (everyone told me in the beginning 'nothing would grow up a Sycamore')!

I was frustrated by the good drainage in the garden that hindered the growing of many of the damp loving plants such as gunnera, rodgersias, candelabra and other primulas, irises, hostas etc., so after much persuasion, a digger was brought in which produced 2 large holes –

one with a small island. For at least a year I didn't know where to start! Today massed plantings thrive with the backdrop of the surrounding glen and each year I add to the banks behind interesting trees which have to survive the force of the prevailing wind. This year's gales proved to be the strongest ever known in May and resulted in much desiccation and blackening of leaves but thankfully no deaths.

The woodland walk along the burn side leads from the Walled Garden to the water gardens and has an increasingly interesting collection of shrubs and plants and bulbs. It then leads back to Lady Murray's Walk on the outside of the wall where huge clumps of Crinum x powellii, hardy geraniums, tree paeonies, shrub roses, azaleas and other shrubs young and old jostle for space.

Having much lifted the canopy of the larger rhododendrons inside the garden, the beds have gradually been filled with all sorts of ground cover plants providing interest all year. Generally throughout the garden, bark or plants have been used to reduce the maintenance. Ardmaddy does not have a full time gardener but I have managed over the years with many hours myself and valuable help from part-timers. The garden has moved on from those early days and most years there has always been something different to see with new stone work; the little pond with surrounding raised bed and water feature at the far end; the Clock Garden now full of

cutting flowers where once vegetables grew; the stone obelisk with surrounding gravel bed and plants propagated or grown from seed available for sale along with all sorts of vegetables and soft fruits.

After browsing round all of that, the more energetic visitor can take themselves up into the 'Donkey Wood' full of paths to meander up and down along the burn with the occasional huge rhododendron, miles of bluebells in spring and several young ornamental trees. There is always another corner to explore at Ardmaddy!

Minette Struthers

See page 96 for Ardmaddy's garden listing.

NEW GARDENS FOR 2012

Aberdeenshire

Alford Village Gardens
Westfield Lodge
Westhall Castle

Angus

Lawton House
Letham Village
The Shrubbery

Argyllshire

Caol Ruadh
Dal an Eas and Dalnaneun
Stratholm

Ayrshire

1 Burnside Cottages, Sundrum

Caithness, Sutherland, Orkney & Shetland

15 Linkshouse
Birch Garden
Fernbank
Gerdi
Holmlea
Springpark House

Dumfriesshire

Drumpark

Dunbartonshire

Parkhead

East Lothian

Pilmuir House

Croftcat Lodge

Edinburgh & West Lothian

Redcroft
Rocheid Garden

Fife

Newton Barns (Fife Diamond Garden Festival)
Newton Mains (Fife Diamond Garden Festival)
Rosewells (Fife Diamond Garden Festival)
46 South Street (Fife Diamond Garden Festival)
St Leonard's School (Fife Diamond Garden Festival)
Strathmore Cottage (Fife Diamond Garden Festival)
Old Inzievar House
St Mary's Road and Fernie Gardens
Tayport Gardens
The Tower

Glasgow & District

Claddagh
Crossburn

Isle of Arran

The Kilmichael Hotel

Kincardine & Deeside

Drumlithie Village

Lanarkshire

Cleghorn
Wellbutts

Lochaber & Badenoch

Ralia Lodge and Milton Lodge

Midlothian

1 Standpretty

Parkhead

15 Linkshouse

Briglands House

Rocheid Garden

Dal an Eas and Dalnaneun

Stratholm

Moray & Nairn

Cuddy's Well
Mill Road Allotments

Peeblesshire

Glen House
Halmyre Mains

Perth & Kinross

Briglands House
Croftcat Lodge
Glenearn

Renfrewshire

31 Kings Road
Hill Cottage
Quarriers Village Gardens

Ross, Cromarty, Skye & Inverness

Sailean Cottage
The Lookout

Roxburghshire

Newcastleton Village Gardens & Floral Festival

Stirlingshire

Lanrick
Park House
Settie
Thornhill Village

Wigtownshire

Dunskey Garden and Maze

Redcroft

Focusing on the things that matter to you

Turcan Connell offers a comprehensive service to private individuals and their families; charities; and the owners and managers of land. Our focus has always been on providing trusted counsel over the long term. Our combination of legal and financial expertise allows us to provide focused and tailored advice on the issues that really matter.

- Asset Protection
- Charity Law
- Turcan Connell Charity Office
- Dispute Resolution
- Employment Law

- Family Business advice
- Family Law
- Financial Planning
- Investment Management

- Land & Property
- Pensions
- Tax Services
- Trust and Succession
- Turcan Connell Family Office

Edinburgh   London   Guernsey

Princes Exchange, 1 Earl Grey Street
Edinburgh EH3 9EE

Tel: 0131 228 8111

enquiries@turcanconnell.com
www.turcanconnell.com

TURCAN CONNELL
SOLICITORS AND ASSET MANAGERS

Turcan Connell is authorised and regulated by the Financial Services Authority for investment business.

BY APPOINTMENT TO
HER MAJESTY THE QUEEN
WINE MERCHANTS
CORNEY & BARROW LIMITED
LONDON

BY APPOINTMENT TO
HRH THE PRINCE OF WALES
WINE MERCHANTS
CORNEY & BARROW LIMITED
LONDON

CORNEY & BARROW

INDEPENDENT WINE MERCHANTS

Established 1780

For tastings, offers, personal cellar
and purchasing advice, please visit
our Edinburgh office or contact
Georgina Leslie on 01875 321 921
or sgs@corneyandbarrow.com

www.corneyandbarrow.com

Corney & Barrow (Scotland) Ltd
with Whighams of Ayr
Oxenfoord Castle, Pathhead,
Midlothian EH37 5UB

VISIT OUR WEBSITE FOR LAST MINUTE OFFERS!

the National Trust for Scotland
a place for everyone

SCOTTISH BREAKS

The National Trust for Scotland has a wide range of self-catering holiday accommodation. Many of the properties are located close to some of Scotland's most breathtaking scenery and glorious gardens making a perfect base for a holiday or short break.

New for 2012

The charming Garden Lodge in the grounds of the world-famous Inverewe Garden.

Find out more and book online at **www.nts.org.uk** or call **0844 493 2108** to request a brochure.

The National Trust for Scotland for Places of Historic Interest or Natural Beauty is a charity registered in Scotland, Charity Number SC 007410

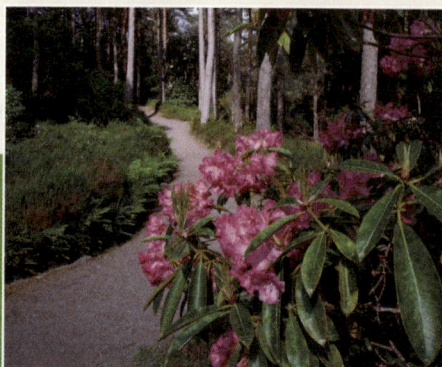

A very different garden centre

Dobbies Garden Centres
Ideas for life inspired by nature

To find your local store
visit us at www.dobbies.com

Dobbies
GARDEN CENTRES

it's in our nature

Cheshire's gardens
Different every day

There are over **25 beautiful Gardens of Distinction** in Cheshire and each promises a unique adventure.

From stately homes and secret gardens, the quintessentially English to exotic oriental planting – Cheshire is Home to England's Finest Gardens.

Discover more at visitcheshire.com/gardens

Cheshire's Gardens of Distinction
Home of England's Finest Gardens

Supported by

INVESTING IN
englandsnorthwest

EUROPEAN REGIONAL DEVELOPMENT FUND

Gardens Etc

DAY TOURS WITH THE NATIONAL GARDENS SCHEME IN 2012

Day trips out of London from April to August with a difference. Mostly around Chelsea and Hampton Court Show weeks, but including spring and late season gardens.

- We start with a bluebell tour in late April
- NEW: A walk through the Inns of Court gardens
- A visit to unusual gardens in East London
- To Kent's picturesque Stour valley in July
- A Thames river tour
- More secret gardens of the City of London
- Gardens with hot colour and exotic shapes in August

Prices from £50 to £95 to include a relaxing lunch with a glass of wine. For full information, dates, and brochure contact Janine Wookey:

4 Piermont Green, East Dulwich, London SE22 0LP
tel: 020 8693 1015 mobile: 07711279636
j.wookey@btinternet.com www.gardentoursetc.co.uk

Garden Day Tours in 2012 to raise funds on behalf of the National Gardens Scheme

ngs gardens open for charity

www.ngs.org.uk

ngs gardens open for charity

OVER 3,700 GARDENS OPEN FOR CHARITY IN ENGLAND AND WALES

1927–2012 EIGHTY FIVE YEARS OF GARDENS AND GIVING

For more information telephone 01483 211535 or visit our website www.ngs.org.uk

The National Gardens Scheme registered charity number 1112664

Discover Special Places to Stay in Britain for Garden Lovers

This beautifully illustrated book contains over 100 B&Bs, self-catering cottages and hotels – an unusual and diverse spread of places to stay, all with gorgeous gardens to discover. Stay on the remote Isle of Gigha where the owner grows rare tropical orchids; take a course with a Chelsea Gold Medal winner in a secluded valley garden in Wales; discover a pretty plot planted to excite the wildlife – and the senses – in Somerset. Owners' gardening tips are listed too, and their ideas for visits to special woodlands, gardens and arboretums close by.

Special Places to Stay in Britain for

Garden Lovers

Alastair Sawday's

Foreword by Tom Hodgkinson

Alastair Sawday has been publishing Special Places to Stay guides since 1994. Each of the 5,000 properties in our guides has been visited by us – we hope that we can take the hard work out of planning your escape.

Special Places to Stay in Britain for Garden Lovers, RRP £19.99, is available to Gardens of Scotland readers at the special price of *£12.99 (35% discount). To order, call 01275 395433 and ask for the Gardens of Scotland discount.

Alastair Sawday's

Visit **www.sawdays.co.uk** for more information about Alastair Sawday's Special Places to Stay
*Postage not included, £2.99 will be added on UK deliveries

Photos: Cambo House – Sir Peter Erskine

Photo: Newtonmill – Roy Summers / Scottish Field

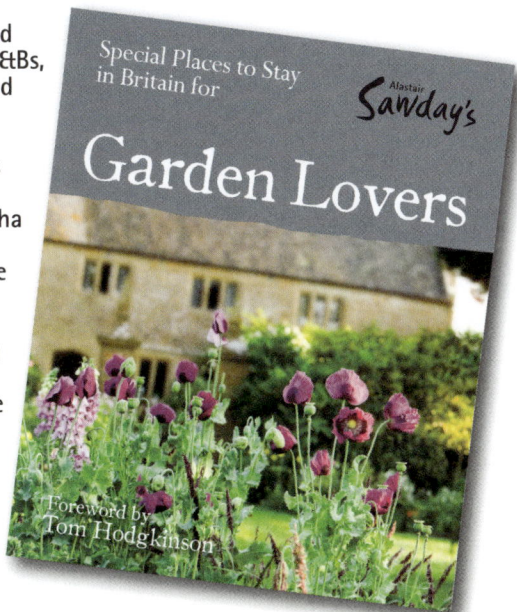

OPEN GARDENS AUSTRALIA

Australia's
Open Gardens
NATIONAL GARDEN GUIDE OVER 500 GARDENS · 2011-2012

Step inside
Your guide to Australia's finest gardens

Nature nurture
GARDENS AS THERAPY
Meet Harvey Ottley
CHOC: CHEATING DEATH AND HER OWN TOP END OASIS
An enduring passion
WHAT DRIVES A LONG-TIME OPEN GARDENER

Around 600 inspiring private gardens drawn from every Australian state and territory feature in our annual program.

Included are tropical gardens in the Northern Territory and Queensland, awe-inspiring arid zone gardens, traditional gardens in the temperate south, gardens which feature Australia's unique flora, and gardens designed by many of Australia's contemporary designers.

Our full colour guide is published each August by Hardie Grant Books and every entry includes a full description, map references and directions, opening details and amenities.

State-by-state calendars make it easy to plan a personal itinerary, and a special index identifies gardens with a particular plant collection or area of interest.

Also included are comprehensive listings of regularly open gardens around the country.

hardie grant magazines

President: Tamie Fraser
Chief Executive Officer: Richard Barley

PO Box 940, Woodend, Victoria 3442
Telephone: +61 3 5424 8061
Email: national@opengarden.org.au
Website: www.opengarden.org.au
Open Gardens Australia
ABN 60 057 467 553

THE GARDEN CONSERVANCY'S
OPEN DAYS PROGRAM

opendaysprogram.org

The Garden Conservancy has been opening America's very best, rarely seen, private gardens to the public through its Open Days program since 1995. Visit us online at **opendaysprogram.org** for more information.

The Open Days program is a project of The Garden Conservancy, a nonprofit organization dedicated to preserving America's gardening heritage.

Photo: Garden of Phillis Warden, Bedford Hills, NY

Nairn Brown

GLASGOW LTD.

Suppliers of the finest quality groundcare
equipment, from walk-behind lawnmowers,
lawn tractors, strimmers and hedge trimmers
to precision golf course and commercial equipment.

JOHN DEERE

Nairn Brown (Glasgow) Ltd
Est. 1964
Busby Station, Busby, Glasgow G76 8HY
Tel: 0141 644 3563
www.nairnbrown.com

Discover a world of plants in Scotland...

Experience
400 years of plant hunting
when you visit the four Gardens of the
Royal Botanic Garden Edinburgh

Royal
Botanic Garden
Edinburgh

RBGE | INVERLEITH ROW | EDINBURGH EH3 5LR

Royal Botanic Garden Edinburgh at **Dawyck**
Dawyck Botanic Garden
Stobo, Scottish Borders EH45 9JU
OPEN DAILY 1 FEB TO 30 NOV

Royal Botanic Garden Edinburgh at **Benmore**
Benmore Botanic Garden
Nr Dunoon, Argyll PA23 8QU
OPEN DAILY 1 MAR TO 31 OCT

Royal Botanic Garden Edinburgh at **Logan**
Logan Botanic Garden
Nr Stranraer, Dumfries & Galloway DG9 9ND
OPEN DAILY 15 MAR TO 31 OCT

Royal Botanic Garden Edinburgh is a Charity registered in Scotland No SC007983

www.rbge.org.uk

A Taste of Mey

Recipes and Memories

Inspired by The Castle of Mey Caithness
Home of Her Majesty Queen Elizabeth The Queen Mother

Available from www.castleofmey.org.uk

PLANT HERITAGE

National Council for the Conservation of Plants & Gardens

NCCPG

Help conserve our beautiful and diverse plant heritage

Join one of our five Scottish Groups for only £25 and meet fellow enthusiasts, hear experts speak and acquire rare and unusual plants.

Your support will help secure the future of our garden plants.

Meconopsis grandis © Stan Farrow

www.plantheritage.com
01483 447540 for further details
Reg Charity: 1004009/SC041785

There are over 60 National Plant Collections in Scotland - 'living libraries' of garden plants – all worth a visit!

HAND-DRAWN GARDEN AND ESTATE LANDSCAPES

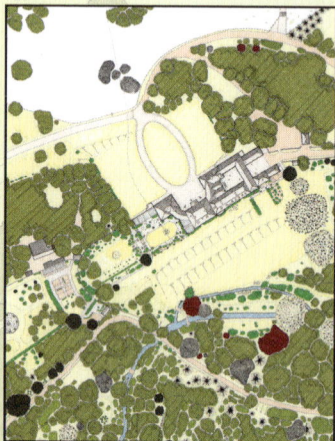

JAMES BYATT BSc (Hons) MLD
Mobile: 07796 591197
Email: enquiries@jamesbyatt.com
Web: www.jamesbyatt.com

Garden & Estate Cartographer
Drawings suitable for framing

© Crown Copyright. All rights reserved. Licence number 100051956

Atholl Estates
Blair Castle & Gardens

Hercules Garden is a stunning 9 acre walled garden, with a herbaceous border that runs along 275 metres of south facing wall. It has recently been restored to its original Georgian design and landscaped with ponds, a Chinese bridge, plantings, vegetables and an orchard of more than 100 fruit trees.

Set within the grounds of Blair Castle and surrounded by magnificent mountain scenery, this hidden jewel provides something to be seen during every season. Take in Diana's Grove woodland walk or the delightful sculpture trail and towards the end of February enjoy the snowdrops at their best. The Tullibardine restaurant and gift shop help make your visit complete.

Tel: 01796 481207 or visit www.blair-castle.co.uk
Blair Castle, Blair Atholl, Pitlochry, Perthshire. PH18 5TL

Bonhams

1793

An invitation to consign
Edinburgh

We are currently consigning jewellery, silver, pictures, furniture, works of art, clocks, rugs, books, whisky, arms and armour, glass, ceramics and Asian and sporting art for our forthcoming 2012 sales.

For more information please contact our Edinburgh saleroom

0131 225 2266
edinburgh@bonhams.com

Powder blue and iron red rouleau vase, Kangxi period

Provenance:
Sold by a direct descendant of Mary Burrell younger sister of the famous 19th century Glasgow collector William Burrell.

International Auctioneers and Valuers - **bonhams.com/edinburgh**

INCHMARLO

Retirement living around 'a garden paradise' on Royal Deeside

Our new neighbourhood - East Park consisting of 7 bungalows and 8 apartments will be available mid 2012

The opening of the Inchmarlo Continuing Care Retirement Community in 1986 pioneered a new way of living in Scotland for those over 55 years old. We are proud that 250 people call Inchmarlo "home"

We offer services that will enable you to live independently in your own home and if, or when, health patterns change we provide additional services, which can be tailored to enable you to continue living in your own home longer than might be the case elsewhere. By postponing a permanent move into a Care Home, significant savings can be made of £35,000 per year.

- 24-hour security warden • care support
- help call system • home delivery of meals
- customer liaison officer
- priority entry to Inchmarlo Care Home
- respite care • social committee and events programme • private function room

1 and 2 bedroom apartments and 2 – 4 bedroom houses are available for resale throughout the year from £95,000 to £350,000.

**HUMPHREY
Therapy Assistant
(canine)**
Read my Blog
http://
inchmarlo.wordpress.com

Tel Sales Office: 01330 826242 or visit www.inchmarlo-retirement.co.uk

HAVE YOU VISITED US YET?

Surrounded by themed gardens you will be entertained, inspired and tempted when you visit us at New Hopetoun Gardens! The Orangery Tearoom is open everyday like the garden centre 10.00am – 5.30pm (last orders 4.30pm)

NEW HOPETOUN GARDENS

…So much more than just a garden centre!

FIND US AND OUR AMAZING PLANTS

On the A904 three miles west of the Forth Road Bridge roundabout heading for Linlithgow in West Lothian

Why not visit us today
www.newhopetoungardens.co.uk
01506 834433

BENNYBEG PLANT CENTRE

Plant Paradise
One of the widest selections of garden plants in Scotland

Muthill Road, Crieff, Perthshire, PH7 4HN T: 01764 656345 info@bennybeg.co.uk

JAMESFIELD GARDEN CENTRE

For all your Garden needs
PERTHSHIRE'S BRAND NEW GARDEN CENTRE
Next to Jamesfield Farm Food Shop & Restaurant

Abernethy, Perthshire, KY14 6EW
T: 01738 851176
www.jamesfieldgardencentre.co.uk

quercus garden plants

*Easy and Unusual Plants for
Contemporary Scottish Gardens*

Phone **01337 810444** *or email* **info@quercus.uk.net**
for further information or to receive a catalogue.

**New for 2012! Wed to Sun 10am - 5pm.
First weekend in April to mid-October.**

Rankeilour Gardens, Rankeilour Estate,
Springfield, Cupar, Fife KY15 5RE

britishplant
nursery guide

A new website supporting quality British Nurseries

Find out what British Nurseries have to offer
Thousands of plants to choose from with expert advice from the growers
and higher plant survival rates

Search for quality nurseries, find information on shows & events
and enjoy a day out with Jolly Jaunts

Jolly Jaunts

www.britishplantnurseryguide.co.uk

42

the NOMADS tent

a warehouse of tribal art

The Nomads Tent
21 St Leonard's Lane
Edinburgh
EH8 9SH
0131 662 1612
nomadstent@tiscali.co.uk

www.nomadstent.co.uk

PRINCES ST
ROYAL MILE
BRIDGES
S. CLERK ST
PLEASANCE
ST. LEONARD'S LANE

RUGS
KILIMS
TEXTILES
CERAMICS
FURNITURE
ARTEFACTS
JEWELLERY
& LARGE CARPETS

rug cleaning and repair service

Mon- Sat 10-5   Sun 12-4

TERRA FIRMA GARDENS

SUSAN GALLACHER BA (HONS) LANDSCAPE ARCHITECTURE

We have been designing and building gardens for almost 20 years, and we cater for all budgets and sizes of projects, from small city courtyards to larger suburban gardens and small country estates.

All of our gardens are designed by qualified Landscape Architects and built by our experienced and qualified in house team. We are fully insured and all work is guaranteed.

We also construct individual features such as fencing, decking, driveways, ponds, pergolas, paths, drainage improvements, planting and turfing.

Call or email Susan to arrange a free initial consultation 0141 429 6267 / 07985 070433

the National Trust
for Scotland

a place for everyone

GIVE A GIFT OF MEMBERSHIP

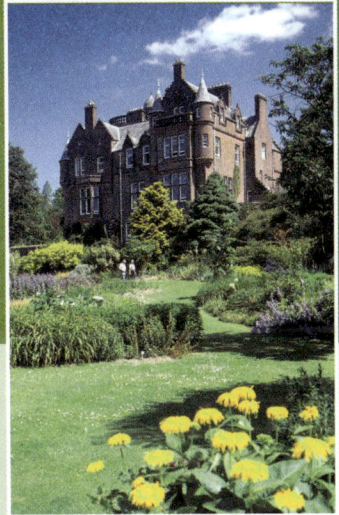

THE PRESENT THAT LASTS A WHOLE YEAR

Join online at www.nts.org.uk
or call 0844 493 2100 quoting *Scotland's Gardens*

The National Trust for Scotland for Places of Historic Interest or Natural Beauty is a charity registered in Scotland, Charity Number SC 007410

Garden Solutions

Specialist Compost & Mulch Suppliers

The value of soil improving and particularly mulching is regularly promoted in all gardening programmes and publications.
Our products are, without doubt, among the best and easiest option for gardeners wanting to get the best from their gardens.

Find out more online at www.gardensolutions.info or call 08000 430 450 to request a catalogue.

HOUSES FOR HENS

"Practical and stylish." The Garden

Fox proof hen houses with a difference

A feature in any garden, orchard or yard our hen houses are beautifully made by local craftsmen and built to last, using quality materials. Your poultry (present or future) will benefit greatly from our 'good welfare' innovations.

The Houses for Hens range is delivered ready assembled to your door, complete with training instructions, helpful hints and a selection of tea for you to enjoy whilst taking in the information.

Tudor Style
3 to 5 Hens

Do visit our website at
www.housesforhens.co.uk

call me on
07976 443742
Edward Tate

Chest Heart & Stroke Scotland

Chest, heart or stroke illness can be devastating for the whole family.
CHSS provides care, information and support when it's needed most – helping people regain their independence.

We also fund research into the causes, prevention and treatment of these illnesses.

To make a donation or find out more about our services, please contact:

Chest Heart & Stroke Scotland
Rosebery House, 9 Haymarket Terrace
EDINBURGH EH12 5EZ
Tel: 0131 225 6963

Working Together for a Healthier Future

Chest Heart & Stroke Scotland and CHSS are operating names of The Chest, Heart & Stroke Association Scotland, a registered Scottish Charity Registration No SC018761

INVESTING IN VOLUNTEERS

Chest Heart & Stroke Scotland

Visit our website
www.chss.org.uk

Munro Greenhouses & Garden Buildings

10 Alexandra Drive Alloa FK10 2DQ

01259 222 811
07785 343 130

info@munrogreenhouses.co.uk
www.munrogreenhouses.co.uk

supply : erection : maintenance : repair : removal : relocation : all accessories

Celebrate
Life with
RBGE

Celebrate Life

A New Commemorative Programme from the Royal Botanic Garden Edinburgh

The Hope Tree | Tree Adoption | Commission a Botanical Painting
Online Commemorative Book | Leave a Legacy

Celebrate Life is a wonderful programme which
allows supporters and friends of the Garden
to commemorate the life of a loved one,
celebrate an event or purchase a
unique gift for someone special
in the beautiful surroundings
of the Royal Botanic
Garden Edinburgh.

For more details please visit **celebratelife.rbge.org.uk**
or call the Development Office on **0131 248 2855**

The Royal Botanic Garden Edinburgh is a Charity registered in Scotland (number SC007983) and is supported by the Rural and Environment Science and Analytical Services (RESAS).

damhead nursery

	Trees and Shrubs	
Fruit Trees and Soft Fruit	**Hardy Plants Online**	Topiary and Climbers
	Herbaceous and Bulbs	

Damhead Farm
Lothianburn
Edinburgh
EH10 7DZ

Hardy plants for Scottish gardens
Garden Design
Horticultural Advice

Plants online at www.damheadnursery.co.uk   t:0131 4454698

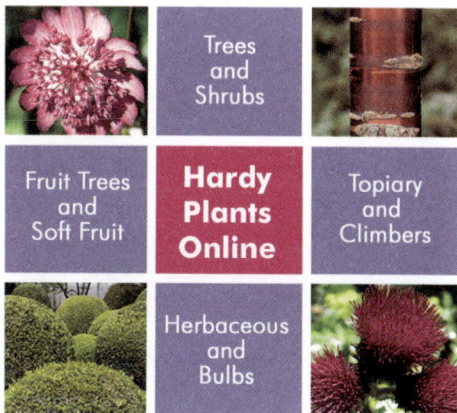

MANY NEW GARDENS OPENING THIS YEAR

We welcome gardens large and small and also groups of gardens.

WHY NOT OPEN YOURS?

CONTACT US
SCOTLAND'S GARDENS
42A NORTH CASTLE STREET
EDINBURGH EH2 3BN
T: 0131 226 3714
E: INFO@SCOTLANDSGARDENS.ORG

WWW.SCOTLANDSGARDENS.ORG

WOODBURY ESTATE

WHOLESALE FOREST TREE AND POTTED STOCK NURSERY

Kiln House, Newton of Glenisla, Blairgowrie, PH11 8PE

Tel/Fax 01575 582288 email: chris@woodburyestate.co.uk

Nursery visits by appointment only. Hours Mon-Sat 8 till 5pm. Ring for your copy of our full catalogue.

Nursery owned and managed by John and Chris Watkinson. John has over 35 years experience in the nursery trade. Our nursery is in the heart of the beautiful Angus Glens and well worth a visit.

Bare root. Nov to April. (Min.order 100) Forestry broadleaves & conifers, hedging, shrubs, willows and game cover. We supply farmers and estates for hedge and woodland planting schemes thoughout Scotland.

Potted stock. All year round. Huge range of potted native and ornamental trees & shrubs from 3L to 20L pot size, 30cm to 3m height. We pot between 10 and 100 of a species and can supply larger numbers than most garden centres. We stock ornamental Rowan, Birches, Crab apples, Acers, Flowering Cherries and many other beautiful and unusual trees, shrubs & fruit trees.

The David Welch Winter Gardens

at Duthie Park, Polmuir Road, Aberdeen are one of Europe's largest indoor gardens. It boasts a beautiful floral paradise all year round, with many rare and exotic plants on show from all around the world.

Open daily from 9:30am Tel: 01224 583 155

Email: wintergardens@aberdeencity.gov.uk
Web-site:www.aberdeencity.gov.uk

Free Admission

SNOWDROP OPENINGS

Snowdrops remain as popular as ever and several properties will be opening in February and March to enable visitors to enjoy the stunning displays of these flowers. Once again VisitScotland will be supporting the openings with their heavily marketed Snowdrop Festival which has become an important part of their successful Winter White campaign.

The following properties will be opening and most will be participating in the Snowdrop Festival:

Angus

Dunninald
Gagie House
Lawton House
Pitmuies Gardens

Argyllshire

Ardkinglas Woodland Garden

Ayrshire

Caprington Castle

Dunbartonshire

Linn Botanic Gardens

East Lothian

Shepherd House

Fife

Cambo House

Kincardine & Deeside

Ecclesgreig Castle

Kirkcudbrightshire

Danevale
Broughton House Garden

Lanarkshire

Cleghorn

Midlothian

Kevock Garden

Peeblesshire

Dawyck Botanic Garden
Kailzie Gardens
Traquair

Perth & Kinross

Blair Castle Gardens
Cluny House
Fingask Castle

Renfrewshire

Ardgowan
Gargunnock House
Kilbryde Castle

Stirlingshire

The Linns
West Plean House

Wigtownshire

Castle Kennedy & Gardens
Dunskey Garden and Maze
Kirkdale

GARDENS OPEN ON A SPECIFIC DATE

January

Saturday 28 January
Kincardine & Deeside   Workshop at Crathes Castle, Banchory

February

To be announced
Kirkcudbrightshire   Danevale Park, Crossmichael

Tuesday 7 February
Kirkcudbrightshire   Broughton House Garden, 12 High Street, Kirkcudbright

Wednesday 8 February
Kirkcudbrightshire   Broughton House Garden, 12 High Street, Kirkcudbright

Saturday 11 February
Ayrshire   Caprington Castle, Kilmarnock

Sunday 12 February
Ayrshire   Caprington Castle, Kilmarnock
Wigtownshire   Kirkdale, Carsluith, Newton Stewart

Saturday 18 February
Wigtownshire   Dunskey Garden and Maze

Sunday 19 February
Renfrewshire   Ardgowan, Inverkip

Saturday 25 February
Ayrshire   Caprington Castle, Kilmarnock
Peeblesshire   Traquair, Innerleithen

Sunday 26 February
Ayrshire   Caprington Castle, Kilmarnock
East Lothian   Shepherd House, Inveresk
Fife   Balmerino Abbey, Newport-on-Tay
Kincardine & Deeside   Ecclesgreig Castle, St Cyrus
Peeblesshire   Traquair, Innerleithen
Stirlingshire   West Plean House, Denny Road, by Stirling

March

Saturday 3 March
Angus   Dunninald, Montrose

Sunday 4 March

Angus	Dunninald, Montrose
Lanarkshire	Cleghorn , Stable House, Cleghorn Farm, Lanark
Midlothian	Kevock Garden, 16 Kevock Road, Lasswade
Peeblesshire	Kailzie Gardens, Peebles
Stirlingshire	Kilbryde Castle, Dunblane

Sunday 11 March

Angus	Lawton House, Inverkeilor, by Arbroath
Stirlingshire	The Linns, Sheriffmuir, Dunblane

Sunday 25 March

Dunbartonshire	Linn Botanic Gardens, Cove, by Helensburgh

April

Sunday 1 April

Edinburgh & West Lothian	Dean Gardens and Belgrave Crescent, Edinburgh

Sunday 8 April

Aberdeenshire	Auchmacoy, Ellon
Edinburgh & West Lothian	61 Fountainhall Road, Edinburgh
Stirlingshire	Milseybank, Bridge of Allan

Thursday 12 April

Ross, Cromarty, Skye & Inverness	Dundonnell House, Dundonnell, Little Loch Broom

Saturday 14 April

Glasgow & District	Greenbank Garden, Flenders Road, Clarkston
Moray & Nairn	Brodie Castle, Brodie, Forres

Sunday 15 April

Aberdeenshire	Westhall Castle, Oyne, Inverurie
East Lothian	Winton House, Pencaitland
Edinburgh & West Lothian	10 Pilton Drive North, Edinburgh
Moray & Nairn	Brodie Castle, Brodie, Forres
Perth & Kinross	Megginch Castle, Errol
Stirlingshire	West Plean House, Denny Road, by Stirling

Sunday 22 April

Argyllshire	Benmore Botanic Garden, Benmore, Dunoon
Argyllshire	Crarae Garden, Inveraray
Dunbartonshire	Kilarden, Rosneath

Sunday 29 April

Dunbartonshire	Milton House, Milton, Dumbarton
East Lothian	Shepherd House, Inveresk, Musselburgh
Edinburgh & West Lothian	101 Greenbank Crescent, Edinburgh
Edinburgh & West Lothian	Redcroft, 23 Murrayfield Road, Edinburgh

Fife	Birkhill Castle, Balmerino, Cupar
Stirlingshire	The Pass House, Kilmahog, Callander

May

Saturday 5 May

Argyllshire	Knock Cottage, Lochgair
Argyllshire	Stratholm, Clachan
East Lothian	Greywalls, Gullane
Lochaber & Badenoch	Canna House Walled Garden, Isle of Canna

Sunday 6 May

Angus	Brechin Castle, Brechin
Argyllshire	Knock Cottage, Lochgair
Argyllshire	Stratholm, Clachan
Dumfriesshire	Portrack House, Holywood
Edinburgh & West Lothian	Redcroft, 23 Murrayfield Road, Edinburgh
Fife	St Andrews Botanic Garden, Canongate, St Andrews
Isle of Arran	Brodick Castle & Country Park, Brodick
Kirkcudbrightshire	Corsock House, Corsock
Lanarkshire	The Scots Mining Company House, Leadhills
Lochaber & Badenoch	Ard-Daraich, Ardgour
Perth & Kinross	Branklyn, 116 Dundee Road
Perth & Kinross	Briglands House, Rumbling Bridge
Perth & Kinross	Glendoick, by Perth
Stirlingshire	Southwood & 1 Laurelhill Place, Stirling
Wigtownshire	Logan Botanic Garden, Port Logan

Saturday 12 May

Argyllshire	Drim na Vullin, Blarbuie Road, Lochgilphead
Argyllshire	Knock Cottage, Lochgair

Sunday 13 May

Angus	Dalfruin, Kirktonhill Road, Kirriemuir
Argyllshire	Arduaine, Oban
Argyllshire	Drim na Vullin, Blarbuie Road, Lochgilphead
Argyllshire	Knock Cottage, Lochgair
Dumfriesshire	Drumpark, Irongray
Dunbartonshire	Ardchapel and Seven The Birches, Shandon
East Lothian	Tyninghame House, Dunbar
Edinburgh & West Lothian	61 Fountainhall Road, Edinburgh
Edinburgh & West Lothian	Hunter's Tryst, 95 Oxgangs Road, Edinburgh
Edinburgh & West Lothian	Moray Place & Bank Gardens, Edinburgh
Fife	Culross Palace, Culross
Fife	Tayfield, Forgan
Fife	Willowhill,Forgan
Kirkcudbrightshire	Threave Garden, Castle Douglas

Perth & Kinross	Fingask Castle, Rait
Perth & Kinross	Glendoick, by Perth
Perth & Kinross	Pitcurran House, Abernethy
Stirlingshire	Auchmar, Drymen
Wigtownshire	Claymoddie Garden, Whithorn, Newton Stewart

Friday 18 May

| Fife | Fife Diamond Garden Festival |

Saturday 19 May

| Argyllshire | Strachur House Flower & Woodland Gardens , Strachur |
| Fife | Fife Diamond Garden Festival |

Sunday 20 May

Angus	Dunninald, Montrose
Argyllshire	Strachur House Flower & Woodland Gardens , Strachur
Dumfriesshire	Dalswinton House, Dalswinton
Dunbartonshire	Ross Priory, Gartocharn
East Lothian	Stobshiel House, Stobshiel House, Humbie
Edinburgh & West Lothian	61 Fountainhall Road, Edinburgh
Fife	Fife Diamond Garden Festival
Glasgow & District	Kilsyth Gardens, Allanfauld Road, Kilsyth
Isle of Arran	Strabane, Brodick
Kincardine & Deeside	Inchmarlo House Garden, Inchmarlo, Banchory
Kirkcudbrightshire	Stockarton, Kirkcudbright
Renfrewshire	Carruth, Bridge of Weir
Renfrewshire	Hill Cottage, Spey Road, Inverkip
Stirlingshire	Kilbryde Castle, Dunblane

Wednesday 23 May

Aberdeenshire	Cruickshank Botanic Gardens, St Machar Drive, Aberdeen
Ross, Cromarty, Skye & Inverness	House of Gruinard, Laide
Ross, Cromarty, Skye & Inverness	Inverewe, Poolewe, Achnasheen, Ross-shire

Thursday 24 May

| Aberdeenshire | Leith Hall, Huntly |

Saturday 26 May

Edinburgh & West Lothian	Rocheid Garden, 20 Inverleith Terrace, Edinburgh
Fife	Tayport Gardens, Tayport
Perth & Kinross	Acres of Keillour, Methven
Ross, Cromarty, Skye & Inverness	Sailean Cottage, 83 Aird Bernisdale, Skeabost Bridge

Sunday 27 May

Angus	Cortachy Castle, Cortachy, by Kirriemuir
Ayrshire	1 Burnside Cottages, Sundrum, Coyton Ayrshire
Berwickshire	Lennel Bank, Coldstream
Caithness, Sutherland, Orkney & Shetland	Shangri-La, 3 Anderson Road, Lerwick, Shetland
East Lothian	Stenton Village

Fife	St. Monans Village Gardens,
Fife	Tayport Gardens, Tayport
Isle of Arran	Strabane, Brodick
Kincardine & Deeside	The Burn House & The Burn Garden House, Glenesk
Lochaber & Badenoch	Conaglen, Ardgour
Peeblesshire	Haystoun, Peebles
Ross, Cromarty, Skye & Inverness	Sailean Cottage, 83 Aird Bernisdale, Skeabost Bridge
Stirlingshire	Thornhill Village, The Gardens of Thornhill

Monday 28 May

Caithness, Sutherland, Orkney & Shetland	Shangri-La, 3 Anderson Road, Lerwick, Shetland

Thursday 31 May

Ross, Cromarty, Skye & Inverness	Dundonnell House, Little Loch Broom

June

Saturday 2 June

Stirlingshire	Lanrick, Doune

Sunday 3 June

Aberdeenshire	Dunecht House Gardens, Dunecht
Aberdeenshire	Kildrummy Castle Gardens, Alford
Aberdeenshire	Tillypronie, Tarland
Angus	Gallery, Montrose
Caithness, Sutherland, Orkney & Shetland	Pentland Firth Gardens, Dunnet
Dumfriesshire	Cowhill Tower, Holywood
East Lothian	Inveresk Village, Musselburgh
East Lothian	Shepherd House, Inveresk
Fife	Earlshall Castle, Leuchars
Kirkcudbrightshire	Cally Gardens, Gatehouse of Fleet
Midlothian	Cousland Smiddy and Village Gardens, Cousland
Peeblesshire	Stobo Japanese Water Garden, Home Farm, Stobo
Perth & Kinross	Delvine, Spittalfield
Stirlingshire	Burnbrae, Killearn

Wednesday 6 June

Ross, Cromarty, Skye & Inverness	Inverewe, Poolewe, Achnasheen

Saturday 9 June

Ayrshire	Holmes Farm, Drybridge, by Irvine
Caithness, Sutherland, Orkney & Shetland	Amat, Ardgay
Caithness, Sutherland, Orkney & Shetland	Birch Garden, 3 Sands of Sound, Shetland
Caithness, Sutherland, Orkney & Shetland	Cruisdale, Sandness, Shetland
East Lothian	Dirleton Village, North Berwick
Glasgow & District	Kew Terrace Secret Gardens, Kew Terrace Lane
Midlothian	The Old Sun Inn, Newbattle
Wigtownshire	Glenwhan Gardens, Dunragit

Sunday 10 June

Aberdeenshire	Esslemont, Ellon
Angus	The Shrubbery, 67 Magdalen Yard Road, Dundee
Ayrshire	Holmes Farm, Drybridge, by Irvine
Caithness, Sutherland, Orkney & Shetland	Amat, Ardgay
Caithness, Sutherland, Orkney & Shetland	Cruisdale, Sandness, Shetland
East Lothian	Dirleton Village, North Berwick
Edinburgh & West Lothian	61 Fountainhall Road, Edinburgh
Fife	Greenhead Farmhouse, Greenhead of Arnot
Fife	Old Inzievar House
Glasgow & District	Crossburn, Stockiemuir Road, Milngavie, Glasgow
Isle of Arran	The Kilmichael Hotel, Glen Cloy, Brodick
Kincardine & Deeside	Kincardine, Kincardine O'Neil
Kincardine & Deeside	Milltown Community Gardens, Arbuthnott
Lochaber & Badenoch	Aberarder, Kinlochlaggan
Lochaber & Badenoch	Ardverikie, Kinlochlaggan
Midlothian	1 Standpretty, Fuschie Bridge by Gorebridge
Ross, Cromarty, Skye & Inverness	Field House, Belladrum, Beauly
Ross, Cromarty, Skye & Inverness	Novar, Evanton
Stirlingshire	Bridge of Allan Gardens, Bridge of Allan
Stirlingshire	Kilbryde Castle, Dunblane

Thursday 14 June

Edinburgh & West Lothian	Malleny Garden, Balerno

Saturday 16 June

Argyllshire	Dal an Eas and Dalnaneun, Kilmore, Oban
Caithness, Sutherland, Orkney & Shetland	Birch Garden, 3 Sands of Sound, Shetland
Edinburgh & West Lothian	National Records of Scotland, 2 Princes Street, Edinburgh
Fife	Falkland's Small Gardens, Falkland
Kincardine & Deeside	Crathes Castle, Banchory
Midlothian	Kevock Garden, 16 Kevock Road, Lasswade
Perth & Kinross	Blair Castle Gardens, Blair Atholl
Perth & Kinross	Explorers Garden, Pitlochry
Stirlingshire	Duntreath Castle, Blanefield

Sunday 17 June

Angus	Letham Village, Letham
Argyllshire	Dal an Eas and Dalnaneun, Kilmore, Oban
East Lothian	Gifford Village, Gifford
Edinburgh & West Lothian	61 Fountainhall Road, Edinburgh
Edinburgh & West Lothian	National Records of Scotland, 2 Princes Street, Edinburgh
Fife	Falkland's Small Gardens, Falkland
Glasgow & District	123 Waterfoot Row, Newton Mearns
Kincardine & Deeside	Ecclesgreig Castle, St Cyrus
Lanarkshire	20 Smithycroft, Hamilton
Lanarkshire	Dippoolbank Cottage, Carnwath

Lanarkshire	New Lanark Roof Garden, Lanark
Midlothian	Kevock Garden, Lasswade
Moray & Nairn	42 Fife Street, Keith
Moray & Nairn	Bents Green, 10 Pilmuir Road West, Forres
Moray & Nairn	Castleview, Auchindoun, Dufftown
Peeblesshire	West Linton Village Gardens, West Linton
Perth & Kinross	Glenearn, Bridge of Earn
Stirlingshire	Duntreath Castle, Blanefield

Wednesday 20 June

Caithness, Sutherland, Orkney & Shetland	Shangri-La, 3 Anderson Road, Lerwick

Thursday 21 June

Caithness, Sutherland, Orkney & Shetland	Shangri-La, 3 Anderson Road, Lerwick

Saturday 23 June

Argyllshire	The Shore Villages, by Dunoon
Caithness, Sutherland, Orkney & Shetland	Birch Garden, 3 Sands of Sound, Shetland
Moray & Nairn	Cuddy's Well, Clephanton

Sunday 24 June

Aberdeenshire	Mansefield, Alford
Angus	Edzell Village & Castle, Edzell
Argyllshire	The Shore Villages, by Dunoon
Dumfriesshire	The Old Mill, Keir Mill, Thornhill
East Lothian	Tyninghame House, Dunbar
Ettrick & Lauderdale	Harmony Garden, St. Mary's Road, Melrose
Ettrick & Lauderdale	Priorwood Gardens, Abbey Road, Melrose
Kincardine & Deeside	Finzean House, Finzean
Kirkcudbrightshire	Blair House, 8 High Street, Kirkcudbright
Kirkcudbrightshire	Oakleigh Bank, Kirkcudbright
Midlothian	Broomieknowe Gardens, Lasswade
Moray & Nairn	Cuddy's Well, Clephanton
Moray & Nairn	Gordonstoun, Duffus, near Elgin
Renfrewshire	Sma' Shot Cottages Heritage Centre, Paisley
Ross, Cromarty, Skye & Inverness	House of Aigas and Field Centre, by Beauly
Stirlingshire	Park House, Blair Drummond

Thursday 28 June

Aberdeenshire	Leith Hall, Huntly

Saturday 30 June

Argyllshire	Ardlussa House Garden, Isle of Jura
Ayrshire	Gardens of West Kilbride and Seamill,
Caithness, Sutherland, Orkney & Shetland	Birch Garden, 3 Sands of Sound, Shetland
Fife	Balcaskie, Pittenweem
Fife	Blebo Craigs Village Gardens, Cupar
Fife	Kellie Castle , Pittenweem

Kincardine & Deeside   Drumlithie Village, Drumlithie

July

Sunday 1 July
Aberdeenshire   Bruckhills Croft, Rothienorman, Inverurie
Angus   Montrose and Hillside Gardens, Montrose
Argyllshire   Ardlussa House Garden, Isle of Jura
Ayrshire   Gardens of West Kilbride and Seamill
Berwickshire   Anton's Hill and Walled Garden, Leitholm, Coldstream
Dumfriesshire   The Garth, Tynron, Thornhill
Fife   Blebo Craigs Village Gardens, Cupar
Glasgow & District   Claddagh, 24 Station Road, Bearsden
Isle of Arran   Dougarie
Kirkcudbrightshire   Southwick House, Southwick
Peeblesshire   Glen House, Glen Estate, Innerleithen
Perth & Kinross   Bradystone House, Murthly
Stirlingshire   Doune Village, Doune Village Gardens

Monday 2 July
Kirkcudbrightshire   Southwick House, Southwick

Tuesday 3 July
Kirkcudbrightshire   Southwick House, Southwick

Wednesday 4 July
Caithness, Sutherland, Orkney & Shetland   The Castle & Gardens of Mey, Mey
Kirkcudbrightshire   Southwick House, Southwick
Ross, Cromarty, Skye & Inverness   House of Gruinard, Laide

Thursday 5 July
Caithness, Sutherland, Orkney & Shetland   15 Linkshouse, Mid Yell
Caithness, Sutherland, Orkney & Shetland   Fernbank, Camb, Yell
Kirkcudbrightshire   Southwick House, Southwick

Friday 6 July
Kirkcudbrightshire   Southwick House, Southwick

Saturday 7 July
Aberdeenshire   Hillockhead, Glendeskry, Strathdon
Argyllshire   Ardlussa House Garden, Isle of Jura
Ayrshire   Barr Village Gardens, by Girvan
Kincardine & Deeside   Drum Castle, Drumoak, by Banchory
Roxburghshire   Corbet Tower, Morebattle, Nr Kelso

Sunday 8 July
Aberdeenshire   23 Don Street, Old Aberdeen
Angus   Gallery, Montrose
Argyllshire   Ardlussa House Garden, Isle of Jura

Ayrshire	Barr Village Gardens, by Girvan
Edinburgh & West Lothian	Merchiston Cottage, Edinburgh
Fife	Kinghorn Village Gardens
Fife	St Mary's Road and Fernie Gardens, by Cupar
Isle of Arran	Brodick Castle & Country Park, Brodick
Kincardine & Deeside	Drum Castle, Drumoak, by Banchory
Kincardine & Deeside	Findrack, Torphins
Perth & Kinross	Wester Cloquhat , Bridge of Cally
Stirlingshire	Settie, Kippen

Thursday 12 July

Caithness, Sutherland, Orkney & Shetland	15 Linkshouse, Mid Yell
Caithness, Sutherland, Orkney & Shetland	Fernbank, Camb, Yell
Caithness, Sutherland, Orkney & Shetland	The Castle & Gardens of Mey, Mey

Saturday 14 July

Edinburgh & West Lothian	9 Braid Farm Road, Edinburgh
Ettrick & Lauderdale	Carolside , Earlston
Perth & Kinross	Achnacloich , Balhomais
Perth & Kinross	Croftcat Lodge, Grandtully

Sunday 15 July

Ayrshire	Carnell, Hurlford
East Lothian	Inwood, Carberry
Edinburgh & West Lothian	9 Braid Farm Road, Edinburgh
Fife	Strathmiglo Village Gardens
Fife	Wormistoune House, Crail
Kincardine & Deeside	Douneside House, Tarland
Kirkcudbrightshire	Crofts, Kirkpatrick Durham
Roxburghshire	Yetholm Village Gardens, Town Yetholm

Tuesday 17 July

Ayrshire	Culzean, Maybole

Thursday 19 July

Caithness, Sutherland, Orkney & Shetland	15 Linkshouse, Mid Yell
Caithness, Sutherland, Orkney & Shetland	Fernbank, Camb, Yell

Saturday 21 July

Edinburgh & West Lothian	45 Northfield Crescent, Longridge
Fife	Crail: Small Gardens in the Burgh
Lanarkshire	Wellbutts, Elsrickle
Moray & Nairn	42 Fife Street, Keith
Roxburghshire	Newcastleton Village Gardens & Floral Festival

Sunday 22 July

Aberdeenshire	Alford Village Gardens, Alford
Aberdeenshire	Leith Hall, Huntly
Argyllshire	Crarae Garden, Inveraray

Ayrshire	Largs Open Gardens, Willowbank Hotel, Greenock Road
East Lothian	Pilmuir House, Haddington
Edinburgh & West Lothian	45 Northfield Crescent, Longridge, Bathgate
Fife	Crail: Small Gardens in the Burgh
Kirkcudbrightshire	Glensone Walled Garden, Southwick
Lanarkshire	Wellbutts, Elsrickle, by Biggar
Lochaber & Badenoch	Glenkyllachy Lodge, Tomatin
Midlothian	Newhall, Carlops
Moray & Nairn	Mill Road Allotments, Mill Road, Nairn
Renfrewshire	Hill Cottage, Spey Road, Inverkip
Ross, Cromarty, Skye & Inverness	House of Aigas and Field Centre, by Beauly

Tuesday 24 July

Ross, Cromarty, Skye & Inverness	Hugh Miller's Museum & Birthplace Cottage, Church Street, Cromarty

Thursday 26 July

Aberdeenshire	Leith Hall, Huntly
Caithness, Sutherland, Orkney & Shetland	15 Linkshouse, Mid Yell
Caithness, Sutherland, Orkney & Shetland	Fernbank, Camb, Yell

Friday 27 July

Aberdeenshire	Fyvie Castle, Fyvie, Turriff

Saturday 28 July

Argyllshire	Caol Ruadh, Colintraive
Caithness, Sutherland, Orkney & Shetland	House of Tongue, Tongue, Lairg

Sunday 29 July

Aberdeenshire	Castle Fraser, Sauchen, Inverurie
Aberdeenshire	Glenkindie House, Glenkindie, Alford
Angus	Kirkton House, Kirkton of Craig, Montrose
Argyllshire	Ardchattan Priory, North Connel
Argyllshire	Caol Ruadh, Colintraive
Ayrshire	Skeldon, Dalrymple
Caithness, Sutherland, Orkney & Shetland	Flagstone Village Gardens, Castletown
Caithness, Sutherland, Orkney & Shetland	Lea Gardens, Tresta, Shetland
Dumfriesshire	Newtonairds Lodge, Newtonairds
Fife	Earlshall Castle, Leuchars
Kincardine & Deeside	Mill of Benholm Project, Benholm by Johnshaven
Kirkcudbrightshire	Borgue Parish Gardens
Lanarkshire	Dippoolbank Cottage, Carnwath
Peeblesshire	8 Halmyre Mains, West Linton

Tuesday 31 July

Stirlingshire	Gean House , Tullibody Road, Alloa

August

Saturday 4 August

Aberdeenshire	Pitscurry Project, Whiteford, Pitcaple, Inverurie
Edinburgh & West Lothian	2 Houstoun Gardens, Uphall

Sunday 5 August

Aberdeenshire	5 Rubislaw Den North, Aberdeen
Aberdeenshire	Pitscurry Project, Whiteford, Pitcaple
Caithness, Sutherland, Orkney & Shetland	Burravoe, North House, Brae
Caithness, Sutherland, Orkney & Shetland	Langwell, Berriedale
Dunbartonshire	Geilston Garden, Cardross
Edinburgh & West Lothian	2 Houstoun Gardens, Uphall
Fife	Ceres Village Gardens
Kincardine & Deeside	Glenbervie House, Drumlithie
Kirkcudbrightshire	Threave Garden, Castle Douglas
Lochaber & Badenoch	Ralia Lodge and Milton Lodge, Newtonmore
Peeblesshire	Broughton Place Farmhouse, Biggar
Perth & Kinross	Drummond Castle Gardens, Crieff
Ross, Cromarty, Skye & Inverness	Woodview, Highfield, Muir of Ord

Monday 6 August

Aberdeenshire	Pitscurry Project, Whiteford, Pitcaple

Tuesday 7 August

Aberdeenshire	Pitscurry Project, Whiteford, Pitcaple

Wednesday 8 August

Aberdeenshire	Pitscurry Project, Whiteford, Pitcaple

Thursday 9 August

Aberdeenshire	Pitscurry Project, Whiteford, Pitcaple

Friday 10 August

Aberdeenshire	Pitscurry Project, Whiteford, Pitcaple

Saturday 11 August

Aberdeenshire	Pitscurry Project, Whiteford, Pitcaple
Caithness, Sutherland, Orkney & Shetland	Cruisdale, Sandness
Edinburgh & West Lothian	Dr Neil's Garden, Duddingston Village

Sunday 12 August

Aberdeenshire	Pitscurry Project, Whiteford, Pitcaple
Caithness, Sutherland, Orkney & Shetland	Burravoe, North House, Brae
Caithness, Sutherland, Orkney & Shetland	Cruisdale, Sandness, Shetland
Caithness, Sutherland, Orkney & Shetland	Langwell, Berriedale
Caithness, Sutherland, Orkney & Shetland	The Old Playground, Old School Road, Trondra
Edinburgh & West Lothian	Dr Neil's Garden, Duddingston Village
Kirkcudbrightshire	Cally Gardens, Gatehouse of Fleet
Lanarkshire	Culter Allers, Coulter, Biggar

Ross, Cromarty, Skye & Inverness	Cardon, Balnafoich, Farr
Stirlingshire	Thorntree, Arnprior

Wednesday 15 August

Lochaber & Badenoch	Canna House Walled Garden, Isle of Canna

Thursday 16 August

Ross, Cromarty, Skye & Inverness	Dundonnell House, Dundonnell, Little Loch Broom

Friday 17 August

Kirkcudbrightshire	Broughton House Garden, 12 High Street, Kirkcudbright

Saturday 18 August

Caithness, Sutherland, Orkney & Shetland	The Castle & Gardens of Mey, Mey

Sunday 19 August

Aberdeenshire	Pitmedden Garden, Ellon
Angus	Airlie Castle, Airlie, by Kirriemuir
Caithness, Sutherland, Orkney & Shetland	Burravoe, North House, Brae, Shetland
Caithness, Sutherland, Orkney & Shetland	Springpark House, Laurie Terrace, Thurso
Renfrewshire	Barshaw Park Walled Garden, Paisley
Roxburghshire	West Leas, Bonchester Bridge
Stirlingshire	Rowberrow, 18 Castle Road, Dollar

Thursday 23 August

Aberdeenshire	Leith Hall, Huntly

Saturday 25 August

Aberdeenshire	Westfield Lodge, Contlaw Road, Milltimber, Aberdeen

Sunday 26 August

Aberdeenshire	Tillypronie, Tarland
Caithness, Sutherland, Orkney & Shetland	Burravoe, North House, Brae, Shetland
Dunbartonshire	Parkhead, Rosneath, Helensburgh
Fife	Falkland Palace and Garden, Falkland
Glasgow & District	Sundrum, 11 Neidpath Road West, Giffnock, Glasgow
Renfrewshire	Knowes End, Auchans Road, Houston

September

Saturday 1 September

Caithness, Sutherland, Orkney & Shetland	Cruisdale, Sandness, Shetland

Sunday 2 September

Caithness, Sutherland, Orkney & Shetland	Cruisdale, Sandness, Shetland
Dunbartonshire	Hill House, Helensburgh
Edinburgh & West Lothian	61 Fountainhall Road, Edinburgh
Fife	Tayfield, Forgan
Fife	Willowhill, Forgan
Renfrewshire	Quarriers Village Gardens
Stirlingshire	Avonmuir House, Muiravonside

Saturday 8 September
Edinburgh & West Lothian   Rocheid Garden, Edinburgh

Sunday 9 September
Edinburgh & West Lothian   61 Fountainhall Road, Edinburgh

Thursday 20 September
Ross, Cromarty, Skye & Inverness   Dundonnell House, Little Loch Broom

Sunday 23 September
Stirlingshire   Gargunnock House, Gargunnock

Sunday 30 September
Aberdeenshire   Kildrummy Castle Gardens, Alford

October

Sunday 7 October
Peeblesshire   Dawyck Botanic Garden, Stobo

Sunday 21 October
Fife   Hill of Tarvit, Cupar
Kincardine & Deeside   Inchmarlo House Garden, Inchmarlo

GARDENS OPEN REGULARLY

Angus

Dunninald, Montrose	28 June - 29 July
Gagie House, Duntrune, by Dundee	15 February - 31 March
Pitmuies Gardens, House of Pitmuies, Guthrie, Forfar	1 - 14 March & 21 March - 31 October

Argyllshire

Achnacloich, Connel, Oban	31 March - 31 October
An Cala, Ellenabeich, Isle of Seil	1 April - 31 October
Ardchattan Priory, North Connel	1 April - 31 October
Ardkinglas Woodland Garden, Cairndow	All year
Ardmaddy Castle, By Oban	All Year
Barguillean's "Angus Garden", Taynuilt	All Year
Benmore Botanic Garden, Benmore, Dunoon	March - October
Crinan Hotel Garden, Crinan	1 May - 31 August
Druimneil House, Port Appin	Easter - October
Fairwinds, 14 George Street, Hunter's Quay, Dunoon	All summer
Inveraray Castle Gardens, Inveraray	1 April - 31 October
Kinlochlaich House Gardens, Appin	All year
Oakbank, Ardrishaig	1 May - 31 August

Berwickshire

Bughtrig, Near Leitholm, Coldstream	1 June - 1 September

Caithness, Sutherland, Orkney & Shetland

Cruisdale, Sandness, Shetland	2 July - 8 July
Holla, Sandwick, Shetland	Open most days
Lea Gardens, Tresta, Shetland	March - October
Nonavaar, Levenwick, Shetland	2 June - 27 August Sats & Mons
The Castle & Gardens of Mey, Mey	1 May - 25 July & 14 August - 30 September
U.R.G.E., 13 Nikkavord Lea, Baltasound, Shetland	11 - 29 July Wednesdays - Sundays

Dunbartonshire

Glenarn, Glenarn Road, Rhu, Helensburgh	21 March - 21 September
Linn Botanic Gardens, Cove, By Helensburgh	All year

East Lothian

Inwood, Carberry, Musselburgh	1 April - 30 September, Tuesday, Thursday & Saturdays
Shepherd House, Inveresk, Musselburgh	14 February - 1 March & 17 April - 5 July, Tues and Thurs

Ettrick & Lauderdale

Carolside, Earlston	23 June - 28 July, Mons, Weds & Sats

Fife

Barham, Bow of Fife	25 April - 26 September, Wednesdays
Cambo House, Kingsbarns	All Year
Willowhill, Forgan, Newport-on-Tay	3 July- 29 August, Wednesdays

Kirkcudbrightshire

Cally Gardens, Gatehouse of Fleet	Easter Saturday - last Sunday in September, ex Mons

Lanarkshire

New Lanark Roof Garden, New Lanark Mills, Lanark	All Year

Lochaber & Badenoch

Ardtornish, By Lochaline, Morvern	1 January - 31 December

Peeblesshire

Dawyck Botanic Garden, Stobo	February - November
Kailzie Gardens, Peebles	All Year
Traquair House, Innerleithen, Peeblesshire	6 April - 31 October, Daily & 1 - 30 November, weekends

Perth & Kinross

Ardvorlich, Lochearnhead	22 April - 27 May
Blair Castle Gardens, Blair Atholl	21 January - 26 October & 3 - 16 November
Bolfracks, Aberfeldy	1 April - 31 October
Braco Castle, Braco	1 February - 31 October
Cloan, by Auchterarder	30 July - 5 August
Cluny House, Aberfeldy	All Year
Dowhill, Cleish	1 May - 31 May, Tuesdays and Thursdays
Drummond Castle Gardens, Crieff	1 May - 31 October
Easter Meikle Fardle, Meikleour	16 April - End of August, Mondays and Fridays
Fingask Castle, Rait	4 February - 18 March
Glendoick, by Perth	1 April - 31 May Daily
Lands of Loyal Hotel, Loyal Road, Alyth, Blairgowrie	All Year

Ross, Cromarty, Skye & Inverness

Abriachan Garden Nursery, Loch Ness Side	1 February - 30 November
Applecross Walled Garden, Strathcarron	15 March - 31 October
Attadale, Strathcarron	1 April - 13 October
Balmeanach House, Struan, Isle of Skye	2 May - 31 October Wednesdays & Saturdays
Clan Donald Skye, Armadale, Isle of Skye	All Year
Dunvegan Castle and Gardens, Isle of Skye	1 April - 15 October
Leathad Ard, Upper Carloway, Isle of Lewis	1 June - 30 August ex Fris & Suns also not open Wed 1 Aug
Leckmelm Shrubbery & Arboretum, By Ullapool	1 April - 31 October
The Lookout, Kilmuir	April - September, Sundays & Tuesdays

Roxburghshire

Floors Castle, Kelso	6 April - 9 April and 1 May - 28 October
Monteviot, Jedburgh	1 April - 31 October

Stirlingshire

Gargunnock House, Gargunnock	4 February - 18 March, Daily & Mid April - Mid June, Weds

Wigtownshire

Ardwell House Gardens, Ardwell, Stranraer	1 April - 30 September
Castle Kennedy & Gardens, Stranraer	4 February - 30 October
Claymoddie Garden, Whithorn, Newton Stewart	1 April - 30 September Fridays, Saturdays & Sundays
Dunskey Garden and Maze, Portpatrick	Easter - October Daily
Glenwhan Gardens, Glenwhan Gardens, Dunragit	1 April - 31 October
Logan Botanic Garden, Port Logan, By Stranraer	1 March - 31 October

GARDENS OPEN BY ARRANGEMENT

Aberdeenshire

5 Rubislaw Den North, Aberdeen	On request
Blairwood House, South Deeside Road, Blairs	18 June - 31 August
Grandhome, Danestone, Aberdeen	On request
Greenridge, Craigton Road, Cults	1 July - 31 August, Monday to Friday only
Hatton Castle, Turriff	On request
Laundry Cottage, Culdrain, Gartly, Huntly	On request
Ploughman's Hall, Old Rayne, Insch	On request
Tillypronie, Tarland	On request
Westfield Lodge, Contlaw Road, Milltimber, Aberdeen	27 August - 31 August

Angus

Dunninald, Montrose	Groups welcome throughout the year
Kirkside of Lochty, Menmuir, by Brechin	On request

Argyllshire

Knock Cottage, Lochgair	Mid-April to mid-June

Berwickshire

Anton's Hill and Walled Garden, Leitholm, Coldstream	1 May - 30 September

Caithness, Sutherland, Orkney & Shetland

Burravoe, North House, Brae, Shetland	On request
Gerdi, Hillswick	15 May to 15 September
Highlands, East Voe, Scalloway, Shetland	On request
Holla, Sandwick, Shetland	On request
Holmlea, Mid Yell	Sundays in July and 3, 12, 19 August
Langwell, Berriedale	On request
Norby, Burnside, Sandness, Shetland	On request
Toam, North Roe, Shetland	18 June - 24 June
U.R.G.E., 13 Nikkavord Lea, Baltasound, Shetland	On request

Dumfriesshire

Grovehill House , Burnhead, Thornhill	April to September

Dunbartonshire

8 Laggary Park, Rhu, Helensburgh	1 June - 31 August

East Lothian

Bowerhouse, Dunbar	15 April - 30 September
Humbie Dean, Humbie	1 May - 30 July
Stobshiel House, Stobshiel House, Humbie	On request

Edinburgh & West Lothian

61 Fountainhall Road, Edinburgh	April to September
Newliston, Kirkliston	2 May - 3 June except Mondays & Tuesdays
Rocheid House, 20 Inverleith Terrace, Edinburgh	On request

Ettrick & Lauderdale

Carolside , Earlston	On request: groups welcome

Fife

Earlshall Castle, Leuchars	On request
Glassmount House, by Kirkcaldy	19 March - 30 September
Teasses Gardens, Nr. Ceres	On request
The Tower, 1 Northview Terrace, Wormit	15 April - 16 September
Willowhill, Forgan	1 May - 30 September

Glasgow & District

Kilsyth Gardens, Allanfauld Road, Kilsyth	April - September

Kincardine & Deeside

Drum Castle, Drumoak, by Banchory	July & August for exclusive evening tour bookings

Kirkcudbrightshire

Corsock House, Corsock, Castle Douglas	April - June
The Waterhouse Gardens at Stockarton, Kirkcudbright	1 April - 31 August

Lanarkshire

Baitlaws, Lamington, Biggar	1 June - 31 August
Biggar Park, Biggar	1 May - 31 July
Carmichael Mill, Hyndford Bridge, Lanark	On request
The Scots Mining Company House, Leadhills, Biggar	On request

Midlothian

Newhall, Carlops	1 May - 31 August
The Old Sun Inn, Newbattle, Dalkeith	1 June - 31 July

Moray & Nairn

Bents Green, 10 Pilmuir Road West, Forres	1 June - 31 August
Carestown Steading, Deskford, Buckie	On request
Cuddy's Well, Clephanton, Inverness	1 June - 31 July

Perth & Kinross

Briglands House, Rumbling Bridge	On request
Croftcat Lodge	1 April - 31 October
Easter Meikle Fardle, Meikleour	On request: large groups welcome
Parkhead House, Burghmuir Road, Perth	1 May - 30 September

Renfrewshire

31 Kings Road, Elderslie, Johnstone	On request

Ross, Cromarty, Skye & Inverness

Brackla Wood, Culbokie, Dingwall	1 - 29 July
Coiltie Garden, Divach, Drumnadrochit	June, July & second two weeks of October
Dundonnell House, Little Loch Broom, Wester Ross	On request
Dunvegan Castle and Gardens, Isle of Skye	16 October - 31 March weekdays
House of Aigas and Field Centre, by Beauly	April - October for groups
Novar, Evanton	On request
Sailean Cottage, 83 Aird Bernisdale, Skeabost Bridge, Isle of Skye	On request
The Lookout, Kilmuir	April - October

Stirlingshire

Arndean, By Dollar	Mid May - Mid June
Camallt, Fintry	1 April - Mid May
Culbuie, Buchlyvie	1 May - 31 October
Gargunnock House, Gargunnock	On request
Kilbryde Castle, Dunblane	On request
Milseybank, Bridge of Allan	On request
Thorntree, Arnprior	On request

Wigtownshire

Castle Kennedy & Gardens, Stranraer	November - December
Claymoddie Garden, Whithorn, Newton Stewart	On request
Craichlaw, Kirkcowan, Newton Stewart	On request
Dunskey Garden and Maze, Portpatrick, Stranraer	November - March

PLANT SALES

Fife

SG Spring Plant Sale at St Andrews Botanic Garden, Canongate, St Andrews, Fife	Sunday 6 May	11:00am - 5:00pm

Dunbartonshire

Glenearn Plant Sale, Glenearn Road, Rhu	Sunday 6 May	2:00pm - 5:00pm

Dunbartonshire

SG Hill House Plant Sale, Helensburgh	Sunday 2 September	11:00am - 4:00pm

Renfrewshire

St Fillans Church Plant Sale, Moss Road, Kilmacolm	Saturday 15 September	10:00am - 1:00pm

Stirlingshire

Gargunnock House, Gargunnock	Sunday 23 September	2:00pm - 5:00pm

Fife

Hill of Tarvit Plant Sale and Autumn Fair, Hill of Tarvit, Cupar	Sunday 21 October	10:30am - 4:00pm

PLANT SALE DONATIONS PLEASE

Donations of plants are always extremely welcome.

MAP OF DISTRICTS

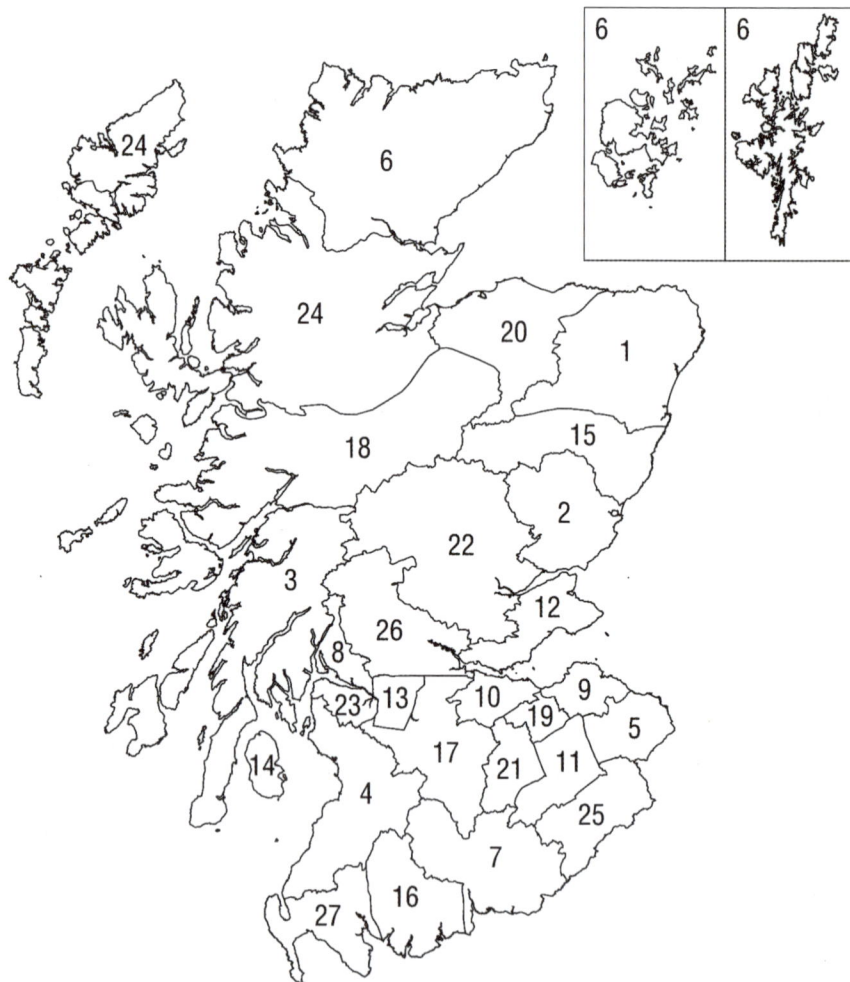

1. Aberdeenshire
2. Angus
3. Argyllshire
4. Ayrshire
5. Berwickshire
6. Caithness, Sutherland, Orkney and Shetland
7. Dumfriesshire
8. Dunbartonshire
9. East Lothian
10. Edinburgh and West Lothian
11. Ettrick and Lauderdale
12. Fife
13. Glasgow and District
14. Isle of Arran
15. Kincardine and Deeside
16. Kircudbrightshire
17. Lanarkshire
18. Lochaber and Badenoch
19. Midlothian
20. Moray and Nairn
21. Peebleshire
22. Perth and Kinross
23. Renfrewshire
24. Ross, Cromarty, Skye and Inverness
25. Roxburghshire
26. Stirlingshire
27. Wigtownshire

GENERAL INFORMATION

MAPS
A map of each district is provided at the start of each section. These show the location of gardens as per the postal codes provided. Directions can be found in the garden descriptions.

HOUSES
Houses are not open unless specifically stated; where the house or part of the house is shown, an additional charge is usually made.

TOILETS
Private gardens do not normally have outside toilets. For security reasons owners have been advised not to admit visitors into their houses.

PHOTOGRAPHY
No photographs taken in a garden may be used for sale or reproduction without the prior permission of the garden owner.

CHILDREN
Children are always welcome but must be accompanied by an adult. Children's activities are often available at openings.

CANCELLATIONS
All cancellations will be posted on our website www.scotlandsgardens.org

KEY TO SYMBOLS

	New in 2012		Homemade teas	B&B	Accommodation
	Teas		Dogs on a lead allowed		Plant stall
	Cream teas		Wheelchair access		Scottish Snowdrop Festival

ABERDEENSHIRE

Scotland's Gardens 2012 Guidebook is sponsored by **INVESTEC WEALTH & INVESTMENT**

District Organiser

Mrs V Walters   Tillychetly, Alford AB33 8HQ

Area Organisers

Mrs H Gibson   6 The Chanonry, Old Aberdeen AB24 1RP
Mrs C Hamilton   Ardneidly, Monymusk, Inverurie AB51 7HX
Mrs F G Lawson   Asloun, Alford AB33 8NR
Mrs A Robertson   Drumblade House, Huntly AB54 6ER
Mrs F M K Tuck   Stable Cottage, Allargue, Gorgarff AB36 8YP

Treasurer

Lesley Mitchell   13 Highgate Gardens, Ferryhill AB11 7TZ

Gardens open on a specific date

Garden	Date	Time
Auchmacoy, Ellon	Sunday 8 April	1:30pm - 4:00pm
Westhall Castle, Oyne, Inverurie	Sunday 15 April	1:00pm - 4:00pm
Cruickshank Botanic Gardens, 23 St Machar Drive	Wednesday 23 May	6:30pm - 8:30pm
Leith Hall, Huntly	Thursday 24 May	7:00pm
Dunecht House Gardens, Dunecht	Sunday 3 June	1:00pm - 5:00pm
Kildrummy Castle Gardens, Alford	Sunday 3 June	10:00am - 5:00pm
Tillypronie, Tarland	Sunday 3 June	2:00pm - 5:00pm
Esslemont, Ellon	Sunday 10 June	1:00pm - 4:30pm
Mansefield, Alford	Sunday 24 June	2:00pm - 5:00pm
Leith Hall, Huntly	Thursday 28 June	7:00pm
Bruckhills Croft, Rothienorman, Inverurie	Sunday 1 July	12:00pm - 5:00pm
Hillockhead, Glendeskry, Strathdon	Saturday 7 July	2:00pm - 5:00pm
23 Don Street, Old Aberdeen	Sunday 8 July	1:30pm - 6:00pm
Alford Village Gardens, Alford	Sunday 22 July	1:30pm - 5:30pm
Leith Hall, Huntly	Sunday 22 July	10:00am - 4:00pm
Leith Hall, Huntly	Thursday 26 July	7:00pm
Fyvie Castle, Fyvie, Turriff.	Friday 27 July	7:00pm - 10:00pm
Castle Fraser, Sauchen, Inverurie	Sunday 29 July	10:00am - 4:30pm

Glenkindie House, Glenkindie, Alford	Sunday 29 July	1:00pm - 5:00pm
Pitscurry Project, Whiteford, Pitcaple, Inverurie	Saturday 4 August	10:00am - 3:00pm
5 Rubislaw Den North, Aberdeen	Sunday 5 August	2:00pm - 5:00pm
Pitscurry Project, Whiteford, Pitcaple, Inverurie	Sunday 5 August	10:00am - 3:00pm
Pitscurry Project, Whiteford, Pitcaple, Inverurie	Monday 6 August	10:00am - 3:00pm
Pitscurry Project, Whiteford, Pitcaple, Inverurie	Tuesday 7 August	10:00am - 3:00pm
Pitscurry Project, Whiteford, Pitcaple, Inverurie	Wednesday 8 August	10:00am - 3:00pm
Pitscurry Project, Whiteford, Pitcaple, Inverurie	Thursday 9 August	10:00am - 3:00pm
Pitscurry Project, Whiteford, Pitcaple, Inverurie	Friday 10 August	10:00am - 3:00pm
Pitscurry Project, Whiteford, Pitcaple, Inverurie	Saturday 11 August	10:00am - 3:00pm
Pitscurry Project, Whiteford, Pitcaple, Inverurie	Sunday 12 August	10:00am - 3:00pm
Pitmedden Garden, Ellon	Sunday 19 August	10:00am - 5:30pm
Leith Hall, Huntly	Thursday 23 August	7:00pm
Westfield Lodge, Contlaw Road, Milltimber, Aberdeen	Saturday 25 August	10:00am - 4:00pm
Tillypronie, Tarland	Sunday 26 August	2:00pm - 5:00pm
Kildrummy Castle Gardens, Alford	Sunday 30 September	10:00am - 5:00pm

Gardens open by arrangement

When organising a visit to a garden open by arrangement, please enquire if there are facilities and catering available

5 Rubislaw Den North, Aberdeen	On request.	01224 317345
Blairwood House, South Deeside Road, Blairs	18 June - 31 August	01224 868301
Grandhome, Danestone, Aberdeen	On request.	01224 722202
Greenridge, Craigton Road, Cults	1 July - 31 August Mons - Fris	01224 860200 or fax 01224 860210
Hatton Castle, Turriff	On request.	01888 562279
Laundry Cottage, Culdrain, Gartly, Huntly	On request.	01466 720768
Ploughman's Hall, Old Rayne, Insch	On request.	01464 851253
Tillypronie, Tarland	On request.	01339 881529 or 07796 946309
Westfield Lodge, Contlaw Road, Milltimber, Aberdeen	27 August - 31 August	07590 808178

Key to symbols

New in 2012	Homemade teas	B&B Accommodation
Teas	Dogs on a lead allowed	Plant stall
Cream teas	Wheelchair access	Scottish Snowdrop Festival

Garden locations

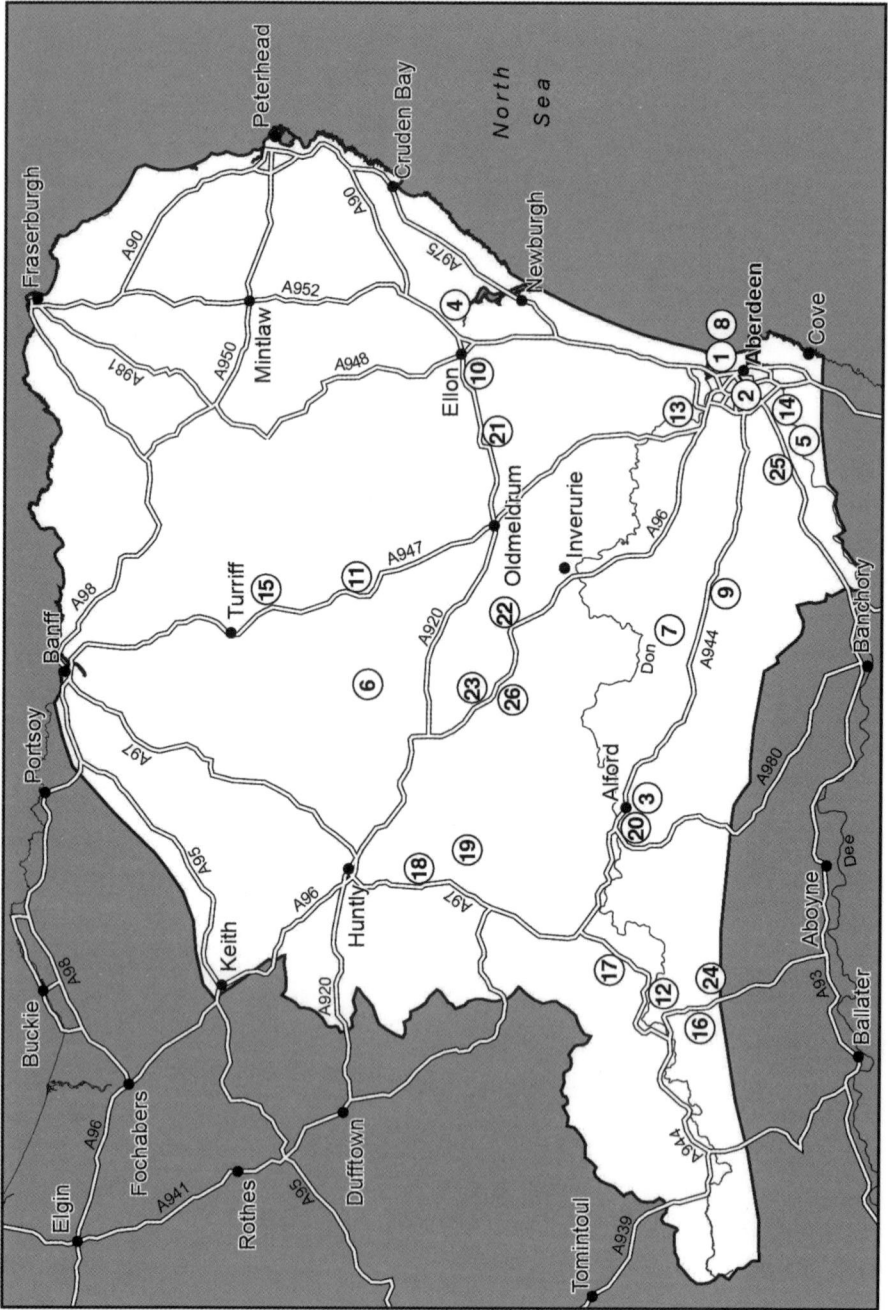

1 23 DON STREET
Old Aberdeen AB24 1UH
Miss M and Mr G Mackechnie

Atmospheric walled garden in historic Old Aberdeen. Wide range of rare and unusual plants and old-fashioned scented roses.

Directions: Park at St Machar Cathedral, short walk down Chanonry to Don Street, turn right. City plan ref: P7.

Disabled Access: Full

Opening Times:
Sunday 8 July 1:30pm - 6:00pm

Admission:
£4.00 Concessions £3.50

Charities: Cat Protection receives 40%, the net remaining to SG Beneficiaries.

2 5 RUBISLAW DEN NORTH
Aberdeen AB15 4AL
Dr. Tom Smith Tel: 01224 317345

Featured in the RHS magazine, this is a beautiful and complex garden of sculptural design with many rare and exotic plants not usually found in north-east Scotland. It reflects the owner's passion for form, science and philosophy, as well as for plants.

Other Details: Teas available at Gordon Highlanders Museum in nearby Viewfield Road.

Directions: Turn North off Queen's Road into Forest Road; Rubislaw Den North is second on left.

Disabled Access: Partial

Opening Times:
Sunday 5 August 2:00pm - 5:00pm

Also by arrangement on request

Admission:
£7.00

Charities: St James' Church Roof Fund receives 40%, the net remaining to SG Beneficiaries.

3 ALFORD VILLAGE GARDENS
Alford AB33
Gardeners of Alford

In the heart of the beautiful Vale of Alford, the village lies near the River Don amid rolling farmland. The eight gardens, both mature and newly established, offer a fascinating range of planting and designs, some quirky, some traditional, but all inspirational. Six gardens lie within the village, with a further two a short drive away across the Don. A warm welcome awaits you.

Other Details: Teas will be available in the Public Hall.

Directions: Tickets and directions available from the Public Hall in Kingsford Road, or in any of the gardens. Look out for the yellow signs.

Disabled Access: Partial

Opening Times:
Sunday 22 July 1:30pm - 5:30pm

Admission:
£4.00 : includes all 8 gardens
Children under 12 Free.

Charities: All proceeds to SG Beneficiaries

4 AUCHMACOY
Ellon AB41 8RB
Mr and Mrs Charles Buchan

Auchmacoy House's attractive policies feature spectacular displays of thousands of daffodils.

Other Details: Produce and homemade jam for sale. Easter games. Tombola.

Directions: A90 from Aberdeen. Turn right to Auchmacoy/Collieston.

Disabled Access: Partial

Opening Times:
Sunday 8 April 1:30pm -
4:00pm

Admission:
£3.00 Concessions £2.00
Children under 12 Free

Charities: Royal National
Mission to Deep Sea Fishermen
receives 40%, the net remaining
to SG Beneficiaries.

5 BLAIRWOOD HOUSE
South Deeside Road, Blairs AB12 5YQ
Ilse Elders Tel: 01224 868301
Email: ilse.elders@yahoo.co.uk

A thirteen year old garden of approx ½ acre designed to sit easily in the surrounding countryside and to provide colour over a long season, without requiring too much maintenance. Herbaceous borders, small beautiful herb garden packed with well over a hundred medicinal and culinary herbs, pebble mosaics and sunken patio area. One garden 'room' has been grown on a landfill site. River walk.

Other Details: Refreshments available at two nearby hotels. Teas for parties of 10 and over by request.

Directions: Blairs, on the B9077, 5 mins by car from Bridge of Dee, Aberdeen. Very close to Blairs Museum.

Disabled Access: Partial

Opening Times:
By arrangement 18 June - 31
August

Admission:
£4.00

Charities: Elvanfoot Trust
receives 40%, the net remaining
to SG Beneficiaries.

6 BRUCKHILLS CROFT
Rothienorman, Inverurie AB51 8YB
Paul and Helen Rushton Tel: 01651 821596
Email: helenrushton1@aol.com

A slate built croft-house is surrounded by an informal country cottage garden. There is an orchard, a productive fruit & vegetable patch with poly tunnel, herbaceous borders & rabbit proof mixed planting areas. The wildflower meadow with its wildlife pond continues to develop and the new deck overhanging the stream (River Ythan) is a lovely place to relax and watch wildlife. Due to the hedges & numerous trees the garden is very sheltered.

Other Details: Large selection of herbaceous perennials from the garden for sale. Produce from the garden available in the form of homemade jams and preserves.

Directions: From Rothienorman take the B9001 north, just after Badenscoth Nursing Home (approx 2.5 miles) turn left, after 1 mile you will be directed into a field behind the Croft.

Disabled Access: Partial

Opening Times:
Sunday 1 July 12:00pm -
5:00pm

Admission:
£4.00 Concessions £3.00
Children Free

Charities: Advocacy Service
Aberdeen receives 40%, the net
remaining to SG Beneficiaries.

7 CASTLE FRASER
Sauchen, Inverurie AB51 7LD
The National Trust for Scotland Tel: 0844 493 2164
Email: castlefraser@nts.org.uk www.nts.org.uk

Castle Fraser is one of the most spectacular of the Castles of Mar built between 1575 & 1635 with designed landscape and parkland, the work of Thomas White in 1794. Includes exciting new garden developments. A traditional walled garden including trees, shrubs and herbaceous borders. Also a medicinal and culinary border, organically grown fruit and vegetables. A newly constructed woodland garden with azaleas and rhododendrons. Woodland secrets adventure playground and trails.

Other Details: Small plant and produce sales. Live music, children's entertainment, raffle. Self-catering accommodation.

Directions: Near Kemnay, off A944.

Disabled Access: Partial

Opening Times:
Sunday 29 July 10:00am - 4:30pm

Admission:
£4.00 Children under 16 Free. Prices are correct on going to print

Charities: Donation to SG Beneficiaries

8 CRUICKSHANK BOTANIC GARDENS
23 St. Machar Drive, Aberdeen AB24 3UU
Cruickshank Botanic Garden Trust/Aberdeen University
www.abdn.ac.uk/botanic-garden/

An evening tour with Head Gardener, Richard Walker. The garden comprises: a sunken garden with alpine lawn, a rock garden built in the 1960s complete with waterfalls and pond system, a long unbroken herbaceous border, a formal rose garden with drystone walling, and an arboretum. Has a large collection of flowering bulbs and rhododendrons, and many unusual shrubs and trees including 2 mature Camperdown Elms. It is sometimes known as The Secret Garden of Old Aberdeen.

Directions: Come down St Machar Drive over the mini-roundabout, at the next set of traffic lights turn left. Garden entrance in the Chanonry. Park by St Machar's Cathedral, at end of Chanonry.

Disabled Access: Partial

Opening Times:
Wednesday 23 May 6:30pm - 8:30pm

Admission:
£5.00 including light refreshments

Charities: Cruickshank Botanic Garden receives 40%, the net remaining to SG Beneficiaries.

9 DUNECHT HOUSE GARDENS
Dunecht AB32 7AW
The Hon Charles A Pearson

A magnificent copper beech avenue leads to Dunecht House built by John and William Smith with a Romanesque addition in 1877 by G Edmund Street. Highlights include rhododendrons, azaleas and a wild garden.

Other Details: Light refreshments.

Directions: Dunecht 1 mile, routes: A944 and B977. Follow signs up drive and park at the house.

Disabled Access: Partial

Opening Times:
Sunday 3 June 1:00pm - 5:00pm

Admission:
£3.00 Concessions £2.50

Charities: Riding for the Disabled, Gordon District receives 40%, the net remaining to SG Beneficiaries.

10 ESSLEMONT
Ellon AB41 8PA
Mr and Mrs Wolrige Gordon of Esslemont

Victorian house set in wooded policies above River Ythan. Roses and shrubs in garden with double yew hedges (17th and 18th centuries).

Directions: A920 from Ellon. On Pitmedden/Oldmeldrum Road.

Disabled Access: Partial

Opening Times:
Sunday 10 June 1:00pm - 4:30pm

Admission:
£3.00 Concessions £2.00

Charities: Ellon Drop In Group receives 40%, the net remaining to SG Beneficiaries.

11 FYVIE CASTLE
Fyvie, Turriff. AB53 8JS
The National Trust for Scotland   Tel: 01651 891363 or 01651 891266
Email: gthomson@nts.org.uk   www.nts.org.uk

An 18th century walled garden developed as a garden of Scottish fruits & vegetables. There is also the American garden, Rhymer's Haugh woodland garden, loch and parkland to visit. An evening guided walk round the gardens with the Head Gardener (meeting in the Walled Garden). Learn about the collection of Scottish fruits and their cultivation, and exciting projects for the future. The evening will end with a 3 course dinner with produce from the kitchen garden and glass of wine in the Victorian Tea Room.

Other Details: Booking essential - by 10 August. Contact 01651 891363 or gthomson@nts.org.uk for more information. Self catering accommodation.

Directions: Off A947 8m SE of Turriff and 25m NW of Aberdeen.

Disabled Access: Full

Opening Times:
Friday 27 July 7:00pm - 10:00pm

Admission:
£28.00 includes guided walk with 3 course dinner and glass of wine. NB: Correct price on going to print.

Charities: Donation to SG Beneficiaries

12 GLENKINDIE HOUSE
Glenkindie, Alford AB33 8SU
Mr & Mrs JP White

Large country garden containing herbaceous borders, rose beds, hedges and topiary surrounded by mature conifers and hardwoods.

Directions: On the A97 Alford/Strathdon road, 12 miles west of Alford.

Disabled Access: Full

Opening Times:
Sunday 29 July 1:00pm - 5:00pm

Admission:
£4.00 Concessions £2.50

Charities: Willow Foundation receives 40%, the net remaining to SG Beneficiaries.

13 GRANDHOME

Danestone, Aberdeen AB22 8AR
Mr and Mrs D R Paton Tel: 01224 722202
Email: davidpaton@btconnect.com

18th century walled garden, incorporating rose garden (replanted 2010); policies with daffodils, tulips, rhododendrons, azaleas, mature trees and shrubs. At its best in April to October.

Directions: From north end of North Anderson Drive, continue on A90 over Persley Bridge, turning left at Tesco roundabout. 1¾ miles on left, through the pillars on a left hand bend.

Disabled Access: Partial

Opening Times:
By arrangement on request

Admission:
£4.00 Concessions £2.00

Charities: Children 1st receives 40%, the net remaining to SG Beneficiaries.

14 GREENRIDGE

Craigton Road, Cults AB15 9PS
BP Exploration Tel: 01224 860200 or Fax 01224 860210
Email: greenrid@bp.com

Large secluded garden surrounding 1840 Archibald Simpson house. For many years winner of Britain in Bloom 'Best Hidden Garden'. Mature specimen trees and shrubs. Sloping walled rose garden and terraces. Kitchen garden.

Directions: Will be advised when booking.

Disabled Access: Partial

Opening Times:
By arrangement 1 July - 31 August, Monday to Friday only

Admission:
£3.50

Charities: Cancer Research Scotland receives 40%, the net remaining to SG Beneficiaries.

15 HATTON CASTLE

Turriff AB53 8ED
Mr and Mrs James Duff Tel: 01888 562279
Email: jjdgardens@btinternet.com

Two acre walled garden featuring mixed borders and shrub roses with yew and box hedges and alleys of pleached hornbeam. Kitchen garden and fan trained fruit trees. Lake and woodland walks.

Other Details: Teas and lunch parties by arrangement.

Directions: On A947, 2 miles south of Turriff.

Disabled Access: Full

Opening Times:
By arrangement on request

Admission:
£4.50 Children Free

Charities: Juvenile Diabetes Research Foundation receives 40%, the net remaining to SG Beneficiaries.

16 HILLOCKHEAD
Glendeskry, Strathdon AB36 8XL
Stephen Campbell and Sue Macintosh

This garden is set against the stunning backdrop of Morven, at an altitude of 1300 feet, where wilderness meets cultivation. Wildflower areas, herbaceous borders, and organic fruit and vegetables are punctuated by numerous sit-ooteries and quiet corners, meandering dry stone dykes, and probably the world's smallest grouse moor!

Directions: From Deeside, take A97 north for 9 miles, turn sharp left at crossroads. After ½ mile take first left at Ardgeith Fishings, go 2 miles, Hillockhead on right. Grass verge parking.

Disabled Access: Partial

Opening Times:
Saturday 7 July 2:00pm - 5:00pm

Admission:
£3.00 Concessions £2.50

Charities: The Silver Circle receives 40%, the net remaining to SG Beneficiaries.

17 KILDRUMMY CASTLE GARDENS
Alford AB33 8RA
Kildrummy Garden Trust Tel: 01975 571203
www.kildrummy-castle-gardens.co.uk

April shows the gold of the lysichitons in the water garden and the small bulbs naturalised beside the copy of the 14th century Brig o' Balgownie. Rhododendrons and azaleas from April (frost permitting). September/October brings colchicums and brilliant colour with acers, fothergillas and viburnums.

Other Details: Play area.

Directions: On A97, 10 miles from Alford, 17 miles from Huntly. Car park free inside hotel main entrance. Coaches park up at hotel delivery entrance.

Disabled Access: Partial

Opening Times:
Sunday 3 June 10:00am - 5:00pm
Sunday 30 September 10:00am - 5:00pm

Admission:
£4.50 Concessions £4.00
Children Free

Charities: Aberdeen Branch Multiple Sclerosis Society receives 40%, the net remaining to SG Beneficiaries.

18 LAUNDRY COTTAGE
Culdrain, Gartly, Huntly AB54 4PY
Simon and Judith McPhun Tel: 01466 720768
Email: simon.mcphun@btinternet.com

An informal, cottage-style garden of about 1½ acres. Upper garden around the house of mixed borders, vegetables and fruit. Steep grass banks to the south and east are planted with native and non-native flowers, specimen trees and shrubs. Narrow grass paths lead down to the River Bogie.

Directions: 4 miles south of Huntly on A97.

Disabled Access: Partial

Opening Times:
By arrangement on request

Admission:
£3.00 Children Free

Charities: Amnesty International receives 40%, the net remaining to SG Beneficiaries.

19 LEITH HALL
Huntly AB54 4NQ
The National Trust for Scotland Tel: 01464 831148
Email: clow@nts.org.uk www.nts.org.uk

An open day & a series of evening guided tours with the head gardener. This attractive old country house, the earliest part dating from 1650, was the home of the Leith & Leith-Hay families for over three centuries. The west garden was made by Mr & The Hon Mrs Charles Leith-Hay around the beginning of the 20th century. The rock garden has been enhanced by the Scottish Rock Garden Club. In summer the magnificent zigzag herbaceous & serpentine catmint borders provide a dazzling display.

Other Details: 24 May, 28 June, 26 July & 23 August: Meet at car park 7:00pm. 22 July: Meet at car park at 11.00 & 2.00pm.

Directions: On B9002 1 mile west of Kennethmont.

Disabled Access: Partial

Opening Times:
Thurs 24 May & 28 Jun 7:00pm
Sunday 22 July 10:00am - 4:00pm
Thurs 26 Jul & 23 Aug 7:00pm

Admission:
£5.00 Tour & Tea £3.00 Garden only. NB: Correct prices on going to print.

Charities: Donation to SG Beneficiaries

---

20 MANSEFIELD
Alford AB33 8NL
Diane and Derek Neilson Tel: 019755 63086
Email: info@mansefieldgarden.co.uk www.mansefieldgarden.co.uk

Developing three acre country garden. Woodland and burnside walks together with a more formal walled garden.

Directions: On A980 Alford/Lumphanan road, adjacent to Alford West Church.

Disabled Access: Partial

Opening Times:
Sunday 24 June 2:00pm - 5:00pm

Admission:
£4.00 Concessions £3.00 Children under 12 Free

Charities: Alford Car Transport Service receives 40%, the net remaining to SG Beneficiaries.

---

21 PITMEDDEN GARDEN
Ellon AB41 7PD
The National Trust for Scotland Tel: 0844 493 2177
Email: sburgess@nts.org.uk www.nts.org.uk

Garden created by Sir Alexander Seton in 1675. Elaborate floral designs in parterres of box edging, inspired by the garden at the Palace of Holyroodhouse, have been re-created by the Trust. Fountains and sundials make fine centrepieces to the garden, filled in summer with 40,000 annual flowers. Also herb garden, herbaceous borders, trained fruit, museum of farming life, visitor centre, nature hut, woodland walk and wildlife garden.

Other Details: Behind the scenes guided walks at 1:30pm and 3:00pm. Self-catering accommodation available. Light refreshments in the restaurant

Directions: On A920, 1 mile west of Pitmedden village and 14 miles north of Aberdeen.

Disabled Access: Partial

Opening Times:
Sunday 19 August 10:00am - 5:30pm

Admission:
£6.00 Concessions £5.00 Family £15.50 NTS/NT Members Free. Correct prices on going to print.

Charities: Donation to SG Beneficiaries

22 PITSCURRY PROJECT
Whiteford, Pitcaple, Inverurie AB51 5DY
Aberdeenshire Council   Tel: 01467 681773

Aberdeenshire Council, together with PEP Ltd and local industry have created a 6 acre garden providing work experience for adults with learning disabilities. The gardens are fully accessible and are divided into several themed areas: sensory, heritage, wildlife and production. There are also displays of sculpture, art and crafts, hand crafted garden furniture and recycling activities.

Other Details: Disabled access toilets and changing facilities. Teas in the environmentally friendly building.

Directions: The site is located next to Pitcaple Quarry which is sign-posted from most local junctions. Be wary of using the post code in a satnav as it covers a number of properties.

Disabled Access: Full

Opening Times:
Saturday 4 August - Sunday 12 August 10:00am - 3:00pm

Admission:
£4.00

Charities: Pitcaple Environmental Project receives 40%, the net remaining to SG Beneficiaries.

23 PLOUGHMAN'S HALL
Old Rayne, Insch AB52 6SD
Mr and Mrs A Gardner Tel: 01464 851253
Email: tony@ploughmanshall.co.uk

One acre garden. Rock, herbaceous, kitchen, herb and woodland gardens.

Directions: Off A96, 9 miles north of Inverurie. Turn off at Pitmachie.

Disabled Access: Partial

Opening Times:
By arrangement on request

Admission:
£3.00

Charities: Wycliffe Bible Translators receives 40%, the net remaining to SG Beneficiaries.

24 TILLYPRONIE
Tarland AB34 4XX
The Hon Philip Astor
Michael Rattray, Head Gardener Tel: 01339 881529 or 07796 946309

Late Victorian house for which Queen Victoria laid a foundation stone. Herbaceous borders, terraced garden, heather beds, water garden and new rockery. New Golden Jubilee garden still being laid out. Shrubs and ornamental trees, including pinetum with rare specimens. Fruit garden and greenhouses. Superb views. In June there is a wonderful show of azaleas and spring heathers.

Other Details: Plant stall June opening only. Homemade teas June opening, cream teas August opening.

Directions: Off A97 between Ballater and Strathdon.

Disabled Access: Partial

Opening Times:
Sunday 3 June 2:00pm - 5:00pm
Sunday 26 August 2:00pm - 5:00pm
Also by arrangement on request

Admission:
£5.00 Children £2.00

Charities: All proceeds to SG Beneficiaries

25 WESTFIELD LODGE

Contlaw Road, Milltimber, Aberdeen AB13 0EX
Mr and Mrs L Kinch Tel: 07590 808178

The gardens have been under redevelopment for the past 3 years, under the present head gardener, with changes to hard and soft landscaping throughout the whole garden. We have an array of water features surrounded by lush planting, a large walled garden, and a tropical house which contains a koi pond and a variety of exotic plants and flowers. There are lots of things to see at Westfield to make a great day out.

Directions: On North Deeside Road (A93), at Milltimber turn into Contlaw Road. Continue approx 1 mile; turn right into single track road signposted Westfield.

From A944 turn off at Mason Lodge on to B979, straight over Carnie Crossroads, turn 2nd left signposted Contlaw, take 1st left and follow road for almost 1 mile. The Westfield turning is on the left.

Disabled Access: Partial

Opening Times:
Saturday 25 August 10:00am - 4:00pm
Also by arrangement 27 August - 31 August

Admission:
£4.00 Children under 12 Free

Charities: CLAN Aberdeen receives 40%, the net remaining to SG Beneficiaries.

26 WESTHALL CASTLE

Oyne, Inverurie AB52 6RW
Mr Gavin Farquhar
Email: enquiries@ecclesgreig.com

Set in an ancient landscape in the foothills of the impressive foreboding hill of Bennachie. A circular walk through glorious daffodils with outstanding views. Interesting garden in early stages of restoration, with large groupings of rhododendrons and specimen trees. Westhall Castle is a 16th century tower house, incorporating a 13th century building of the bishops of Aberdeen. There were additions in the 17th, 18th & 19th centuries. The castle is semi derelict, but stabilized from total dereliction. A fascinating house encompassing 600 years of alteration and additions.

Other Details: Archery, children's activities.

Directions: Marked from the A96 at Old Rayne and from Oyne village.

Disabled Access: Partial

Opening Times:
Sunday 15 April 1:00pm - 4:00pm

Admission:
£3.00 Accompanied Children Free

Charities: Scottish Civic Trust receives 20%, Scottish Guides receives 20%, the net remaining to SG Beneficiaries.

ANGUS

Scotland's Gardens 2012 Guidebook is sponsored by **INVESTEC WEALTH & INVESTMENT**

District Organiser

Mrs Terrill Dobson   Logie House, Kirriemuir DD8 5PN

Area Organisers

Mrs Katie Dessain	Lawton House, Inverkeilor, by Arbroath DD11 4RU
Mrs Susan Macgregor	Lundie Castle, Edzell DD9 7QW
Mrs Rosanne Porter	West Scryne, By Carnoustie DD7 6LL
Mrs Nici Rymer	Murroes House, Murroes, Broughty Ferry DD5 3PB
Mrs Clare Smoor	Gagie House, Duntrune, by Dundee DD4 0PR
Mrs Gladys Stewart	Ugie-Bank, Ramsay Street, Edzell DD9 7TT
Mrs Annabel Stormonth Darling	Lednathie, Glen Prosen, Kirriemuir DD8 4RR

Treasurer

Mrs Mary Stansfeld   Dunninald, By Montrose DD10 9TD

Gardens open on a specific date

Dunninald, Montrose	Saturday 3 March	12:00pm - 4:00pm
Dunninald, Montrose	Sunday 4 March	12:00pm - 4:00pm
Lawton House, Inverkeilor, by Arbroath	Sunday 11 March	1:00pm - 4:00pm
Brechin Castle, Brechin	Sunday 6 May	2:00pm - 5:00pm
Dalfruin, Kirktonhill Road, Kirriemuir	Sunday 13 May	2:00pm - 5:00pm
Dunninald, Montrose	Sunday 20 May	2:00pm - 5:00pm
Cortachy Castle, Cortachy, By Kirriemuir	Sunday 27 May	2:00pm - 6:00pm
Gallery, Montrose	Sunday 3 June	2:00pm - 5:00pm
The Shrubbery, 67 Magdalen Yard Road, Dundee	Sunday 10 June	2:00pm - 5:00pm
Letham Village, Letham	Sunday 17 June	12:00pm - 6:00pm
Edzell Village & Castle, Edzell	Sunday 24 June	2:00pm - 5:00pm
Montrose and Hillside Gardens, Montrose	Sunday 1 July	1:00pm - 6:00pm
Gallery, Montrose	Sunday 8 July	2:00pm - 5:00pm
Kirkton House, Kirkton of Craig, Montrose	Sunday 29 July	2:00pm - 5:00pm
Airlie Castle, Airlie, By Kirriemuir	Sunday 19 August	2:00pm - 5:00pm

Gardens open regularly

Dunninald, Montrose	28 June - 29 July	12:00pm - 5:00pm
Gagie House, Duntrune, by Dundee	15 February - 31 March	10:00am - 5:00pm
Pitmuies Gardens, House of Pitmuies, Guthrie	1 - 14 March	10:00am - 5:00pm
	21 March - 31 October	10:00am - 5:00pm

Gardens open by arrangement

When organising a visit to a garden open by arrangement, please enquire if there are facilities and catering available.

Dunninald, Montrose	Groups welcome.	01674 672031
Kirkside of Lochty, Menmuir, by Brechin	On request.	01356 660431

Key to symbols

New in 2012	Homemade teas	B&B Accommodation
Teas	Dogs on a lead allowed	Plant stall
Cream teas	Wheelchair access	Scottish Snowdrop Festival

SCOTTISH SNOWDROP FESTIVAL

Scotland's Gardens season starts with the Snowdrop Openings which are extremely popular.

We are very keen to have more Snowdrop properties opening in 2013 so please let us know if you have good snowdrops and would like to participate.

Garden locations

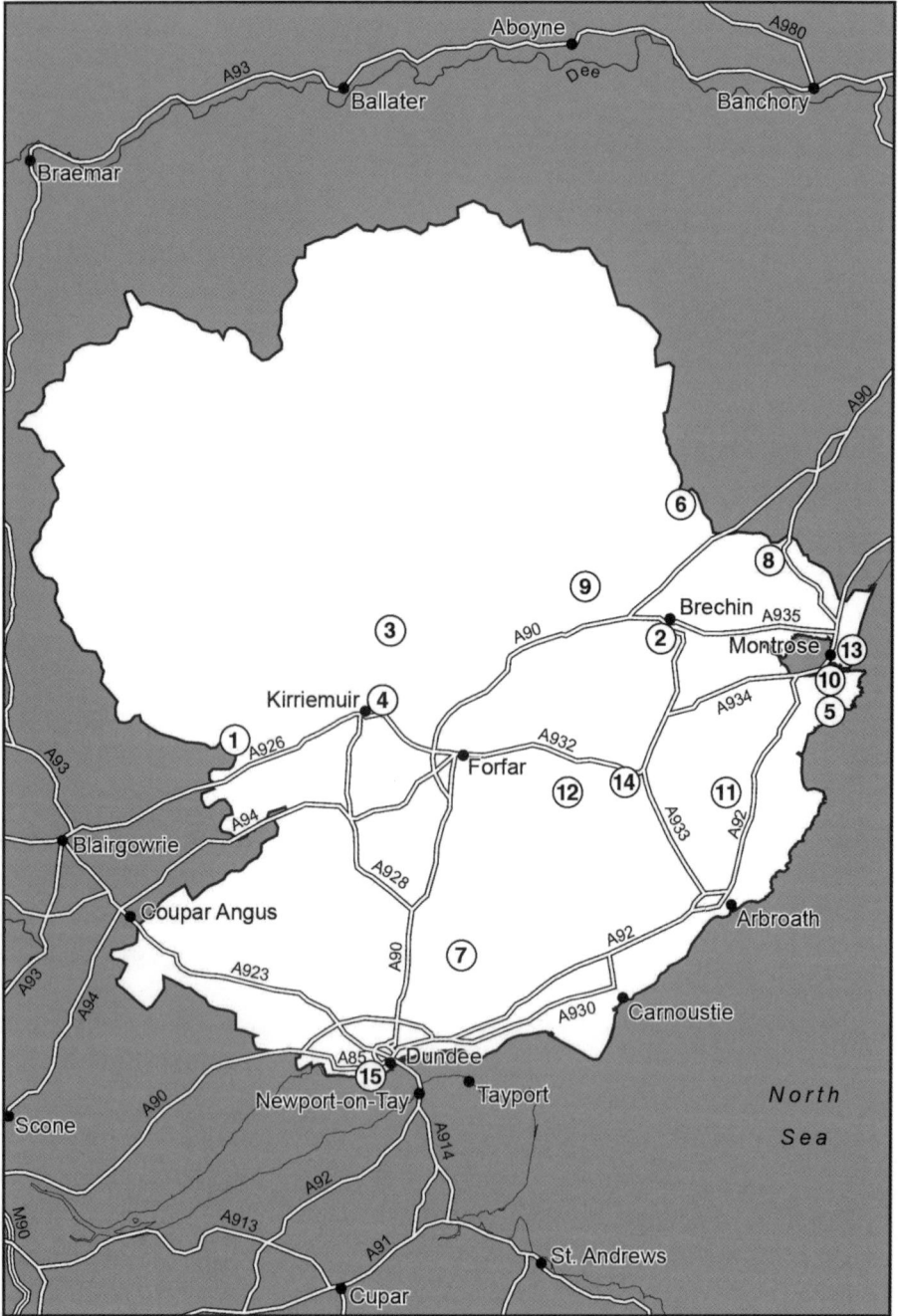

1 AIRLIE CASTLE
Airlie, By Kirriemuir DD8 5NG
Lord and Lady Ogilvy
Email: office@airlieestates.com www.airlieestates.com

An 18th century walled garden with topiary and herbaceous borders, laburnum arch and river walk.

Directions: Take B951 from Kirriemuir signposted Glen Isla. Pass Kinnordy Loch and then turn left signposted Airlie and Alyth. Keep on for 3.5 miles, pass Mains of Airlie farm on left. Entrance to castle is just beyond on the right.

Disabled Access: None

Opening Times:
Sunday 19 August 2:00pm - 5:00pm

Admission:
£4.00

Charities: Maggies Centre Dundee receives 40%, the net remaining to SG Beneficiaries.

2 BRECHIN CASTLE
Brechin DD9 6SG
The Earl and Countess of Dalhousie Tel: 01356 624566
Email: mandyferries@dalhousieestates.co.uk www.dalhousieestates.co.uk

The uniquely curving walls of the garden at Brechin Castle are just the first of many delightful surprises in store. The luxurious blend of ancient and modern plantings is the second. Find charm and splendour in the wide gravelled walks, secluded small paths and corners. May sees the Rhododendrons and Azaleas hit the peak of their flowering to wonderful effect; and with complementary under-planting and a framework of great and beautiful trees to set the collection in the landscape, this is a lovely garden at any time of year and a knock-out in the spring.

Other Details: Tombola and childrens' activities.

Directions: A90 southernmost exit to Brechin, 1 mile past Brechin Castle Centre, Castle gates on right.

Disabled Access: Partial

Opening Times:
Sunday 6 May 2:00pm - 5:00pm

Admission:
£4.00, OAPs £3.50, Children under 12 Free.

Charities: Dalhousie Day Centre receives 20%, Unicorn Preservation Society receives 20%, the net remaining to SG Beneficiaries.

3 CORTACHY CASTLE
Cortachy, By Kirriemuir DD8 4LX
The Earl and Countess of Airlie Tel: 01575 570108
Email: office@airlieestates.com www.airlieestates.com

16th century castellated house. Additions in 1872 by David Bryce. Spring garden and wild pond garden with a mass of azaleas, primroses and rhododendrons. Garden of fine American species trees and river walk along South Esk.

Other Details: Ice cream, pipe band.

Directions: B955 Kirriemuir 5 miles.

Disabled Access: None

Opening Times:
Sunday 27 May 2:00pm - 6:00pm

Admission:
£5.00

Charities: The New School Butterstone, Dunkeld, Perthshire receives 40%, the net remaining to SG Beneficiaries.

4 DALFRUIN
Kirktonhill Road, Kirriemuir DD8 4HU
Mr and Mrs James A Welsh

A well stocked connoisseur's garden of about one-third of an acre situated at the end of a short cul-de-sac. There are many less common plants like varieties of trilliums, meconopsis (blue poppies), tree peonies (descendants of ones collected by George Sherriff and grown at Ascreavie), dactylorhiza and codonopsis. There is a scree and collection of ferns. Vigorous climbing roses, Kiftsgate and Paul's Himalayan Musk, grow over pergolas. Interconnected ponds encourage wildlife.

Other Details: Plant stall may include trilliums, meconopsis and tree peonies. Teas at St Mary's Episcopal Church.

Directions: From centre of Kirriemuir turn left up Roods. Kirktonhill Rd is on left near top of hill. Please park on Roods or at St Mary's Episcopal Church. Disabled parking only in Kirktonhill Road.

Disabled Access: Full

Opening Times:
Sunday 13 May 2:00pm -
5:00pm

Admission:
£3.00 Accompanied Children Free.

Charities: St Mary's Episcopal Church receives 40%, the net remaining to SG Beneficiaries.

5 DUNNINALD
Montrose DD10 9TD
The Stansfeld Family   Tel: 01674 672031
Email: visitorinformation@dunninald.com   www.dunninald.com

Dunninald is a family home built in 1824, set in policies developed during the seventeenth and eighteenth centuries, it offers many attractive features to the visitor including a beech avenue planted around 1670. Snowdrops in spring and bluebells in May carpet the woods and wild garden. The garden is at its best in July, the highlight of Dunninald is the walled garden planted with traditional mixed borders, vegetables, soft fruits, fruit trees and a greenhouse.

Other Details: Children's trail. Groups are welcome throughout the year by prior arrangement.

Directions: 2 miles south of Montrose, signposted off A92 Arbroath/Montrose road (Usan turning).

Disabled Access: Partial

Opening Times:
Sat & Sun 3/4 Mar 12:00pm -
4:00pm
Sun 20 May 2:00pm - 5:00pm
28 Jun - 29 Jul 12:00pm -
5:00pm
Also by arrangement

Admission:
Gardens £3.50 Under 12 Free.

Charities: Scott Jubilee Hall (Montrose) Refurbishment Fund receives 40%, the net remaining to SG Beneficiaries.

6 EDZELL VILLAGE & CASTLE
Edzell DD9 7TT
The Gardeners of Edzell & Historic Scotland

Walk round several fabulous and different gardens in Edzell village including those of Edzell Castle. Tickets are on sale in the village and a map is issued with the tickets.

Directions: On B966.

Disabled Access: None

Opening Times:
Sunday 24 June 2:00pm -
5:00pm

Admission:
£4.00

Charities: Stracathro Cancer Care Fund UK receives 40%, the net remaining to SG Beneficiaries.

7 GAGIE HOUSE
Duntrune, by Dundee DD4 0PR
France and Clare Smoor Tel: 01382 380207
Email: smoor@gagie.com www.gagie.com

A one mile springtime woodland walk in a delightful secluded den along the Sweet Burn and its artesian ponds. Semi-wild pond garden in the policies of early 17th century Gagie House. Naturalised and more recent plantations of snowdrops, followed by daffodils, bluebells, hellebores, erythroniums, primroses and candelabra primulas. Snowdrops at their best late February to mid March.

Other Details: Rustic do-it-yourself tea facilities in farm building.

Directions: From A90 about 2 miles north of Dundee take turning to east signposted Murroes. Continue for 2 miles, wood on left, sharp right bend ahead; turn left along far side of wood, signpost Gagie; follow this road through stone gateposts at end (marked Private Road). Car park immediately to right.

Disabled Access: None

Opening Times:
15 February - 31 March
10:00am - 5:00pm for the
Snowdrop Festival

Admission:
£4.00

Charities: Donation to SG
Beneficiaries

---

8 GALLERY
Montrose DD10 9LA
Mr John Simson
Email: galleryhf@googlemail.com

Redesign and replanting of this historic garden have preserved and extended its traditional framework of holly, privet and box. A grassed central alley, embellished with circles, links themed gardens, incl. a fine collection of old roses, yellow and blue floral borders of the entrance garden and the fountain and pond in the formal white garden. A walk through the woodland garden, home to rare breed sheep, with its extensive border of mixed heathers, leads to the river North Esk. From there rough paths lead both ways along the bank.

Directions: From A90 south of Northwater Bridge take exit to Hillside and next left to Gallery & Marykirk. From A937 west of rail underpass follow signs to Gallery & Northwater Bridge.

Disabled Access: Partial

Opening Times:
Sunday 3 June 2:00pm -
5:00pm
Sunday 8 July 2:00pm -
5:00pm

Admission:
£4.00 Children £0.50.

Charities: Practical Action
receives 40%, the net remaining
to SG Beneficiaries.

---

9 KIRKSIDE OF LOCHTY
Menmuir, by Brechin DD9 6RY
James & Irene Mackie Tel: 01356 660431

The garden contains a large collection of plants, several rare and unusual, also many different varieties of ferns. It is approached by a strip of woodland and expands into various compartments in an overall area of two acres, part of which is cultivated as a flowering meadow.

Other Details: No dogs allowed.

Directions: Leave the A90 two miles south of Brechin and take the road to Menmuir. After a further two miles pass a wood on the left and a long beech hedge in front of the house.

Disabled Access: None

Opening Times:
By arrangement on request

Admission:
£3.50

Charities: All proceeds to SG
Beneficiaries

10 KIRKTON HOUSE
Kirkton of Craig, Montrose DD10 9TB
Campbell Watterson

18th century Manse, built by the Ross family of The Craig and Rossie Castle. Walled garden including herbaceous borders, pond, and rose garden. New woodland garden and pond.

Directions: 1 mile south of Montrose, off A92. Balgove turn-off.

Disabled Access: Partial

Opening Times:
Sunday 29 July 2:00pm - 5:00pm

Admission:
£3.50, Children Free.

Charities: Scottish Wildlife Trust receives 40%, the net remaining to SG Beneficiaries.

11 LAWTON HOUSE
Inverkeilor, by Arbroath DD11 4RU
Katie & Simon Dessain

Woodland garden of beech trees carpeted with snowdrops and crocuses in spring set around a Georgian House. There is also a walled garden planted with fruit trees and vegetables.

Directions: Take B965 between Inverkeiler and Friockheim. Turn right at sign for Angus Chain Saws. Drive approximately 200 metres, then take 2nd right into drive with green gate.

Disabled Access: Partial

Opening Times:
Sunday 11 March 1:00pm - 4:00pm

Admission:
£3.00

Charities: Yorkhill Children's Foundation receives 40%, the net remaining to SG Beneficiaries.

12 LETHAM VILLAGE
Letham DD8 2PP
Letham Gardening Club

Be inspired by the diverse range of gardens from cottage style to shady gardens to small gardens and those newly developed by keen gardeners. Tickets and maps available in the village with tea and plant stall at Letham Church Hall in the village centre.

Other Details: Homemade cakes and jams for sale.

Directions: From north take A90 exiting for Forfar town centre, then take A932 towards Arbroath and pickup signs to Letham. From south via Dundee take B978 Kellas/Wellbank Rd, pickup signs.

Disabled Access: Partial

Opening Times:
Sunday 17 June 12:00pm - 6:00pm

Admission:
£4.00

Charities: The Basement Youth Project receives 20%, Letham Village Church Fund receives 20%, the net remaining to SG Beneficiaries.

13 MONTROSE AND HILLSIDE GARDENS
Montrose DD10 8SB
Montrose & Hillside Gardeners

An eclectic mix of fascinating and sometimes hidden gardens in Montrose and neighbouring Hillside. These range from older established gardens to newly designed and planted. Parking around the town. Tickets & maps available in the town, at Dorward House, and in Hillside.

Other Details: No dogs allowed. Homemade teas at Dorward House.

Directions: Approach Montrose on A92 or A90 via Brechin. Head towards town centre to Murray Street. Turn into North Street, Dorward House, 24 Dorward Road is opposite Murray Lodge Hotel.

Disabled Access: None

Opening Times:
Sunday 1 July 1:00pm - 6:00pm

Admission:
£4.00

Charities: Dorward House receives 40%, the net remaining to SG Beneficiaries.

14 PITMUIES GARDENS
House of Pitmuies, Guthrie, By Forfar DD8 2SN
Mrs Farquhar Ogilvie

Two semi-formal wall gardens adjoin 18th century house and shelter long borders of herbaceous perennials, superb delphiniums, old fashioned roses and pavings with violas and dianthus. Spacious lawns, river and lochside walks beneath fine trees. A wide variety of shrubs with good autumn colours. Interesting picturesque turreted doocot and 'Gothick' wash-house. Myriad spring bulbs include carpets of crocus following the massed snowdrops.

Directions: A932. Friockheim 1½ miles.

Disabled Access: Partial

Opening Times:
1-14 March 10:00am - 5:00pm for the Snowdrop Festival
21 March - 31 October 10:00am - 5:00pm

Admission:
£4.00 Children Free.

Charities: Donation to SG Beneficiaries

15 THE SHRUBBERY
67 Magdalen Yard Road, Dundee DD2 1AL
Mrs E Kuwahara

Home of famed Dundee artist McIntosh Patrick for many years, the garden and house were the subject of several of his paintings. The Georgian townhouse was designed and built by Dundee architect David Neave in 1817. The garden has been sympathetically restored to McIntosh Patrick's time and features mainly herbaceous perennials and shrubs. It also includes surviving fruit trees from its original layout as a working garden. Pond with goldfish and koi carp.

Directions: From Riverside Drive in Dundee, take slip road at the old rail bridge and follow road to left round Magdalen Green.

Disabled Access: Full

Opening Times:
Sunday 10 June 2:00pm - 5:00pm

Admission:
£3.00

Charities: Dundee Civic Trust/ Shelter receives 40%, the net remaining to SG Beneficiaries.

ARGYLLSHIRE

Scotland's Gardens 2012 Guidebook is sponsored by **INVESTEC WEALTH & INVESTMENT**

District Organiser

Minette Struthers	Ardmaddy Castle, Balvicar, By Oban PA34 4QY

Area Organisers

Mrs G Cadzow	Duachy, Kilninver, Oban PA34 4RH
Mrs E B Ingleby	Braighbhaille, Crarae, Inveraray PA32 8YA
Mrs P McArthur	Bute Cottage, Newton, Strachlachan PA27 8DB
Mrs M Lindsay	Dal an Eas, Kilmore, Oban PA34 4XD

Treasurer

Minette Struthers	Ardmaddy Castle, Balvicar, By Oban PA34 4QY

Gardens open on a specific date

Benmore Botanic Garden, Benmore, Dunoon	Sunday 22 April	10:00am -	6:00pm
Crarae Garden, Inveraray	Sunday 22 April	10:00am -	5:00pm
Knock Cottage, Lochgair	Saturday 5 May	1:00pm -	5:30pm
Stratholm, Clachan	Saturday 5 May	10:00am -	5:00pm
Knock Cottage, Lochgair	Sunday 6 May	1:00pm -	5:30pm
Stratholm, Clachan	Sunday 6 May	10:00am -	5:00pm
Drim na Vullin, Blarbuie Road, Lochgilphead	Saturday 12 May	2:00pm -	5:00pm
Knock Cottage, Lochgair	Saturday 12 May	1:00pm -	5:30pm
Arduaine, Oban	Sunday 13 May	9:30am -	6:00pm
Drim na Vullin, Blarbuie Road, Lochgilphead	Sunday 13 May	2:00pm -	5:00pm
Knock Cottage, Lochgair	Sunday 13 May	1:00pm -	5:30pm
Strachur House Flower & Woodland Gardens, Strachur	Saturday 19 May	1:00pm -	5:00pm
Strachur House Flower & Woodland Gardens, Strachur	Sunday 20 May	1:00pm -	5:00pm
Dal an Eas and Dalnaneun, Kilmore, Oban	Saturday 16 June	2:00pm -	6:00pm
Dal an Eas and Dalnaneun, Kilmore, Oban	Sunday 17 June	2:00pm -	6:00pm
The Shore Villages, by Dunoon	Saturday 23 June	1:00pm -	5:00pm
The Shore Villages, by Dunoon	Sunday 24 June	1:00pm -	5:00pm
Ardlussa House Garden, Isle of Jura	Saturday 30 June	1:00pm -	5:00pm
Ardlussa House Garden, Isle of Jura	Sunday 1 July	1:00pm -	5:00pm
Ardlussa House Garden, Isle of Jura	Saturday 7 July	1:00pm -	5:00pm
Ardlussa House Garden, Isle of Jura	Sunday 8 July	1:00pm -	5:00pm
Crarae Garden, Inveraray	Sunday 22 July	10:00am -	5:00pm

Caol Ruadh, Colintraive	Saturday 28 July	2:00pm	-	5:00pm
Ardchattan Priory, North Connel	Sunday 29 July	12:00pm	-	4:00pm
Caol Ruadh, Colintraive	Sunday 29 July	2:00pm	-	5:00pm

Gardens open regularly

Achnacloich, Connel, Oban	31 March - 31 October	10:00am	-	6:00pm
An Cala, Ellenabeich, Isle of Seil	1 April - 31 October	10:00am	-	6:00pm
Ardchattan Priory, North Connel	1 April - 31 October	9:30am	-	5:30pm
Ardkinglas Woodland Garden, Cairndow	All year	Dawn	-	Dusk
Ardmaddy Castle, By Oban	All year	9:00am	-	Dusk
Barguillean's "Angus Garden", Taynuilt	All year	9:00am	-	Dusk
Benmore Botanic Garden, Benmore, Dunoon	March and October	10.00am	-	5.00pm
	April - September	10:00am	-	6:00pm
Crinan Hotel Garden, Crinan	1 May - 31 August	Dawn	-	Dusk
Druimneil House, Port Appin	Easter to October	Dawn	-	Dusk
Fairwinds, 14 George Street, Hunter's Quay, Dunoon	All summer	9:00am	-	6:00pm
Inveraray Castle Gardens, Inveraray	1 April - 31 October	10:00am	-	5:45pm
Kinlochlaich House Gardens, Appin	All year	9:30am	-	5:00pm
Oakbank, Ardrishaig	1 May - 31 August	10:30am	-	5:30pm

Gardens open by arrangement

When organising a visit to a garden open by arrangement, please enquire if there are facilities and catering available.

Knock Cottage, Lochgair	Mid April to mid June	01546 886 331

Key to symbols

🌳	New in 2012	☕	Homemade teas	B&B	Accommodation
☕	Teas	🐕	Dogs on a lead allowed	🌷	Plant stall
☕	Cream teas	♿	Wheelchair access	🌸	Scottish Snowdrop Festival

Garden locations

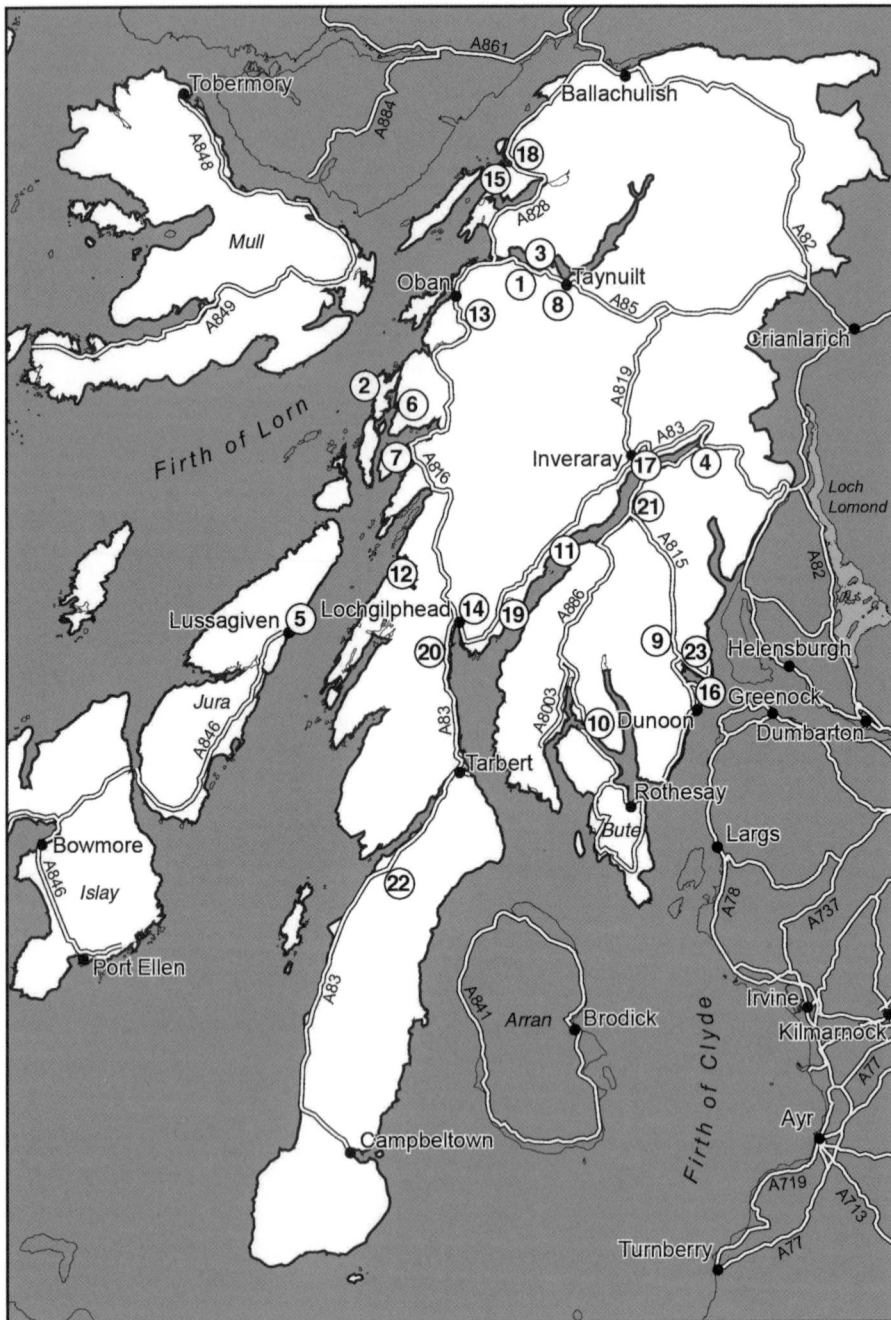

1 **ACHNACLOICH**
Connel, Oban PA37 1PR
Mr T E Nelson Tel: 01631 710796
Email: charlie_milne@msn.com

Scottish baronial house by John Starforth of Glasgow. Succession of wonderful
bulbs, flowering shrubs, rhododendrons, azaleas, magnolias and primulas. Woodland
garden with ponds above Loch Etive. Good autumn colours.

Directions: On A85 3 miles east of Connel.

Disabled Access: Partial

Opening Times:
31 March - 31 October
10:00am - 6:00pm

Admission:
£3.50 OAPs £3.00 Children
Free

Charities: Donation to SG
Beneficiaries

---

2 **AN CALA**
Ellenabeich, Isle of Seil PA34 4RF
Mrs Thomas Downie Tel: 01852 300237

A wonderful example of a 1930s designed garden, An Cala sits snugly in its
horseshoe shelter of surrounding cliffs. A spectacular and very pretty garden with
streams, waterfall, ponds, many herbaceous plants as well as azaleas, rhododendrons
and cherry trees in spring. Archive material of Mawson's design found recently.

Directions: Proceed south from Oban on Campbeltown road for 8 miles, turn right
at Easdale sign, a further 8 miles on B844; garden between school and village.

Disabled Access: Partial

Opening Times:
1 April - 31 October 10:00am
- 6:00pm

Admission:
£3.00

Charities: Cancer Research UK
receives 40%, the net remaining
to SG Beneficiaries.

---

3 **ARDCHATTAN PRIORY**
North Connel PA37 1RQ
Mrs Sarah Troughton Tel: 01796 481355
Email: sh.troughton@virgin.net www.gardens-of-argyll.co.uk

Beautifully situated on the north side of Loch Etive. In front of the house there is a
rockery, extensive herbaceous and rose borders, with excellent views over the loch.
West of the house there are shrub borders and a wild garden, numerous roses and
over 30 different varieties of sorbus providing excellent autumn colour. The Priory,
founded in 1230, is now a private house. The ruins of the chapel and graveyard, with
fine early stones, are in the care of Historic Scotland and open with the garden.

Other Details: Garden fete - catering, plant and other stalls, 29 July only.

Directions: Oban 10 miles. From north, left off A828 at Barcaldine onto B845 for
6 miles. From East/Oban on A85, cross Connel Bridge and turn first right, proceed
east on Bonawe Road. Well signed.

Disabled Access: Partial

Opening Times:
Sunday 29 July 12:00pm -
4:00pm
1 April - 31 October 9:30am -
5:30pm

Admission:
£3.50

Charities: Donation to SG
Beneficiaries

❹ ARDKINGLAS WOODLAND GARDEN
Cairndow PA26 8BH
Ardkinglas Estate   Tel: 01499 600261
www.ardkinglas.com

In a peaceful setting overlooking Loch Fyne the garden contains one of the finest collections of rhododendrons and conifers in Britain. This includes the tallest tree in Britain, a 'Grand Fir' measured at over 64m as well as many other champion trees. Gazebo with unique "Scriptorium" based around a collection of literary quotes. Woodland lochan, ancient mill ruins and many woodland walks. VisitScotland 3* garden.

Other Details: Nearby Tree Shop offers take away food.

Directions: Entrance through Cairndow village off A83 Loch Lomond/Inveraray road.

Disabled Access: Partial

Opening Times:
All year Dawn - Dusk

Admission:
£4.50, Concessions £3.50, Children under 16 Free.

Season Ticket available for £16

Charities: Donation to SG Beneficiaries

---

❺ ARDLUSSA HOUSE GARDEN
Isle of Jura PA60 7XW
Andrew and Claire Fletcher   Tel: 01496 820323
Email: fletchers1234@btinternet.com   www.ardlussaestate.com

Ardlussa House garden, one of the most remote in Argyll, is at the north end of the Isle of Jura. Cultivated over three generations, there is an acre of walled garden and atmospheric woodland walks along the coastline.

Directions: Follow single track road from Feolin (on leaving Jura Ferry) for 25 miles. Go over cattlegrid signposted 'Ardlussa Estate', through farm buildings and pull in at cream house.

Disabled Access: None

Opening Times:
Sat & Sun 30 June & 1 July 1:00pm - 5:00pm
Sat & Sun 7 & 8 July 1:00pm - 5:00pm

Admission:
£3.00

Charities: Small Isles Primary School, Craighouse, Jura receives 40%, the net remaining to SG Beneficiaries.

---

❻ ARDMADDY CASTLE
By Oban PA34 4QY
Mr and Mrs Charles Struthers   Tel: 01852 300353
Email: ardmaddycastle@btinternet.com   www.gardens-of-argyll.co.uk

Set in a spectacular setting the gardens are shielded by mature woodlands carpeted with bluebells & daffodils and protected from the atlantic winds by the Castle. The Walled Garden is full of magnificent rhododendrons, a collection of rare & unusual shrubs & plants, the 'Clock Garden' with cutting flowers, fruit & vegetables grown with labour saving formality, all within dwarf box hedging. A woodland walk, with hydrangea climbing to 60 feet, leads to the water gardens - in early summer a riot of candelabra primulas, irises, rodgersias & other damp loving plants & grasses. Lovely autumn colour. A garden for all seasons.

Other Details: Stall for veg & summer fruits in season. Toilet suitable for disabled.

Directions: Take A816 south of Oban for 8 miles. Turn right B844 to Seil Island/Easdale. 4 miles on, take Ardmaddy road for further 2 miles.

Disabled Access: Full

Opening Times:
All Year 9:00am - Dusk

Admission:
£3.50 Children Free

Charities: Donation to SG Beneficiaries

7 ARDUAINE
Oban PA34 4XQ
The National Trust for Scotland   Tel: 0844 493 2216
Email: mwilkins@nts.org.uk   www.nts.org.uk

Outstanding 20 acre coastal garden created over a 100 years ago on the south facing slope of a promontory separating Asknish Bay from Loch Melfort. This remarkable hidden paradise, protected by tall shelterbelts and influenced favourably by the North Atlantic Drift, grows a wide variety of plants from all over the globe. Internationally known for the rhododendron species collection, the garden also features magnolias, camellias, azaleas & other wonderful trees & shrubs, many being tender and rarely seen. A broad selection of perennials, bulbs, ferns & water plants ensure year-long interest.

Other Details: Teas in local hotel. Garden staff walks at 11:00am and 2:30pm.

Directions: Off A816 Oban-Lochgilphead, sharing an entrance with the Loch Melfort Hotel.

Disabled Access: Partial

Opening Times:
Sunday 13 May 9:30am - 6:00pm

Admission:
£5.50
N.B. Correct prices on going to print.

Charities: Donation to SG Beneficiaries

8 BARGUILLEAN'S "ANGUS GARDEN"
Taynuilt PA35 1HY
The Josephine Marshall Trust   Tel: 01866 822 333
Email: info@barguillean.co.uk   www.barguillean.co.uk

Nine acre woodland garden around an eleven acre loch set in the Glen Lonan hills. Spring flowering shrubs and bulbs, extensive collection of rhododendron hybrids, deciduous azaleas, conifers and unusual trees. The garden contains a large collection of North American rhododendron hybrids from famous contemporary plant breeders. Some paths can be steep. Three marked walks from thirty minutes to one and a half hours.

Other Details: Self catering accommodation. Coach Tours by Arrangement - contact Sean Honeyman Tel: 01866 822 335

Directions: 3 miles south off A85 Glasgow/Oban road at Taynuilt; road marked Glen Lonan; 3 miles up single track road; turn right at sign.

Disabled Access: None

Opening Times:
Open all year 9:00am - Dusk

Admission:
£3.00 Children under 14 Free

Charities: Donation to SG Beneficiaries

9 BENMORE BOTANIC GARDEN
Benmore, Dunoon PA23 8QU
Regional Garden of the Royal Botanic Garden Edinburgh   Tel: 01369 706261
Email: benmore@rbge.org.uk   www.rbge.org.uk

World famous for magnificent conifers and its extensive range of flowering trees and shrubs, including over 250 species of rhododendron. From a spectacular avenue of Giant Redwoods numerous marked walks lead via a formal garden and pond through hillside woodlands to a dramatic viewpoint overlooking the Eachaig valley and the Holy Loch. The newly restored Benmore Fernery is open from 11am, closing an hour before the Garden closes. Guided tours Tue, Wed, Thu & Sun at 2pm.

Directions: 7 miles north of Dunoon or 22 miles south from Glen Kinglass below Rest and Be Thankful pass. On A815.

Disabled Access: Partial

Opening Times:
Sunday 22 April 10:00am - 6:00pm
Mar & Oct 10.00am - 5.00pm
Apr to Sept 10:00am - 6:00pm

Admission:
£5.50 Concessions £4.50
Children £1.00 Families (2 adults and up to 4 children) £11.00.

Charities: Donation to SG Beneficiaries

10 CAOL RUADH
Colintraive PA22 3AR
Mr and Mrs C Scotland

Delightful seaside garden on the old B866 shore road looking out over Loch Riddon and the Kyles of Bute in this very beautiful corner of Argyll.

Directions: Turn right off A886 Strachur - Colintraive onto B866 about 2½ miles before Colintraive. From Dunoon take A815 north about 3½ miles, left on to B836 and then left on to A886

Disabled Access: None

Opening Times:
Saturday 28 July 2:00pm - 5:00pm
Sunday 29 July 2:00pm - 5:00pm

Admission:
£6.00 includes tea

Charities: All proceeds to SG Beneficiaries

11 CRARAE GARDEN
Inveraray PA32 8YA
The National Trust for Scotland   Tel: 0844 493 2210
Email: nprice@nts.org.uk   www.nts.org.uk

A spectacular 50 acre garden in a dramatic setting. Crarae has a wonderful collection of woody plants centered on the Crarae Burn, which is spanned by several bridges and tumbles through a rocky gorge in a series of cascades. A wide variety of shrubs and trees chosen for spring flowering and autumn colour grow in the shelter of towering conifers. The lush naturalistic planting and rushing water gives the garden the feel of a valley in the Himalayas. Crarae garden is the most northerly holder of the National Collection of Nothofagus (Southern Beech) in the UK.

Other Details: NCCPG Collection of Nothofagus. Self-catering accommodation. Sturdy shoes advised.

Directions: On A83, ten miles south of Inveraray.

Disabled Access: Partial

Opening Times:
Sunday 22 April 10:00am - 5:00pm
Sunday 22 July 10:00am - 5:00pm

Admission:
£6.00 Concessions £5.00
N.B. Correct prices on going to print.

Charities: Donation to SG Beneficiaries

12 CRINAN HOTEL GARDEN
Crinan PA31 8SR
Mr and Mrs N Ryan   Tel: 01546 830261
Email: nryan@crinanhotel.com   www.crinanhotel.com

Small rock garden with azaleas and rhododendrons created into a steep hillside over a century ago with steps leading to a sheltered, secluded garden with sloping lawns, herbaceous beds and spectacular views of the canal and Crinan Loch.

Other Details: Raffle of painting by Frances Macdonald (Ryan), tickets at coffee shop, art gallery & hotel. Homemade teas available in the coffee shop.

Directions: Lochgilphead A83, then A816 to Oban, then A841 Cairnbaan to Crinan.

Disabled Access: None

Opening Times:
1 May - 31 August Dawn - Dusk

Admission:
By donation.

Charities: Feedback Madagascar receives 40%, the net remaining to SG Beneficiaries.

13 DAL AN EAS AND DALNANEUN
Kilmore, Oban PA34 4XU
Mary Lindsay and Ms C Boswell   Tel: 01631 770246 or 770209
Email: dalaneas@live.com

Recently created informal country garden with the aim of increasing the biodiversity of native plants and insects while adding interest and colour with introduced trees, shrubs and naturalised perennials. A structured garden with pond, a burn with pool, wildflower meadow with 5 different species of native orchid and a vegetable plot. Grass paths lead to waterfalls, views and ancient archaeological sites. The enclosed garden of Dalnaneun is accessed through the Dal an Eas garden and comprises lawns, flowerbeds, vegetables and herbs. A burn runs through the garden and local stone has been imaginatively used for various features.

Other Details: Sturdy footwear is recommended.

Directions: A816 to Kilmore turn (3½ miles S of Oban) marked Barran and Musdale. Keep left at junction. Follow the Connel road. Dal an Eas is on the left.

Disabled Access: Partial

Opening Times:
Saturday 16 June 2:00pm - 6:00pm
Sunday 17 June 2:00pm - 6:00pm

Admission:
£4.00

Charities: Mary's Meals receives 40%, the net remaining to SG Beneficiaries.

14 DRIM NA VULLIN
Blarbuie Road, Lochgilphead PA31 8LE
Mr and Mrs Robin Campbell Byatt   Tel: 01546 602615
Email: byatt.drim@virgin.net

Originally a mill & its woodland garden, owned by the same family since 1829. Most of the development of the garden was landscaped & planted in the 1950s by Sybil Campbell OBE, Britain's 1st woman professional magistrate, assisted by Percy Cane the garden designer. It lies along a cleft formed by the Cuilarstitch Burn with a spectacular waterfall at the top. Mature species & hybrid rhododendrons, magnolias, azaleas & other shrubs under a canopy of mostly native trees. The present owners' planting brings the developed area to about 5 acres.

Other Details: Waterproof shoes are recommended. Uphill walking.

Directions: A83 to Lochgilphead. At the top of main street in front of parish church, turn right. Garden is ⅓ mile up hill on left. Beyond the houses on left a high fence leads to Drim na Vullin's entrance. Please park on road.

Disabled Access: None

Opening Times:
Saturday 12 May 2:00pm - 5:00pm
Sunday 13 May 2:00pm - 5:00pm

Admission:
£3.00

Charities: Wildfowl & Wetlands Trust, Caerlaverock receives 20%, Save the Children Fund receives 20%, the net remaining to SG Beneficiaries.

15 DRUIMNEIL HOUSE
Port Appin PA38 4DQ
Mrs J Glaisher (Gardener - Mr Andrew Ritchie)   Tel: 01631 730228

Large garden overlooking Loch Linnhe with many fine varieties of mature trees and rhododendrons and other woodland shrubs. Nearer the house, an impressive bank of deciduous azaleas underplanted with a block of camassia and a range of other bulbs. A small Victorian walled garden is currently being restored.

Other Details: Teas normally available. Lunch by prior arrangement.

Directions: Turn in for Appin off A828 (Connel/Fort William Road). 2 miles, sharp left at Airds Hotel, second house on right.

Disabled Access: None

Opening Times:
Easter to October Dawn - Dusk

Admission:
By Donation.

Charities: All proceeds to SG Beneficiaries

16 FAIRWINDS
14 George Street, Hunter's Quay, Dunoon PA23 8JU
Mrs Carol Stewart   Tel: 01369 702666
Email: carol.argyll@talk21.com

This mature garden was created in the fifties from a small orchard. The present
owner is constantly trying to add colour and interest for all seasons. Spring brings
a flourish of spring flowers, rhododendrons and azaleas. Trees of all kinds display
their constantly changing shades throughout the year and in Autumn the acers and
copper beech are at their very best. Around every corner there is yet another plant
of interest, or a goldfish pond and a swing.

Other Details: Please call to confirm if coming from a distance. Tea on request.

Directions: On A815. Enter Dunoon on loch side road, right up Cammesreinach
Brae just before the Royal Marine Hotel opposite West Ferries terminal. The Brae
becomes George St, Fairwinds is on left.

Disabled Access: Partial

Opening Times:
All summer 9:00am - 6:00pm

Admission:
£2.50, Children Free.

Charities: The Cowal Hospice
receives 40%, the net remaining
to SG Beneficiaries.

---

17 INVERARAY CASTLE GARDENS
Inveraray PA32 8XF
The Duke & Duchess of Argyll   Tel: 01499 302203
Email: enquiries@inveraray-castle.com   www.inveraray-castle.com

Rhododendrons & Azaleas abound & flower from April to June. Fine specimens
of Cedrus Deodars, Sequoiadendron Wellingtonia, Cryptomeria Japonica, Taxus
Baccata & others thrive in the damp climate. The 'Flag-Borders' on each side of
the main drive, with paths in the shape of Scotland's flag, the St. Andrew's Cross,
are outstanding in spring with Prunus "Ukon" & "Subhirtella", underplanted with
Rhododendrons, Eucryphias, shrubs & herbaceous plants giving interest all year.

Other Details: Only Guide Dogs allowed. Tearoom open for teas, coffees,
homebaking & light lunches.

Directions: Inveraray is 60 miles north of Glasgow on the banks of Loch Fyne on
the A 83 with a regular bus service from Glasgow and 15 miles from Dalmally on
A819.

Disabled Access: Partial

Opening Times:
1 April - 31 October 10:00am
- 5:45pm

Admission:
£4.00

Charities: Donation to SG
Beneficiaries

---

18 KINLOCHLAICH HOUSE GARDENS
Appin PA38 4BD
Mr & Mrs D E Hutchison and Miss F M M Hutchison   Tel: 07881 525 754
Email: gardens@kinlochlaich-house.co.uk   www.kinlochlaichgardencentre.co.uk

Walled garden incorporating the Western Highlands' largest Nursery Garden
Centre. Amazing variety of plants growing and for sale. Extensive grounds with
woodland walk, spring garden, vegetable gardens, fruit polyhouse and formal garden.
Fantastic display of rhododendrons, azaleas, shrubs and herbaceous, including many
unusuals - embothrium, davidia, magnolia, eucryphia and tropaeolum.

Other Details: Plant stall at Western Highlands' largest Nursery Garden Centre.
Self-catering accommodation. We don't sell teas, but are happy to make you one if
possible.

Directions: A828. Oban 18 miles, Fort William 27 miles. Look out for the Police
Station, the entrance is next to it.

Disabled Access: Partial

Opening Times:
All year round 9:30am -
5:00pm

Admission:
£2.50
Garden Centre Customers Free
Supervised Children Free

Charities: Appin Village Hall
receives 40%, the net remaining
to SG Beneficiaries.

19 KNOCK COTTAGE
Lochgair PA31 8RZ
Mr David Sillar   Tel: 01546 886 331
Email: Birkhill@btinternet.com

A five acre woodland and water garden centred round a small loch and lily pond. Shrubs and trees were planted around the house in the 1960s but the present garden began with the creation of the lochan in 1989 and the plantings of the 1990s. Development continues. Camelias, rhododendrons, azaleas and other shrub species are sheltered by mixed conifer, eucalyptus, birch, rowan, alder and beech. Several of the 70 different rhododendron varieties are scented including Rh. Fragrantissimum and some early flowering species.

Other Details: Waterproof footwear recommended.

Directions: On the A83, ½ mile south of Lochgair Hotel on west side of the road between two sharp bends. Very limited parking.

Disabled Access: Partial

Opening Times:
Sat & Sun 5 & 6 May 1:00pm - 5:30pm
Sat & Sun 12 & 13 May 1:00pm - 5:30pm
Also by arrangement mid April to mid June

Admission:
£3.50

Charities: Marie Curie Nursing receives 40%, the net remaining to SG Beneficiaries.

20 OAKBANK
Ardrishaig PA30 8EP
Helga Macfarlane   Tel: 01546 603405
Email: helgamacfarlane@onetel.com   www.gardenatoakbank.blogspot.com

An unusual and delightful garden which has been transformed by the removal of overgrown trees and scrub, which covered a hillside of 3 acres. Paths have been created and they wind through a varied collection of trees, shrubs, bulbs and wild flowers. There are several small ponds, many wonderful wood carvings and a secret garden. A viewpoint looks over Loch Fyne to the Isle of Arran.

Directions: On the Tarbert side of Ardrishaig. Entry to the garden is at the junction of Tarbert and Oakfield Roads and immediately opposite the more southerly Scottish Water lay-by.

Disabled Access: None

Opening Times:
1 May - 31 August 10:30am - 5:30pm

Admission:
£3.00 Children Free

Charities: Diabetes UK receives 40%, the net remaining to SG Beneficiaries.

21 STRACHUR HOUSE FLOWER & WOODLAND GARDENS
Strachur PA27 8BX
Sir Charles and Lady Maclean

Directly behind Strachur House the flower garden is sheltered by magnificent beeches, limes, ancient yews and Japanese maples. There are herbaceous borders, a burnside rhododendron and azalea walk and a rockery. Old fashioned and species roses, lilies, tulips, spring bulbs and Himalayan poppies make a varied display in this informal haven of beauty and tranquillity. The garden gives onto Strachur Park, laid out by General Campbell in 1782, which offers spectacular walks through natural woodland with 200-year-old trees, rare shrubs and a lochan rich in native wildlife.

Directions: Turn off A815 at Strachur House Farm entrance. Park in farm square.

Disabled Access: Full

Opening Times:
Saturday 19 May 1:00pm - 5:00pm
Sunday 20 May 1:00pm - 5:00am

Admission:
£3.50

Charities: CLASP receives 40%, the net remaining to SG Beneficiaries.

22 STRATHOLM
Clachan PA29 6XL
Don and Paddy Alderson Tel: 01880 740 654
Email: dons.barite@btopenworld.com

This sheltered 2 acre garden on a south-facing hillside has pleasant views across the fields & woodland of the opposite side of the valley. There are many & varied mature camellias, azaleas, rhododendrons & other shrubs planted by the first owner, Jeanie McCallum. Over 5 years the present owners have added pergolas with roses, clematis, honeysuckle etc; herbaceous beds; a gravel area with hostas and ferns; pools and watercourse; a greenhouse; fruit trees; soft fruits; vegetable beds. There is a burnside pathway plus extra pathways and steps accessing all parts of the garden.

Other Details: There is a delightful summerhouse at highest point where you can have tea.

Directions: On A83, on the right, before Clachan Filling Station, if approaching from Tarbert. Turn immediately after first 40 mph sign.

Disabled Access: Partial

Opening Times:
Saturday 5 May 10:00am - 5:00pm
Sunday 6 May 10:00am - 5:00pm

Admission:
£3.00 Accompanied Children under 16 Free.

Charities: Clachan Village Hall receives 40%, the net remaining to SG Beneficiaries.

23 THE SHORE VILLAGES
by Dunoon PA23 8SE
The Gardeners of The Shore Villages

19-20 Graham's Point, Kilmun (Mr & Mrs A McClintock)
Dunclutha, Strone (Mr & Mrs R Aldam)
Belhaven, Blairmore (Mr & Mrs J Hampson)
Saltire House, Blairmore (Mr & Mrs I McEwan)
4 Swedish Houses, Ardentinny (E Connell)
5 Swedish Houses, Ardentinny (Mr & Mrs B Waldapfel)
Garden Cottage, Ardentinny (Mr & Mrs A McLundie).
Seven very different gardens on a 7 mile stretch off the A880, overlooking the Holy Loch, the Clyde and Loch Long. Gardening for wildlife, colour combinations and for low maintenance, with terracing, sculpture, wildflower meadows and ponds, herbaceous borders and trees from seed. Some gardens are on steep slopes with limited disabled access.

Other Details: Several Plant Stalls. Teas at Dunclutha, Strone.

Directions: Approaching Dunoon from the north on the A815, take the left hand turning for Kilmun and follow the yellow arrows.

Disabled Access: Partial

Opening Times:
Saturday 23 June 1:00pm - 5:00pm
Sunday 24 June 1:00pm - 5:00pm

Admission:
£4.00 Accompanied Children Free (Tickets, with information sheet, can be purchased at all gardens)

Charities: All proceeds to SG Beneficiaries

AYRSHIRE

Scotland's Gardens 2012 Guidebook is sponsored by **INVESTEC WEALTH & INVESTMENT**

District Organisers

Mrs Glen Collins	Grougarbank House, Kilmarnock KA3 6HP
Mrs R F Cuninghame	Caprington Castle, Kilmarnock KA2 9AA

Area Organisers

Mrs Hywel Davies	Peatland, Gatehead, Kilmarnock KA2 9AN
Mrs Michael Findlay	Carnell, Hurlford, Kilmarnock KA1 5JS
Mrs John MacKay	Pierhill, Annbank KA6 5AW
Mrs A J Sandiford	Harrowhill Cottage, Kilmarnock KA3 6HX
Mrs Stewart Selbie	Glenhaven, Kirkmichael KA19 7PR
Mrs Heidi Stone	3 Noddsdale Cottage, Brisbane Glen Rd, Largs KA30 8SL

Treasurer

Brigadier A J Sandiford	Harrowhill Cottage, Kilmarnock KA3 6HX

Gardens open on a specific date

Caprington Castle, Kilmarnock	Saturday 11 February	12:00pm - 3:30pm
Caprington Castle, Kilmarnock	Sunday 12 February	12:00pm - 3:30pm
Caprington Castle, Kilmarnock	Saturday 25 February	12:15pm - 4:00pm
Caprington Castle, Kilmarnock	Sunday 26 February	12:15pm - 4:00pm
1 Burnside Cottages, Sundrum, Coyton	Sunday 27 May	2:00pm - 5:00pm
Holmes Farm, Drybridge, By Irvine	Saturday 9 June	12:00pm - 5:00pm
Holmes Farm, Drybridge, By Irvine	Sunday 10 June	12:00pm - 5:00pm
Gardens of West Kilbride and Seamill	Saturday 30 June	1:00pm - 5:00pm
Gardens of West Kilbride and Seamill	Sunday 1 July	1:00pm - 5:00pm
Barr Village Gardens, By Girvan	Saturday 7 July	1:00pm - 5:00pm
Barr Village Gardens, By Girvan	Sunday 8 July	1:00pm - 5:00pm
Carnell, Hurlford	Sunday 15 July	2:00pm - 5:00pm
Culzean, Maybole	Tuesday 17 July	10:30am - 5:00pm
Largs Open Gardens, Willowbank Hotel, Greenock Road	Sunday 22 July	1:30pm - 5:00pm
Skeldon, Dalrymple	Sunday 29 July	2:00pm - 5:00pm

Key to symbols

New in 2012	Homemade teas	Accommodation
Teas	Dogs on a lead allowed	Plant stall
Cream teas	Wheelchair access	Scottish Snowdrop Festival

Garden locations

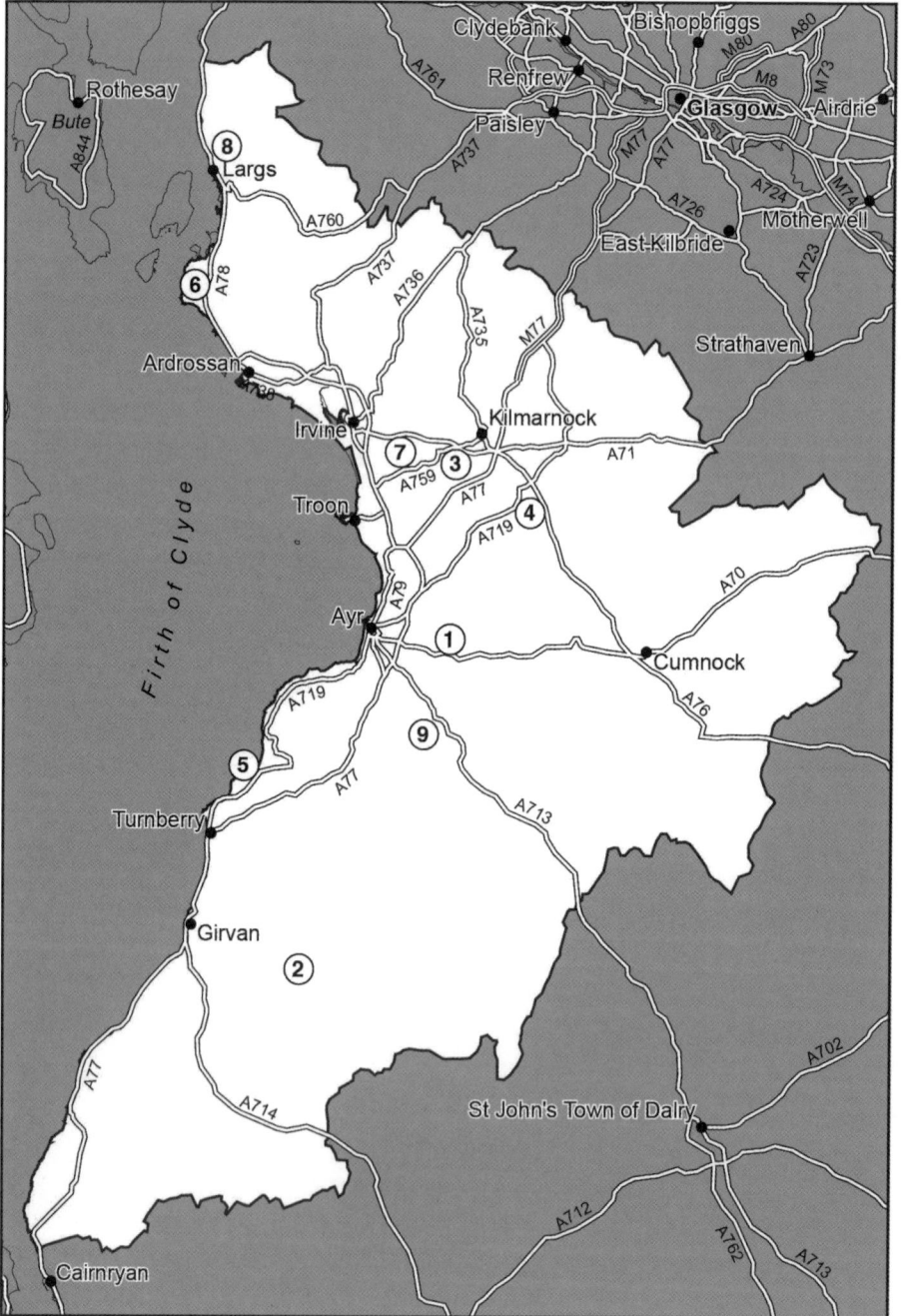

1 BURNSIDE COTTAGES, SUNDRUM
Coyton, Ayrshire KA6 5JX
Carol Freireich

A sheltered Cottage Garden of 1.3 acres. Organically cultivated, native trees and many wild flowers encourage wide varieties of bird and insect life. A stream runs through, a small wood, an old orchard with newer plantings of varieties chosen to tolerate northern conditions, a pond, vegetable garden and ornamental plantings all with plenty of places to sit.

Other Details: The garden can be muddy during wet spells.

Directions: A70 3 miles from Ayr signed left at Sundrum Castle Caravan Park. Up road ¾ mile left down dirt track. Limited parking. Or continue Coylton 1st left Barclauch Drive round right, park Woodhead Road, walk 5 mins to garden. Bus 45 or 48 Ayr/Cumnock to foot Barclaugh Drive and follow signed route.

Disabled Access: None

Opening Times:
Sunday 27 May 2:00pm - 5:00pm

Admission:
£3.50 Children Free

Charities: Ayrshire Hospice receives 40%, the net remaining to SG Beneficiaries.

BARR VILLAGE GARDENS
By Girvan KA26 9TU
Barr Village Gardeners

This July weekend features a number of attractive gardens, mostly well established but some new, within this small beautiful conservation village. Included will be the garden of Barr Primary School, featuring the pupils' barrel garden. Map and tickets available at Barr Community Hall.

Other Details: Garden photography and model railway exhibitions as well as other attractions. See map provided on the day for wheelchair access.

Directions: Barr is on the B734. Girvan 8 miles, Ballantrae 17 miles, Ayr 24 miles.

Disabled Access: Partial

Opening Times:
Saturday 7 July 1:00pm - 5:00pm
Sunday 8 July 1:00pm - 5:00pm

Admission:
£3.50 Children £0.50

Charities: CHAS receives 40%, the net remaining to SG Beneficiaries.

SCOTTISH SNOWDROP FESTIVAL

Scotland's Gardens season starts with the popular Snowdrop Openings.

We are very keen to add more Snowdrop Gardens in 2013 so please let us know if you would like to share your snowdrops with us next year.

All our Snowdrop Gardens are listed on page 49

3 CAPRINGTON CASTLE

Kilmarnock KA2 9AA
Captain and Mrs Robert Cuninghame and Mr William Cuninghame Tel: 07748 280036
Email: caprington@googlemail.com

Caprington stands in a landscape bordered by the River Irvine, close to Kilmarnock. The mixed woodland policies are well carpeted with snowdrops with early daffodils from late February. There is a walled garden with fruit trees, vegetables and flowers in season. Strong waterproof footwear recommended. Longer trails for the energetic signposted.

Other Details: Teas on 12 and 26 February only.

Directions: From M77 take the A71 to Irvine and go off at first roundabout to Troon, Dundonald and Gatehead. In Gatehead go over railway line and river bridge and take first left at Old Rome Farmhouse. The twin lodges are about ½ mile on.

Disabled Access: Partial

Opening Times:
Sat & Sun 11 & 12 February
12:00pm - 3:30pm
Sat & Sun 25 & 26 February
12:15pm - 4:00pm

Admission:
£3.50

Charities: The Order of St. John receives 40%, the net remaining to SG Beneficiaries.

4 CARNELL

Hurlford KA1 5JS
Mr & Mrs J R Findlay and Mr & Mrs Michael Findlay   Tel: 01563 884236
Email: carnellestates@aol.com   www.carnellestates.com

The 16th century Peel Tower looks down over a 10 acre garden which has featured in the "Beechgrove Garden", "Country Life", "The Good Gardens Guide" as well as Suki Urquhart's book "The Scottish Gardener". Carnell has a traditional walled garden with a 100 yard long herbaceous border, as well as a rock and water garden, Gazebo with Burmese statues, lawns and many other features of interest. Herbaceous, rose and phlox borders are in full bloom during July.

Other Details: Arts and crafts, food stalls, gallery.

Directions: From A77 (Glasgow / Kilmarnock) take A76 (Mauchline / Dumfries) then right on to the A719 to Ayr for 1½ miles.

Disabled Access: Partial

Opening Times:
Sunday 15 July 2:00pm - 5:00pm

Admission:
£4.00 Children under 12 Free.

Charities: Craigie Church receives 10%, Craigie Village Hall receives 10%, British Red Cross Society receives 10%, SSPCA receives 10%, the net remaining to SG Beneficiaries.

5 CULZEAN

Maybole KA19 8LE
The National Trust for Scotland   Tel: 0844 493 2148
Email: culzean@nts.org.uk   www.nts.org.uk

A major Scottish attraction and a perfect day out for all the family. Robert Adam's romantic 18th-century masterpiece is perched on a cliff high above the Firth of Clyde. The Fountain Garden lies in front of the castle with terraces and herbaceous borders reflecting its Georgian elegance. The extensive country park offers beaches and rock pools, parklands, gardens, woodland walks and adventure playground. It contains fascinating restored buildings contemporary with the castle.

Other Details: Guided Walk with the Head Gardener at 2:00pm: £2.00 Accompanied Children Free. Homemade wine and light refreshments.

Directions: On A719 12m south of Ayr, 4m W of Maybole. Bus: Stagecoach No 60, Ayr/Girvan via Maidens to entrance. 1m walk downhill from stop to castle/visitor centre.

Disabled Access: None

Opening Times:
Tuesday 17 July 10:30am - 5:00pm

Admission:
£12.00 Concessions £8.00
NB: Correct prices on going to print.

Charities: Donation to SG Beneficiaries

6 GARDENS OF WEST KILBRIDE AND SEAMILL
KA23
The Gardeners of West Kilbride and Seamill

A selection of varied gardens, some new this year, close to the sea in Scotland's Craft Town.

Other Details: Map provided on the day shows wheelchair access availability.

Directions: Heading from Dalry take B781 for 7 miles. Alternatively take the A78 south for 8 miles from Largs or the A78 north for 7 miles from Kilwinning. Signposted to Village Hall for tickets and maps marked with gardens opening, disabled access shown as applicable.

Disabled Access: Partial

Opening Times:
Saturday 30 June 1:00pm - 5:00pm
Sunday 1 July 1:00pm - 5:00pm

Admission:
£4.00 School Children Free
Charities: North Ayrshire Cancer Care receives 40%, MND receives 40% (Motor Neuron Disease), the net remaining to SG Beneficiaries.

7 HOLMES FARM
Drybridge, By Irvine KA11 5BS
Mr Brian A Young Tel: 01294 311210
Email: yungi@fsmail.net

A plantsman's garden created by a confirmed plantaholic. Meandering paths guide the eye through plantings of predominantly herbaceous plantings with small trees and shrubs. Some plant collections are housed permanently in polytunnels. The garden opening will hopefully be timed for peak bloom of some of the 300 iris in the garden. Some areas of the garden are currently undergoing a partial replant and redesign.

Other Details: Arts and crafts, food stalls, gallery. Please no dogs.

Directions: Holmes is the only farm between Drybridge and Dreghorn on B730.

Disabled Access: None

Opening Times:
Saturday 9 June 12:00pm - 5:00pm
Sunday 10 June 12:00pm - 5:00pm

Admission:
£4.00 Children Free

Charities: Glenkens Playgroup receives 40%, the net remaining to SG Beneficiaries.

8 LARGS OPEN GARDENS
Willowbank Hotel, Greenock Road KA30 8PG
Largs Gardening Club Tel: 01475 673155
Email: heidistone@btinternet.com

Largs Gardening Club are opening three new gardens along with two favourites from last year. The first new garden is a tiered tapestry of beautiful colours, created by an artist and talented embroiderer, also a town garden full of varied plants, the award winning hotel gardens and two new glen gardens, one providing homemade teas and a plant stall.

Directions: A78 south from Greenock and north from Irvine. Ticket Point and maps at the Willowbank Hotel, 96 Greenock Road (A78), Largs KA30 8PG

Disabled Access: Partial

Opening Times:
Sunday 22 July 1:30pm - 5:00pm

Admission:
£4.00 Children Free

Charities: UNICEF receives 20%, MND receives 20%, the net remaining to SG Beneficiaries.

9 SKELDON
Dalrymple KA6 6AT
Mr S E Brodie QC

Disabled Access: Partial

Opening Times:
Sunday 29 July 2:00pm -
5:00pm

Admission:
£4.00 Children Free

Charities: Princess Royal
Trust for Carers receives
40%, the net remaining to SG
Beneficiaries.

One and a half acres of formal garden with herbaceous borders and arched pathways. Large Victorian glasshouse with a substantial collection of plants. Four acres of woodland garden within a unique setting on the banks of the River Doon.

Other Details: Silver Band on Lawn to be confirmed.

Directions: From Dalrymple take B7034 Dalrymple/Hollybush road and follow yellow signs

2011 AYRSHIRE DISTRICT RAFFLE

Thank you to everyone who bought a ticket for our raffle which succeeded in raising over £2,000. It was drawn at the Turnberry Hotel on 14 September and won by a gentleman from Barassie. The second prize was won by a lady from Dundonald.

WITH
THANKS

BERWICKSHIRE

Scotland's Gardens 2012 Guidebook is sponsored by **INVESTEC WEALTH & INVESTMENT**

District Organiser

Mrs F Wills	Anton's Hill, Coldstream TD12 4JD

Treasurer

Mr F Wills	Anton's Hill, Coldstream TD12 4JD

Gardens open on a specific date

Lennel Bank, Coldstream	Sunday 27 May	10:30am - 5:00pm
Anton's Hill and Walled Garden, Leitholm, Coldstream	Sunday 1 July	2:00pm - 5:30pm

Gardens open regularly

Bughtrig, Near Leitholm, Coldstream	1 June - 1 September	11:00am - 5:00pm

Gardens open by arrangement

When organising a visit to a garden open by arrangement, please enquire if there are facilities and catering available.

Anton's Hill and Walled Garden, Leitholm, Coldstream	1 May - 30 September	01890 840203/468

Key to symbols

	New in 2012		Homemade teas		Accommodation
	Teas		Dogs on a lead allowed		Plant stall
	Cream teas		Wheelchair access		Scottish Snowdrop Festival

WOULD YOU LIKE TO OPEN YOUR GARDEN FOR CHARITY?
We welcome gardens large and small and also groups of gardens.

Garden locations

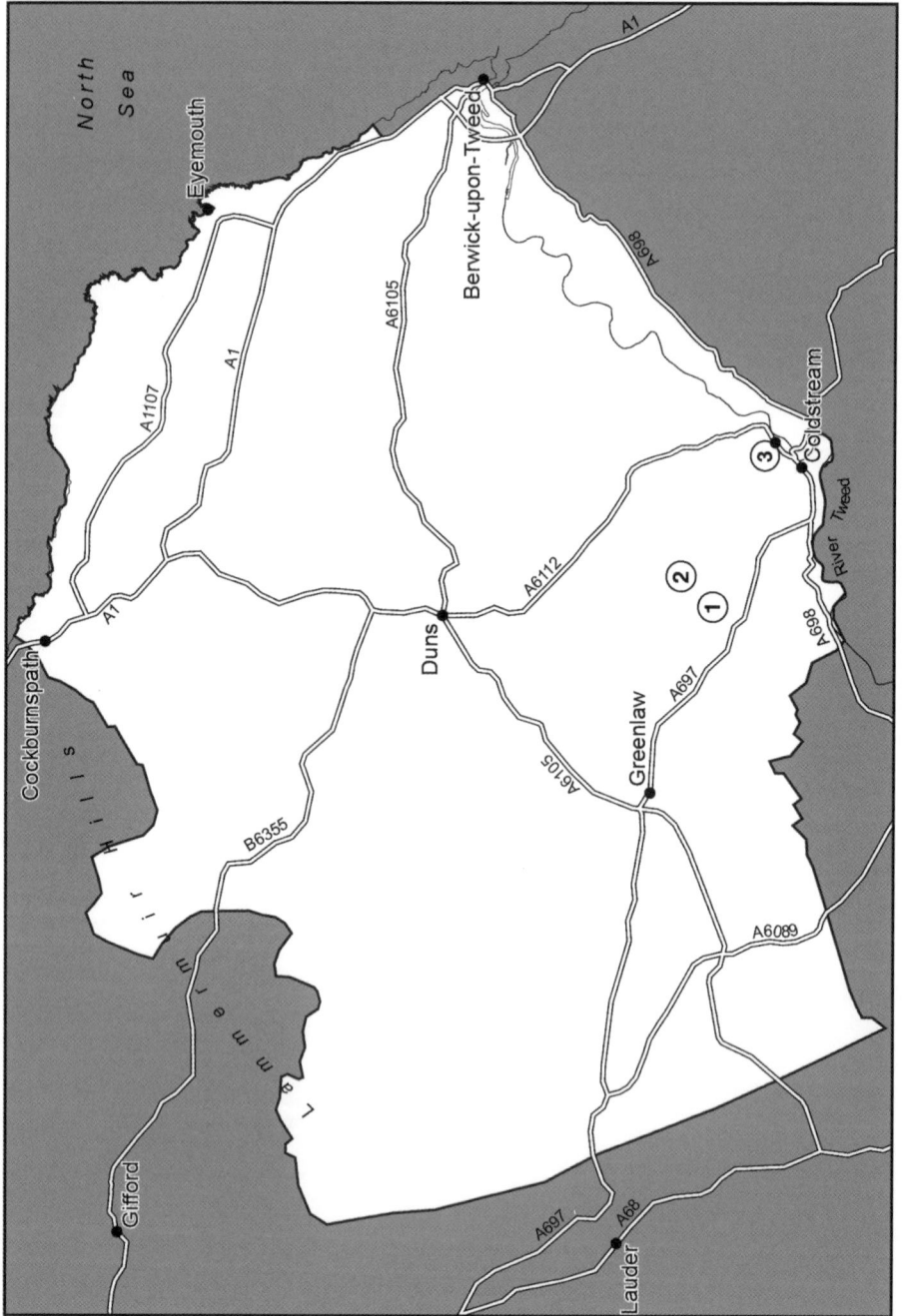

ANTON'S HILL AND WALLED GARDEN
Leitholm, Coldstream TD12 4JD
Mr & Mrs F Wills   Tel: 01890 840203
Alec West & Pat Watson Tel: 01890 840468
Email: cillawills@antonshill.co.uk

Well treed mature garden which has been improved and added to since 1999. There are woodland walks including a stumpery and a large well planted pond, shrubberies and herbaceous borders. Topiary elephant family of yew and a new woodland pond. A restored organic walled garden and greenhouse with an apple and pear orchard containing a growing collection of over 230 varieties.

Other Details: Model railway rides.

Directions: Signed off B6461 west of Leitholm.

Disabled Access: Full

Opening Times:
Sunday 1 July 2:00pm -
5:30pm
Also by arrangement 1 May - 30 September

Admission:
£4.00 Children under 14 Free

Charities: Christ Church, Duns receives 40%, the net remaining to SG Beneficiaries.

BUGHTRIG
Near Leitholm, Coldstream TD12 4JP
Major General C and The Hon Mrs Ramsay   Tel: 01890 840678
Email: ramsay@bughtrig.co.uk

A traditional hedged Scottish family garden with an interesting combination of herbaceous plants, shrubs, annuals and fruit. It is surrounded by fine specimen trees which provide remarkable shelter.

Other Details: Small picnic area.

Directions: ¼ mile east of Leitholm on B6461.

Disabled Access: Partial

Opening Times:
1 June - 1 September 11:00am
- 5:00pm

Admission:
£3.00 Children under 18 £1.00

Charities: Donation to SG Beneficiaries

LENNEL BANK
Coldstream TD12 4EX
Mrs Honor Brown   Tel: 01890 882297

Lennel Bank is a terraced garden overlooking the River Tweed, consisting of wide borders packed with shrubs and perennial planting, some unusual. The water garden, built in 2008, is surrounded by a rockery and utilises the slope ending in a pond. There is a small kitchen garden with raised beds in unusual shapes. Different growing conditions throughout the garden from dry, wet, shady and sun lends itself to a variety of plants, which hopefully enhance the garden's interest.

Directions: On A6112 Coldstream to Duns road. 1 mile from Coldstream.

Disabled Access: None

Opening Times:
Sunday 27 May 10:30am -
5:00pm

Admission:
£3.50 Children £1.50

Charities: British Heart Foundation receives 40%, the net remaining to SG Beneficiaries.

CAITHNESS, SUTHERLAND, ORKNEY & SHETLAND

For Shetland Gardens see page xx

Scotland's Gardens 2012 Guidebook is sponsored by **INVESTEC WEALTH & INVESTMENT**

District Organiser

Mrs Judith Middlemas	22 Miller Place, Scrabster, Thurso KW14 7UH

Area Organisers

Mrs Kathy Greaves	Shangri-La, 3 Anderson Road, Lerwick, Shetland ZE1 0HP
Mrs Mary Leask	VisitShetland, Market Cross, Lerwick, Shetland ZE1 0LU
Mr Steve Mathieson	VisitShetland, Market Cross, Lerwick, Shetland ZE1 0LU
Mrs Jonny Shaw	Amat, Ardgay, Sutherland IV24 3BS

Treasurer

Mr Chris Hobson	Braeside, Dunnet, Caithness KW14 8YD

Gardens open on a specific date

Pentland Firth Gardens, Dunnet	Sunday 3 June	1:00pm	- 5:00pm
Amat, Ardgay	Saturday 9 June	2:00pm	- 5:00pm
Amat, Ardgay	Sunday 10 June	2:00pm	- 5:00pm
The Castle & Gardens of Mey	Wednesday 4 July	10:00am	- 5:00pm
The Castle & Gardens of Mey	Thursday 12 July	10:00am	- 5:00pm
House of Tongue, Tongue, Lairg	Saturday 28 July	2:00pm	- 6:00pm
Flagstone Village Gardens, Castletown	Sunday 29 July	1:00pm	- 5:00pm
Langwell, Berriedale	Sunday 5 August	2:00pm	- 5:00pm
Langwell, Berriedale	Sunday 12 August	2:00pm	- 5:00pm
The Castle & Gardens of Mey	Saturday 18 August	10:00am	- 5:00pm
Springpark House, Laurie Terrace, Thurso	Sunday 19 August	11:00am	- 5:00pm

Gardens open regularly

The Castle & Gardens of Mey	1 May - 25 Jul & 14 Aug - 30 Sep	10:00am - 5:00pm

Gardens open by arrangement

Langwell, Berriedale	On request	01593 751278/751237

Key to symbols

New in 2012	Homemade teas	B&B	Accommodation
Teas	Dogs on a lead allowed		Plant stall
Cream teas	Wheelchair access		Scottish Snowdrop Festival

Garden locations

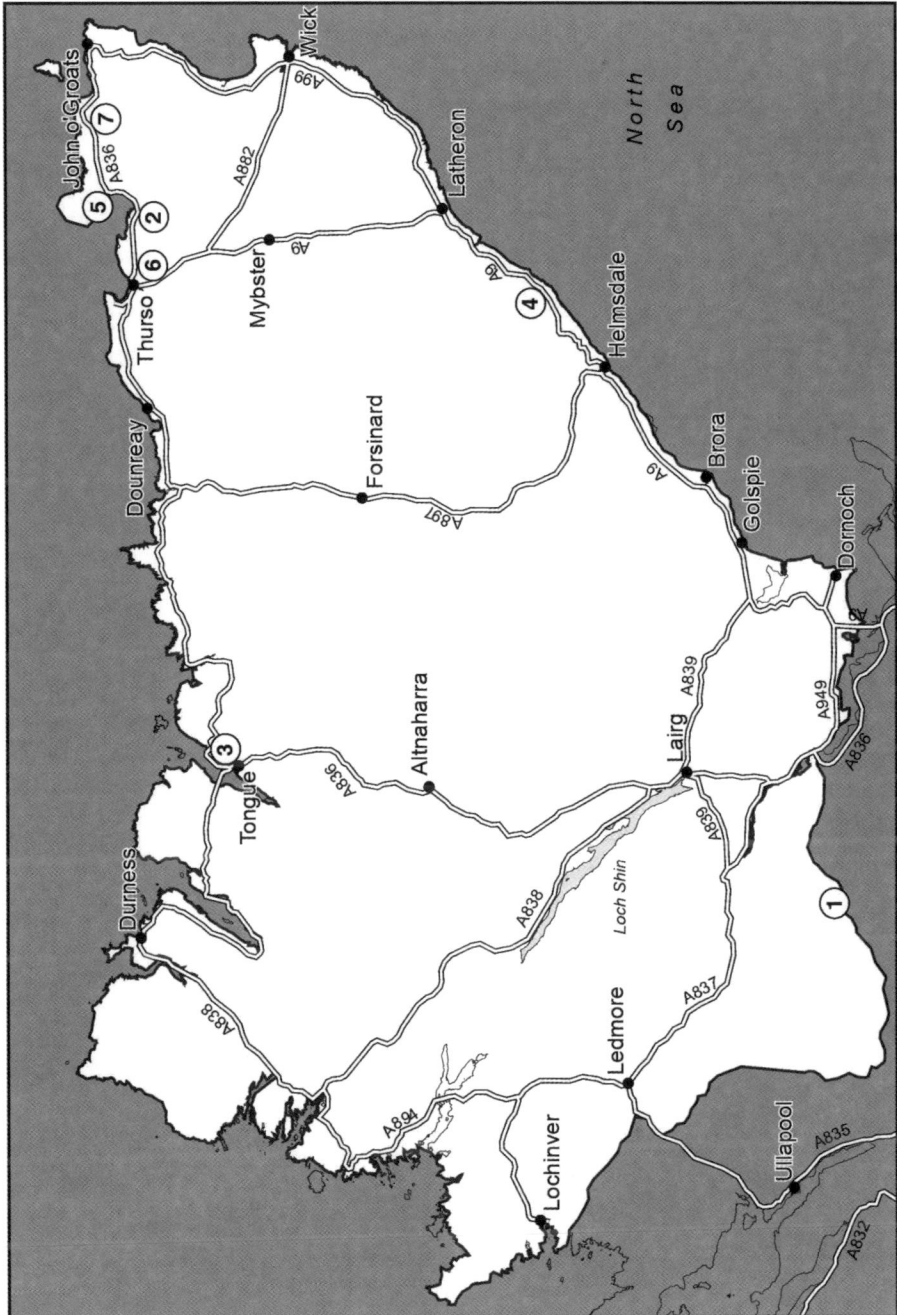

1 AMAT

Ardgay IV24 3BS
Jonny and Sara Shaw
Email: saraamat@btinternet.com

Riverside garden set in Amat forest. Herbaceous borders and rockery set in large lawn looking onto salmon pool. Old and new rhododendrons with woodland and river walk.

Directions: Take road from Ardgay to Croick 9 miles. Turn left at red phone box. 500 yards on left.

Disabled Access: Partial

Opening Times:
Saturday 9 June 2:00pm - 5:00pm
Sunday 10 June 2:00pm - 5:00pm

Admission:
£4.00

Charities: Croick Church receives 20%, Maggie's Centres receives 20%, the net remaining to SG Beneficiaries.

2 FLAGSTONE VILLAGE GARDENS

Castletown KW14 8TG
Flagstone Village Gardeners   Tel: 01847 821 204
Email: castletown.heritage@talk21.com   www.castletownheritage.co.uk

In a range of challenging situations: quarry-edge, former midden yard or next to a busy main road, Castletown gardeners present glorious floral surprises.

Other Details: Toilets at Castlehill. Woodland walk. Heritage exhibition. Homemade teas at Castlehill.

Directions: Start at Castlehill Heritage Centre, Castletown KW14 8TG, where a map of all gardens will be available on payment of admission fee.

Disabled Access: Partial

Opening Times:
Sunday 29 July 1:00pm - 5:00pm

Admission:
£4.00 Concession £3.00
Under 12 Free.

Charities: All proceeds to SG Beneficiaries

3 HOUSE OF TONGUE

Tongue, Lairg IV27 4XH
The Countess of Sutherland
Email: ginrik@btopenworld.com

17th century house on Kyle of Tongue. Superb walled garden, herbaceous borders, old fashioned roses, vegetables, soft fruit and small orchard.

Directions: Tongue half a mile. House just off main road approaching causeway.

Disabled Access: Partial

Opening Times:
Saturday 28 July 2:00pm - 6:00pm

Admission:
Adult £4.00, OAPs £3.00, Children under 12 £0.50.

Charities: Children 1st receives 40%, the net remaining to SG Beneficiaries.

4 LANGWELL
Berriedale KW7 6HD
Welbeck Estates Tel: 01593 751278/751237
Email: macanson@hotmail.com

A beautiful and spectacular old walled-in garden with outstanding borders situated in the secluded Langwell Strath. Charming access drive with a chance to see deer.

Other Details: Homemade teas will be under cover.

Directions: A9 Berriedale 2 miles.

Disabled Access: Partial

Opening Times:
Sunday 5 August 2:00pm - 5:00pm
Sunday 12 August 2:00pm - 5:00pm
Also by arrangement on request

Admission:
£4.00, OAPs £3.00, Children under 12 Free.

Charities: RNLI receives 40%, the net remaining to SG Beneficiaries.

5 PENTLAND FIRTH GARDENS
Dunnet KW14 8YD
The Pentland Firth Gardeners Tel: 01847 851757

With panoramic views of the Pentland Firth, these gardens show what is possible when gardening on the exposed northern coast of Scotland. Two varied gardens, one with a rock garden and herb wheel, greenhouse and container; grown veg, the other with a good selection of trees, a pond and vegetable garden. Both gardens have a good variety of hardy plants and shrubs to enjoy. Transport required in order to visit both gardens.

Other Details: Toilets and teas available at Britannia Hall.

Directions: Start at Britannia Hall, Dunnet KW14 8YD where a map of gardens will be available on payment of admission fee.

Disabled Access: Partial

Opening Times:
Sunday 3 June 1:00pm - 5:00pm

Admission:
£3.00 Children under 12 Free

Charities: Dunnet Forest Trust receives 40%, the net remaining to SG Beneficiaries.

6 SPRINGPARK HOUSE
Laurie Terrace, Thurso KW14 8NR
Mr Ronald and Mrs Kirsty Gunn Tel: 01847 894797

Several individually styled gardens within one walled garden. Collection of old farming implements and household memorabilia on show. Vegetable garden with large polytunnel. The garden is on one level with good wheelchair access and plenty of parking space.

Other Details: Teas £2.00.

Directions: In Thurso off the Castletown road at Mount Pleasant Road, continue up the hill until you see Laurie Terrace (last road on the right), house is at the end. Park in garden or road.

Disabled Access: Full

Opening Times:
Sunday 19 August 11:00am - 5:00pm

Admission:
£3.50

Charities: Cancer Research UK receives 40%, the net remaining to SG Beneficiaries.

THE CASTLE & GARDENS OF MEY
Mey KW14 8XH
The Queen Elizabeth Castle of Mey Trust   Tel: 01847 851473
Email: enquiries@castleofmey.org.uk   www.castleofmey.org.uk

Originally a Z plan castle bought by the Queen Mother in 1952 and then restored and improved. The walled garden and the East Garden were also created by the Queen Mother. An animal centre has been established over the last 3 years and is proving very popular with all ages.

Other Details: Tearoom, shop and animal centre. Check castle website as 14 August date may change.

Directions: On A836 between Thurso and John O'Groats, 1½ miles from Mey.

Disabled Access: Partial

Opening Times:
Wed 4 July 10:00am - 5:00pm
Thur 12 July 10:00am - 5:00pm
Sat 18 Aug. 10:00am - 5:00pm
1 May - 25 July and 14 August -
30 Sept. 10:00am - 5:00pm

Admission:
Adults £10.00 Conc. £9.00.
Children £5.50 Family £26.00
Gardens & Grounds only £5.50.

Charities: Cardiac Unit
Raigmore Hospital receives
40%, the net remaining to SG
Beneficiaries.

WOULD YOU LIKE TO OPEN YOUR GARDEN FOR CHARITY?

If you are interested in opening your garden for charity and would like more information, call 0131 226 3714, email info@scotlandsgardens.org or fill in the form at the back of this book.

We welcome gardens large and small and also groups of gardens.

SHETLAND

Scotland's Gardens 2012 Guidebook is sponsored by **INVESTEC WEALTH & INVESTMENT**

Gardens open on a specific date

Shangri-La, 3 Anderson Road, Lerwick	Sunday 27 May	1:00pm - 5:00pm
Shangri-La, 3 Anderson Road, Lerwick	Monday 28 May	1:00pm - 5:00pm
Birch Garden, 3 Sands of Sound	Saturday 9 June	2:00pm - 4:00pm
Cruisdale, Sandness	Saturday 9 June	10:00am - 7:00pm
Cruisdale, Sandness	Sunday 10 June	10:00am - 7:00pm
Birch Garden, 3 Sands of Sound	Saturday 16 June	2:00pm - 4:00pm
Shangri-La, 3 Anderson Road, Lerwick	Wednesday 20 June	1:00pm - 5:00pm
Shangri-La, 3 Anderson Road, Lerwick	Thursday 21 June	1:00pm - 5:00pm
Birch Garden, 3 Sands of Sound	Saturday 23 June	2:00pm - 4:00pm
Birch Garden, 3 Sands of Sound	Saturday 30 June	2:00pm - 4:00pm
15 Linkshouse, Mid Yell	Thursday 5 July	11:00am - 4:00pm
Fernbank, Camb, Yell	Thursday 5 July	11:00am - 4:00pm
15 Linkshouse, Mid Yell	Thursday 12 July	11:00am - 4:00pm
Fernbank, Camb, Yell	Thursday 12 July	11:00am - 4:00pm
15 Linkshouse, Mid Yell	Thursday 19 July	11:00am - 4:00pm
Fernbank, Camb, Yell	Thursday 19 July	11:00am - 4:00pm
15 Linkshouse, Mid Yell	Thursday 26 July	11:00am - 4:00pm
Fernbank, Camb, Yell	Thursday 26 July	11:00am - 4:00pm
Lea Gardens, Tresta	Sunday 29 July	2:00pm - 5:00pm
Burravoe, North House, Brae	Sunday 5 August	2:00pm - 5:00pm
Cruisdale, Sandness	Saturday 11 August	10:00am - 7:00pm
Burravoe, North House, Brae	Sunday 12 August	2:00pm - 5:00pm
Cruisdale, Sandness	Sunday 12 August	10:00am - 7:00pm
The Old Playground, Old School Road, Trondra	Sunday 12 August	2:00pm - 5:00pm
Burravoe, North House, Brae	Sunday 19 August	2:00pm - 5:00pm
Burravoe, North House, Brae	Sunday 26 August	2:00pm - 5:00pm
Cruisdale, Sandness	Saturday 1 September	10:00am - 7:00pm
Cruisdale, Sandness	Sunday 2 September	10:00am - 7:00pm

Gardens open regularly

Cruisdale, Sandness	2 July - 8 July	10:00am - 7:00pm
Holla, Sandwick	Open most days	10:00am - 5:00pm
Lea Gardens, Tresta	March - October	2:00pm - 5:00pm
Nonavaar, Levenwick	2 June - 25 August, Saturdays	10:00am - 2:00pm
	4 June - 27 August, Mondays	10:00am - 4:00pm
U.R.G.E., 13 Nikkavord Lea, Baltasound, Unst	11-15, 18-22, and 25-29 July	12:00pm - 4:00pm

Gardens open by arrangement

Burravoe, North House, Brae	On request	07765 606429
Gerdi, Hillswick	15 May to 15 September	01806 503776
Highlands, East Voe, Scalloway	On request	01595 880526
Holla, Sandwick	On request	01950 431369
Holmlea, Mid Yell	Suns in July & 3, 12, 19 Aug	01957 702062
Norby, Burnside, Sandness	On request	01595 870246
Toam, North Roe	18 June - 24 June	01806 533217
U.R.G.E., 13 Nikkavord Lea, Baltasound, Unst	On request	01957 711367

Key to symbols

🌳	New in 2012	H☕	Homemade teas	C☕	Accommodation
☕	Teas	🐕	Dogs allowed	🌷	Plant stall
C☕	Cream teas	♿	Wheelchair access	🌱	Scottish Snowdrop Festival

NEW GARDENS

Over 50 new gardens opening this year. For a full listing and photographs go to pages 20 - 23 .

Garden locations

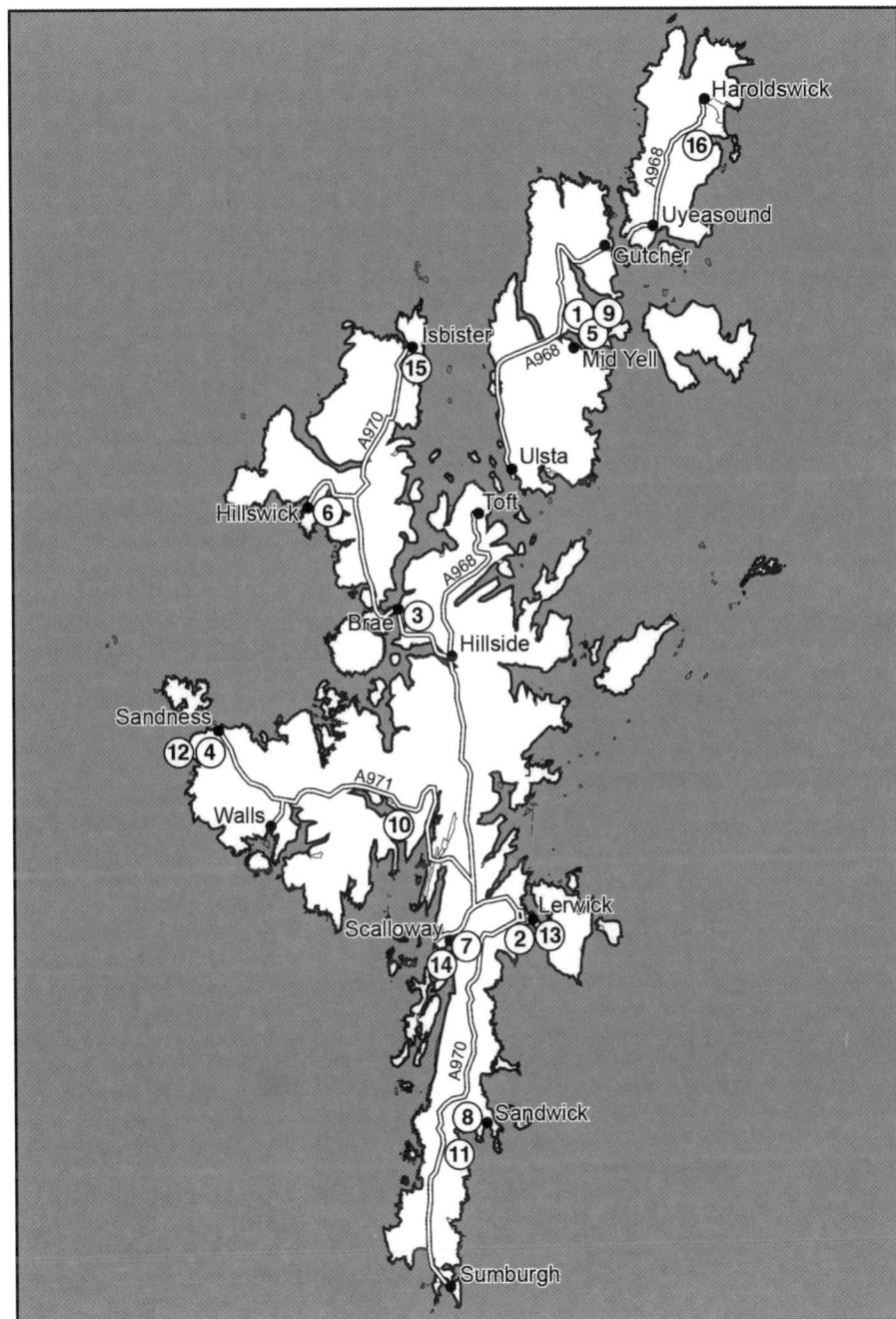

1 15 LINKSHOUSE (IN CONJUNCTION WITH FERNBANK)
Mid Yell ZE2 9BP
Mr Charlie Inkster   Tel: 01957 702049
Email: cjinkster@btinternet.com

A small cottage garden with a greenhouse full of plants and colour, a pond complete with fountain and water lilies, and a small aviary with canaries and finches.The garden is well established with trees, bushes and a good variety of plants giving plenty of colour. Fuschias are a favourite providing a good selection of different varieties both in the garden and in the greenhouse. Also in the greenhouse are many varieties of streptocarpus adding to the colourful display.

Directions: In Yell head north on the A968, turn right to Mid Yell. Drive down through Mid Yell and turn towards Linkshouse Pier. The garden is at the far end of the row of white cottages.

Disabled Access: None

Opening Times:
Thursdays: 5, 12, 19 & 26 July
11:00am - 4:00pm

Admission:
£4.00 (joint entry charge payable at either garden)

Charities: Yell for Cancer Support receives 20%, British Heart Foundation receives 20%, the net remaining to SG Beneficiaries.

2 BIRCH GARDEN
3 Sands of Sound ZE1 0SZ
Mr and Mrs WJ Johnston

Overlooking the Ness of Sound the garden is sheltered by a selection of hardy trees. The garden has three main areas. Front is a low level rockery with a mix of alpines, perennials and smaller shrubs. The back garden consists of four main borders which have a wide variety of perennials, shrubs, bulbs and roses and we have a grass border with two large Gunneras. A feature is a summer house from which to view the garden and provide winter protection for non-hardy plants.

Directions: Drive south out of Lerwick, go left at roundabout before the Sound School. After Blyd 'O' It shop take next left, second right along Braefield, turn right, we are the second bungalow.

Disabled Access: None

Opening Times:
Saturdays 9, 16, 23 & 30 June
2:00pm - 4:00pm

Admission:
£3.00

Charities: Mind Your Head receives 40%, the net remaining to SG Beneficiaries.

3 BURRAVOE
North House, Brae, Shetland ZE2 9QJ
Mr and Mrs A B Hall   Tel: 07765 606429

This garden is on a working croft. It is a large area ideal for a leisurely stroll through the woodland plantation, then enjoy the flowers in a sheltered walled garden with a pond to complete your visit.

Directions: Head north to Brae, take first left after the 'Welcome to Brae' sign (just before the Indian takeaway and the hairdressers), go left again and continue to the bottom of the road.

Disabled Access: Full

Opening Times:
Sundays 5, 12, 19 & 26 August
2:00pm - 5:00pm
Also by arrangement on request

Admission:
£3.00

Charities: Mind Your Head receives 40%, the net remaining to SG Beneficiaries.

4 CRUISDALE
Sandness, Shetland ZE2 9PL
Alfred Kern   Tel: 01595 870739

The garden is in a natural state with many willows, several ponds and a variety of colourful hardy plants that grow well in the Shetland climate. It is a work in progress, started about six years ago and growing bigger over the years with more work planned.

Directions: In Sandness, on the west side of Shetland. Opposite the school, on the right hand side with a wind generator in the field.

Disabled Access: None

Opening Times:
Sat & Sun 9 & 10 June
10:00am - 7:00pm
Sat & Sun 11 & 12 August
10:00am - 7:00pm
Sat & Sun 1 & 2 September
10:00am - 7:00pm
2 - 8 July 10:00am - 7:00pm

Admission:
£3.00

Charities: WRVS receives 40%, the net remaining to SG Beneficiaries.

5 FERNBANK (IN CONJUCTION WITH 15 LINKSHOUSE)
Camb, Yell ZE2 9DA
Helen and Matthew Nicholson   Tel: 01957 702414

An established garden with two arches through hedges into different areas where you can admire the selection of herbaceous plants, annuals and shrubs. There are several varieties of trees such as sycamore, horse chestnut, Japanese larch, witch elm and holly. In the greenhouse is a colourful selection of flowers and you will find apples, plums and blackcurrants growing in the fruit house. An unusual feature in the garden is a shed using the hull of an old boat for the roof.

Directions: Once in Yell, go north, turn right at Camb then right at the crossroads. Fernbank is below the road at the Clingra Park housing scheme. A big long house with a garage at the back.

Disabled Access: None

Opening Times:
Thursdays: 5, 12, 19 & 26 July
11:00am - 4:00pm

Admission:
£4.00 - joint entry charge payable at either garden.

Charities: British Heart Foundation receives 20%, Yell for Cancer Support receives 20%, the net remaining to SG Beneficiaries.

6 GERDI
Hillswick ZE2 9RW
Alison Charleson   Tel: 01806 503776

A small, new garden, surrounded by moorland full of wild flowers. The beds surrounding the house contain a mixture of herbaceous plants and grasses with trees and shrubs to give shelter and colour throughout the summer. Meandering stone paths allow the plants to be enjoyed close up.

Directions: Follow the A970 north from Lerwick to Hillswick, continuing on past the public hall and Stucca. Gerdi is a pale blue wooden chalet on the left just before the Hillswick Hotel.

Disabled Access: None

Opening Times:
Open by arrangement 15 May - 15 September

Admission:
£3.00

Charities: All proceeds to SG Beneficiaries

7 HIGHLANDS
East Voe, Scalloway, Shetland ZE1 0UR
Sarah Kay   Tel: 01595 880526
Email: info@easterhoull.co.uk

The garden is in two parts. The upper garden includes a rockery built with large rocks and a wide selection of plants. The lower garden is on a steep slope with a spectacular sea view over village of Scalloway. Path to lead visitors around. Wide selection of plants, pond and vegetable patch.

Directions: Follow A970 main road towards village of Scalloway. Take a sharp turn on the left, signposted for Easterhoull Chalets and follow road, stop at greenhouse!

Disabled Access: None

Opening Times:
By arrangement on request

Admission:
£3.50

Charities: All proceeds to SG Beneficiaries

8 HOLLA
Sandwick, Shetland ZE2 9HW
Mrs Margaret Johnson Tel: 01950 431369

Created from a bare field, this is now a beautiful established garden surrounded by over 10 varieties of trees creating shelter for a mixture of shrubs, herbaceous, perennial and annual plants, including a great show of spring bulbs. Paths wind throughout the garden. Next to the pond is an old boat filled with flowers and there are flowers and plants tumbling over the drystane dykes. A greenhouse, conservatory and a woody section for chickens complete the garden experience.

Other Details: Seating areas available for picnics.

Directions: From Lerwick head south. Take the first turnoff to Sandwick. Follow sea road towards Sandlodge taking the first right turn after the house. Holla is the only house on the left.

Disabled Access: Partial

Opening Times:
Open most days - look for open sign on gate 10:00am - 5:00pm.
By arrangement on request for groups

Admission:
£3.00

Charities: Lerwick Lifeboat Guild receives 40%, the net remaining to SG Beneficiaries.

9 HOLMLEA
Mid Yell ZE2 9BT
John and Sandra Robertson Tel: 01957 702062

The garden has a greenhouse, conservatory and drystane dyke, with a mixture of flowers, shrubs and vegetables. Enjoy wandering around admiring the variety of different shrubs and herbaceous plants interspersed with colourful annuals, then see the plot of mixed vegetables before moving on into the greenhouse where tomatoes, cucumber and peppers grow.

Directions: Once on the island of Yell head for Mid Yell, going down to Linkshouse Pier. From there go up past the shop about 150yds. Holmlea is right on the corner with garage and basement.

Disabled Access: Partial

Opening Times:
By arrangement on request
Sundays 1, 8, 15, 22, 29 July & 3, 12, 19 August 2.00pm - 5.00pm

Admission:
£3.00

Charities: RNLI receives 40%, the net remaining to SG Beneficiaries.

LEA GARDENS
Tresta, Shetland ZE2 9LT
Rosa Steppanova Tel: 01595 810454

Lea Gardens, started in the early 1980s, now covers almost 2 acres. The plant collection, the largest north of Inverewe Gardens, consists of 1,500 different species and cultivars from all over the world, including phyto-geographic elements of collections of plants from New Zealand, South Africa and South America. Planted to provide all-year-round interest it has been divided into a variety of habitats: woodland & shade, borders, wetland, raised beds, and acid and lime lovers.

Directions: From Lerwick take A970 north, turn left at Tingwall onto A971 past Weisdale along Weisdale Voe and up Weisdale hill. Coming down, Lea Gardens is on your right surrounded by trees.

Disabled Access: Partial

Opening Times:
Sunday 29 July 2:00pm -
5:00pm
March - October 2:00pm -
5:00pm

Admission:
£3.00

Charities: All proceeds to SG Beneficiaries for 29 July and donation to SG Beneficiaries for other dates.

NONAVAAR
Levenwick, Shetland ZE2 9HX
James B Thomason Tel: 01950 422447

This is a delightful country garden, sloping within drystone walls, overlooking magnificent coastal views. It contains ponds, terraces, areas of lawn, trees, bushes, varied perennials, annuals, vegetable garden and greenhouse.

Other Details: Art and craft studio. Teas and soft drinks on request - by donation.

Directions: Head south from Lerwick. Turn left at Levenwick sign soon after Bigton turnoff. Follow road to third house on left after Midway stores. Park where there is a 'Garden Open' sign.

Disabled Access: None

Opening Times:
Saturdays 2 June - 25 August
10:00am - 2:00pm
Mondays 4 June - 27 August
10:00am - 4:00pm

Admission:
£3.00

Charities: Leukaemia Research receives 40%, the net remaining to SG Beneficiaries.

NORBY
Burnside, Sandness, Shetland ZE2 9PL
Mrs Gundel Grolimund Tel: 01595 870246
Email: gislinde@tiscali.co.uk

A small but perfectly formed garden and a prime example of what can be achieved in a very exposed situation. Blue painted wooden pallets provide internal wind breaks and form a background for shrubs, climbers and herbaceous plants, while willows provide a perfect wildlife habitat. There are treasured plants such as Chionocloa rubra, pieris, Chinese tree peonies, and a selection of old-fashioned shrub roses. Narrow raised beds contain salads and herbs decorated by beach finds.

Other Details: Historic old house.

Directions: At Sandness, take road to Norby, turn right at Methodist Church, 'Burnside' at end.

Disabled Access: None

Opening Times:
By arrangement on request.
Due to remote location, phone or email before visit.

Admission:
£3.00

Charities: Survival International receives 40%, the net remaining to SG Beneficiaries.

13 SHANGRI-LA
3 Anderson Road, Lerwick, Shetland ZE1 0HP
Mike & Kathy Greaves Tel: 01595 693225
Email: kathy_greaves@tiscali.co.uk

Suburban garden close to local leisure centre and parks. Gardens to front and side of house with courtyard garden and secluded converted peat shed/summerhouse/atelier, BBQ decking and greenhouse to the rear. Variety of small trees, shrubs and vegetables. Shows a good example of living in Shetland in Summertime at 60N.

Directions: Half mile from town centre, via Town Hall. Head through Gilbertson Park. Leisure centre nearby.

Disabled Access: Partial

Opening Times:
Sunday & Monday 27 & 28 May
1:00pm - 5:00pm
Wednesday & Thursday 20 & 21
June 1:00pm - 5:00pm

Admission:
£3.00

Charities: RNLI receives 40%, the net remaining to SG Beneficiaries.

14 THE OLD PLAYGROUND
Old School Road, Trondra, Shetland ZE1 0XL
Maureen Christie

Former school playground surrounded by drystane dyke containing a pond, four seating areas and gravel walkways around various beds. There are trees, shrubs, flowers and bird feeding stations. The garden has wonderful views of Scalloway and the sea.

Directions: After crossing Trondra bridge, take right turn to Cauldhame and then immediate left for Old School Road. Middle house of three at end of the road.

Disabled Access: Full

Opening Times:
Sunday 12 August 2:00pm -
5:00pm

Admission:
£3.00

Charities: Scalloway Public Hall receives 40%, the net remaining to SG Beneficiaries.

15 TOAM
North Roe, Shetland ZE2 9RY
Neil and Iwona Charleson Tel: 01806 533217
Email: iwonacharleson@hotmail.com

Small recently established croft garden, with perennial borders, large polytunnel and large vegetable area. A 'prairie' style garden is currently under construction. There is a variety of livestock including chickens, geese, ducks and shetland sheep. There is also an art and crafts studio on the premises.

Other Details: Art and craft studio. Teas available by prior arrangement.

Directions: From Lerwick head north to North Roe. Once there look for the school (on left side) and take the second turning right (signposted Burravoe). Toam is the first cottage on the right.

Disabled Access: Partial

Opening Times:
By arrangement 18 - 24 June
11.30am - 5.00pm

Admission:
£3.00

Charities: Border Collie Rescue receives 40%, the net remaining to SG Beneficiaries.

16 U.R.G.E.

13 Nikkavord Lea, Baltasound, Unst, Shetland ZE2 9XL
Unst Regeneration Growers Enterprise Tel: 01957 711367
Email: postmaster@unstmarketgardens.shetland.co.uk

A combination of fresh food production and recycling, the U.R.G.E. gardens have been developed on the most marginal land using manure, seaweed and compost to create the soil; pallets and waste wood for raised beds. U.R.G.E. grow herbs, vegetables, fruit, soft fruit, flowers and mushrooms. The intense growing season is extended by use of polytunnels. We have free range ducks and chickens.

Other Details: Website: www.unstmarketgardens.shetland.co.uk

Directions: From ferry Terminal follow main road to T junction in Baltasound, turn right and first left into Nikkavord Lea. No 13 is in top right hand car park. Access to site through No 13.

Disabled Access: None

Opening Times:
Weds - Suns 11-15, 18-22, and 25-29 July 12:00pm - 4:00pm
Also by arrangement on other days from 10.00am to 4.00pm

Admission:
£4.00

Charities: CLAN receives 40%, the net remaining to SG Beneficiaries.

TWITTER

We have been busy tweeting in order to help increase the awareness of our activities amongst the online community.

Follow us on Twitter at:

http://twitter.com/scotgardens

DUMFRIESSHIRE

Scotland's Gardens 2012 Guidebook is sponsored by **INVESTEC WEALTH & INVESTMENT**

District Organiser

Mrs Sarah Landale	Dalswinton House, Dalswinton DG2 0XZ

Area Organisers

Ms Fiona Bell-Irving	Bankside, Kettleholm, Lockerbie DG11 1BY

Treasurer

Mr Harold Jack	The Clachan, Newtonairds DG2 0JL

Gardens open on a specific date

Portrack House, Holywood	Sunday 6 May	12:00pm - 5:00pm
Drumpark, Irongray	Sunday 13 May	2:00pm - 5:00pm
Dalswinton House, Dalswinton	Sunday 20 May	2:00pm - 5:00pm
Cowhill Tower, Holywood	Sunday 3 June	2:00pm - 5:00pm
The Old Mill, Keir Mill, Thornhill	Sunday 24 June	2:00pm - 5:00pm
The Garth, Tynron, Thornhill	Sunday 1 July	2:00pm - 5:00pm
Newtonairds Lodge, Newtonairds	Sunday 29 July	2:00pm - 5:00pm

Gardens open by arrangement

When organising a visit to a garden open by arrangement, please enquire if there are facilities and catering available.

Grovehill House , Burnhead, Thornhill	April to September	01848 331637

Key to symbols

🌳	New in 2012	☕	Homemade teas	B&B	Accommodation
☕	Teas	🐕	Dogs on a lead allowed	🌷	Plant stall
☕	Cream teas	♿	Wheelchair access	🌿	Scottish Snowdrop Festival

Garden locations

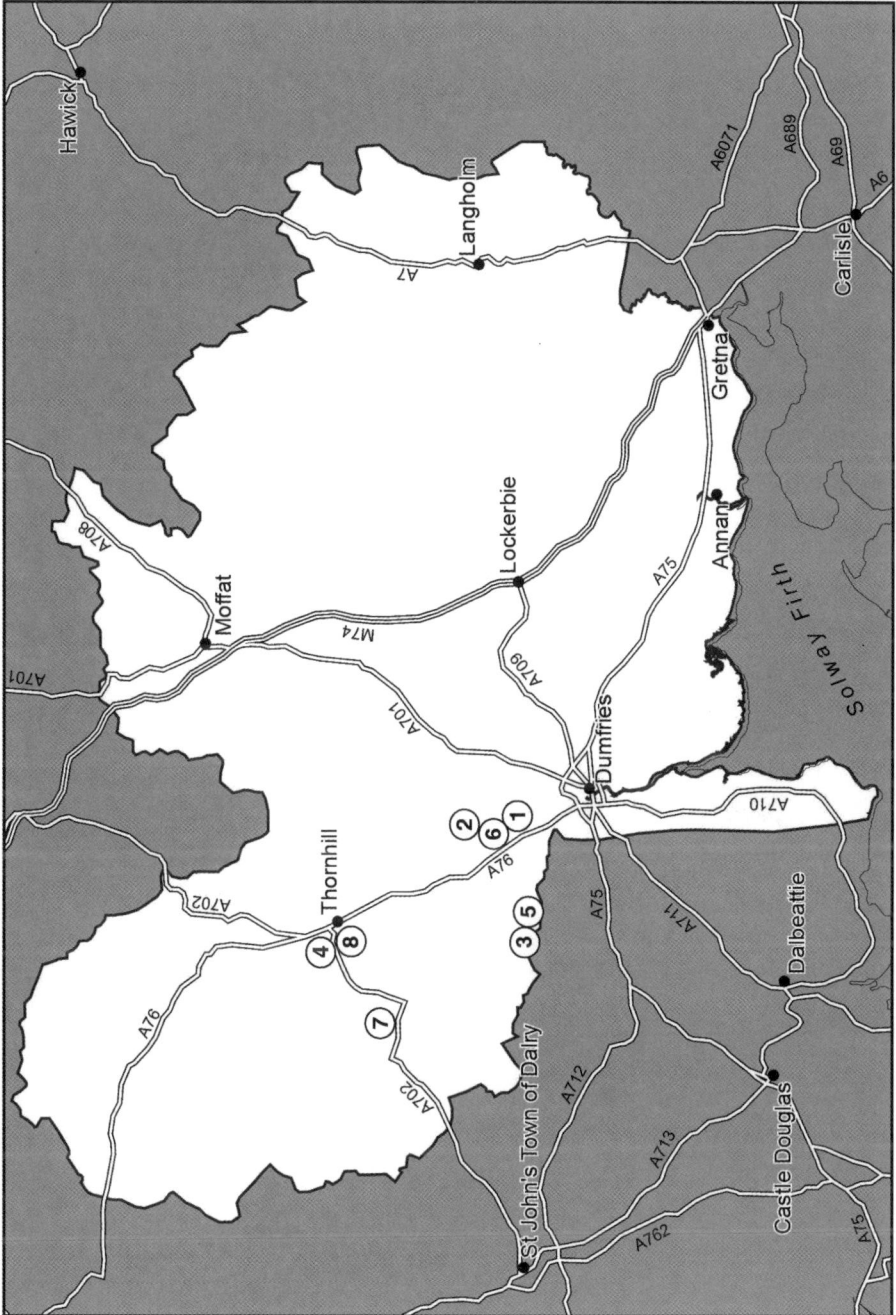

1 COWHILL TOWER
Holywood DG2 0RL
Mr and Mrs P Weatherall   Tel: 01387 720304

Interesting walled garden. Topiary animals, birds and figures. Woodland walk. Splendid views from lawn down the Nith valley. Variety of statues from the Far East.

Directions: Holywood 1½ miles off A76, 5 miles north of Dumfries.

Disabled Access: Partial

Opening Times:
Sunday 3 June 2:00pm - 5:00pm

Admission:
£4.00 Children £0.50

Charities: Maggie's Cancer Caring Centres receives 40%, the net remaining to SG Beneficiaries.

2 DALSWINTON HOUSE
Dalswinton DG2 0XZ
Mr and Mrs Peter Landale   Tel: 01387 740220

Late 18th century house sits on top of a hill surrounded by herbaceous beds and well established shrubs, including rhododendrons and azaleas overlooking the loch. Attractive walks through woods and around the loch. It was here that the first steamboat in Britain made its maiden voyage in 1788 and there is a life-size model beside the water to commemorate this.

Directions: Seven miles North of Dumfries off A76.

Disabled Access: Partial

Opening Times:
Sunday 20 May 2:00pm - 5:00pm

Admission:
£4.00 Children Free

Charities: Kirkmahoe Parish Church receives 40%, the net remaining to SG Beneficiaries.

3 DRUMPARK
Irongray DG2 9TX
Mr & Mrs Iain Mitchell   Tel: 01387 820223

Well contoured woodland garden and extensive policies with mature azaleas, rhodadendrons and rare shrubs among impressive specimen trees. Water garden with primulas and meconopsis. Victorian walled garden with fruit trees and garden produce. Herbaceous border. All set in a natural bowl providing attractive vistas.

Directions: From Dumfries by-pass, head north on A76 for ½ mile, turn left at signpost to "Lochside Industrial Estates" and immediately right onto Irongray Road; continue for 5 miles; gates in sandstone wall on left (½ mile after Routin' Brig).

Disabled Access: Partial

Opening Times:
Sunday 13 May 2:00pm - 5:00pm

Admission:
£4.00 Children Free

Charities: Loch Arthur Community (Camphill Trust) receives 40%, the net remaining to SG Beneficiaries.

GROVEHILL HOUSE
Burnhead, Thornhill DG3 4AD
Mr & Mrs Allen & Penelope Paterson   Tel: 01848 331637

Two acre plantsman's garden designed for year-round interest. The steep site has been terraced to offer sheltered borders and garden 'rooms'. Small productive walled garden. There are fine views down the Nith Valley and to the surrounding hills.

Directions: In Burnhead on the A702. Approx 1 mile, coming from Thornhill. House on left on steep corner with sandstone lodge and red phone box opposite.

Disabled Access: None

Opening Times:
By arrangement April to September

Admission:
£3.00

Charities: Loch Arthur Community (Camphill Trust) receives 40%, the net remaining to SG Beneficiaries.

NEWTONAIRDS LODGE
Newtonairds DG2 0JL
Mr and Mrs J Coutts

An interesting 1.2 acre Plantsman's garden punctuated with topiary, trees and shrubs, surrounding a 19th century listed baronial lodge. The National Collection is integrated with a further 150 other Hosta varieties on a natural terraced wooded bank.

Other Details: NCPPG collection of Hosta Plantagirea Hybrids and CVS. Scottish Piper between 2.00pm-5.00pm.

Directions: From Dumfries take A76 north. At Holywood take B729 (Dunscore). After 1 mile turn left (Morrinton). After 3 miles red sandstone lodge is on right behind black iron railings.

Disabled Access: Partial

Opening Times:
Sunday 29 July 2:00pm - 5:00pm

Admission:
£3.00

Charities: Peter Pan Moat Brae Trust receives 40%, the net remaining to SG Beneficiaries.

PORTRACK HOUSE
Holywood DG2 0RW
Charles Jencks
www.charlesjencks.com

Original 18th century manor house with Victorian addition; octagonal folly-library. Twisted undulating landforms and terraces designed by Charles Jencks as "The Garden of Cosmic Speculation"; lakes designed by Maggie Keswick; rhododendrons, large new greenhouse in a geometric kitchen garden of the Six Senses; Glengower Hill plantation and view; woodland walks with Nonsense Building (architect: James Stirling); Universe cascade and rail garden of the Scottish Worthies; interesting sculpture including that of DNA and newly completed Comet Bridge.

Other Details: Local pipe band.

Directions: Holywood 1½ miles off A76, five miles north of Dumfries.

Disabled Access: Partial

Opening Times:
Sunday 6 May 12:00pm - 5:00pm

Admission:
£6.00

Charities: Maggie's Cancer Caring Centres receives 40%, the net remaining to SG Beneficiaries.

7 THE GARTH
Tynron, Thornhill DG3 4JY
Mimi and Christopher Craig   Tel: 01848 200364

Old Manse, established 1750 with additions. Two acre garden: woodland, waterside and walled.

Other Details: Teas available in Village Hall nearby.

Directions: Off A702 between Penpont and Moniaive.

Disabled Access: Partial

Opening Times:
Sunday 1 July 2:00pm -
5:00pm

Admission:
£3.50 Children £0.50.

Charities: Village Hall Fund receives 40%, the net remaining to SG Beneficiaries.

8 THE OLD MILL
Keir Mill, Thornhill DG3 4DF
Mr Robin and Mrs Margaret Thomson

Maturing garden of shrubs and and azaleas with herbaceous borders. Naturalised pond and riverside boundary.

Directions: Situated in the village of Keir Mill on C125, 1 mile from Penpont on Auldgirth road. Car Parking at Village Hall.

Disabled Access: Partial

Opening Times:
Sunday 24 June 2:00pm -
5:00pm

Admission:
£3.00

Charities: Diabetes Scotland receives 20%, Scottish Ornithology Club receives 20%, the net remaining to SG Beneficiaries.

DUNBARTONSHIRE

Scotland's Gardens 2012 Guidebook is sponsored by **INVESTEC WEALTH & INVESTMENT**

District Organiser

Mrs K Murray	7 The Birches, Shandon, Helensburgh G84 8HN

Area Organisers

Mrs M Greenwell	Avalon, Shore Road, Mambeg, Garelochhead G84 0EN
Mrs R Lang	Ardchapel, Shandon, Helensburgh G84 8NP
Mrs R Macaulay	Denehard, Garelochhead G84 0EL
Mrs S Miller	8 Laggary Park, Rhu G84 8LY
Mrs M Rogers	Station House, Station Road, Tarbet G83 7DA
Mrs J Theaker	19 Blackhill Drive, Helensburgh G84 9AF
Mrs H Wands	Lindowan, Rhu G84 8NH

Treasurer

Mrs S Miller	8 Laggary Park, Rhu G84 8LY

Gardens open on a specific date

Linn Botanic Gardens, Cove, By Helensburgh	Sunday 25 March	2:00pm	-	5:00pm
Kilarden, Rosneath	Sunday 22 April	2:00pm	-	5:00pm
Milton House, Milton, Dumbarton	Sunday 29 April	2:00pm	-	5:00pm
Ardchapel and Seven The Birches, Shandon, Helensburgh	Sunday 13 May	2:00pm	-	5:00pm
Ross Priory, Gartocharn	Sunday 20 May	2:00pm	-	5:00pm
Geilston Garden, Main Road, Cardross	Sunday 5 August	12:00pm	-	5:00pm
Parkhead, Rosneath, Helensburgh	Sunday 26 August	2:00pm	-	5:00pm
Hill House, Helensburgh	Sunday 2 September	11:00am	-	4:00pm

Gardens open regularly

Glenarn, Glenarn Road, Rhu, Helensburgh	21 March - 21 September	Dawn	-	Dusk
Linn Botanic Gardens, Cove, By Helensburgh	All year	Dawn	-	Dusk

Gardens open by arrangement

When organising a visit to a garden open by arrangement, please enquire if there are facilities and catering available.

8 Laggary Park, Rhu, Helensburgh   1 June - 31 August   01436 821314

Plant sales

Glenarn Plant Sale, Glenarn Road, Rhu   Sunday 6 May   2:00pm - 5:00pm
SG Hill House Plant Sale, Helensburgh   Sunday 2 September   11:00am - 4:00pm

Key to symbols

🌳	New in 2012	H	Homemade teas	B&B	Accommodation
☕	Teas	🐕	Dogs on a lead allowed	🌷	Plant stall
☕	Cream teas	♿	Wheelchair access	🌱	Scottish Snowdrop Festival

PLANT SALE DONATIONS PLEASE

DONATIONS OF PLANTS ARE ALWAYS EXTREMELY WELCOME

Garden locations

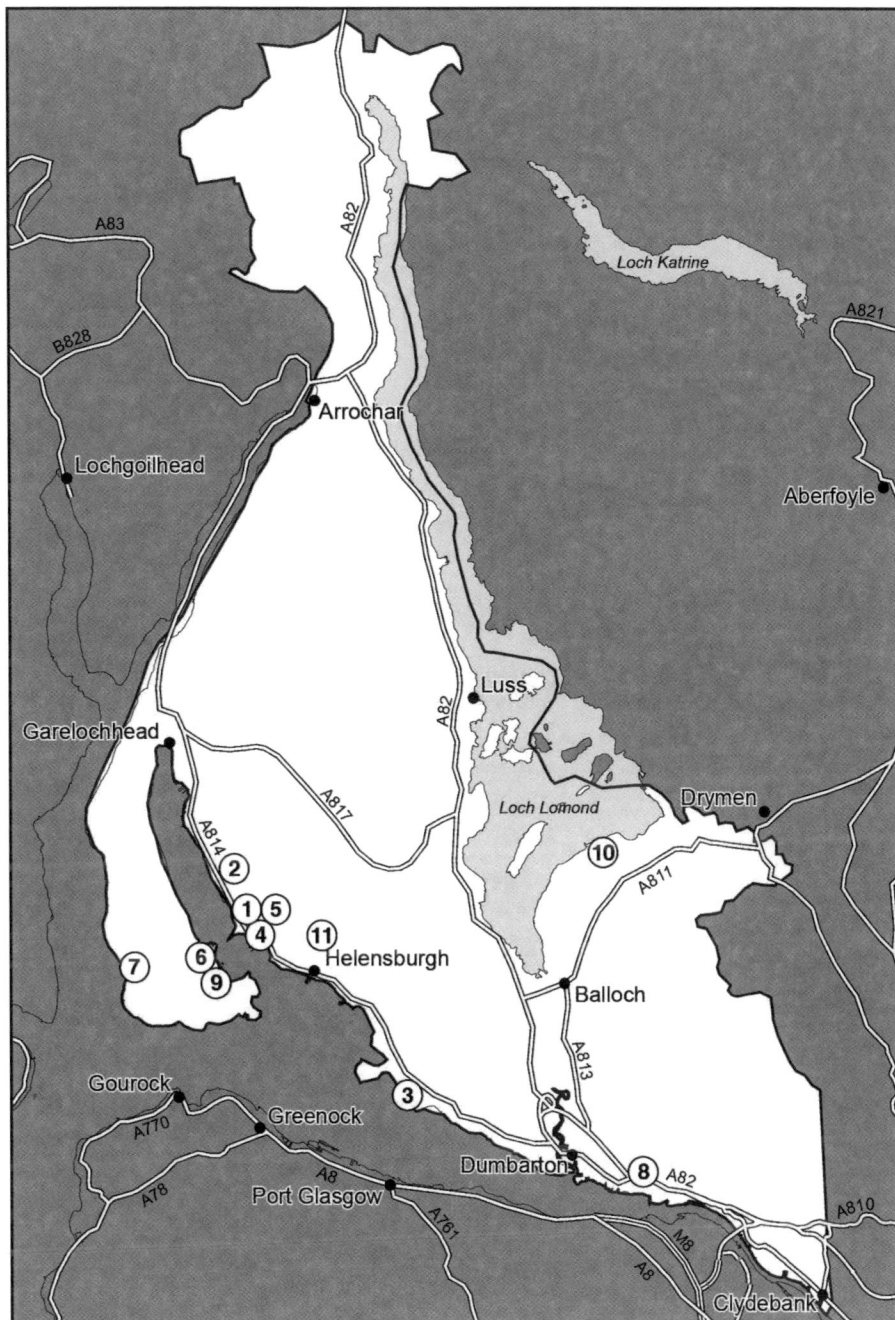

1 8 LAGGARY PARK
Rhu, Helensburgh G84 8LY
Susan and Jim Miller   Tel: 01436 821314
Email: susan.miller17@btinternet.com

Half acre garden with formal and informal plantings of flowering shrubs and specimen trees. Clematis arbour and pergola, fernery and winding woodland walk with secluded seating areas. All giving an interesting structure. Mixed shrub and herbaceous borders featuring dahlias, hardy geraniums, hydrangeas, penstemons and violas.

Other Details: Gravel paths, some slopes and steps. Home grown plants for sale.

Directions: Take A814 shore road from Helensburgh to Rhu Marina. Turn right into Pier Road and take second turn right (signposted) into Laggary Park and bear right.

Disabled Access: Partial

Opening Times:
By arrangement 1 June - 31 August : No parties under ten.

Admission:
£3.00

Charities: SSPCA receives 40%, the net remaining to SG Beneficiaries.

2 ARDCHAPEL AND SEVEN THE BIRCHES
Shandon, Helensburgh G84 8HN
Mr & Mrs J S Lang and Mr & Mrs R I Murray

Ardchapel: Mr & Mrs J S Lang. Established 3½ acres with a variety of mature trees overlooking the Gareloch. It retains the rough layout drawn by architect James Smith in 1854 when the house was built. Woodland walks with burn, rhododendrons, azaleas and camellias. Bank of bluebells. Herbaceous & rose garden. Apple orchard and vegetable garden.

Seven the Birches: Mr & Mrs R Murray. New features in this re-designed garden include raised beds, gravel garden & rockery. Good mixed planting.

Directions: 3¾ miles north of Helensburgh on A814. Parking on service road below houses.

Disabled Access: Partial

Opening Times:
Sunday 13 May 2:00pm - 5:00pm

Admission:
£4.00 (includes both gardens) Children Free

Charities: Erskine Hospital receives 40%, the net remaining to SG Beneficiaries.

3 GEILSTON GARDEN
Main Road, Cardross G82 5HD
The National Trust for Scotland   Tel: 0844 493 2219
Email: jgough@nts.org.uk   www.nts.org.uk

Geilston garden has many attractive features including the walled garden with the herbaceous border providing summer colour, the tranquil woodland walks along the Geilston Burn and a large working kitchen garden which will be the focus of this year's Open Day.

Other Details: The fresh produce from the kitchen garden will be on sale and there will be inspiring cookery demonstrations on how to use some of the wide variety of fresh fruit and vegetables grown at Geilston.

Directions: On the A814, 1 mile from Cardross.

Disabled Access: Partial

Opening Times:
Sunday 5 August 12:00pm - 5:00pm

Admission:
£4.00 Children under 12 Free

Charities: Donation to SG Beneficiaries

4 GLENARN

Glenarn Road, Rhu, Helensburgh G84 8LL
Michael & Sue Thornley   Tel: 01436 820493
Email: masthome@dsl.pipex.com   www.gardens-of-argyll.co.uk

Glenarn survives as a complete example of a 10 acre garden that spans from 1850 to the present day. There are winding paths through glens under a canopy of oak and lime, sunlit open spaces, a vegetable garden with beehives, and a rock garden with views over the Gareloch. It is famous for its collection of rare and tender rhododendrons but horticulturally there is much more besides.

Other Details: Catering for groups by prior arrangement.

Directions: On A814, two miles north of Helensburgh. Cars to be left at gate unless passengers are infirm.

Disabled Access: Partial

Opening Times:
21 March - 21 September Dawn - Dusk

Admission:
£4.00   Accompanied children under 16 free

Charities: Donation to SG Beneficiaries

5 GLENARN PLANT SALE

Glenarn Road, Rhu G84 8LL
Michael and Sue Thornley   Tel: 01436 820493
Email: masthome@dsl.pipex.com   www.gardens-of-argyll.co.uk

Large plant sale with a selection of rhododendrons and magnolias propagated from the collection of special plants at Glenarn. Also unusual shrubs, woodland and rock garden plants.

Other Details: Honey may be for sale.

Directions: On A814, two miles north of Helensburgh. Cars to be left at gate unless passengers are infirm.

Disabled Access: Partial

Opening Times:
Sunday 6 May 2:00pm - 5:00pm

Admission:
Free but normal admission charges apply for those wishing to go round the garden.

Charities: Contact the Elderly receives 40%, the net remaining to SG Beneficiaries.

6 KILARDEN

Rosneath G84 0PU
Mr & Mrs J.E. Rowe

Sheltered hilly 10 acre woodland with notable collection of species and hybrid rhododendrons gathered over a period of 50 years by the late Neil and Joyce Rutherford as seen on "Beechgrove Garden". Paths may be muddy.

Other Details: St. Modan's church open. Organ music. Homemade tea in church hall.

Directions: ¼ mile from Rosneath off B833.

Disabled Access: Partial

Opening Times:
Sunday 22 April 2:00pm - 5:00pm

Admission:
£2.50, Children Free

Charities: Friends of St Modan's receives 40%, the net remaining to SG Beneficiaries.

7 LINN BOTANIC GARDENS
Cove, By Helensburgh G84 0NR
Jamie Taggart   Tel: 01436 842084
Email: jamie@linnbotanicgardens.org.uk   www.linnbotanicgardens.org.uk

Designed landscape with a very diverse range of plants, developed over the past 40 years by the Taggart family. There is a marked one kilometre walk with descriptive leaflet for visitors. Formal pond, fountain, glen with waterfalls. Large collection of bamboo species. Cliff garden, rockery and New Zealand alpine lawn. Views over Loch Long to Cowal peninsula and down the Firth of Clyde.

Directions: ¾ mile north of Cove village (B833), 13 miles from Helensburgh, 18 miles from Balloch.

Disabled Access: None

Opening Times:
Sunday 25 March 2:00pm - 5:00pm
All year Dawn - Dusk

Admission:
£5.00
Students/Teenagers £3.00
Children £1.00 under 5s Free

Charities: Friends of the Linn Gardens receives 40%, the net remaining to SG Beneficiaries.

8 MILTON HOUSE
Milton, Dumbarton G82 2TU
Mr & Mrs Charles Villiers

Beautiful rhododendron garden: many mature species and old hybrids as well as new plantings over the past decade. Fine extensive views out high above the Clyde estuary. Large lawn sweeps down in front of late 18th century house which is sheltered by extensive arboretum of mature trees. Large variety of interesting shrubs including azaleas, camellias, magnolia wilsonii, stewartia. Spring flowers across the lawn and borders.

Directions: On north side of the Clyde, off A82 at Milton. East of Dumbarton/Loch Lomond junction, before BP Service Station, turn left up Milton Brae. Entrance to garden is on the left.

Disabled Access: Partial

Opening Times:
Sunday 29 April 2:00pm - 5:00pm

Admission:
£3.00 Children under 16 Free

Charities: Hope and Homes for Children receives 40%, the net remaining to SG Beneficiaries.

9 PARKHEAD
Rosneath, Helensburgh G84 0QR
Ian and Susan McKellar

Early 18th century building attached to an older walled garden which was a field by 1960s. Since then the current owners have restored the burnt out property and laid out the architectural Italianate garden, featuring Box Yew Beech Hornbeam Holly and Prunus in hedges parterre and topiary. Pots & bedding plants set off the clipped evergreens. A lily pond, foot maze and sundial garden occupy three circular Yew "rooms". There is a hen run and walled enclosure for vegetables and soft fruit.

Other Details: Teas by Friends of St Modan's.

Directions: One mile beyond Rosneath, fork left off B833, left again for 400m. Parking in Rosneath Castle Caravan Park by kind arrangement (10 min walk). Disabled parking space at garden.

Disabled Access: Partial

Opening Times:
Sunday 26 August 2:00pm - 5:00pm

Admission:
£4.00 Children Free

Charities: Friends of St. Modan's receives 40%, the net remaining to SG Beneficiaries.

10 ROSS PRIORY
Gartocharn G83 8NL
University of Strathclyde

1812 Gothic addition by James Gillespie Graham to house of 1693 overlooking Loch Lomond. Rhododendrons, azaleas, selected shrubs and trees. Walled garden with glasshouses, pergola, ornamental plantings. Family burial ground. Nature and garden trails. House not open to view.

Other Details: Putting green. Teas are served in the house.

Directions: Gartocharn 1½ miles off A811. Bus: Balloch to Gartocharn leaves Balloch at 1:00pm and 3:00pm.

Disabled Access: Full

Opening Times:
Sunday 20 May 2:00pm - 5:00pm

Admission:
£4.00 Children Free

Charities: CHAS receives 40%, the net remaining to SG Beneficiaries.

11 SG HILL HOUSE PLANT SALE
Helensburgh G84 9AJ
The National Trust for Scotland/SG Tel: 01436 673900
Email: gsmith@nts.org.uk www.nts.org.uk

The Plant Sale is held in the garden of The Hill House which has fine views over the Clyde estuary and is considered Charles Rennie Mackintosh's domestic masterpiece. The sale includes nursery grown perennials and locally grown trees, shrubs, herbaceous, alpine and house plants. The gardens continue to be restored to the patron's planting scheme with many features that reflect Mackintosh's design.

Other Details: Teas served in House from 12.00pm.

Directions: Follow signs to The Hill House.

Disabled Access: Full

Opening Times:
Sunday 2 September 11:00am - 4:00pm

Admission:
No admission charge but donations to Scotland's Gardens welcome.

Charities: All proceeds to SG Beneficiaries

OPEN
FOR
DISCOVERY

EAST LOTHIAN

Scotland's Gardens 2012 Guidebook is sponsored by **INVESTEC WEALTH & INVESTMENT**

District Organiser

Mr W Alder — Granary House, Kippielaw, Haddington EH41 4PY

Area Organisers

Mr P Atkins	Mizzentop, Westerdunes Pk, North Berwick EH39 5HJ
Mrs C Gwyn	The Walled Garden, Tyninghame, Dunbar EH42 1XY
Mr M Hedderwick	Gifford Bank, Gifford EH41 4JE
Mr T W Jackson	Highbury, Whim Road, Gullane EH31 2BD
Mrs J Lindsay	Kirkland, Whittingehame EH41 4QA
Mrs N Parker	Steading Cottage, Stevenson, Haddington EH41 4PU

Treasurer

Mr S M Edington — Meadowside Cottage, Strathearn Road, North Berwick EH39 5BZ

Gardens open on a specific date

Shepherd House, Inveresk, Musselburgh	Sunday 26 February	2:00pm	5:00pm
Winton House, Pencaitland	Sunday 15 April	12:00pm	4:30pm
Shepherd House, Inveresk, Musselburgh	Sunday 29 April	2:00pm	5:00pm
Greywalls, Gullane	Saturday 5 May	2:00pm	5:00pm
Tyninghame House, Dunbar	Sunday 13 May	1:00pm	5:00pm
Stobshiel House, Humbie	Sunday 20 May	2:00pm	5:00pm
Stenton Village	Sunday 27 May	2:00pm	5:30pm
Inveresk Village, Musselburgh	Sunday 3 June	2:00pm	5:00pm
Shepherd House, Inveresk, Musselburgh	Sunday 3 June	2:00pm	5:00pm
Dirleton Village, North Berwick	Saturday 9 June	2:00pm	5:00pm
Dirleton Village, North Berwick	Sunday 10 June	2:00pm	5:00pm
Gifford Village, Gifford	Sunday 17 June	1:00pm	6:00pm
Tyninghame House, Dunbar	Sunday 24 June	1:00pm	5:00pm
Inwood, Carberry, Musselburgh	Sunday 15 July	2:00pm	5:00pm
Pilmuir House, Haddington	Sunday 22 July	2:00pm	5:00pm

Gardens open regularly

Inwood, Carberry, Musselburgh	1 April - 30 September	
	Tues, Thurs & Sats	2:00pm - 5:00pm
Shepherd House, Inveresk, Musselburgh	14 February - 1 March	
	& 17 April - 5 July	
	Tuesdays & Thursdays	2:00pm - 4:00pm

Gardens open by arrangement

When organising a visit to a garden open by arrangement, please enquire if there are facilities and catering available.

Bowerhouse, Dunbar	15 April - 30 September	rebecca@tyndall.co.uk
Humbie Dean, Humbie	1 May - 30 July	07768 996382
Stobshiel House, Humbie	On request	01875 833 646

Key to symbols

🌳	New in 2012	H	Homemade teas	B&B	Accommodation
☕	Teas	🐕	Dogs on a lead allowed	🌷	Plant stall
C	Cream teas	♿	Wheelchair access		Scottish Snowdrop Festival

CANCELLATIONS

On the rare occasions that garden openings are cancelled, details will be posted on the Cancellation page at:

WWW.SCOTLANDSGARDENS.ORG

Garden locations

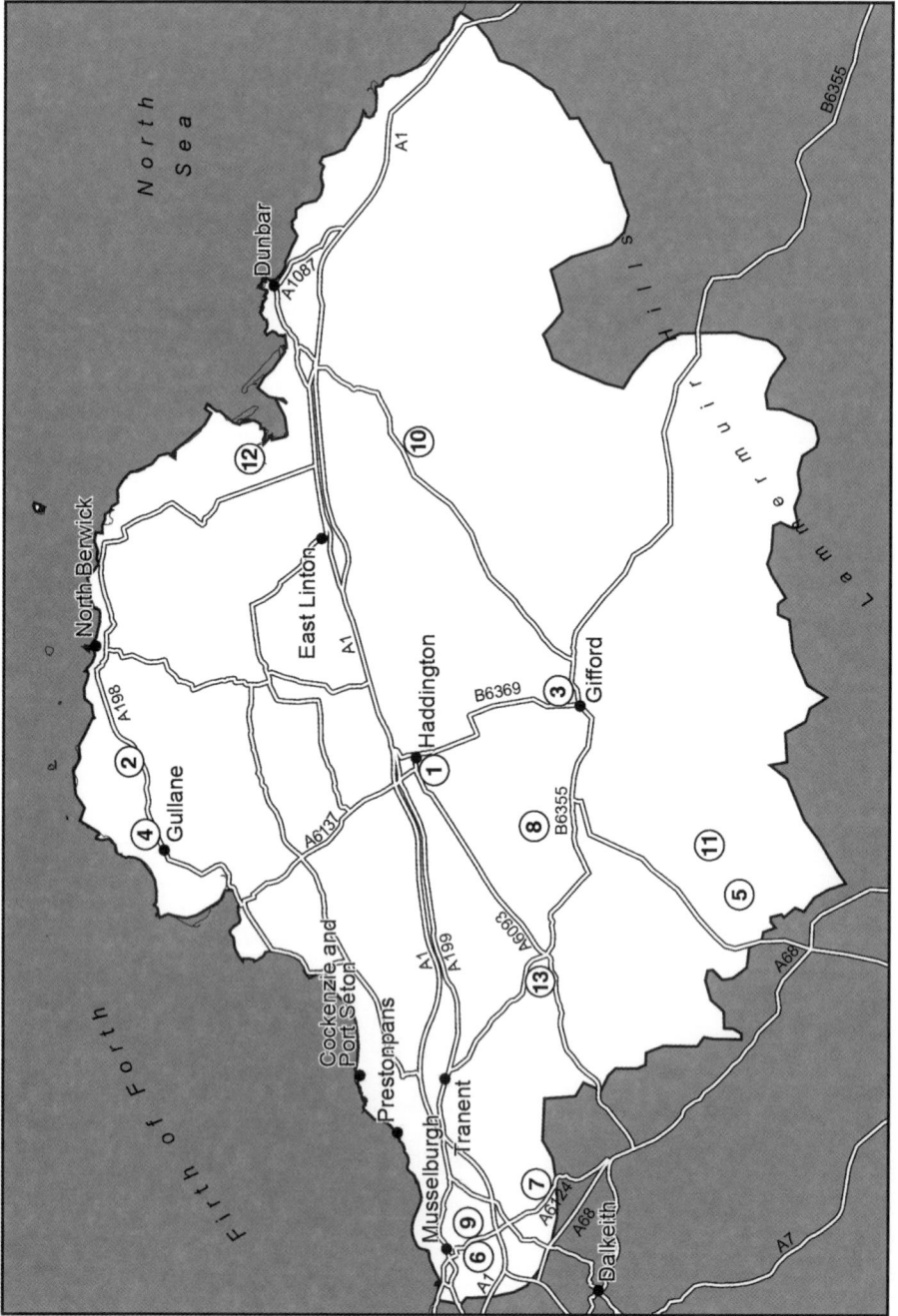

North Sea

Dunbar

North Berwick

East Linton

Gullane

Haddington

Gifford

Cockenzie and Port Seton

Prestonpans

Musselburgh

Tranent

Dalkeith

Firth of Forth

Lammermuir Hills

A1

A1087

A198

A6137

B6369

B6355

B6355

A6093

A199

A6124

A68

A7

A68

1 BOWERHOUSE
Dunbar EH41 1RE
Mark and Rebecca Tyndall
Email: rebecca@tyndall.co.uk

The formal gardens with courtyards and water features enhance the 1835 David Bryce Mansion House set in 17 acres of parkland, orchard and woodland walks.

Directions: 1 mile south of Dunbar off the westbound carriage of the A1.

Disabled Access: Full

Opening Times:
By arrangement 15 April - 30 September : Groups welcome

Admission:
£4.00

Charities: Leuchie House receives 40%, the net remaining to SG Beneficiaries.

2 DIRLETON VILLAGE
North Berwick EH39 5EH
The Gardeners of Dirleton & Historic Scotland

Dirleton is a beautiful conservation village with a large green, historic church and castle. Gardens of various sizes and types are open throughout the village, including the famous castle gardens. Parking, tickets and maps are available at the green and teas are served in the Church Hall.

Other Details: Flower Festival in Dirleton Kirk. Teas in church hall.

Directions: Dirleton Village is 2 miles west of North Berwick.

Disabled Access: Partial

Opening Times:
Saturday 9 June 2:00pm - 5:00pm
Sunday 10 June 2:00pm - 5:00pm

Admission:
£4.00 Children Free

Charities: RNLI receives 40%, the net remaining to SG Beneficiaries.

3 GIFFORD VILLAGE
Gifford EH41 4QY
The Gardeners of Gifford

Gifford was laid out early in the 18th century and has retained much of its original charm. The village includes a beautiful church built in 1708, the Lime Avenue of Yester House, the Goblin Ha' and Tweeddale hotels and a wide range of gardens all within walking distance of the village hall where tickets and garden maps will be available. The gardens vary in size and types, from the compact to the informal, to the large and formal with a wide range of plants, shrubs and trees.

Directions: Gifford sits between the A1 and A68 roads about 5 miles south of Haddington. The village is well signposted from Haddington, Pencaitland and Duns.

Disabled Access: Partial

Opening Times:
Sunday 17 June 1:00pm - 6:00pm

Admission:
£5.00

Charities: Local Charities receives 40%, the net remaining to SG Beneficiaries.

4 GREYWALLS
Gullane EH31 2EG
Mr and Mrs Giles Weaver
www.greywalls.co.uk

Six acres of formal garden attributed to Gertrude Jekyll complements the Edwardian house built by Sir Edwin Lutyens in 1901. Formal garden, tulips, shrub and annual borders.

Directions: Signposted on the A198 SE of Gullane.
From Edinburgh take A1 south, then A198 to Gullane last turning on left side.
From south take A1 north to Haddington, Gullane is signposted.
Further information on website.

Disabled Access: None

Opening Times:
Saturday 5 May 2:00pm - 5:00pm

Admission:
£4.00 Accompanied Children Free

Charities: All proceeds to SG Beneficiaries

5 HUMBIE DEAN
Humbie EH36 5PW
Frank Kirwan & Sarah Wedgwood   Tel: 07768 996382
Email: frank.kirwan@which.net

A two acre woodland garden at 600 feet with the core created in the 1960s, under renovation and major extension since 2008. It is bounded by burns & woodland and on different levels. Renovation entails tree clearance, creation of light, access to the woodland, replanting, making of paths, steps, a bridge, and a partially completed woodland walk. Planting includes an Oudolf-type autumn border; drifts of candelabra primula & hosta. Erythroniums enrich the extensive 1960s daffodil underplanting & the mature azalea & rhododendron planting has been extended.

Other Details: Stout footwear recommended.

Directions: Enter Humbie from A68, pass school and village hall on left then turn right into lane (Shell sign in hedge). Take 2nd left. Humbie Dean is first house on left between two small bridges.

Disabled Access: None

Opening Times:
By arrangement 1 May - 30 July

Admission:
£4.00

Charities: Oxfam receives 40%, the net remaining to SG Beneficiaries.

6 INVERESK VILLAGE
Musselburgh EH21
The Gardeners of Inveresk

A collection of walled gardens in a historic village. Each has its own individual character displaying a wide variety of interesting and unusual trees, shrubs and plants.

Directions: South side of Musselburgh, Inveresk Village Road - A6124.

Disabled Access: Partial

Opening Times:
Sunday 3 June 2:00pm - 5:00pm

Admission:
£5.00 Children Free

Charities: Thistle Foundation receives 40%, the net remaining to SG Beneficiaries.

7 INWOOD
Carberry, Musselburgh EH21 8PZ
Mr and Mrs I Morrison Tel: 0131 665 4550
Email: lindsay@inwoodgarden.com www.inwoodgarden.com

The garden sits snugly around the house with a fine Cornus contraversa variagata as the centerpiece and a backdrop of mature woodland. Springtime includes masses of tulips and rhododendrons whilst rambling roses romp through the trees in high summer. Hydrangeas, dahlias and perennials bring the season to a close. In the glasshouse there is a colourful display of begonias and streptocarpus whilst the depths of the pond can be explored for newts and frogs. A RHS Recommended Garden.

Directions: From the A1 take A6094 exit signed Wallyford and Dalkeith. At roundabout turn left on A6124. Continue up hill for 1½ miles. Turn left at Inwood sign on left.

Disabled Access: Partial

Opening Times:
Sunday 15 July 2:00pm - 5:00pm
1 April to 30 September, Tuesday, Thursday & Saturdays 2:00pm - 5:00pm

Admission:
£3.00 Children Free

Charities: All proceeds to SG Beneficiaries

---

8 PILMUIR HOUSE
Haddington EH41 4HS
Sir Henry Wade Pilmuir Trust

A four to five acre walled garden in a parkland setting in the grounds of 400 year old house. Specimen trees, herbaceous border and dovecot. Ideal for families.

Directions: From Hadddington take A6093 signposted Pentcaitland, turn off left to Samuelson and then follow signs. Also from East Saltoun follow signs.

Disabled Access: Full

Opening Times:
Sunday 22 July 2:00pm - 5:00pm

Admission:
£4.00 Children Free

Charities: East Lothian Special Needs Play Group receives 40%, the net remaining to SG Beneficiaries.

---

9 SHEPHERD HOUSE
Inveresk, Musselburgh EH21 7TH
Sir Charles and Lady Fraser Tel: 0131 665 2570
Email: annfraser@talktalk.net www.shepherdhousegarden.co.uk

The house and its 1-acre garden form a walled triangle in the middle of the village. The main garden is to the rear of the house where the formality of the front garden is continued with a herb parterre and two symmetrical potagers. A formal rill runs the length of the garden, beneath a series of rose, clematis and wisteria pergolas and arches and connects the ponds. Snowdrops are mainly grown in beds and borders. However there is a growing collection of "specialist snowdrops" around 50 different cultivars at present some of which will be displayed in our "Snowdrop Theatre".

Other Details: Plant stall and teas on Sunday openings only. Sun 3 June opening is in conjunction with Inveresk Village.

Directions: Near Musselburgh. From A1 take A6094 signed Wallyford/Dalkeith and follow signs to Inveresk.

Disabled Access: Full

Opening Times:
Sun 26 Feb 2:00pm - 5:00pm
Sun 29 April 2:00pm - 5:00pm
Sun 3 June 2:00pm - 5:00pm
14 Feb - 1 Mar & 17 Apr- 5 Jul
Tues & Thurs 2:00pm - 4:00pm

Admission:
£4.00 Children under 12 Free

Charities: Battle of Prestonpans Heritage Trust receives 40%, the net remaining to SG Beneficiaries.

10 STENTON VILLAGE
East Lothian EH42
The Gardeners of Stenton Village

Stenton is a lovely conservation village at the edge of the Lammermuir hills with a great variety of gardens.

Directions: Follow signs from A199/A1.

Disabled Access: Partial

Opening Times:
Sunday 27 May 2:00pm - 5:30pm

Admission:
£4.00 Children Free

Charities: Leuchie House receives 40%, the net remaining to SG Beneficiaries.

11 STOBSHIEL HOUSE
Stobshiel House, Humbie, East Lothian EH36 5PD
Max and Sarah Ward   Tel: 01875 833 646
Email: stobshiel@gmail.com

A large garden to see for all seasons. Walled garden adjacent to the house, box-edged borders filled with herbaceous plants, bulbs, roses and lavender beds. Rustic summerhouse. Glasshouse. Shrubbery with rhododendrons, azaleas and bulbs. Water and woodland garden with meconopsis and primulas. Formal lily pond. Woodland walks.

Other Details: Kate Denton garden sculpture exhibition on 20 May only.

Directions: B6368 Haddington/Humbie; Sign to Stobshiel 1 mile.

Disabled Access: None

Opening Times:
Sunday 20 May 2:00pm - 5:00pm
Also by arrangement on request

Admission:
£4.00 Children under 12 Free

Charities: Camphill Blair Drummond receives 40%, the net remaining to SG Beneficiaries.

12 TYNINGHAME HOUSE
Dunbar EH42 1XW
Tyninghame Gardens Ltd

Splendid 17th century pink sandstone Scottish baronial house, remodelled in 1829 by William Burn, rises out of a sea of plants. Herbaceous border, formal rose garden, Lady Haddington's secret garden with old fashioned roses, formal walled garden with sculpture and yew hedges. The "wilderness" spring garden with magnificent rhododendrons, azaleas, flowering trees and bulbs. Grounds include 1 mile beech avenue to sea, "apple walk", Romanesque ruin of St Baldred's Church, views across Tyne estuary and Lammermuir Hills. Tyninghame is one of only seven estates in Scotland to have been awarded 'Outstanding' for every category in the Inventory of Gardens and Designed Landscapes of Scotland.

Other Details: Plant stall on May opening only.

Directions: Gates on A198 at Tyninghame Village.

Disabled Access: Full

Opening Times:
Sunday 13 May 1:00pm - 5:00pm
Sunday 24 June 1:00pm - 5:00pm

Admission:
£5.00 Children Free

Charities: Leuchie House receives 40% on Sunday 13 May, Camphill Blair Drummond Trust receives 40% on Sunday 24 June, the net remaining to SG Beneficiaries.

3 WINTON HOUSE

Pencaitland EH34 5AT
Sir Francis Ogilvy Winton Trust   Tel: 01875 340222
www.wintonhouse.co.uk

The gardens continue to develop and improve, in addition to the natural areas around Sir David's loch and the Dell, extensive mixed borders are taking shape for the terrace borders and walled garden. In spring a glorious covering of daffodils make way for cherry and apple blossoms. Enjoy an informative tour of this historic house and walk off delicious lunches and home baking around the estate.

Directions: Entrance off B6355 Tranent/Pencaitland Road.

Disabled Access: Full

Opening Times:
Sunday 15 April 12:00pm - 4:30pm

Admission:
Estate: £4.00.
Guided House Tours: £5.00/ £3.00 Children under 10 Free

Charities: Maggie's Centres receives 40%, the net remaining to SG Beneficiaries.

GUIDEBOOK

Copies of our guidebook can be purchased on our website www.scotlandsgardens.org or use the order form on page 277.

EDINBURGH & WEST LOTHIAN

Scotland's Gardens 2012 Guidebook is sponsored by **INVESTEC WEALTH & INVESTMENT**

District Organisers

Mrs Victoria Reid Thomas   Riccarton Mains Farmhouse, Currie EH14 4AR
Mrs Charles Welwood   Kirknewton House, Kirknewton EH27 8DA

Treasurer

Mrs Charles Welwood   Kirknewton House, Kirknewton EH27 8DA

Gardens open on a specific date

Dean Gardens and Belgrave Crescent, Edinburgh	Sunday 1 April	2:00pm - 5:00pm
61 Fountainhall Road, Edinburgh	Sunday 8 April	2:00pm - 5:00pm
10 Pilton Drive North, Edinburgh	Sunday 15 April	11:00am - 4:30pm
101 Greenbank Crescent, Edinburgh	Sunday 29 April	2:00pm - 5:00pm
Redcroft, 23 Murrayfield Road, Edinburgh	Sunday 29 April	2:00pm - 5:00pm
Redcroft, 23 Murrayfield Road, Edinburgh	Sunday 6 May	2:00pm - 5:00pm
61 Fountainhall Road, Edinburgh	Sunday 13 May	2:00pm - 5:00pm
Hunter's Tryst, 95 Oxgangs Road, Edinburgh	Sunday 13 May	2:00pm - 5:00pm
Moray Place & Bank Gardens, Edinburgh	Sunday 13 May	2:00pm - 5:00pm
61 Fountainhall Road, Edinburgh	Sunday 20 May	2:00pm - 5:00pm
Rocheid Garden, 20 Inverleith Terrace, Edinburgh	Saturday 26 May	2:00pm - 5:00pm
61 Fountainhall Road, Edinburgh	Sunday 10 June	2:00pm - 5:00pm
Malleny Garden, Balerno	Thursday 14 June	6:00pm - 8:00pm
National Records of Scotland, 2 Princes Street, Edinburgh	Saturday 16 June	2:00pm - 5:00pm
61 Fountainhall Road, Edinburgh	Sunday 17 June	2:00pm - 5:00pm
National Records of Scotland, 2 Princes Street, Edinburgh	Sunday 17 June	2:00pm - 5:00pm
Merchiston Cottage, 16 Colinton Road, Edinburgh	Sunday 8 July	2:00pm - 5:00pm
9 Braid Farm Road, Edinburgh	Saturday 14 July	2:00pm - 5:00pm
9 Braid Farm Road, Edinburgh	Sunday 15 July	2:00pm - 5:00pm
45 Northfield Crescent, Longridge, Bathgate	Saturday 21 July	2:00pm - 5:00pm
45 Northfield Crescent, Longridge, Bathgate	Sunday 22 July	2:00pm - 5:00pm
2 Houstoun Gardens, Uphall	Saturday 4 August	2:00pm - 5:00pm
2 Houstoun Gardens, Uphall	Sunday 5 August	2:00pm - 5:00pm
Dr Neil's Garden, Duddingston Village	Saturday 11 August	2:00pm - 5:00pm
Dr Neil's Garden, Duddingston Village	Sunday 12 August	2:00pm - 5:00pm
61 Fountainhall Road, Edinburgh	Sunday 2 September	2:00pm - 5:00pm
Rocheid Garden, 20 Inverleith Terrace, Edinburgh	Saturday 8 September	2:00pm - 5:00pm
61 Fountainhall Road, Edinburgh	Sunday 9 September	2:00pm - 5:00pm

Gardens open by arrangement

When organising a visit to a garden open by arrangement, please enquire if there are facilities and catering available.

61 Fountainhall Road, Edinburgh	April to September	0131 667 6146
Newliston, Kirkliston	2 May - 3 June	
	ex. Mondays & Tuesdays	0131 333 3231
Rocheid Garden, 20 Inverleith Terrace, Edinburgh	On request	0131 311 7000

Key to symbols

⚘	New in 2012	HP	Homemade teas	B&B	Accommodation
☕	Teas	🐕	Dogs on a lead allowed	🌷	Plant stall
CP	Cream teas	♿	Wheelchair access	🌿	Scottish Snowdrop Festival

TWITTER

We have been busy tweeting in order to help increase the awareness of our activities amongst the online community.

Follow us on Twitter at:

http://twitter.com/scotgardens

twitter

Garden locations

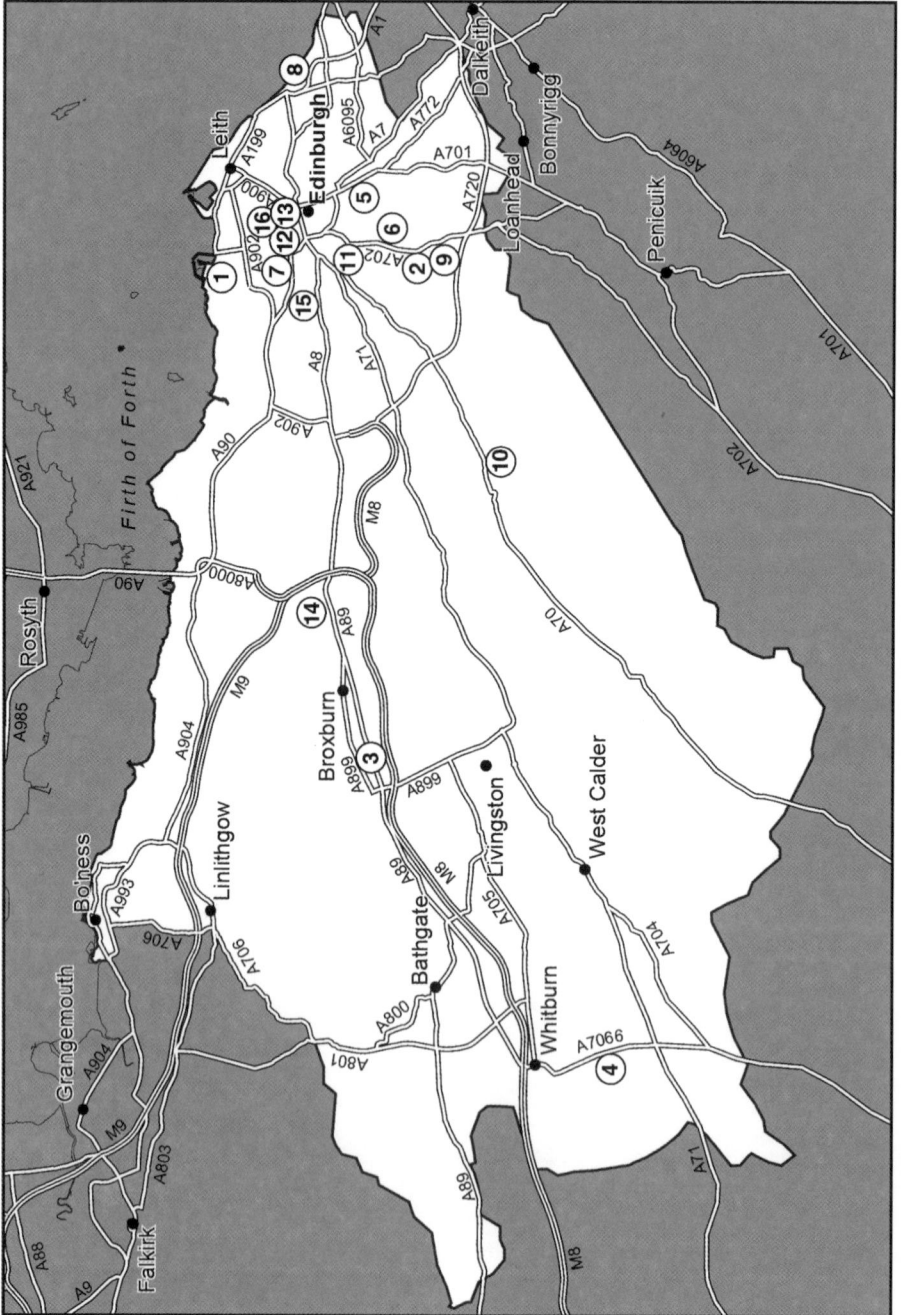

10 PILTON DRIVE NORTH
Edinburgh EH5 1NX
Fraser Drummond   Tel: 0131 467 6811
Email: fdrummond@hotmail.co.uk

Divided into 3 areas, the garden is 90 x 40 feet. In April, fritillarias, erythronium 'Pagoda' and other plants flower in the woodland area. In May the rockery and herbaceous bed are in flower. There are ponds, a greenhouse and numerous unusual species, e.g. vestia, actinidia. kolomikta and ribes Speciosum. The last area is evergreen with Polyanthus and Tulips.

Other Details: Teas to include scone or similar.

Directions: From Crewe Road roundabout, pass the nearby Morrisons on Ferry Road and turn left into Pilton Drive, carry on straight down to Pilton Drive North. On Numbers 9 and 18 Bus Routes.

Disabled Access: None

Opening Times:
Sunday 15 April 11:00am - 4:30pm

Admission:
£3.00

Charities: Maggie's Cancer Caring Centres receives 40%, the net remaining to SG Beneficiaries.

---

101 GREENBANK CRESCENT
Edinburgh EH10 5TA
Mr and Mrs Jerry and Christine Gregson   Tel: 0131 447 6492
Email: jerry_gregson@yahoo.co.uk

Interesting spacious terraced garden with water feature, variety of shrubs and spring flowers, and wandering paths and steps. Marvellous views over hills and neighbouring park.

Directions: From Edinburgh centre, via Morningside Station. Turn right at Greenbank Church crossing. Nos 16 and 5 buses. Stop opposite Greenbank Row.

Disabled Access: None

Opening Times:
Sunday 29 April 2:00pm - 5:00pm

Admission:
£3.00

Charities: Macmillan Cancer Support receives 40%, the net remaining to SG Beneficiaries.

---

2 HOUSTOUN GARDENS
Uphall, West Lothian EH52 5PX
John & Isabel Macdonald
Email: houstounmacs@gmail.com   www.macsgarden.com

A detached 1980s bungalow garden. Large variety of shrubs and plants. Fruit and vegetables are also grown. An outstanding feature of this garden is its summer bedding with over 120 baskets and containers.

Other Details: Admission includes homemade teas.

Directions: Leave A89 at the B8046 junction towards Uphall. Travel 80 yards and turn right into Stankards Road, take 2nd left into Houstoun Gardens. From Uphall village travel west.

Disabled Access: None

Opening Times:
Saturday 4 August 2:00pm - 5:00pm
Sunday 5 August 2:00pm - 5:00pm

Admission:
£4.00

Charities: The Bennie Museum, receives 40%, the net remaining to SG Beneficiaries.

4 45 NORTHFIELD CRESCENT

Longridge, Bathgate EH47 8AL
Mr Jamie Robertson Tel: 07885 701642
Email: jamierobertson04@hotmail.co.uk

A delightful garden with a wide variety of shrubs and herbaceous plants. Large pond with a small waterfall and a colourful decked area with an attractive selection of bedding plants. Good vegetable patch and a 12' x 8' greenhouse. The owner has held the "West Lothian Gardener of the Year" award.

Directions: From A71: turn right after Breith at traffic lights, go about a mile and turn right into the Crescent. From Whitburn: take A706 Longridge Rd to Longridge and last left into Crescent.

Disabled Access: None

Opening Times:
Saturday 21 July 2:00pm - 5:00pm
Sunday 22 July 2:00pm - 5:00pm

Admission:
£4.00

Charities: World Cancer Research Fund receives 40%, the net remaining to SG Beneficiaries.

5 61 FOUNTAINHALL ROAD

Edinburgh EH9 2LH
Dr J A and Mrs A Hammond Tel: 0131 667 6146
Email: froglady@blueyonder.co.uk   www.froglady.pwp.blueyonder.co.uk

Large walled town garden in which trees and shrubs form an architectural backdrop to a wide variety of flowering plants. The growing collection of hellebores and trilliums and a large variety of late blooming flowers provide interest from early March to late October. In addition there are now several alpine beds which include a large collection of Sempervivums. Three ponds, with and without fish, have attracted a lively population of frogs.

Other Details: Coffee, chocolate, juice and spring water available.

Directions: See "Contact Details" on website.

Disabled Access: Full

Opening Times:
Sundays: 8 April, 13 & 20 May 10 & 17 June, 2 & 9 September 2:00pm - 5:00pm
Also by arrangement April to September

Admission:
£4.00

Charities: Froglife receives 40%, the net remaining to SG Beneficiaries.

6 9 BRAID FARM ROAD

Edinburgh EH10 6LG
Mr and Mrs R Paul Tel: 0131 447 3482
Email: raymondpaul@btinternet.com

A fabulous medium sized town garden of different styles. Cottage garden with pond. Mediterranean courtyard and colourful decked area with water feature and exotic plants. Mosaics and unusual features throughout. A few changes this year.

Directions: Near Braid Hills Hotel, on the 11 and 15 bus routes.

Disabled Access: Full

Opening Times:
Saturday 14 July 2:00pm - 5:00pm
Sunday 15 July 2:00pm - 5:00pm

Admission:
£4.00 Children Free

Charities: CHAS receives 40%, the net remaining to SG Beneficiaries.

7 DEAN GARDENS AND BELGRAVE CRESCENT
Edinburgh EH4
Dean Gardens and Belgrave Crescent Management Committees

Disabled Access: Partial

Dean Gardens: Private 13.5 acre gardens on north bank of the Water of Leith. Spring bulbs, daffodils and shrubs with lovely views over the Dean Valley. The Victorian Pavilion has been reinstated and there is seating throughout.

Belgrave Crescent Gardens: Private 7.5 acre gardens sloping down to the Water of Leith with good flower borders, shrubs and woodland.

Other Details: Teas in Belgrave Crescent Gardens. Plant stall in Dean Gardens.

Directions: Dean Gardens - Entrance at Ann Street or Eton Terrace. Belgrave Gardens - Entrance off Belgrave Crescent.

Opening Times:
Sunday 1 April 2:00pm - 5:00pm

Admission:
£4.00 to each garden £6.00 for entry to both.

Charities: All proceeds to SG Beneficiaries.

8 DR NEIL'S GARDEN
Duddingston Village EH15 7DG
Dr Neil's Garden Trust
Email: info@drneilsgarden.co.uk www.drneilsgarden.co.uk

Landscaped garden on the lower slopes of Arthur's Seat using conifers, heathers, alpines and herbaceous borders.

Directions: Kirk car park on Duddingston Road West. Then follow signposts.

Disabled Access: None

Opening Times:
Saturday 11 August 2:00pm - 5:00pm
Sunday 12 August 2:00pm - 5:00pm

Admission:
£3.00

Charities: Dr Neils Garden Trust receives 40%, the net remaining to SG Beneficiaries.

9 HUNTER'S TRYST
95 Oxgangs Road, Edinburgh EH10 7BA
Jean Knox Tel: 0131 477 2919
Email: jean.knox@blueyonder.co.uk

Well stocked mature town garden comprising herbaceous/shrub beds, lawn, vegetables and fruit. Seating areas and trees.

Directions: From Fairmilehead crossroads head down Oxgangs Road to Hunter's Tryst roundabout, last house on the left. Bus Nos. 4, 5, 18, 27. Bus Stop at Hunter's Tryst. Garden opposite Hunter's Tryst.

Disabled Access: Partial

Opening Times:
Sunday 13 May 2:00pm - 5:00pm

Admission:
£3.00

Charities: Lothian Cat Rescue receives 40%, the net remaining to SG Beneficiaries.

10 MALLENY GARDEN
Balerno EH14 7AF
National Trust for Scotland   Tel: 0844 493 2123
Email: pdeacon@nts.org.uk www.nts.org.uk

A rare opportunity to savour the scents of Malleny with an evening stroll through this beautiful garden on midsummer's eve.

Other Details: NCCPG National Collection: 19th century Shrub Roses. Wine.

Directions: In Balerno off A70 Lanark Road. Bus: LRT No 44. First No 44.

Disabled Access: Full

Opening Times:
Thursday 14 June 6:00pm - 8:00pm

Admission:
By Donation.

Charities: Donation to SG Beneficiaries.

11 MERCHISTON COTTAGE
16 Colinton Road, Edinburgh EH10 5EL
Esther Mendelssohn

Small, walled, urban wildlife friendly, organic, bee keeper's garden. Open for the fourth time, this eco friendly tapestry of wildlife habitats encourages birds, insects and frogs as pest control. In addition the bees not only provide honey, but also act as pollinators for the many fruit trees including blueberries and mulberries. When possible the bees can be seen at close quarters in an observation hive.

Directions: Near Holy Corner, opposite Watson's College School. Bus: nos. 11 and 16

Disabled Access: Partial

Opening Times:
Sunday 8 July 2:00pm - 5:00pm

Admission:
£4.00

Charities: Alyn Children's Hospital receives 40%, the net remaining to SG Beneficiaries.

12 MORAY PLACE & BANK GARDENS
Edinburgh EH3 6BX
The Gardeners of Moray Place and Bank Gardens

Moray Place: Private garden of 3½ acres in Georgian New Town recently benefited from five-year programme of replanting. Shrubs, trees and beds offering atmosphere of tranquillity in the city centre.

Bank Gardens: Nearly six acres of secluded wild gardens with lawns, trees and shrubs with banks of bulbs down to the Water of Leith. Stunning vistas across Firth of Forth.

Directions: Moray Place - Enter by north gate in Moray Place.
Bank Gardens - Enter by gate at top of Doune Terrace.

Disabled Access: None

Opening Times:
Sunday 13 May 2:00pm - 5:00pm

Admission:
£3.00

Charities: Queen Elizabeth Spinal Unit receives 40%, the net remaining to SG Beneficiaries.

13 NATIONAL RECORDS OF SCOTLAND
HM General Register House, 2 Princes Street, Edinburgh EH1 3YY
David Brownlee, Deputy Keeper Tel: 0131 535 1313
Email: tristram.clarke@nas.gov.uk www.scotlandspeoplehub.gov.uk

The Archivists' Garden is an open courtyard, a garden planted with 57 species, these include heather, iris, birch, violet, male fern, rosemary and Scotch thistle. The plants are all connected in some way to Scotland's collective memory, whether through myth and folklore, heraldry or association with Famous Scots. A visit to the garden shows the role that plants play in our national heritage.

Other Details: Cafe open in Scotland's People Centre.

Directions: The garden is at the rear of the Register House Campus at the east end of Princes Street. Enter through the iron gates on West Register Street (next to the Guilford Bar). Close to Waverley Station and on several bus routes.

Disabled Access: None

Opening Times:
Saturday 16 June 2:00pm - 5:00pm
Sunday 17 June 2:00pm - 5:00pm

Admission:
£3.00

Charities: Maggie's Centre receives 40%, the net remaining to SG Beneficiaries.

---

14 NEWLISTON
Kirkliston EH29 9EB
Mr and Mrs R C Maclachlan Tel: 0131 333 3231
Email: mac@newliston.fsnet.co.uk

18th century designed landscape with good rhododendrons and azaleas. The house, designed by Robert Adam, is open. On Sundays there is a ride-on steam model railway from 2:00pm - 5:00pm.

Other Details: Please note there are no catering facilities.

Directions: Four miles from Forth Road Bridge, entrance off B800.

Disabled Access: Full

Opening Times:
By arrangement 2 May - 3 June ex. Mondays & Tuesdays

Admission:
£3.00 Children Free

Charities: Children's Hospice Association. receives 40%, the net remaining to SG Beneficiaries.

---

15 REDCROFT
23 Murrayfield Road, Edinburgh EH12 6EP
James and Anna Buxton Tel: 0131 337 1747
Email: annabuxton@aol.com

A walled garden surrounding an Arts and Crafts villa which provides an unexpected haven off a busy road. Interest in spring comes from many different features - the herbaceous border just coming into growth, the species peony bed, the rockery with its pond and cloud pruned conifer, the orchard covered in daffodils, shrubberies and a working greenhouse. Planted and maintained with form and texture in mind. A fine display of spring bulbs, flowering shrubs rhododendrons and blossom.

Other Details: Small plant stall.

Directions: Murrayfield Road runs North from Corstorphine Road to Ravelston Dykes. Easy Parking. Nos 26 and 31 buses.

Disabled Access: Full

Opening Times:
Sunday 29 April 2:00pm - 5:00pm
Sunday 6 May 2:00pm - 5:00pm

Admission:
£4.00

Charities: Leuchie House Short Breaks Centre receives 40%, the net remaining to SG Beneficiaries.

⊃ GARDEN

ouse, 20 Inverleith Terrace, Edinburgh EH3 5NS
Guest Tel: 0131 311 7000
na@afguest.co.uk

A young but rapidly maturing garden with an impressive diversity of plants, shrubs, trees, including native, exotic and rare, providing a tranquil retreat in the midst of the city. The transition from Eastern leads one through ribbons of bamboo and ornamental grasses into the Mediterranean. The natural swimming pond forms a dramatic focus and is surrounded by rich planting and overlooked by olive trees. The planted tunnel leads to the woodland by the river. Mature trees above an exciting variety of planting, creating a mosaic of colour, diversity and interest. Award-winning compost shed with a roof creating waves of ornamental grasses.

Directions: The Garden is on the southern side of the Royal Botanic Garden, Edinburgh.

Disabled Access: Partial

Opening Times:
Saturday 26 May 2:00pm - 5:00pm
Saturday 8 September 2:00pm - 5:00pm
Also by arrangement. Please telephone or email.

Admission:
£4.00

Charities: The Safe Garden at Ferryfield Nursing Home receives 40%, the net remaining to SG Beneficiaries.

WOULD YOU LIKE TO OPEN YOUR GARDEN FOR CHARITY?

If you are interested in opening your garden for charity and would like more information, call 0131 226 3714, email info@scotlandsgardens.org or fill in the form at the back of this book.

We welcome gardens large and small and also groups of gardens.

ETTRICK & LAUDERDALE

Scotland's Gardens 2012 Guidebook is sponsored by **INVESTEC WEALTH & INVESTMENT**

District Organiser

Mrs D Muir	Torquhan House, Stow TD1 2RX

Area Organiser

Mrs M Kostoris	Wester Housebyres, Melrose TD6 9BW

Treasurer

Mrs D Muir	Torquhan House, Stow TD1 2RX

Gardens open on a specific date

Harmony Garden, St. Mary's Road, Melrose	Sunday 24 June	1:00pm - 4:00pm
Priorwood Gardens, Abbey Road, Melrose	Sunday 24 June	1:00pm - 4:00pm
Carolside, Earlston	Saturday 14 July	2:00pm - 6:00pm

Gardens open regularly

Carolside, Earlston	23 June - 28 July Mons, Weds, Sats	11:00am - 5:00pm

Gardens open by arrangement

When organising a visit to a garden open by arrangement, please enquire if there are facilities and catering available.

Carolside, Earlston	On request, Groups Welcome	01896 8 49272

Key to symbols

🌳	New in 2012	☕	Homemade teas	B&B	Accommodation
☕	Teas	🐕	Dogs on a lead allowed	🌷	Plant stall
☕	Cream teas	♿	Wheelchair access		Scottish Snowdrop Festival

Garden locations

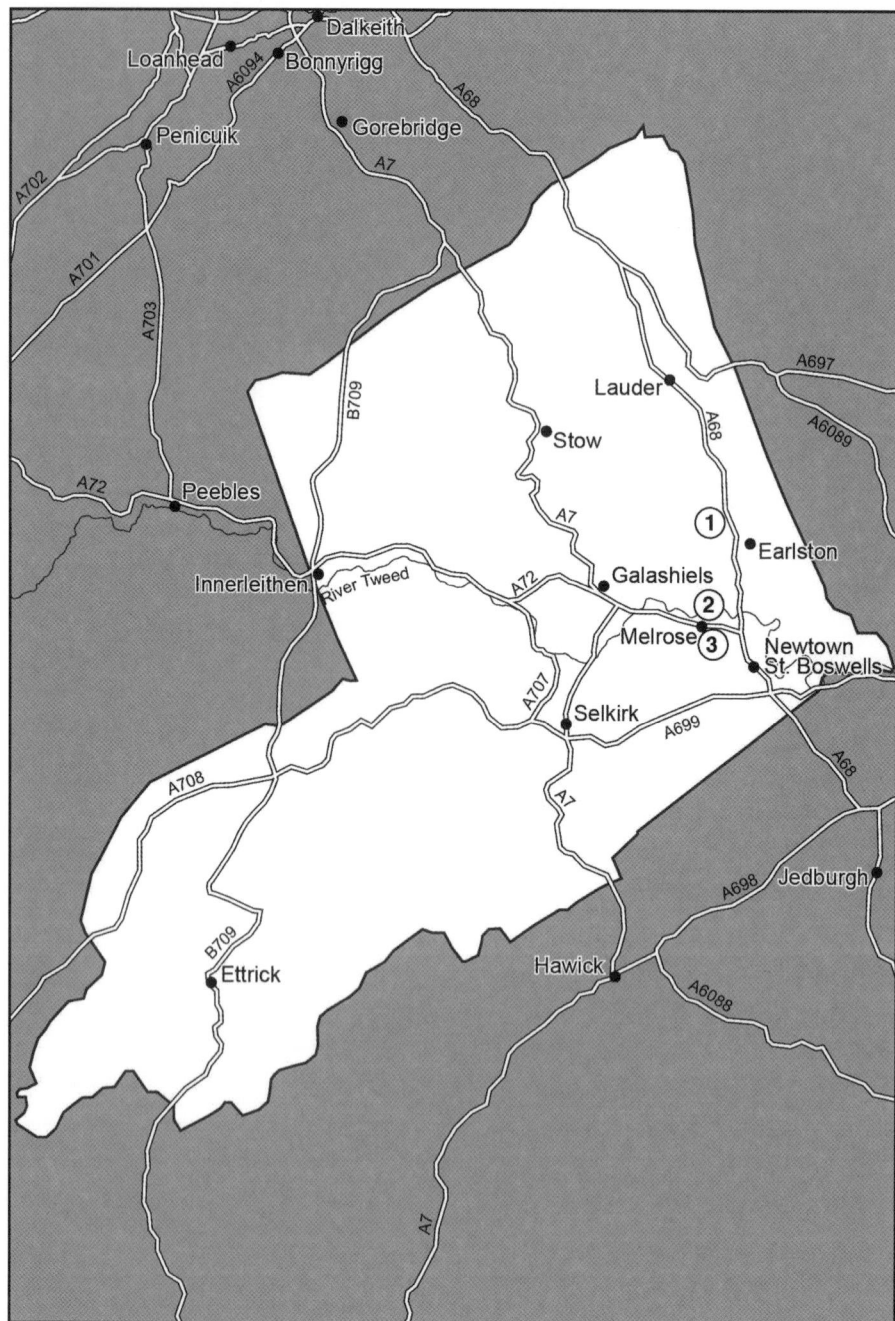

CAROLSIDE
Earlston TD4 6AL
Mr and Mrs Anthony Foyle   Tel: 018968 49272
Email: a.foyle@virgin.net

Traditional garden set in a beautiful 18th century landscape, comprising lawns, shrubberies, borders and a particularly lovely oval walled garden, containing traditional herbaceous borders, fruits, vegetables, parterres and a historically important collection of roses that has been carefully assembled over 20 years. Kenneth Cox in his book 'Scotland for Gardeners' describes Carolside as "one of Scotland's finest private gardens".

Other Details: Teas available 14 July only.

Directions: One mile north of Earlston on A68. Entrance faces south.

Disabled Access: Full

Opening Times:
Saturday 14 July 2:00pm - 6:00pm
23 June - 28 July: Mons, Weds, Sats 11:00am - 5:00pm
Also groups welcome by arrangement.

Admission:
£4.00 Concessions £3.00
Children Free

Charities: All proceeds to SG Beneficiaries

HARMONY GARDEN (JOINT OPENING WITH PRIORWOOD GARDENS)
St. Mary's Road, Melrose TD6 9LJ
The National Trust for Scotland   Tel: 0844 493 2251
Email: ggregson@nts.org.uk www.nts.org.uk

Wander through this tranquil garden, wonderful herbaceous borders, lawns and fruit and vegetable plots, and enjoy fine views of the Abbey and Eildon Hills.

Other Details: Self-catering accommodation available.

Directions: Road: Off A6091, in Melrose, opposite the Abbey. Bus: First from Edinburgh and Peebles.

Disabled Access: Full

Opening Times:
Sunday 24 June 1:00pm - 4:00pm

Admission:
£6.00 for both Harmony and Priorwood Gardens. N.B Correct price on going to print

Charities: Donation to SG Beneficiaries

PRIORWOOD GARDENS (JOINT OPENING WITH HARMONY GARDEN)
Abbey Road, Melrose TD6 9PX
The National Trust for Scotland Tel: 01896 822493
Email: ggregson@nts.org.uk   www.nts.org.uk

In Melrose, overlooked by the Abbey ruins, this unique garden produces plants for a superb variety of dried flower arrangements made and sold here. The orchard contains many historic apple varieties.

Other Details: Self-catering accommodation available.

Directions: Road: Off A6091, in Melrose opposite the Abbey. Bus: First from Edinburgh and Peebles.

Disabled Access: Full

Opening Times:
Sunday 24 June 1:00pm - 4:00pm

Admission:
£6.00 for both Priorwood and Harmony Gardens. Correct price on going to print.

Charities: Donation to SG Beneficiaries

FIFE

Scotland's Gardens 2012 Guidebook is sponsored by **INVESTEC WEALTH & INVESTMENT**

District Organiser

Lady Erskine	Cambo House, Kingsbarns KY16 8QD

Area Organisers

Mrs Jeni Auchinleck	2 Castle Street, Crail KY10 3SQ
Mrs Jayne Clarke	Marine House, Ordnance Road, Crombie KY12 8JZ
Mrs Evelyn Crombie	West Hall, Cupar KY15 4NA
Mrs Sue Eccles	Whinhill, Upper Largo KY8 5QS
Mrs Kate Elliott	Lucklaw House, Logie, Cupar KY15 4SJ
Mrs Lisa Hall	Old Inzievar House, Oakley, Dunfermline KY12 8HA
Mrs Lindsay Murray	Craigfoodie, Dairsie KY15 4RU
Ms Louise Roger	Chesterhill, Boarhills, St Andrews KY16 8PP
Mrs April Simpson	The Cottage, Boarhills, St Andrews KY16 8PP
Mrs Fay Smith	37 Ninian's Field, Pittenweem, Anstruther KY10 2QU
Mrs Lucy Wright	91 Main Street, Newmills KY12 8ST
Mrs Julia Young	South Flisk, Blebo Craigs, Cupar KY15 5UQ

Area Plant Sales Organiser

Mrs Caroline MacPherson	Edenside, Strathmiglo KY14 7PX

Treasurer

Mrs Sally Lorimore	Willowhill, Forgan, Newport-on-Tay DD6 8RA

Gardens open on a specific date

Balmerino Abbey, Balmerino Village, Newport-on-Tay	Sunday 26 February	10:00am -	4:00pm
Birkhill Castle, Balmerino, Cupar	Sunday 29 April	2:00pm -	5:30pm
St Andrews Botanic Garden, Canongate	Sunday 6 May	11:00am -	5:00pm
Culross Palace, Culross	Sunday 13 May	12:00pm -	5:00pm
Tayfield, Forgan, Newport-on-Tay	Sunday 13 May	2:00pm -	5:00pm
Willowhill, Forgan, Newport-on-Tay	Sunday 13 May	2:00pm -	5:00pm
Fife Diamond Garden Festival	Friday 18 May	1:00pm -	5:00pm
Fife Diamond Garden Festival	Saturday 19 May	11:00am -	5:00pm
Fife Diamond Garden Festival	Sunday 20 May	11:00am -	5:00pm
Tayport Gardens, Tayport	Saturday 26 May	2:00pm -	5:00pm

St. Monans Village Gardens	Sunday 27 May	2:00pm -	5:00pm
Tayport Gardens, Tayport	Sunday 27 May	2:00pm -	5:00pm
Earlshall Castle, Leuchars	Sunday 3 June	2:00pm -	5:00pm
Greenhead Farmhouse, Greenhead of Arnot	Sunday 10 June	2:00pm -	5:00pm
Old Inzievar House	Sunday 10 June	2:00pm -	5:00pm
Falkland's Small Gardens, Falkland	Saturday 16 June	11:00am -	5:00pm
Falkland's Small Gardens, Falkland	Sunday 17 June	1:00pm -	5:00pm
Balcaskie, Pittenweem	Saturday 30 June	12:00pm -	5:00pm
Blebo Craigs Village Gardens, Cupar	Saturday 30 June	12:00pm -	5:00pm
Kellie Castle, Pittenweem	Saturday 30 June	12:00pm -	5:00pm
Blebo Craigs Village Gardens, Cupar	Sunday 1 July	12:00pm -	5:00pm
Kinghorn Village Gardens	Sunday 8 July	12:00pm -	5:00pm
St Mary's Road and Fernie Gardens, By Cupar	Sunday 8 July	2:00pm -	5:00pm
Strathmiglo Village Gardens	Sunday 15 July	1:00pm -	5:00pm
Wormistoune House, Crail	Sunday 15 July	12:00pm -	5:00pm
Crail: Small Gardens in the Burgh	Saturday 21 July	1:00pm -	5:30pm
Crail: Small Gardens in the Burgh	Sunday 22 July	1:00pm -	5:30pm
Earlshall Castle, Leuchars	Sunday 29 July	2:00pm -	5:00pm
Ceres Village Gardens	Sunday 5 August	12:00pm -	5:00pm
Falkland Palace and Garden, Falkland	Sunday 26 August	10:00pm -	5:00pm
Tayfield, Forgan, Newport-on-Tay	Sunday 2 September	2:00pm -	5:00pm
Willowhill, Forgan, Newport-on-Tay	Sunday 2 September	2:00pm -	5:00pm
Hill of Tarvit, Cupar	Sunday 21 October	10:30am -	4:00pm

Gardens open regularly

Barham, Bow of Fife	25 April - 26 Sept Weds	2:00pm -	5:00pm
Cambo House, Kingsbarns	All Year	10:00am -	5:00pm
Willowhill, Forgan, Newport-on-Tay	3 July- 29 August Weds	2:00pm -	5:00pm

Gardens open by arrangement

When organising a visit to a garden open by arrangement, please enquire if there are facilities and catering available.

Earlshall Castle, Leuchars	On request	01334 839205
Glassmount House, by Kirkcaldy	19 March - 30 September	01592 890214
Teasses Gardens, Nr. Ceres	On request	01334 828048
The Tower, 1 Northview Terrace, Wormit	15 April - 16 September	01382 541635 07768 406946
Willowhill, Forgan, Newport-on-Tay	1 May - 30 September	07948 286031

Plant sales

SG Spring Plant Sale at St Andrews
Botanic Garden, Canongate | Sunday 6 May | 11:00am - 5:00pm
Hill of Tarvit Plant Sale and Autumn Fair, Cupar | Sunday 21 October | 10:30am - 4:00pm

Key to symbols

	New in 2012		Homemade teas	B&B	Accommodation
	Teas		Dogs on a lead allowed		Plant stall
C	Cream teas		Wheelchair access		Scottish Snowdrop Festival

JOIN OUR GARDEN TOURS

Following the two very successful garden tours which took place in 2011, the Fife committee is delighted to announce there are plans for a trip to the north which will probably take place in June 2012.

For full details of this trip or any other trips which may be organised please contact Fay Smith on 01333 311046 or faysmith70@btinternet.com.

Garden locations

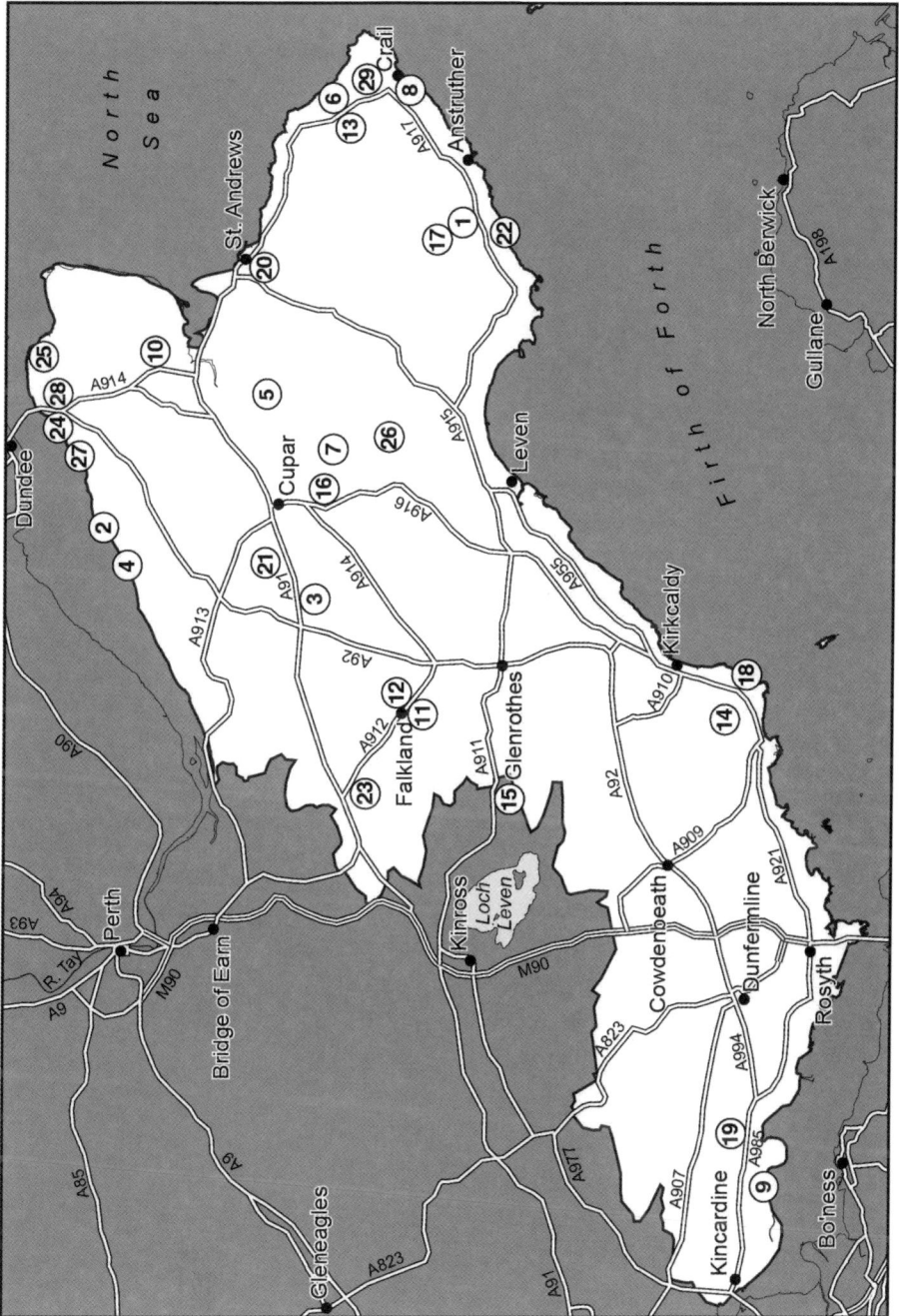

1 BALCASKIE (IN CONJUNCTION WITH KELLIE CASTLE)
Pittenweem KY10 2RD
The Anstruther Family

In 1905 George Elgood wrote that Balcaskie was 'one of the best and most satisfying gardens in the British Isles'. Over the centuries, the gardens have seen input from Gilpin, Bryce and Nesfield. Today the gardens are at the start of a period of restoration. As part of a collaboration with the National Trust for Scotland, the gardens are being restored by the gardening team from Kellie Castle.

Directions: Access is via Kellie Castle only, a free minibus will take visitors from Kellie Castle to Balcaskie. OS ref: NO520052 Road: B9171, 3m NNW of Pittenweem. Bus: Flexible from local villages by pre-booking.

Disabled Access: Partial

Opening Times:
Saturday 30 June 12:00pm - 5:00pm

Admission:
£6.00 includes both gardens.

Charities: Donation to SG Beneficiaries

2 BALMERINO ABBEY
Balmerino Village, Newport-on-Tay, Fife DD6 8SB
The National Trust for Scotland   Tel: 0844 4932184
Email: robrown@nts.org.uk   www.nts.org.uk

This is a small park enclosing the ruins of 13th century Balmerino Abbey. The grounds comprise lawns, grass meadow and wooded area. A small nature trail winds through the woods. The heritage Sweet Chestnut is approximately 450 years old. Stunning displays of aconites and some snowdrops.

Other Details: Partial wheelchair access by side gate at Memorial Cottage. Ground may be soft or difficult going.

Directions: Off the A914, 5 miles west of Tay Road Bridge. 10 miles NW of St Andrews. Bus service to Gauldry with 1 mile walk to the Abbey. Situated on the Fife Coastal Path.

Disabled Access: Partial

Opening Times:
Sunday 26 February 10:00am - 4:00pm

Admission:
By Donation.

Charities: Donation to SG Beneficiaries

3 BARHAM
Bow of Fife KY15 5RG
Sir Robert & Lady Spencer-Nairn Tel: 01337 810227

A small woodland garden with snowdrops, spring bulbs, trilliums, rhododendrons and ferns. Also a summer garden with rambler roses, herbaceous borders and island beds.

Other Details: Small plant nursery selling unusual plants.

Directions: A914 miles west of Cupar.

Disabled Access: None

Opening Times:
25 April - 26 September:
Wednesdays 2:00pm - 5:00pm

Admission:
£3.00 OAPs £2.50 Children Free

Charities: Pain Association Scotland receives 40%, the net remaining to SG Beneficiaries.

BIRKHILL CASTLE
Balmerino, Cupar KY15 4QP
The Earl and Countess of Dundee
www.birkhillcastle.org.uk

Outstanding woodland garden with 100ft magnolias and specieshododendrons. Moss paths under-planted with erythroniums and narcissi with orchids growing along a burn. Stunning views across the 'silvery' Tay. Formal walled garden with vegetables and orchard. Rose walks and wild flowers. Cliff walks and beach.

Directions: By Balmerino. Take the road off the A92 at Rathillet sign-posted Hazelton.

Disabled Access: Partial

Opening Times:
Sunday 29 April 2:00pm - 5:30pm

Admission:
£5.00

Charities: Motor Neurone Disease Scotland receives 40%, the net remaining to SG Beneficiaries.

BLEBO CRAIGS VILLAGE GARDENS
Cupar KY15 5UF
The Gardeners of Blebo Craigs

A wide variety of gardens, including some new ones, will be open in this beautifully situated former quarry and farm village with stunning views over the Fife countryside.

Directions: From St Andrews: B939 for 4 miles. Small sign on left pointing to right hand turn. From Cupar: B940 and take left at Pitscottie then after 2 miles left at sign onto B939.

Disabled Access: Partial

Opening Times:
Saturday 30 June 12:00pm - 5:00pm
Sunday 1 July 12:00pm - 5:00pm

Admission:
£4.50

Charities: Village Hall Fund receives 40%, the net remaining to SG Beneficiaries.

CAMBO HOUSE
Kingsbarns KY16 8QD
Sir Peter and Lady Erskine   Tel: 01333 450313
Email: cambo@camboestate.com   www.camboestate.com

Renowned for snowdrops (mail order in February), this traditional walled garden with some of Scotland's best herbaceous displays is constantly evolving. Head Gardener, Elliott Forsyth, has created irresistible planting combinations with drifts of bold perennials and grasses in the style originally devised by Piet Oudolf and an outrageous annual potager garden. Outside the main garden, a recently planted North American prairie, spectacular in August, is developing. Woodland walks to the sea. Tulip and Rose Festival. Events throughout the year. Featured in 'Gardens Illustrated' and 'The Beechgrove Garden'.

Other Details: NCCPG National Plant Collection: Snowdrops. Large selection of plants for sale. Snowdrop gift shop. Tearoom.

Directions: A917 between Crail and St Andrews.

Disabled Access: Full

Opening Times:
All Year 10:00am - 5:00pm

Admission:
£5.00

Charities: Donation to SG Beneficiaries

7 CERES VILLAGE GARDENS
KY15 5NF
The Gardeners of Ceres

♿ 🏠 🌱

Ceres is often described as the most beautiful village in Scotland. The open gardens will offer a variety of shapes and sizes. A footbridge from Ceres car park leads directly into the Museum garden where tickets (maps indicating the gardens) can be purchased. From there a pleasant stroll around the village includes all the gardens.

Other Details: No dogs allowed, except guide dogs.

Directions: Map indicating gardens at entry to Fife Folk Museum garden which is adjacent to Ceres car park.

Disabled Access: Partial

Opening Times:
Sunday 5 August 12:00pm - 5:00pm

Admission:
£4.50

Charities: Fife Folk Museum receives 40%, the net remaining to SG Beneficiaries.

8 CRAIL: SMALL GARDENS IN THE BURGH
KY10 3SQ
The Gardeners of Crail

🏠 🌱

A number of small gardens in varied styles: cottage, historic, plantsman's, bedding. Tickets and maps available from Mrs Auchinleck, 2 Castle Street and Mr Ian Robertson & Mrs Lisa Hughes, The Old House, 9 Marketgate.

Other Details: Teas in British Legion Hall

Directions: Approach Crail from either St Andrews or Anstruther by A917. Park in the Marketgate.

Disabled Access: None

Opening Times:
Saturday 21 July 1:00pm - 5:30pm
Sunday 22 July 1:00pm - 5:30pm

Admission:
£5.00 Children Free

Charities: Crail British Legion Hall receives 10%, Crail Preservation Society receives 30%, the net remaining to SG Beneficiaries.

9 CULROSS PALACE
Culross KY12 8JH
The National Trust for Scotland Tel: 0844 493 2189
Email: mjeffery@nts.org.uk www.nts.org.uk

🏠 🌱

Relive the domestic life of the 16th and 17th centuries amid the old buildings and cobbled streets of this Royal Burgh on the River Forth. A model 17th century garden has been recreated behind Culross Palace to show the range of plants available and includes vegetables, culinary and medicinal herbs, soft fruits and ornamental shrubs. Don't miss the adorable Scots Dumpy chickens!

Other Details: Fruit and vegetable stall. Light refreshments.

Directions: Off A985, 12m E of Kincardine Bridge, 6m W of Dunfermline. Stagecoach Stirling to Dunfermline or First Edinburgh to Dunfermline. Falkirk station 12 miles, Dunfermline station 6 miles.

Disabled Access: None

Opening Times:
Sunday 13 May 12:00pm - 5:00pm

Admission:
£5.00 includes tea/coffee and cakes. N.B. These prices are correct at time of going to print.

Charities: Donation to SG Beneficiaries

EARLSHALL CASTLE

Leuchars KY16 0DP
Paul & Josine Veenhuijzen   Tel: 01334 839205

♿ ☕ ❧

Disabled Access: Partial

Garden designed by Sir Robert Lorimer. Topiary lawn, for which Earlshall is renowned, rose terrace, croquet lawn with herbaceous borders, shrub border, box garden, orchard, kitchen and herb garden.

Other Details: Wheelchair access difficult but possible.

Directions: On Earlshall road, ¾ of a mile east of Leuchars Village (off A919).

Opening Times:
Sunday 3 June 2:00pm - 5:00pm
Sunday 29 July 2:00pm - 5:00pm
Also by arrangement on request

Admission:
£5.00 Children Free

Charities: RAF Benevolent Fund receives 40% June Opening, St Athernaise Church receives 40% July Opening, the net remaining to SG Beneficiaries.

FALKLAND PALACE AND GARDEN

Falkland KY15 7BU
The National Trust for Scotland   Tel: 0844 493 2186
Email: gardens@nts.org.uk   www.nts.org.uk

♿ B&B

Disabled Access: Partial

Set in a medieval village, the Royal Palace of Falkland is a superb example of Renaissance architecture. Garden enthusiasts will appreciate the work of Percy Cane, who designed and cultivated the gardens between 1947 and 1952. There are colourful herbaceous borders, unusual shrubs and trees and a small herb garden. Meet the Head Gardener at 2:00pm and 4:00pm for free guided walks and see the stunning herbaceous border at it's best!

Other Details: Self-catering accommodation available.

Directions: Road: A912, 10m from M90, junction 8, 11m N of Kirkcaldy. Bus: Stagecoach Fife stops in High Street (100 metres). OS Ref: NO253075

Opening Times:
Sunday 26 August 10:00pm - 5:00pm.

Admission:
£5.00 N.B. These prices are correct at time of going to print.

Charities: Donation to SG Beneficiaries

FALKLAND'S SMALL GARDENS

Falkland KY15
The Gardeners of Falkland

♿ ☕ ❧

Disabled Access: Partial

A wonderful selection of small, secret and private gardens in this interesting historic village.

Other Details: Organic cafe and pubs. Homemade teas in village tearooms.

Directions: On A912 and B936

Opening Times:
Saturday 16 June 11:00am - 5:00pm
Sunday 17 June 1:00pm - 5:00pm

Admission:
£4.50

Charities: Alzheimer Scotland receives 20%, British Heart Foundation receives 20%, the net remaining to SG Beneficiaries.

13 FIFE DIAMOND GARDEN FESTIVAL
KY16
The Fife Gardeners
Email: info@scotlandsgardens.org www.scotlandsgardens.org

The official opening of the Garden Festival will take place at Cambo House, Kingsbarns (Sir Peter & Lady Erskine) with a walkabout in the Walled Garden. A further 11 gardens will be open during the following 2 days, many opening to the public for the first time. The festival participants are:

- Barham, Bow of Fife (Sir Robert & Lady Spencer-Nairn)
- Glassmount House, by Kirkcaldy (James & Irene Thomson)
- Micklegarth, Aberdour (Mr and Mrs Gordon Maxwell)
- The Murrel, Aberdour (Mr and Mrs Alistair Bowen)
- Newton Barns, Auchtermuchty (Mr and Mrs John Anderson)
- Newton Mains, Auchtermuchty (Mr & Mrs Tony Lear)
- Rosewells, Pitscottie (Mr and Mrs Gordon MacDonald)
- 46 South Street, St Andrews (Mrs E J Baxter)
- St Leonards School Grounds and the Headmaster's Garden, South Street, St Andrews (Dr and Mrs Michael Carslaw)
- Strathmore Cottage, Drumeldrie (Barbara Whitelaw & Willie Duncan)
- Teasses Garden, Nr Ceres (Sir Frazer and Lady Morrison)

Other Details: Mega plant sale at Barham with a wide selection of interesting and unusual plants. Teas in St Andrews at 46 South Street on Saturday and in St Leonards School Grounds on Sunday.
For further details see pages 14 and 15.

Directions: Details will be shown in booklet provided on purchase of ticket(s).

Disabled Access: None

Opening Times:
Friday 18 May 1:00pm - 5:00pm for Cambo House Only
Saturday 19 May 11:00am - 5:00pm
Sunday 20 May 11:00am - 5:00pm

Admission:
£20.00 to include all gardens. Tickets limited and must be purchased in advance from www.scotlandsgardens.org for Credit Card Sales or by cheque payable to Scotland's Gardens from S. Lorimore, Willowhill, Forgan, Newport on Tay Fife DD6 8RA

Charities: AICR (The Association for International Cancer Research) receives 40%, the net remaining to SG Beneficiaries.

14 GLASSMOUNT HOUSE
by Kirkcaldy KY2 5UT
James and Irene Thomson Tel: 01592 890214
Email: peterlcmclaren@yahoo.co.uk

Intriguing densely planted walled garden with surrounding woodland. An A-listed sundial, Mackenzie & Moncur greenhouse and historical doocot are complemented by newer structures including an atmospheric water feature/fish pond. Snowdrops and daffodils are followed by a mass of candelabra and cowslip primula, meconopsis and cardiocrinum giganteum. Then hedges and topiary form backdrops for an abundance of bulbs, clematis, rambling roses and perennials, creating interest through the summer into September. Featured in 'Country Living'. Winner: The Times/Fetzer Back Gardens of the Year 2008.

Other Details: Green garden category.

Directions: From Kirkcaldy take the B9157 Invertiel Road. Turn left onto Kinghorn Road, then 50 yards up second road on right. Surrounded by trees, Glassmount House overlooks Kinghorn and Kirkcaldy.

Disabled Access: None

Opening Times:
By arrangement 19 March - 30 September

Admission:
£3.00

Charities: Parkinsons UK receives 40%, the net remaining to SG Beneficiaries.

15 GREENHEAD FARMHOUSE
Greenhead Of Arnot KY6 3JQ
Mr and Mrs Malcolm Strang Steel   Tel: 01592 840459
www.fife-bed-breakfast-glenrothes.co.uk

Open garden surrounding renovated farmhouse and steadings. Mixed borders and rose trellis. Kitchen plot with herbs and vegetables.

Directions: A911 between Auchmuir Bridge and Scotlandwell.

Disabled Access: None

Opening Times:
Sunday 10 June 2:00pm - 5:00pm

Admission:
£3.00 Children under 10 Free

Charities: St Paul's Scottish Episcopal Church, Kinross receives 40%, the net remaining to SG Beneficiaries.

16 HILL OF TARVIT PLANT SALE AND AUTUMN FAIR
Hill of Tarvit, Cupar KY15 5PB
The National Trust for Scotland

A wide range of interesting and unusual plants for sale plus generous clumps of herbaceous plants for any size of garden at bargain prices. A celebration of local food will include a cookery demonstration and various stalls selling local produce. Demonstrations of country crafts will be on show and a nature quiz trail around the estate will be available. A fun day out for families and gardeners alike.

Directions: 2 miles south of Cupar off A916.

Disabled Access: Partial

Opening Times:
Sunday 21 October 10:30am - 4:00pm

Admission:
£2.00 Children Free

Charities: Save the Children Fund receives 40%, the net remaining to SG Beneficiaries.

17 KELLIE CASTLE (IN CONJUNCTION WITH BALCASKIE)
Pittenweem KY10 2RF
The National Trust for Scotland Tel: 0844 4932184
Email: marmour@nts.org.uk   www.nts.org.uk

This superb garden around 400 years old was sympathetically restored by the Lorimer family in the late 19th century. The Arts and Crafts style garden has a selection of old-fashioned roses and herbaceous plants, cultivated organically and hosts an amazing 30 varieties of rhubarb and 75 different types of apple.

Other Details: Garden team will be available for questions. Light refreshments: soup, sandwiches and a selection of cakes available.

Directions: Road: B9171, 3m NNW of Pittenweem Bus: Flexible from local villages by pre-booking. Access to Balcaskie and Kellie Castle via Kellie Castle only. A free minibus will transport visitors between both gardens.

Disabled Access: Partial

Opening Times:
Saturday 30 June 12:00pm - 5:00pm

Admission:
£6.00, Children Free. N.B. These prices are correct at time of going to print

Charities: Donation to SG Beneficiaries

18 KINGHORN VILLAGE GARDENS
KY3
The Gardeners of Kinghorn Village

Kinghorn is a large coastal village boasting an interesting variety of gardens, some directly on the sea front and some hidden treasures tucked away! Tickets and maps from Community Centre.

Directions: Kinghorn village is between Kirkcaldy and Burntisland.

Disabled Access: Partial

Opening Times:
Sunday 8 July 12:00pm - 5:00pm

Admission:
£4.00 Children Free

Charities: Kinghorn Community Centre receives 20%, Kinghorn in Bloom receives 20%, the net remaining to SG Beneficiaries.

19 OLD INZIEVAR HOUSE
KY12 8HA
Mr and Mrs Tim Hall

A recently restored walled garden with lime walk, herbaceous borders, knot garden, rose gardens, gravel garden, fruit trees and a small amount of vegetables. Lovely views over the lower south facing wall.

Other Details: Other attractions include Hebridean sheep and Highland cattle.

Directions: A985 heading west for Kincardine Bridge turn right at sign to Oakley 2 miles after Cairneyhill roundabout. After ½ mile take a right turn to Linvid Pet Hotel. Follow SG signs.

Disabled Access: Partial

Opening Times:
Sunday 10 June 2:00pm - 5:00pm

Admission:
£3.50

Charities: Holy Name Church restoration fund receives 40%, the net remaining to SG Beneficiaries.

20 SG SPRING PLANT SALE AT ST ANDREWS BOTANIC GARDEN
Canongate, St Andrews, Fife KY16 8RT
St Andrews Botanic Garden

Stock up your borders with a wide selection of interesting and unusual plants, grown locally and sourced from private gardens, at Scotland's Gardens Spring Plant Sale held in the beautiful grounds of St Andrews Botanic Garden. Free conducted tours of renowned rhododendron collection, scree garden and herb garden.

Directions: On the Canongate off A915.

Disabled Access: Full

Opening Times:
Sunday 6 May 11:00am - 5:00pm

Admission:
Donations Only

Charities: Friends of the Botanic Garden receives 40%, the net remaining to SG Beneficiaries.

21 ST MARY'S ROAD AND FERNIE GARDENS
By Cupar KY15 4NA
The Gardeners of St Mary's Road and Fernie Gardens

St Mary's Farm KY15 4NF (Michael Innes and Carolyn Scott) A rare chance to see how a garden designer has laid out and planted his small garden around the converted steading buildings.
West Hall KY15 4NA (Ian and Evelyn Crombie) An interesting and attractive south facing garden with pond, greenhouse, borders etc and open views across the Fife countryside.
3 Fernie Mill Cottages KY15 7RU (May and Sandy Watson): A true 'cottage garden' full of herbaceous colour and interest.

Other Details: Only guide dogs allowed. Teas and plant stall at West Hall.

Directions: From Cupar: off the A913 on the outskirts of the town. From A92: turn off at Fernie, between Letham and the junction between A92/A913.

Disabled Access: Partial

Opening Times:
Sunday 8 July 2:00pm - 5:00pm

Admission:
£4.00

Charities: Camphill, Blair Drummond and Monimail Church, Letham receives 40%, the net remaining to SG Beneficiaries.

22 ST. MONANS VILLAGE GARDENS
KY10 2BX
The Gardeners of St. Monans Tel: 01333 730792

Several gardens will be opening, many for the first time in this picturesque seaside village. The medieval church welcomes visitors.

Other Details: Plant stall with a large selection of interesting and unusual plants at 'Inverie'. Homemade teas by the Ladies of the Guild in the Church Hall.

Directions: Enter village, drive to harbour, turn right and follow road to top of hill where tickets can be bought from Mr & Mrs Gardner at Inverie. Large church car park is just beyond.

Disabled Access: None

Opening Times:
Sunday 27 May 2:00pm - 5:00pm

Admission:
£4.00

Charities: Auld Kirk, St Monans receives 40%, the net remaining to SG Beneficiaries.

23 STRATHMIGLO VILLAGE GARDENS
Fife KY14 7PR
The Gardeners of Strathmiglo
Tel: 01337 860676
Email: scottishgardens@btinternet.com

Strathmiglo offers a selection of lovely village and walled gardens, nestling beneath the stunning Lomond Hills. Beautiful walks in and around the village; an historic tollbooth and a pictish standing stone provide further interest.
For further information contact Raine and David Du Puy, Clunie House, 89 High Street, Strathmiglo. KY14 7PR. For further information by telephone or email see above.

Directions: Off the A91, two miles west of Auchtermuchty, enter village from the west end, passing the primary school on the left. Follow signs in the High Street to parking and ticket sales.

Disabled Access: None

Opening Times:
Sunday 15 July 1:00pm - 5:00pm

Admission:
£4.00

Charities: SSPCA receives 20%, Save the Children (Fife) receives 20%, the net remaining to SG Beneficiaries.

24 TAYFIELD (IN CONJUNCTION WITH WILLOWHILL)
Forgan, Newport-on Tay DD6 8RA
William and Elizabeth Berry

A wide variety of fine trees and shrubs established over the past 200 years in the extensive attractive grounds of Tayfield House.

Other Details: Craft Stalls at Forgan Arts Centre on 13 May.

Directions: 1½ miles south of Tay Road Bridge. Take the B995 to Newport off the Forgan roundabout.

Disabled Access: Partial

Opening Times:
Sunday 13 May 2:00pm - 5:00pm
Sunday 2 September 2:00pm - 5:00pm

Admission:
£4.00

Charities: Forgan Arts Centre receives 40% on 13 May, Rio Community Centre receives 40% on 2 September, the net remaining to SG Beneficiaries.

25 TAYPORT GARDENS
Tayport DD6 9BH
The Gardeners of Tayport

Located at the mouth of the river Tay, Tayport is a historic harbour town with attractive views of the Broughty Ferry coastline and Tentsmuir Forest. Six gardens of varied styles and age are opening for the first time.

Other Details: Plants and trees for sale. Teas on Sunday opening only.

Directions: On the south of the Tay Road Bridge take the B946 to Tayport. Follow signs to harbour. Tickets and maps available from Mr and Mrs Bayliss, 47 Tay Street.

Disabled Access: None

Opening Times:
Saturday 26 May 2:00pm - 5:00pm
Sunday 27 May 2:00pm - 5:00pm

Admission:
£4.00

Charities: Tayport Community Trust receives 40%, the net remaining to SG Beneficiaries.

26 TEASSES GARDENS
Nr. Ceres KY8 5PG
Sir Fraser and Lady Morrison   Tel: 01334 828048
Email: kirsten@teasses.com

Teasses Gardens have been developed by the present owners for 12 yrs and now extend to approximately 60 acres. In addition to the traditional oval walled garden with fruit, vegetables, cut flowers and large greenhouse, there are formal and informal areas of garden linked by numerous woodland walks with many woodland gardens. There are extensive areas of spring bulbs. Please allow two hours for a tour with a member of the gardening staff to enjoy these large and peaceful gardens.

Directions: Between Ceres and Largo. Enter by farm entrance two miles west of New Gilston village. Follow tarmac road to Estate Office.

Disabled Access: None

Opening Times:
By arrangement on request - for individuals or groups.

Admission:
£5.00 (includes tour)

Charities: All proceeds to SG Beneficiaries

27 THE TOWER
1, Northview Terrace, Wormit DD6 8PP
Peter and Angela Davey   Tel: 01382 541635 or 07768 406946

Situated 4 miles south of Dundee, this one acre Edwardian landscaped garden has panoramic views over the river Tay. Special features include rhododendron walk, rockeries, informal woodland planting schemes using native and exotic plants, offering year round interest. Original raised paths lead to a granite grotto with waterfall pool. A boardwalk leads to four further ponds joined by a stream. Of additional interest are raised vegetable beds made from granite sets.

Other Details: Garden set into a hill with steep paths. Not suitable for those with poor mobility.

Directions: On request.

Disabled Access: None

Opening Times:
By arrangement 15 April - 16 September

Admission:
£3.00

Charities: St Fillan's Roman Catholic Parish Church receives 40%, the net remaining to SG Beneficiaries.

28 WILLOWHILL (IN CONJUNCTION WITH TAYFIELD)
Forgan, Newport-on-Tay DD6 8RA
Eric Wright & Sally Lorimore Tel: 07948 286031

An evolving 3 acre garden as featured in "Scotland for Gardeners" and "Scotland on Sunday". The house is surrounded by a vegetable plot and a series of mixed borders with different vibrant colour combinations containing bulbs, shrubs and herbaceous perennials. A stepped terrace of alpines leads to a wild-life pond in grassland planted with trees, bulbs and herbaceous perennials through which wide sweeping paths are mown.

Other Details: Craft Stalls at Forgan Arts Centre on 13 May.

Directions: 1½ miles south of Tay Road Bridge. Take the B995 to Newport off the Forgan roundabout. Willowhill is the first house on the left hand side next to the Forgan Arts Centre.

Disabled Access: Partial

Opening Times:
Sun 13 May 2:00pm - 5:00pm
Sun 2 Sept 2:00pm - 5:00pm
3 July - 29 August Wednesdays 2:00pm - 5:00pm
Also by arrangement 1 May - 30 September

Admission:
£4.00 Willowhill and Tayfield
£3.00 Willowhill

Charities: Forgan Arts Centre receives 40% on 13 May, RIO Community Centre receives 40% on 2 September, the net remaining to SG Beneficiaries.

29 WORMISTOUNE HOUSE
Crail KY10 3XH
Baron and Lady Wormiston
Email: gemmawormiston@aol.com

17th century formal walled garden restored over the last 10 years including orchard, formal ponds and rill, parterre and potager. Woodland walk around natural lochan. Mosaic celtic cross in new pleasance garden. Splendid herbaceous border and largest listed Grisselinia in Scotland.

Other Details: Dogs are not allowed in the walled garden.

Directions: On A917 Crail - St Andrews.

Disabled Access: None

Opening Times:
Sunday 15 July 12:00pm - 5:00pm

Admission:
£4.50

Charities: Crail Development Trust receives 40%, the net remaining to SG Beneficiaries.

GLASGOW & DISTRICT

Scotland's Gardens 2012 Guidebook is sponsored by **INVESTEC WEALTH & INVESTMENT**

District Organiser

Mrs A Barlow	5 Auchencruive, Milngavie G62 6EE

Area Organisers

Mrs S Elliot	46 Corrour Road, Newlands G42 2DX
Mrs P Macnair	36 Gartconnell Road, Bearsden G61 3BZ
Mrs Jan Millar	3 Cochrane Court, Milngavie G62
Mrs A Murray	44 Gordon Road, Netherlee G44 3TW
Mr A Simpson	48 Thomson Drive, Bearsden G61 3NZ

Treasurer

Mr J Murray	44 Gordon Road, Netherlee G44 3TW

Gardens open on a specific date

Greenbank Garden, Flenders Road, Clarkston	Saturday 14 April	9:30am	- 5:00pm
Kilsyth Gardens, Allanfauld Road, Kilsyth	Sunday 20 May	2:00pm	- 5:00pm
Kew Terrace Secret Gardens, Kew Terrace Lane	Saturday 9 June	2:00pm	- 5:00pm
Crossburn, Stockiemuir Road, Milngavie, Glasgow	Sunday 10 June	2:00pm	- 5:00pm
123 Waterfoot Row, Newton Mearns	Sunday 17 June	2:00pm	- 5:00pm
Claddagh, 24 Station Road, Bearsden	Sunday 1 July	2:00pm	- 5:00pm
Sundrum, 11 Neidpath Road West, Giffnock, Glasgow	Sunday 26 August	2:00pm	- 5:00pm

Gardens open by arrangement

When organising a visit to a garden open by arrangement, please enquire if there are facilities and catering available.

Kilsyth Gardens, Allanfauld Road, Kilsyth	April - September	01236 821667

Key to symbols

🌳	New in 2012	🅗	Homemade teas	B&B	Accommodation
☕	Teas	🐕	Dogs on a lead allowed	🌷	Plant stall
☕	Cream teas	♿	Wheelchair access	🌿	Scottish Snowdrop Festival

Garden locations

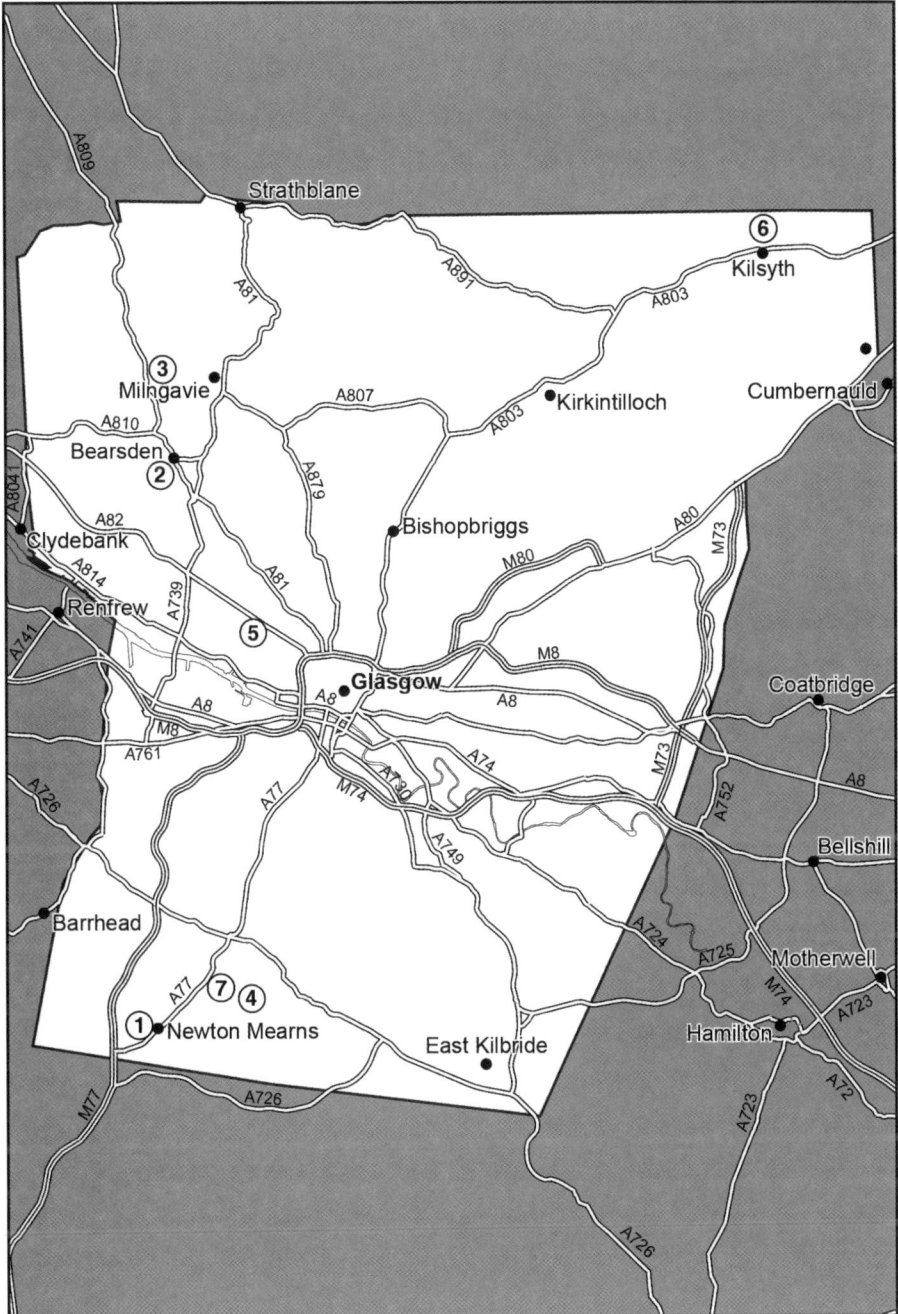

1 123 WATERFOOT ROW
123 Waterfoot Road, Newton Mearns, Glasgow. G77
Mrs Evi Berlow

From the entrance on Waterfoot Road the garden slopes down towards the house. There is a lawned area and the planting is mostly shrubs, trees and perennials. There is a good view of the garden from a decked terrace near the house. To the back of the house there is a small patio area with colourful potted plants standing on pebbles and slate and sheltered by wall climbing plants.

Other Details: Home baking stall.

Directions: From Glasgow: M77 exit 3, turn left onto A726. After 1½ miles, take the A77 Ayr Road. Turn left on to Eaglesham Road. Turn left at junction and immediately right at the traffic lights on to Waterfoot Road.

Disabled Access: Partial

Opening Times:
Sunday 17 June 2:00pm - 5:00pm

Admission:
£5.00 including teas Children Free

Charities: Cosgrove Care receives 40%, the net remaining to SG Beneficiaries.

2 CLADDAGH
24 Station Road, Bearsden, Glasgow G61 4AL
Mr Ian McMillan

An unusual garden with the rear totally hidden from the road and most visitors are surprised by its size and design. It has a semi-circular lawn bordered by vegetable and flower beds with a mix of herbaceous, annuals and delphiniums. Surrounding the lawn are several steep terraces linked by stairs and paths, some of these may be closed on the day. The terraces are planted with a mixed variety including rhododendrons, lilies, poppies alstroemeria, sidalcea and geraniums.

Other Details: Admission includes teas and home baking.

Directions: Travel along Drymen Road, at Bearsden Station turn into Station Road, keep straight on, bearing right under the railway bridge and Claddach, number 24, is the third house on the right.

Disabled Access: Partial

Opening Times:
Sunday 1 July 2:00pm - 5:00pm

Admission:
£5.00 Children Free

Charities: MS Revive receives 40%, the net remaining to SG Beneficiaries.

3 CROSSBURN
Stockiemuir Road, Milngavie, Glasgow G62 7HJ
Willie & Pat Anderson and Annika Sandell & Robert Johnston

Two neighbouring gardens set around a converted farm steading. One, a south facing wooded garden dominated by a large pond, the banks of which are left for natural growth. There is a fruit and vegetable plot within the cultivated garden plus a number of mixed borders with a good variety of plants. The other, a 1 acre garden with mature woodland, a lily pond and bog garden, mixed and herbaceous borders with choice plants; hardy geraniums, irises, paeonies, oriental poppies and others.

Directions: From Glasgow take A739 to Bearsden, Drymen Road, turn right on to A809 Stockiemuir Road, signposted Drymen, go straight through Baljaffrey Roundabout continue to Crossburn Roundabout, take first left road to Douglasmuir Quarry. Bus: First Bus 119 from Buchanan St, stops at 'Mains Estate' just before Crossburn Roundabout.

Disabled Access: None

Opening Times:
Sunday 10 June 2:00pm - 5:00pm

Admission:
£5.00 including teas.

Charities: Allergy UK receives 40%, the net remaining to SG Beneficiaries.

4 GREENBANK GARDEN
Flenders Road, Clarkston G76 8RB
The National Trust for Scotland   Tel: 0844 493 2201
Email: dferguson@nts.org.uk   www.nts.org.uk

A unique walled garden with plants and designs of particular interest to suburban gardeners. Fountains, woodland walk and special area for disabled visitors. There will be a a garden walk on 'Daffodils and how best to grow them'.

Other Details: NCCPG National Colletion: Bergenia. Shop, plant sales and gardening demonstrations throughout the year. Soup and sandwiches, teas and cake.

Directions: Flenders Road, off Mearns Road, Clarkston. Off M77 and A727, follow signs for East Kilbride to Clarkston Toll. Bus: No44a, Glasgow to Newton Mearns. Rail: Clarkston station, 1¼m.

Disabled Access: Full

Opening Times:
Saturday 14 April 9:30am - 5:00pm

Admission:
£6.00 Concessions £5.00
Guided walk £2.00.
NB. These prices are correct at time of going to print.

Charities: Donation to SG Beneficiaries.

---

5 KEW TERRACE SECRET GARDENS
Kew Terrace Lane G12 7NT
Professor George G Browning and other Owners

Kew Terrace is one of the grand terraces that line Great Western Road and when built in 1845 to 1849 only one of the 20 houses had a mews, the others had back gardens. Over the years the temptation to use them as car storage spaces has been resisted and now there is a series of 'Secret Gardens' all different in their handling, but all enhancing green living in a town environment. Access is from tree-lined, cobbled Kew Terrace Lane.

Other Details: Teas in the marquee in West End garden.

Directions: From M8 take junction 17 (A82) and turn right onto Great Western Road. Continue one mile to cross over the Great Western Road/Byres Road junction. Kew Terrace is on the left and access is 250 yards beyond traffic lights.

Disabled Access: None

Opening Times:
Saturday 9 June 2:00pm - 5:00pm

Admission:
£5.00 includes several gardens and tea with home baking.

Charities: Kew on Great Western Road Garden Fund receives 40%, the net remaining to SG Beneficiaries.

---

6 KILSYTH GARDENS
Allanfauld Road, Kilsyth G65 9DE
Mr and Mrs George Murdoch and Mr and Mrs Alan Patrick Tel: 01236 821667

Aeolia (Mr and Mrs G Murdoch) Third of an acre garden developed since 1960 by the owners. Mature specimen trees and shrubs, a large variety of rhododendrons, primulas, hardy geraniums and herbaceous plants.

Blackmill (Mr and Mrs Alan Patrick) Across the road from Aeolia. An acre of mature and recent planting of specimen trees and shrubs on the site of an old mill. There is an ornamental plant and rockpool. A further acre of natural woodland glen. Paths along the Garrel Burn with views to the cascading waterfalls. WC available but unsuitable for disabled.

Directions: A803 to Kilsyth, through main roundabout. Turn left into Parkburn Road up to the crossroads. Short walk up Allanfauld Rd, unsuitable for parking. Buses: No27 Glasgow-Falkirk, No24 Glasgow-Stirling NoX86 Glasgow-Kilsyth (not Sunday).

Disabled Access: Partial

Opening Times:
Sunday 20 May 2:00pm - 5:00pm
Also by arrangement April - September

Admission:
£5.00 includes both gardens and homemade teas.

Charities: Strathcarron Hospice receives 40%, the net remaining to SG Beneficiaries.

7 SUNDRUM
11 Neidpath Road West, Giffnock, Glasgow G46 6SS
Mr and Mrs M. Goldberg

This is a large urban garden and shows an approach to coping with a very steep hill front and back. There has been no attempt to create a structured or organized layout and in some areas, there is just random planting of vegetables, fruit, and flowers. No site is available for a greenhouse so there is a continual struggle to protect and promote these against clay soil and weather. Ours could be described as hotch-potch or haphazard garden - I prefer to say "a random one".

Directions: M77 exit Paisley and follow signs for Giffnock (E. Kilbride) to Eastwood Toll. Take last exit A77 (Ayr). After first set of traffic lights third on left is Cul-de-Sac Neidpath Road West.

Disabled Access: None

Opening Times:
Sunday 26 August 2:00pm - 5:00pm

Admission:
£5.00. Tea and cake £2.00.

Charities: Cosgrave Care receives 40%, the net remaining to SG Beneficiaries.

WOULD YOU LIKE TO OPEN YOUR GARDEN FOR CHARITY?

If you are interested in opening your garden for charity and would like more information, call 0131 226 3714, email info@scotlandsgardens.org or fill in the form at the back of this book.

We welcome gardens large and small and also groups of gardens.

ISLE OF ARRAN

Scotland's Gardens 2012 Guidebook is sponsored by **INVESTEC WEALTH & INVESTMENT**

District Organiser

Mrs S C Gibbs	Dougarie, Isle of Arran KA27 8EB

Treasurer

Mrs E Adam	Bayview, Pirnmill, Isle of Arran KA27 8HP

Gardens open on a specific date

Brodick Castle & Country Park, Brodick	Sunday 6 May	10:00am	-	5:00pm
Strabane, Brodick	Sunday 20 May	11:00am	-	5:00pm
Strabane, Brodick	Sunday 27 May	11:00am	-	5:00am
The Kilmichael Hotel, Glen Cloy, Brodick	Sunday 10 June	12:00am	-	4:00pm
Dougarie KA27 8EB	Sunday 1 July	2:00pm	-	5:00pm
Brodick Castle & Country Park, Brodick	Sunday 8 July	10:00am	-	5:00pm

Key to symbols

🌳	New in 2012	🅗	Homemade teas	B&B	Accommodation
☕	Teas	🐕	Dogs on a lead allowed	🌷	Plant stall
ᴄᴾ	Cream teas	♿	Wheelchair access	🌱	Scottish Snowdrop Festival

OPEN FOR DISCOVERY

1 BRODICK CASTLE & COUNTRY PARK

Brodick KA27 8HY
The National Trust for Scotland   Tel: 0844 493 2152
Email: brodickcastle@ nts.org.uk www.nts.org.uk

At any time of year the gardens are well worth a visit, though especially in spring when the internationally acclaimed rhododendron collection bursts into full bloom. Venture out into the country park and discover wildflower meadows where Highland cows graze, woodland trails and tumbling waterfalls. Exotic plants and shrubs. Walled garden. Woodland garden.

Other Details: NCCPG Collection: Three Rhododendron Collections

Directions: Brodick 2 miles. Service buses from Brodick Pier to Castle. Regular sailings from Ardrossan & Claonaig (Argyll). Information from Caledonian MacBrayne, Gourock. (Tel: 01475 650100)

Disabled Access: Partial

Opening Times:
Sunday 6 May 10:00am -
5:00pm

Sunday 8 July 10:00am -
5:00pm

Admission:
£5.50 Concessions £4.50
Family £15.00. NB: Correct
prices on going to print

Charities: Donation to SG
Beneficiaries

2 DOUGARIE

KA27 8EB
Mr and Mrs S C Gibbs
Email: office@dougarie.com

Terraced garden in castellated folly. Tender shrubs, herbaceous border, traditional kitchen garden.

Other Details: Free Parking. Cream teas in the 19th century Boathouse. Self-catering accommodation available, please email.

Directions: Blackwaterfoot 5 miles. Regular ferry sailing from Ardrossan and Claonaig (Argyll). Information from Caledonian MacBrayne, Gourock. (Telephone 01475 650100)

Disabled Access: None

Opening Times:
Sunday 1 July 2:00pm -
5:00pm

Admission:
£3.50 Children Free

Charities: Pirnmill Village
Association receives 40%,
the net remaining to SG
Beneficiaries.

3 STRABANE

Brodick KA27 8DP
Lady Jean Fforde

Woodland Garden with fine rhododendrons and azaleas. Walled garden with good herbaceous borders

Directions: On east side of Brodick - Corrie road 100 yards before Duchess's Shopping Centre. Parking in front of house.

Disabled Access: None

Opening Times:
Sunday 20 May 11:00am -
5:00pm
Sunday 27 May 11:00am -
5:00am

Admission:
£4.00 Children Free

Charities: Royal Agricultural
Benevolent Institution receive
40% on 20 May, Arran Youth
Foundation receives 40% on 2
May, the net remaining to SG
Beneficiaries.

4 **THE KILMICHAEL HOTEL**
Glen Cloy, Brodick KA27 8BY
Mr Geoffrey Botterill
www.kilmichael.com

Attractive mixed borders and woodland surrounding historic house. Mature beeches, oaks and giant redwoods. "Chickenopolis" collection of chickens and variety of ducks. Peacocks roam freely.

Other Details: Hotel open April-October. Self catering deluxe cottages available all year.

Directions: Parking for disabled only. Please park in village or on Knowe Road, then walk if at all possible. Follow signs from junction of Shore Road and Knowe Road, Brodick. Pleasant 15 minute walk down country lane to garden.

Disabled Access: Partial

Opening Times:
Sunday 10 June 12:00am - 4:00pm

Admission:
£3.50

Charities: Sightsavers.org receives 40%, the net remaining to SG Beneficiaries.

FOR NEW GARDENS IN 2012 SEE PAGES 20 - 23

OVER 50 NEW GARDENS OPENING THIS YEAR.

KINCARDINE & DEESIDE

Scotland's Gardens 2012 Guidebook is sponsored by **INVESTEC WEALTH & INVESTMENT**

District Organisers

Mrs Tina Hammond	Bardfield, Inchmarlo, Banchory AB31 4AT
Mrs Julie Nicol	Bogiesheil, Ballogie, Aboyne AB34 5DU

Area Organisers

Mrs Andrea Bond	Rosebank, Crathes, Banchory AB31 5JE
Mrs Helen Jackson	
Ms Frieda Morrison	
Mr and Mrs David Younie	Bealltainn, Ballogie, Aboyne AB34 5DL

Treasurer

Lesley Mitchell	13 Highgate Gardens, Ferryhill, Aberdeen AB11 7TZ

Gardens open on a specific date

Workshop at Crathes Castle, Banchory	Saturday 28 January	10:00am -	5:00pm
Ecclesgreig Castle, St Cyrus	Sunday 26 February	1:00pm -	4:00pm
Inchmarlo House Garden, Inchmarlo, Banchory	Sunday 20 May	1:30pm -	4:30pm
The Burn House & The Burn Garden House, Glenesk	Sunday 27 May	2:00pm -	5:00pm
Kincardine, Kincardine O'Neil	Sunday 10 June	2:00pm -	5:00pm
Milltown Community Gardens, Arbuthnott	Sunday 10 June	1:30pm -	5:00pm
Crathes Castle, Banchory	Saturday 16 June	11:00am -	4:00pm
Ecclesgreig Castle, St Cyrus	Sunday 17 June	1:00pm -	5:00pm
Finzean House, Finzean, Banchory	Sunday 24 June	2:00pm -	5:00pm
Drumlithie Village, Drumlithie	Saturday 30 June	2:00pm -	5:00pm
Drum Castle, Drumoak, by Banchory	Saturday 7 July	7:00pm	
Drum Castle, Drumoak, by Banchory	Sunday 8 July	11:00am -	5:00pm
Findrack, Torphins	Sunday 8 July	2:00pm -	5:00pm
Douneside House, Tarland	Sunday 15 July	2:00pm -	5:00pm
Mill of Benholm Project, Benholm by Johnshaven	Sunday 29 July	10:00am -	5:00pm
Glenbervie House, Drumlithie, Stonehaven	Sunday 5 August	2:00pm -	5:00pm
Inchmarlo House Garden, Inchmarlo, Banchory	Sunday 21 October	1:30pm -	4:30pm

Gardens open by arrangement

When organising a visit to a garden open by arrangement, please enquire if there are facilities and catering available

Drum Castle, Drumoak, by Banchory

July and August for exclusive evening tour bookings.   0844 4932161

Key to symbols

🌳	New in 2012	H	Homemade teas	B&B	Accommodation
☕	Teas	🐴	Dogs on a lead allowed	🌷	Plant stall
C	Cream teas	♿	Wheelchair access	🌱	Scottish Snowdrop Festival

OPEN FOR EVENTS

CRATHES CASTLE EVENTS

28 JANUARY:
A day workshop about the principles and practicalities of pruning a garden.

16 JUNE:
An exciting family fun day in celebration of the anniversary of Crathes becoming a Trust garden.

For more information on these events see the Crathes entry on page 183 or check out the NTS website: www.nts.org.uk

Garden locations

1 CRATHES CASTLE

Banchory AB31 5QJ
The National Trust for Scotland   Tel: 0844 493 2166
Email: crathes@nts.org.uk   www.nts.org.uk

The walled garden is really eight gardens, ranging from the formal to the modern. Massive yew hedges planted as early as 1702. Famous June Borders, two lavish beds of herbaceous colour.
28 January: Join our expert Head Gardener for a day workshop about the principles and practicalities of pruning a garden. The programme will cover practical sessions on roses, renovations and removals as well as trees, shrubs and formative pruning.
16 June: Exciting family fun in celebration of the anniversary of Crathes becoming a Trust garden. For full details check NTS website.

Other Details: NCCPG Collection: Dianthus. Self-catering accommodation. 28 January: includes soup & sandwich lunch (booking essential).

Directions: On A93, 15m W of Aberdeen and 3m E of Banchory.

Disabled Access: Partial

Opening Times:
Saturday 28 January 10:00am - 5:00pm
Saturday 16 June 11:00am - 4:00pm

Admission:
28 Jan: £50.00 - includes tea/coffee and light lunch (booking essential)

16 Jun: £4.00 Concessions £2.00

Charities: Donation to SG Beneficiaries

2 DOUNESIDE HOUSE

Tarland AB34 4UD
The MacRobert Trust

The former home of Lady MacRobert who designed and developed the gardens from farmland in the early to mid 1900s. The house and gardens are now in Trust and from March to October are used exclusively by retired and serving officers of the armed forces. Overlooking the Deeside hills, ornamental terraced borders, woodland and water gardens surround a spectacular elevated lawn. The house is supplied with vegetables and cut flowers from the well-stocked walled garden, which also houses an ornamental greenhouse. There are fine walks along the beech belts with uninterrupted views over the Howe of Cromar.

Other Details: Local Pipe Band.

Directions: B9119 towards Aberdeen. Tarland 1½ miles.

Disabled Access: Partial

Opening Times:
Sunday 15 July 2:00pm - 5:00pm

Admission:
£4.00 OAP's £2.00 Children under 12 Free

Charities: Perennial receives 40%, the net remaining to SG Beneficiaries.

3 DRUM CASTLE

Drumoak, by Banchory AB31 5EY
The National Trust for Scotland   Tel: 0844 493 2161
www.nts.org.uk

In the walled garden the Trust has established a collection of old-fashioned roses which is at its peak during July. The pleasant parkland contains the 100 acre Old Wood of Drum and offers fine views and walks.
7 July: Romancing the rose. An evening walk around the rose garden. Tickets £6.00 including refreshments. Booking essential.
8 July: SG open day. Celebrating 21 years of roses at Drum; afternoon teas in the garden; garden volunteers will be on hand to demonstrate summer pruning; Tai chi and poetry readings. Silent garden book auction.

Other Details: Opening dates correct at time of going to print. Tearoom open at Castle 11:00am-4:00pm with a fine selection of baking and savouries.

Directions: A93, 3mW of Peterculter. 10mW of Aberdeen and 8mE of Banchory.

Disabled Access: Partial

Opening Times:
Sat 7 July 7:00pm
Sun 8 July 11:00am - 5:00pm
Also by arrangement July & Aug for inclussive tour bookings.

Admission:
7, 8 July: £6.00 incl. Gardens and Guided Walk
Other dates: Gardens: £4.00
Castle & Garden: £9.00

Charities: Donation to SG Beneficiaries

4 DRUMLITHIE VILLAGE
Drumlithie AB39 3YF
Jon Hayati Tel: 01569 740378
Email: jon.hayati@yahoo.co.uk

Walk round the delightful village of Drumlithie and visit a variety of attractive colourful village gardens. Tickets and plan of the gardens available at the Village Hall.

Other Details: Plant stall, art exhibition, strawberry teas and homebaking in the Village Hall.

Directions: Drumlithie, six miles south of Stonehaven, is 1 mile off the A90. It is well signed and on entering the village there are directions to the Village Hall for parking.

Disabled Access: Partial

Opening Times:
Saturday 30 June 2:00pm - 5:00pm

Admission:
£3.50

Charities: RSPB receives 40%, receives 40%, the net remaining to SG Beneficiaries.

5 ECCLESGREIG CASTLE
St Cyrus DD10 0DP
Mr Gavin Farquhar
Email: enquiries@ecclesgreig.com www.ecclesgreig.com

Ecclesgreig Castle, Victorian Gothic on a 16thC core, is internationally famous as an inspiration for Bram Stoker's Dracula. The snowdrop walk starts at the castle, meanders around the estate, along woodland paths and the pond, ending at the garden. The woodlands contain some very interesting trees and shrubs. The Italian Renaissance style garden is below a terrace of decorative stone balustrades and has classical statues, round and sculptured topiary with views across St Cyrus to the sea. Development began 10 years ago from a derelict state and continues.

Other Details: June opening: Children's colouring competition, archery, bouncy castle (provisional)

Directions: Ecclesgreig will be signposted from the A92 Coast Road and from the A937 Montrose / Laurencekirk Road.

Disabled Access: Partial

Opening Times:
Sunday 26 February 1:00pm - 4:00pm for Snowdrop Festival
Sunday 17 June 1:00pm - 5:00pm

Admission:
£3.00 Accompanied Children Free

Charities: Scottish Guide Association (Montrose) receives 20%, Scottish Civic Trust receives 20%, the net remaining to SG Beneficiaries.

6 FINDRACK
Torphins AB31 4LJ
Mr and Mrs Andrew Salvesen

The gardens of Findrack are set in beautiful wooded countryside and are a haven of interesting plants and unusual design features. There is a walled garden with circular lawns and deep herbaceous borders, stream garden leading to a wildlife pond, vegetable garden and woodland walk. Excellent selection of plants for sale all grown in the garden.

Directions: Leave Torphins on A980 to Lumphanan after ½ mile turn off signposted Tornaveen. Stone gateway 1 mile up on left.

Disabled Access: Partial

Opening Times:
Sunday 8 July 2:00pm - 5:00pm

Admission:
£4.00 Children under 12 £1.00

Charities: The Breadmaker receives 40%, the net remaining to SG Beneficiaries.

FINZEAN HOUSE
Finzean, Banchory AB31 6NZ
Mr and Mrs Donald Farquharson

An evolving country house garden with beautiful views in a walled setting. Finzean House was the family home of Joseph Farquharson, the Victorian landscape painter, and the garden was the backdrop for several of his paintings. There are newly planted herbaceous borders and a recently laid out cutting garden alongside shrubs, trees and the historic holly hedge to the front.

Directions: On B976, South Deeside Road, between Banchory and Aboyne.

Disabled Access: Full

Opening Times:
Sunday 24 June 2:00pm - 5:00pm

Admission:
£4.00 OAPs £3.00 Children Free

Charities: Forget Me Not Club receives 40%, the net remaining to SG Beneficiaries.

GLENBERVIE HOUSE
Drumlithie, Stonehaven AB39 3YB
Mr and Mrs A Macphie

Nucleus of present day house dates from 15th century with additions in 18th and 19th centuries. A traditional Scottish walled garden on a slope with roses, herbaceous and annual borders along with fruit and vegetables. One wall is taken up with a fine Victorian style conservatory with many varieties of pot plants and climbers giving a dazzling display. There is also a woodland garden by a burn with primulas and ferns. Please note paths are quite steep in parts of the garden.

Other Details: Baking stall.

Directions: Drumlithie 1 mile. Garden 1½ miles off A90.

Disabled Access: None

Opening Times:
Sunday 5 August 2:00pm - 5:00pm

Admission:
£4.00 Children over 12, £1.00 Children under 12 Free

Charities: West Mearn's Parish Church receives 40%, the net remaining to SG Beneficiaries.

INCHMARLO HOUSE GARDEN
Inchmarlo, Banchory AB31 4AL
Skene Enterprises (Aberdeen) Ltd   Tel: 01330 826242
Email: info@inchmarlo-retirement.co.uk   www.inchmarlo-retirement.co.uk

An ever-changing 5 acre Woodland Garden, featuring ancient Scots Pines, Douglas Firs and Silver Firs, some over 42 metres tall, beeches and rare and unusual trees, including Pindrow Firs, Père David's Maple, Erman's Birch and a mountain snowdrop tree. The Oriental Garden features a Kare Sansui, a dry slate stream designed by Peter Roger, a RHS Chelsea gold medal winner. The Rainbow Garden, within the keyhole-shaped purple Prunus Cerasifera hedge, has been designed by Billy Carruthers, an eight times gold medal winner at the RHS Scottish Garden Show.

Directions: From Aberdeen via North Deeside Road on A93, one mile west of Banchory turn right at the main gate to Inchmarlo House.

Disabled Access: Partial

Opening Times:
Sun 20 May 1:30pm - 4:30pm
Sun 21 Oct 1:30pm - 4:30pm

Admission:
£5.00 OAPs £4.00 Children under 14 Free

Charities: Alzheimer Scotland Action on Dementia receives 40% May Opening, Rotal Deeside Forget-Me-Not Dementia Support receives 40% October Opening, the net remaining to SG Beneficiaries.

10 KINCARDINE
Kincardine O'Neil AB34 5AE
Mr and Mrs Andrew Bradford

A woodland or wilderness garden in development with some mature rhododendrons and azaleas and new planting amongst mature trees. A walled garden with a mixture of herbaceous and shrub borders, a sensational laburnum walk, vegetables and fruit trees. Extensive lawns and wild-flower meadows and a thought-provoking Planetary Garden. All with a background of stunning views across Royal Deeside.

Other Details: Treasure Trail for children included in admission.

Directions: Kincardine O'Neil on A93. Gates and lodge are opposite village school.

Disabled Access: Partial

Opening Times:
Sunday 10 June 2:00pm - 5:00pm

Admission:
£5.00, Children £2.00.

Charities: Children 1st receives 20%, Miss Edith Coutts Trust (A Kincardine O'Neil Charity) receives 20%, the net remaining to SG Beneficiaries.

11 MILL OF BENHOLM PROJECT
Benholm by Johnshaven DD10 0HT
Mill of Benholm Project   Tel: 01561 362466
Email: mill_of_benholm@btconnect.com

The Project provides training for SVQ gardening awards (with Aberdeen College). There are student gardens and a cottage garden. There is a delightful river and woodland walk through Millbrae Wood where there is an abundance of wildlife. Mill wheel demonstrations and guided tours of the mill as well as plants for sale, raised by the students. This is a work in progress which warrants an annual visit to follow the efforts of students, staff, volunteers and members.

Other Details: Mill wheel demonstrations and mill tour included in admission. Disabled toilet.

Directions: Turn off the A92 onto the Kirk of Benholm road. We are south of Inverbervie and North of Johnshaven. Large visitors parking area with disabled parking for two cars directly by tearoom.

Disabled Access: None

Opening Times:
Sunday 29 July 10:00am - 5:00pm

Admission:
£3.50

Charities: Mill of Benholm receives 40%, the net remaining to SG Beneficiaries.

12 MILLTOWN COMMUNITY GARDENS
Arbuthnott AB30 1PB
Milltown Day Workshop   Tel: 01561362882

The 8.5 acre gardens are comprised of 'The Day Workshop' and three house gardens. As a charity, we provide accommodation and a safe, productive work environment for residents and clients from all over Scotland. We aim to make the gardens colourful and stimulating all year round as well as providing a wildlife haven. There is a good mix of mature trees and shrubs, herbaceous, mixed borders, rose and vegetable beds. There are ponds, 'living willow structures' and wooden sculptures.

Other Details: Willow and chainsaw demonstrations.   Pottery and artwork stall.

Directions: Three miles from Inverbervie on the B967 off the A92, or turn left from the A90 southbound onto the B967 Arbuthnott road for three miles.

Disabled Access: Full

Opening Times:
Sunday 10 June 1:30pm - 5:00pm

Admission:
£3.50 Children Free

Charities: Milltown Community Ltd receives 40%, the net remaining to SG Beneficiaries.

13

THE BURN HOUSE & THE BURN GARDEN HOUSE
Glenesk DD9 7YP
The Bursar   Tel: 01356 648281
Email: burn@goodenough.ac.uk

Beautiful 18th century mansion house with magnificent walled garden nearby. Stunning 190 acre estate set in area of outstanding beauty including dramatic walk along the famous gorge in the North Esk river. An added feature of the garden is the labyrinth.

Other Details: Tombola. Homemade teas £2.50.

Directions: 1 mile north of Edzell Village. 3 miles from the A90. Front entrance situated on North side of River North Esk Bridge on B966 between Edzell and Fettercairn.

Disabled Access: Partial

Opening Times:
Sunday 27 May 2:00pm - 5:00pm

Admission:
£4.00

Charities: Marie Curie Hospices receives 40%, the net remaining to SG Beneficiaries.

CANCELLATIONS

On the rare occassions that garden openings are cancelled, details will be posted on the Cancellation page of our website www.scotlandsgardens.org

KIRKCUDBRIGHTSHIRE

Scotland's Gardens 2012 Guidebook is sponsored by **INVESTEC WEALTH & INVESTMENT**

District Organiser

Mrs C Cathcart	Culraven, Borgue, Kirkcudbright DG6 4SG

Area Organisers

Mrs P Addison	Killeron Farm, Gatehouse of Fleet, Castle Douglas DG7 2BS
Mrs Val Bradbury	Glenisle, Jubilee Path, Kippford DG5 4LW
Mrs W N Dickson	Chipperkyle, Kirkpatrick, Durham DG7 3EY
Mrs B Marshall	Cairnview, Carsphairn DG7 3TQ
Mrs M McIlvenna	Braeneuk, Balmaclellan, Castle Douglas DG7 3QS
Mrs C McIver	Loxley, Abercrombie Road, Castle Douglas DG7 1BA
Mrs K Ross	Slate Row, Auchencairn, Castle Douglas DG7 1QL
Mrs C V Scott	14 Castle Street, Kirkcudbright DG6 4JA

Treasurer

Mr P Phillips	The Old Manse, Crossmichael DG7 3AT

Gardens open on a specific date

Danevale Park, Crossmichael	Date to be advised	
Broughton House Garden, 12 High Street, Kirkcudbright	Tuesday 7 February	12:00pm - 4:30pm
Broughton House Garden, 12 High Street, Kirkcudbright	Wednesday 8 February	12:00pm - 4:30pm
Corsock House, Corsock, Castle Douglas	Sunday 6 May	2:00pm - 5:00pm
Threave Garden, Castle Douglas	Sunday 13 May	10:00am - 5:00pm
Stockarton, Kirkcudbright	Sunday 20 May	2:00pm - 5:00pm
Cally Gardens, Gatehouse of Fleet	Sunday 3 June	10:00pm - 5:30pm
Blair House, 8 High Street, Kirkcudbright	Sunday 24 June	2:00pm - 5:00pm
Oakleigh Bank, Kirkcudbright	Sunday 24 June	2:00pm - 5:00pm
Southwick House, Southwick	Sunday 1 July	2:00pm - 5:00pm
Southwick House, Southwick	Monday 2 July	9:00am - 5:00pm
Southwick House, Southwick	Tuesday 3 July	9:00am - 5:00pm
Southwick House, Southwick	Wednesday 4 July	9:00am - 5:00pm
Southwick House, Southwick	Thursday 5 July	9:00am - 5:00pm
Southwick House, Southwick	Friday 6 July	9:00am - 5:00pm
Crofts, Kirkpatrick Durham, Castle Douglas	Sunday 15 July	2:00pm - 5:00pm
Glensone Walled Garden, Southwick	Sunday 22 July	2:00pm - 5:00pm
Borgue Parish Gardens,	Sunday 29 July	1:00pm - 4:00pm

Threave Garden, Castle Douglas	Sunday 5 August	10:00am - 5:00pm
Cally Gardens, Gatehouse of Fleet	Sunday 12 August	10:00pm - 5:30pm
Broughton House Garden, 12 High Street, Kirkcudbright	Friday 17 August	12:00pm - 5:00pm

Gardens open regularly

Cally Gardens, Gatehouse of Fleet	Easter Sat - last Sun in Sept	
	Sats & Suns	10:30am - 5:30pm
	Tues - Fris	2:00pm - 5:30pm

Gardens open by arrangement

When organising a visit to a garden open by arrangement, please enquire if there are facilities and catering available.

Corsock House, Corsock, Castle Douglas	April - June	01644 440250
The Waterhouse Gardens at Stockarton, Kirkcudbright	1 April - 31 August	01557 331266

Key to symbols

	New in 2012		Homemade teas	B&B	Accommodation
	Teas		Dogs on a lead allowed		Plant stall
	Cream teas		Wheelchair access		Scottish Snowdrop Festival

We welcome gardens large and small and also groups of gardens.

WOULD YOU LIKE TO OPEN YOUR GARDEN FOR CHARITY?

If you are interested in opening your garden for charity and would like more information, call 0131 226 3714, email info@scotlandsgardens.org or fill in the form at the back of this book

Garden locations

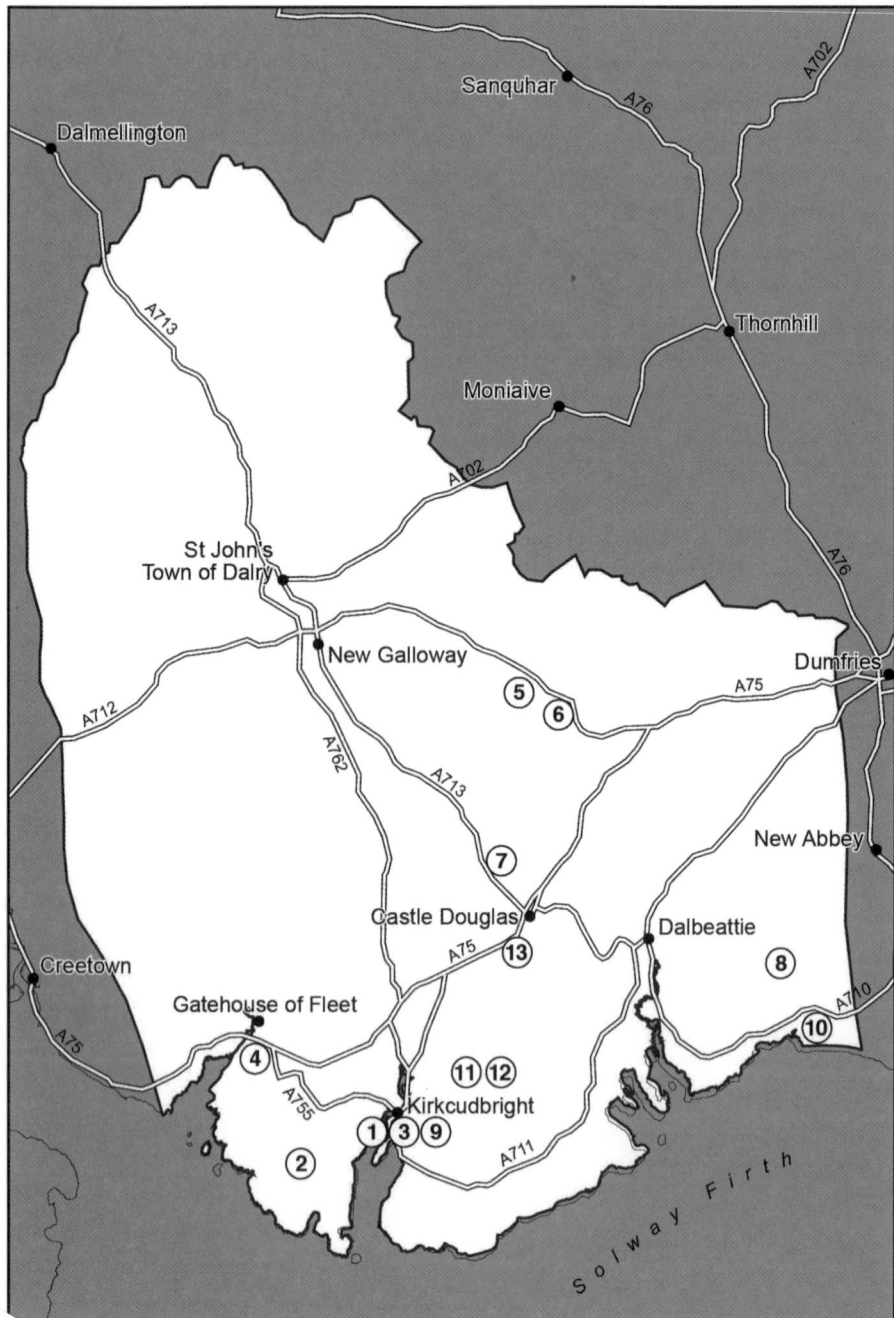

1

BLAIR HOUSE (IN CONJUNTION WITH OAKLEIGH BANK)
8 High Street, Kirkcudbright DG6 4JX
Mr R Reddaway

Georgian town house with newly created garden running to the River Dee and
Solway with views of Kirkcudbright Marina and to distant hills. Shrub borders with
winding paths through a spring garden, a folly, formal rose gardens, a herb garden
and traditional double herbaceous borders.

Directions: From Harbour Square car park walk round behind McLellan's Castle
into the High Street. Blair House is on the right.

Disabled Access: Partial

Opening Times:
Sunday 24 June 2:00pm -
5:00pm

Admission:
£4.00

Charities: Kirkcudbright
Summer Festivities receives
40%, the net remaining to SG
Beneficiaries.

2

BORGUE PARISH GARDENS
DG6 4SH
The Gardeners of Borgue Parish Gardens

Cosy Cottage Borgue DG6 4SH (Mr & Mrs A Broome) Garden with herbaceous
borders, rockeries greenhouse and alpine troughs.
Gardener's Cottage Senwick DG6 4TP (Mr & Mrs M Agnew) Colourful country
cottage garden with lilies, herbaceous and more varieties.
Kirkbank Borgue DG6 4SG (Mr & Mrs R Bell) colourful garden with polytunnel
and greenhouses full of exhibition plants.
Margrie Cottage Borgue DG6 4UE (Mr & Mrs G Hill) Larger garden with mature
shrubs and trees, natural rock features and pond.

Directions: Go to Borgue Village and follow the arrows. Borgue is on the B727
between Kirkcudbright and Gatehouse of Fleet three miles off the A75 route to
Stranraer.

Disabled Access: Partial

Opening Times:
Sunday 29 July 1:00pm -
4:00pm

Admission:
£4.00

Charities: Cancer Research UK
receives 40%, the net remaining
to SG Beneficiaries.

3

BROUGHTON HOUSE GARDEN
12 High Street, Kirkcudbright DG6 4JX
The National Trust for Scotland   Tel: 01557 330 437
Email: broughtonhouse@nts.org.uk   www.nts.org.uk

Fascinating town house garden that belonged to E A Hornel - artist, collector
and one of the 'Glasgow boys'. Full of colour, mostly herbaceous, old apple trees,
greenhouse with old pelargonium varieties, fruit and vegetable garden. Garden
walks (please phone garden for details). Self-catering accommodation available.

Other Details: 17 August opening in celebration of E A Hornel's birthday.
Horticultural demonstration.

Directions: In Kirkcudbright High Street.

Disabled Access: Partial

Opening Times:
Tuesday & Wednesday 7 & 8
February 12:00pm - 4:30pm
Friday 17 August 12:00pm -
5:00pm

Admission:
£3.00 N.B. These prices are
correct at time of going to print.

Charities: Donation to SG
Beneficiaries

4 CALLY GARDENS
Gatehouse of Fleet DG7 2DJ
Mr Michael Wickenden   Tel: 01557 814703
Email: info@callygardens.co.uk   www.callygardens.co.uk

A specialist nursery in a fine 2.7 acre 18th century walled garden with old vinery and bothy, all surrounded by the Cally Oak woods. Our collection of 3,500 varieties of plants can be seen and a selection will be available pot-grown. Excellent range of rare herbaceous perennials. Forestry nature trails nearby.

Directions: From Dumfries take the Gatehouse turning off A75 and turn left through the Cally Palace Hotel gateway from where the gardens are well signposted.

Disabled Access: Full

Opening Times:
Sunday 3 June 10:00pm - 5:30pm
Sunday 12 August 10:00pm - 5:30pm
Easter Sat - last Sun in Sept
Sats & Suns 10:30am - 5:30pm
Tues - Friday 2:00pm - 5:30pm

Admission:
£2.50

Charities: ROKPA Tibetan Charity receives 40%, the net remaining to SG Beneficiaries.

5 CORSOCK HOUSE
Corsock, Castle Douglas DG7 3DJ
Mrs M L Ingall   Tel: 01644 440250

Rhododendrons, woodland walks with temples, water gardens and loch. One acre formal walled garden being re-made. David Bryce turretted "Scottish Baronial" house in background.

Directions: Off A75 Dumfries 14 miles, Castle Douglas 10 miles, Corsock village ½ mile on A712.

Disabled Access: Partial

Opening Times:
Sunday 6 May 2:00pm - 5:00pm
Also by arrangement April - June

Admission:
£4.00 Concessions £3.00
Children Free

Charities: Corsock & Kirkpatrick Durham Church receives 40%, the net remaining to SG Beneficiaries.

6 CROFTS
Kirkpatrick Durham, Castle Douglas DG7 3HX
Mrs Andrew Dalton   Tel: 01556 650235

Victorian garden with mature trees, a walled garden, hydrangea garden and a water garden.

Directions: A75 to Crocketford, then 3 miles on A712 to Corsock & New Galloway

Disabled Access: Partial

Opening Times:
Sunday 15 July 2:00pm - 5:00pm

Admission:
£4.00

Charities: Kirkpatrick Durham Church receives 40%, the net remaining to SG Beneficiaries.

7 DANEVALE PARK
Crossmichael DG7 2LP
Mrs M R C Gillespie   Tel: 01556 670223
Email: danevale@tiscali.co.uk

Mature policies with woodland walk alongside the River Dee. One of the finest displays of snowdrops in Scotland. We also get great praise for our teas.

Other Details: Opening date to be advised, date when known will be shown on our website: www.scotlandsgardens.org.

Directions: On the A713. Crossmichael 1 mile, Castle Douglas 2 miles.

Disabled Access: Partial

Opening Times:
To be advised

Admission:
£2.50

Charities: Poppyscotland receives 40%, the net remaining to SG Beneficiaries.

---

8 GLENSONE WALLED GARDEN
Southwick DG2 8AW
William & Josephine Millar   Tel: 01387 780215
Email: josephine.millar@btconnect.com

A restored walled garden complete with central water feature. Borders of perennials; shrubs with beds interspersed through the lawn. Large kitchen garden with a variety of vegetables; fruit occupies a section of the garden. Bee Bowls, a unique feature, are positioned in two opposite corners of the wall. Set in an idyllic valley with views of the Solway Firth and the Cumbrian hills.

Directions: Off the A710 Dumfries to Dalbeattie coast road at Caulkerbush. Take the B793 to Dalbeattie for two miles then turn right and follow the arrows.

Disabled Access: Full

Opening Times:
Sunday 22 July 2:00pm - 5:00pm

Admission:
£3.50

Charities: Combat Stress receives 40%, the net remaining to SG Beneficiaries.

---

9 OAKLEIGH BANK (IN CONJUNCTION WITH BLAIR HOUSE)
Oakleigh Bank DG6 4AH
Mr & Mrs Robert Mitchell   Tel: 01557 330780
Email: ramkbt@btinternet.com

Garden evolved from scratch with favourite trees and shrubs for all seasons.

Directions: On A711 road out of Kirkcudbright to Dundrennan between end of High Street & Castledykes Road.

Disabled Access: Full

Opening Times:
Sunday 24 June 2:00pm - 5:00pm

Admission:
£4.00 for both gardens

Charities: Kirkcudbright Summer Festivities receives 40%, the net remaining to SG Beneficiaries.

10 SOUTHWICK HOUSE
Southwick DG2 8AH
Mr and Mrs R H L Thomas

Traditional formal walled garden with greenhouses and potager containing fruit, vegetables and cutting flowers. Roses now a prominent feature together with herbaceous borders, shrubs and a lily pond. A water garden with trees, shrubs, ponds and lawns running alongside the Southwick Burn.

Directions: On A710 near Caulkerbush. Dalbeattie 7 miles, Dumfries 17 miles.

Disabled Access: Partial

Opening Times:
Sunday 1 July 2:00pm - 5:00pm
Monday - Friday 2 - 6 July 9:00am - 5:00pm

Admission:
£4.00

Charities: Loch Arthur Community receives 20%, Gardener's Royal Benevolent Society receives 20%, the net remaining to SG Beneficiaries.

11 STOCKARTON
Kirkcudbright DG6 4XS
Lt. Col. and Mrs Richard Cliff   Tel: 01557 330 430

A garden begun in 1994. Our aim has been to create informal and small gardens around a Galloway farmhouse, leading down to a lochan.

Directions: On B727 Kirkcudbright to Gelston Road. Kirkcudbright 3 miles, Castle Douglas 7 miles.

Disabled Access: Partial

Opening Times:
Sunday 20 May 2:00pm - 5:00pm

Admission:
£3.00

Charities: Friends of Loch Arthur Community receives 40%, the net remaining to SG Beneficiaries.

12 THE WATERHOUSE GARDENS AT STOCKARTON
Kirkcudbright DG6 4XS
Martin Gould & Sharon O'Rourke Tel: 01557 331266
Email: waterhousekbt@aol.com www.waterhousekbt.co.uk

One acre of densely planted terraced cottage style gardens attached to a Galloway cottage. Three ponds surround the oak framed eco-polehouse 'The Waterhouse' available to rent 52 weeks a year. Climbing roses, clematis and honeysuckles are a big feature as well as pond-side walk. Over 50 photos on our website. Featured on BBC Scotland's 'Beechgrove Garden' 2007.

Directions: On B727 Kirkcudbright to Gelston - Dalbeattie road. Kirkcudbright 3 miles, Castle Douglas 7 miles.

Disabled Access: None

Opening Times:
By arrangement 1 April - 31 August

Admission:
By Donation

Charities: Loch Arthur Community receives 40%, the net remaining to SG Beneficiaries.

3

THREAVE GARDEN

Castle Douglas DG7 1RX

The National Trust for Scotland   Tel: 01556 502 575

Email: sinnes@nts.org.uk   www.nts.org.uk

Home of the Trust's School of Practical Gardening. Spectacular daffodils in spring. Colourful herbaceous borders in summer, striking autumn trees and heather garden. Working walled garden. Meet with Head Gardener for tour of the beautiful garden. 13 May and 5 August - two tours: Morning and afternoon. Contact the property for more information.

Other Details: Garden trail (quiz) and tours with Head Gardener. Self-catering accommodation available. Restaurant open for full dining.

Directions: Off A75, one mile west of Castle Douglas.

Disabled Access: Full

Opening Times:
Sunday 13 May 10:00am - 5:00pm
Sunday 5 August 10:00am - 5:00pm

Admission:
£6.50 Concessions £5.50.
Correct prices on going to print.

Charities: Donation to SG Beneficiaries

SCOTTISH SNOWDROP FESTIVAL

Scotland's Gardens season starts with the Snowdrop Openings which are extremely popular.

We are very keen to have more Snowdrop properties opening in 2013 so please let us know if you have good snowdrops and would like to participate.

LANARKSHIRE

Scotland's Gardens 2012 Guidebook is sponsored by **INVESTEC WEALTH & INVESTMENT**

District Organiser

Mrs M Maxwell Stuart	Baitlaws, Lamington ML12 6HR

Press Officer

Mr G Crouch	2 Castlehill Court, Symington, Biggar ML12 6JR

Treasurer

Mrs E Munro	High Meadows, Nemphlar, Lanark ML11 9JF

Gardens open on a specific date

Cleghorn , Stable House, Cleghorn Farm, Lanark	Sunday 4 March	2:00pm - 4:00pm
The Scots Mining Company House, Leadhills, Biggar	Sunday 6 May	2:00pm - 6:00pm
20 Smithycroft, Hamilton	Sunday 17 June	2:00pm - 6:00pm
Dippoolbank Cottage, Carnwath	Sunday 17 June	2:00pm - 6:00pm
New Lanark Roof Garden, New Lanark Mills, Lanark	Sunday 17 June	5:00pm - 8:00pm
Wellbutts, Elsrickle, by Biggar	Saturday 21 July	12:00pm - 4:00pm
Wellbutts, Elsrickle, by Biggar	Sunday 22 July	12:00pm - 4:00pm
Dippoolbank Cottage, Carnwath	Sunday 29 July	2:00pm - 6:00pm
Culter Allers, Coulter, Biggar	Sunday 12 August	2:00pm - 5:00pm

Gardens open regularly

New Lanark Roof Garden, New Lanark Mills, Lanark	All year	11:00am - 5:00pm

Gardens open by arrangement

When organising a visit to a garden open by arrangement, please enquire if there are facilities and catering available.

Baitlaws, Lamington, Biggar	1 June - 31 August	01899 850240
Biggar Park, Biggar	1 May - 31 July	01899 220185
Carmichael Mill, Hyndford Bridge, Lanark	On request.	01555 665880
The Scots Mining Company House, Leadhills, Biggar	On request.	01659 74235

Key to symbols

🌳	New in 2012	H	Homemade teas	B&B	Accommodation
☕	Teas	🐕	Dogs on a lead allowed	❀	Plant stall
☕	Cream teas	♿	Wheelchair access	🌱	Scottish Snowdrop Festival

Garden locations

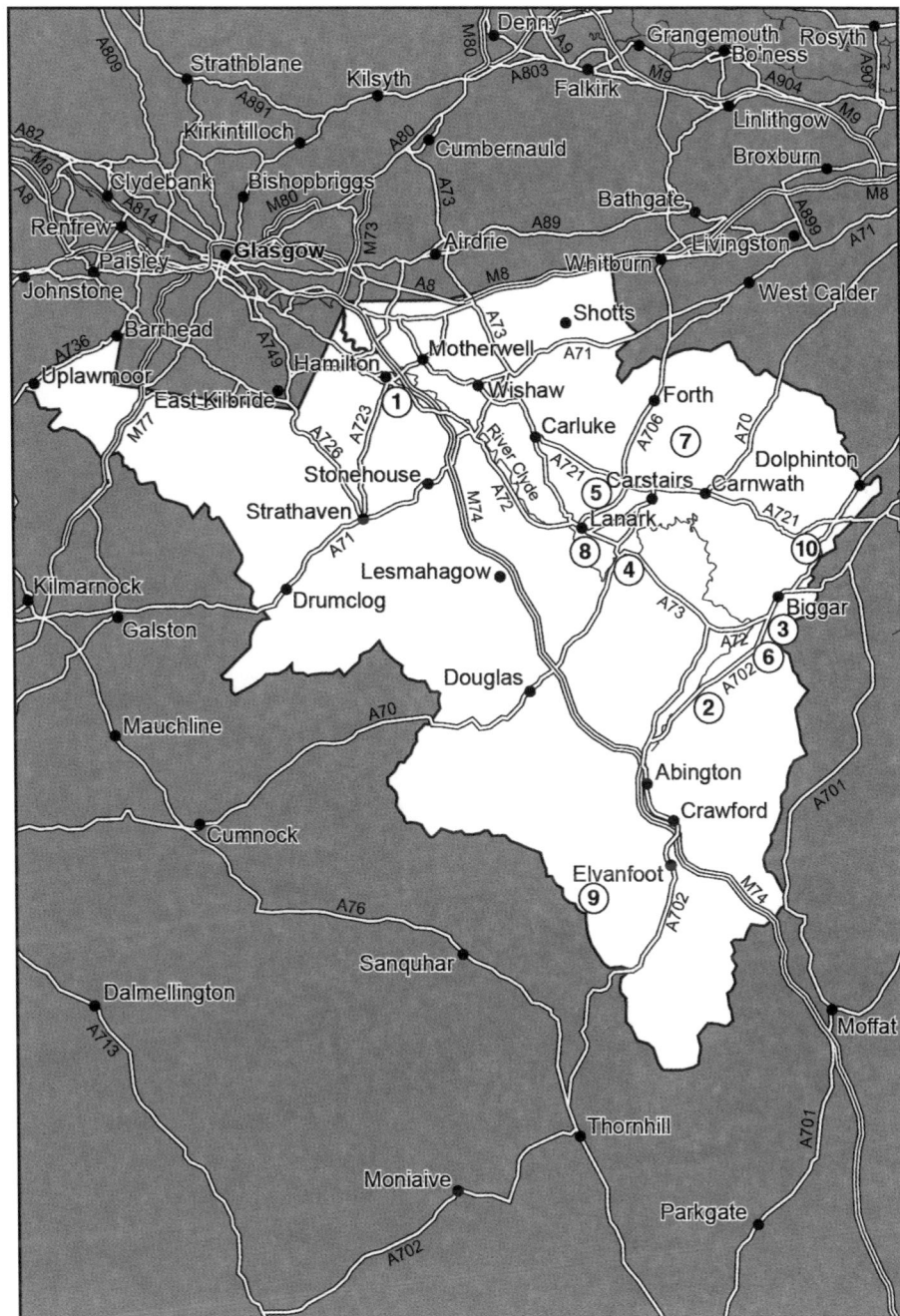

A map of Lanarkshire and surrounding areas showing garden locations numbered 1–10. Place names and roads marked include:

Strathblane, Kilsyth, Denny, Grangemouth, Bo'ness, Rosyth, Falkirk, Kirkintilloch, Cumbernauld, Linlithgow, Broxburn, Clydebank, Bishopbriggs, Bathgate, Renfrew, Glasgow, Airdrie, Livingston, Paisley, Whitburn, West Calder, Johnstone, Barrhead, Shotts, Uplawmoor, Hamilton, Motherwell, Forth, East Kilbride, Wishaw, Carluke, Dolphinton, Stonehouse, Carstairs, Carnwath, Strathaven, Lanark, Kilmarnock, Lesmahagow, Biggar, Galston, Drumclog, Douglas, Mauchline, Abington, Crawford, Cumnock, Elvanfoot, Sanquhar, Dalmellington, Moffat, Thornhill, Moniaive, Parkgate.

Roads: A809, A891, A82, A80, A803, M80, A73, M9, A904, A901, M8, A89, A814, A899, A71, A8, A736, A749, A728, A723, A706, A70, A721, A72, A702, M77, M74, A72, A76, A701, A113, A702.

1 20 SMITHYCROFT
Hamilton ML3 7UL
Mr and Mrs R I Fionda

A plantswoman's award-winning garden which has developed into a mature oasis. Eucalyptus, phormiums and clematis abound and there is a large range of unusual plants which only flourish in sheltered parts of Scotland.

Directions: Off M74 at Junction 6. 1 mile on A72 - well signed.

Disabled Access: None

Opening Times:
Sunday 17 June 2:00pm - 6:00pm

Admission:
£3.00

Charities: St. Mary's Church, Hamilton for Mary's Meals receives 40%, the net remaining to SG Beneficiaries.

2 BAITLAWS
Lamington, Biggar ML12 6HR
Mr and Mrs M Maxwell Stuart Tel: 01899 850240

The garden is set at over 900 ft. above sea level and has been developed over the past 25 years with a particular emphasis on colour combinations of shrubs and herbaceous perennials which flourish at that height. A small pond is a recent addition. The surrounding hills make an imposing backdrop. Featured in "Good Gardens Guide".

Directions: Off A702 above Lamington Village. Biggar 5 miles, Abington 5 miles, Lanark 10 miles.

Disabled Access: None

Opening Times:
By arrangement 1 June - 31 August: Groups Welcome

Admission:
£4.00

Charities: Biggar Museum Trust, Lamington Chapel Restoration Fund receives 40%, the net remaining to SG Beneficiaries.

3 BIGGAR PARK
Biggar ML12 6JS
Mr and Mrs David Barnes   Tel: 01899 220185
Email: sue@smbarnes.com

Ten acre garden starred in "Good Gardens Guide", featured on "The Beechgrove Garden" and in "Country Life" "Scottish Field" and many others. Incorporating traditional walled garden with long stretches of herbaceous borders, shrubberies, fruit, vegetables and a potager. Lawns, walks, pools, small Japanese garden and other interesting features. Glades of rhododendrons, azaleas and blue poppies in May and June. Good collection of old fashioned roses in June and July; interesting young trees.

Directions: On A702, ¼ mile south of Biggar.

Disabled Access: Partial

Opening Times:
By arrangement 1 May - 31 July: Groups Welcome

Admission:
£5.00

Charities: ZANE receives 40%, the net remaining to SG Beneficiaries.

4 CARMICHAEL MILL
Hyndford Bridge, Lanark ML11 8SJ
Chris, Ken & Gemma Fawell   Tel: 01555 665880
Email: ken.fawell@btinternet.com

Riverside gardens surrounding the only remaining workable water powered grain mill in Clydesdale. Admission includes entry to the mill which will be turning, river levels permitting. Diverse plant habitats from saturated to bone dry allow a vast range of trees and shrubs, both ornamental and fruit, with a vegetable garden. Herbaceous perennials, annuals and biennials with ornamental/wildlife pond complementing the landscape. Also archaeological remains of medieval grain mills from C.1200 and foundry, lint mill and threshing mill activity within the curtilage of the Category B Listed Building.

Other Details: Teas and light refreshments by prior arrangement.

Directions: Just off A73 Lanark to Biggar road ½ mile east of the Hyndford Bridge.

Disabled Access: Partial

Opening Times:
By arrangement on request

Admission:
£4.00 Children over 12 £2.00

Charities: Donation to SG Beneficiaries

---

5 CLEGHORN
Stable House, Cleghorn Farm, Lanark. ML11 7RN
Mr and Mrs R Elliott Lockhart   Tel: 01555 663792
Email: info@cleghornestategardens.com   www.cleghornestategardens.com

18th century garden which is currently being renovated. Mature trees and shrubs, with masses of snowdrops spread around. Beautiful views to the south of Tinto Hill and the Cleghorn glen.

Directions: Cleghorn Farm is situated 2 miles north of Lanark on the A706.

Disabled Access: None

Opening Times:
Sunday 4 March 2:00pm - 4:00pm

Admission:
By Donation

Charities: Marie Curie Cancer Care receives 40%, the net remaining to SG Beneficiaries.

---

6 CULTER ALLERS
Coulter, Biggar ML12 6PZ
The McCosh Family

Culter Allers, a late-Victorian baronial house, has maintained its traditional one-acre walled kitchen garden, half with fruit and vegetables, the other half with mainly cut flowers and herbaceous. The policies of the house are open and include woodland walks and an avenue of 125 year old lime trees leading to the Village Church.

Directions: In the village of Coulter, 3 miles south of Biggar on A702.

Disabled Access: Partial

Opening Times:
Sunday 12 August 2:00pm - 5:00pm

Admission:
£4.00 Children Free

Charities: Coulter Library Trust receives 40%, the net remaining to SG Beneficiaries.

7 DIPPOOLBANK COTTAGE
Carnwath ML11 8LP
Mr Allan Brash

Artist's intriguing cottage garden. Vegetables grown in small beds. Herbs, fruit, flowers, pond in woodland area with tree house and summer house. Fernery completed in 2007. This is an organic garden mainly constructed with recycled materials.

Directions: Off B7016 between Forth and Carnwath near the village of Braehead on the Auchengray road. Approx 8 miles from Lanark. Well signed.

Disabled Access: None

Opening Times:
Sunday 17 June 2:00pm - 6:00pm
Sunday 29 July 2:00pm - 6:00pm

Admission:
£3.00

Charities: The Little Haven receives 40%, the net remaining to SG Beneficiaries.

8 NEW LANARK ROOF GARDEN
New Lanark Mills, Lanark ML11 9DB
New Lanark Visitor Centre   Tel: 01555 661345
Email: visit@newlanark.org   www.newlanarkroofgarden.co.uk

This amazing 9,000 sq. ft. garden has been created on the roof of the historic A Listed Mill No. 2, in the heart of the New Lanark World Heritage Site. Designed by Douglas Coltart of Viridarium to meet these challenging conditions, the garden and viewing platform offer splendid and seasonally changing views. The Roof Garden is part of the New Lanark Visitor Centre, and is accessed by lift or stairs.

Other Details: Full details of the special June event will be posted on our website nearer the time. Refreshments and light snacks available in the Mill Pantry Coffee Shop.

Directions: New Lanark is 1 mile south of Lanark and around an hour from Glasgow (M74/A72) and Edinburgh (A70). From the south, the village is 30 mins from M74 Junction 13/Abington - main trunk road to Edinburgh.

Disabled Access: Full

Opening Times:
Sunday 17 June 5:00pm - 8:00pm for a special midsummer roof garden event. Open daily as part of New Lanark Visitor Centre. 11:00am - 5:00pm

Admission:
Price to be confirmed: visit our website for event details and admission charges.

Charities: Donation to SG Beneficiaries

9 THE SCOTS MINING COMPANY HOUSE
Leadhills, Biggar ML12 6XP
Charlie & Greta Clark   Tel: 01659 74235

The site is c.400m above sea level, which is high for a cultivated garden. The surrounding landscape is open moorland with sheep grazing. The garden is largely enclosed by dense planting, but the various walks allow views through the trees into the surrounding countryside. Historic Scotland in their register of "Gardens and designed landscapes" describe the garden as "An outstanding example of a virtually unaltered, small, 18thC garden layout connected with James Stirling, the developer of the profitable Leadhills mining enterprise, and possibly William Adam." Say goodbye to spring walking among what must be amongst the last daffodils of the year.

Directions: On Main Street, Leadhills (B797) 6 miles from M74 Junction 13 (Abington).

Disabled Access: Partial

Opening Times:
Sunday 6 May 2:00pm - 6:00pm
Also by arrangement on request

Admission:
£3.50 Children Free

Charities: Scots Mining Company Trust receives 40%, the net remaining to SG Beneficiaries.

WELLBUTTS
Elsrickle, by Biggar ML12 6QZ
Mr and Mrs N Slater

Started in 2000 from a bare brown site around a renovated croft cottage, with additional field ground obtained in 2005, the garden is now approximately 2 acres. Due to the exposed and elevated (960 ft.) position the ongoing priority is hedge and shrub planting to give some protection for the many and varied herbaceous borders leading to the duckhouse, two large ponds and 'boggery'.

Directions: Parking on main road (A721) near to bus stop. Walk to garden (approx. 200 yards)

Disabled Access: None

Opening Times:
Saturday 21 July 12:00pm - 4:00pm
Sunday 22 July 12:00pm - 4:00pm

Admission:
£4.00

Charities: Marie Curie Cancer Care receives 40%, the net remaining to SG Beneficiaries.

TWITTER

We have been busy tweeting in order to help increase the awareness of our activities amongst the online community.

Follow us on Twitter at:

http://twitter.com/scotgardens

twitter

LOCHABER & BADENOCH

Scotland's Gardens 2012 Guidebook is sponsored by **INVESTEC WEALTH & INVESTMENT**

District Organiser

Mr and Mrs Norrie Maclaren	Ard-Daraich, Ardgour, Nr. Fort William PH33 7AB

Area Organisers

Mrs Sally MacDonald	Keppoch House, Roy Bridge PH31 4AE
Mrs Philip MacKenzie	Glenkyllachy, Tomatin IV13 7YA
Mrs Anne Moore	Polgreggan, Newtonmore PH20 1BD

Treasurer

Mr Norrie Maclaren	Ard-Daraich, Ardgour, Nr. Fort William PH33 7AB

Gardens open on a specific date

Canna House Walled Garden, Isle of Canna	Saturday 5 May	10:30am -	4:00pm
Ard-Daraich, Ardgour, By Fort William	Sunday 6 May	2:00pm -	5:30pm
Conaglen, Ardgour, By Fort William	Sunday 27 May	2:00pm -	5:30pm
Aberarder, Kinlochlaggan	Sunday 10 June	2:00pm -	5:30pm
Ardverikie, Kinlochlaggan	Sunday 10 June	2:00pm -	5:30pm
Glenkyllachy Lodge, Tomatin	Sunday 22 July	2:00pm -	6:00pm
Ralia Lodge and Milton Lodge, Newtonmore	Sunday 5 August	2:00pm -	5:00pm
Canna House Walled Garden, Isle of Canna	Wednesday 15 August	10:30am -	4:00pm

Gardens open regularly

Ardtornish, By Lochaline, Morvern	1 January - 31 December	10:00am -	6:00pm

Key to symbols

🌳	New in 2012	H	Homemade teas	B&B	Accommodation
☕	Teas	🐕	Dogs on a lead allowed	🌷	Plant stall
C	Cream teas	♿	Wheelchair access	🌿	Scottish Snowdrop Festival

Garden locations

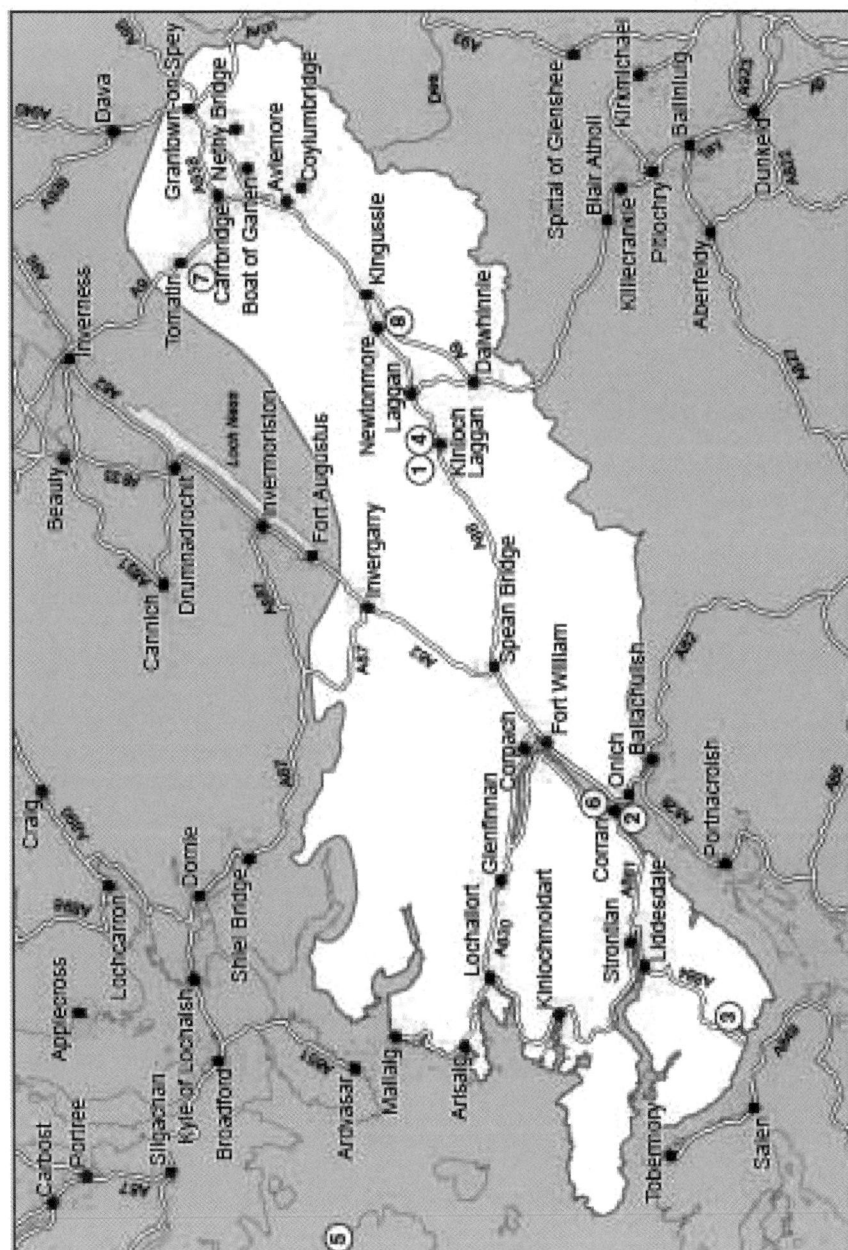

① ABERARDER (JOINT OPENING WITH ARDVERIKIE)
Kinlochlaggan PH20 1BX
The Feilden Family   Tel: 01528 544 300

The garden has been laid out over the last twenty years to create a mixture of spring and autumn plants and trees, including rhododendrons, azaleas and acers. The elevated view down Loch Laggan from the garden is exceptional.

Directions: On A86 between Newtonmore and Spean Bridge at east end of Loch Laggan.

Disabled Access: Partial

Opening Times:
Sunday 10 June 2:00pm - 5:30pm

Admission:
£5.00 includes entrance to Ardverikie

Charities: Marie Curie receives 20%, Laggan Church receives 20%, the net remaining to SG Beneficiaries.

② ARD-DARAICH
Ardgour, By Fort William PH33 7AB
Norrie and Anna Maclaren
www.arddaraich.co.uk

Seven acre hill garden, in a spectacular setting, with many fine and uncommon rhododendrons, an interesting selection of trees and shrubs and a large collection of camellias, acers and sorbus.

Directions: West from Fort William, across the Corran Ferry, turn left and a mile on the right further west.

Disabled Access: None

Opening Times:
Sunday 6 May 2:00pm - 5:30pm

Admission:
£4.00

Charities: Ardgour Memorial Hall receives 40%, the net remaining to SG Beneficiaries.

③ ARDTORNISH
By Lochaline, Morvern PA80 5UZ
Mrs John Raven

Wonderful gardens of interesting mature conifers, rhododendrons, deciduous trees, shrubs and herbaceous set amidst magnificent scenery.

Directions: A884 Lochaline 3 miles.

Disabled Access: None

Opening Times:
1 January - 31 December
10:00am - 6:00pm or Dusk

Admission:
£3.50

Charities: Donation to SG Beneficiaries

4 ARDVERIKIE (JOINT OPENING WITH ABERARDER)
Kinlochlaggan PH20 1BX
Mrs P Laing and Mrs E T Smyth-Osbourne

Lovely setting on Loch Laggan with magnificent trees. Walled garden with large collection of acers, shrubs and herbaceous. Architecturally interesting house (not open). Site of the filming of the TV series "Monarch of the Glen".

Other Details: Teas at Aberarder.

Directions: On A86 between Newtonmore and Spean Bridge. Entrance at east end of Loch Laggan by gate lodge over bridge.

Disabled Access: Partial

Opening Times:
Sunday 10 June 2:00pm - 5:30pm

Admission:
£5.00 - includes entrance to Aberarder

Charities: Laggan Church receives 20%, Marie Curie receives 20%, the net remaining to SG Beneficiaries.

5 CANNA HOUSE WALLED GARDEN
Isle of Canna PH44 4RS
National Trust for Scotland   Tel: 01687 462998
Email: sconnor@nts.org.uk   www.nts.org.uk

Formerly derelict 2 acre walled garden 4 years into a 5 year restoration. Soft fruit, top fruit, vegetables, ornamental lawns and flower beds. 80ft Escallonia arch. Garden being replanted to attract bees, butterflies and moths. Woodland walks outside walls. Spectacular views of neighbouring islands.

Other Details: Dogs welcome but must be kept under close control around livestock. Self-catering accommodation. Light refreshments available at adjacent Island Tearoom.

Directions: Access Isle of Canna via Calmac ferry from Mallaig pier. Head Gardener will meet boat at Canna pier for tour of garden.

Disabled Access: Partial

Opening Times:
Saturday 5 May 10:30am - 4:00pm
Wednesday 15 August 10:30am - 4:00pm

Admission:
£3.00 N.B. These prices are correct at time of going to print.

Charities: Donation to SG Beneficiaries

6 CONAGLEN
Ardgour, By Fort William PH33 7AH
Mr & Mrs J Guthrie   Tel: 01855 841234

A fabulous west coast garden. Rhododendrons, azaleas, herbaceous borders, herb and cut flower gardens, shrubs and mature conifers.

Other Details: Baking stall and other activities.

Directions: From Fort William or Glencon: cross Corran Ferry. Turn right and proceed for 4½ miles.
From Glenfinnan: turn right along west side of Loch Eil then alongside Loch Linnhe for 6 miles.

Disabled Access: Partial

Opening Times:
Sunday 27 May 2:00pm - 5:30pm

Admission:
£4.00

Charities: Abernethy Trust receives 40%, the net remaining to SG Beneficiaries.

7 **GLENKYLLACHY LODGE**
Tomatin, IV13 7YA
Mr and Mrs Philip Mackenzie
Email: emmaglenkyllachy@gmail.com

In a remote highland glen and at an altitude of 1150 feet this is a "wilderness" garden of shrubs, herbaceous, rhododendrons and trees planted round a pond with a backdrop of a juniper and birch covered hillside. Vegetable garden and polytunnel. Short wooded walk with stunning views down the Findhorn. Various garden sculptures.

Directions: Turn off the A9 at Tomatin and take the Coignafearn and Garbole single track road down north side of River Findhorn, cattle grid and gate on right after sign to Farr.

Disabled Access: Partial

Opening Times:
Sunday 22 July 2:00pm - 6:00pm

Admission:
£6.00 (includes tea)

Charities: Marie Curie Cancer Care receives 40%, the net remaining to SG Beneficiaries.

---

8 **RALIA LODGE AND MILTON LODGE**
Newtonmore PH20 1BD
Mrs Eira Drysdale and Alasdair & Charlotte Findlay
www.raliaestate.com

Two Highland gardens, Ralia Lodge and Milton Lodge, 300 yards apart with connecting grass path. Both are at 600ft with water gardens, shrubs and herbaceous with spectacular views.

Other Details: Light refreshments will be available.

Directions: From Perth: take the A9 for 65 miles north to Newtonmore (sign-posted Newtonmore, Spean Bridge, Fort William) after taking this exit drive for approx 250 metres down a long straight to a single tracked tarmac road to your right sign-posted Ralia and Nuide take this turning and drive for approx 250 metres. Ralia Lodge is 1st house and Milton is 3rd entrance on the left.
From North or Aberdeen: On A9, take Kingussie, Newtonmore turning, head through Kingussie and Newtonmore go over Spey Bridge and Railway Bridge with traffic lights. Approx 100 metres after traffic lights take sharp left down a single tracked tarmac road, Ralia Lodge is approximately 250 metres on left.

Disabled Access: Partial

Opening Times:
Sunday 5 August 2:00pm - 5:00pm

Admission:
£4.00 Children up to age 12 Free

Charities: Caberfeidh Horizons receives 20% and Emergency Medical Equipment, the net remaining to SG Beneficiaries.

MIDLOTHIAN

Scotland's Gardens 2012 Guidebook is sponsored by **INVESTEC WEALTH & INVESTMENT**

District Organiser

Mrs Sarah Barron	Laureldene, Kevock Road, Lasswade EH18 1HT

Area Organisers

Mrs Margaret Drummond	Pomathorn House, Penicuik EH26 8PJ
Mrs R Hill	Law House, 27 Biggar Road, Silverburn EH26 9LJ
Mrs Eilidh Liddle	21 Craigiebeild Crescent, Penicuik EH26 9EQ

Treasurer

Mrs Margaret Drummond	Pomathorn House, Penicuik EH26 8PS

Gardens open on a specific date

Kevock Garden, 16 Kevock Road, Lasswade	Sunday 4 March	12:00pm - 3:00pm
Cousland Smiddy and Village Gardens, Cousland	Sunday 3 June	12:00pm - 5:00pm
The Old Sun Inn, Newbattle, Dalkeith	Saturday 9 June	2:00pm - 5:00pm
1 Standpretty, Fuschie Bridge by Gorebridge	Sunday 10 June	2:00pm - 5:00pm
Kevock Garden, 16 Kevock Road, Lasswade	Saturday 16 June	2:00pm - 5:00pm
Kevock Garden, 16 Kevock Road, Lasswade	Sunday 17 June	2:00pm - 5:00pm
Broomieknowe Gardens, Lasswade	Sunday 24 June	2:00pm - 5:30pm
Newhall, Carlops	Sunday 22 July	2:00pm - 5:00pm

Gardens open by arrangement

When organising a visit to a garden open by arrangement, please enquire if there are facilities and catering available.

Newhall, Carlops	1 May - 31 August	01968 660206
The Old Sun Inn, Newbattle, Dalkeith	1 June - 31 July	0131 663 2648

Key to symbols

	New in 2012		Homemade teas	B&B	Accommodation
	Teas		Dogs on a lead allowed		Plant stall
C	Cream teas		Wheelchair access		Scottish Snowdrop Festival

Garden locations

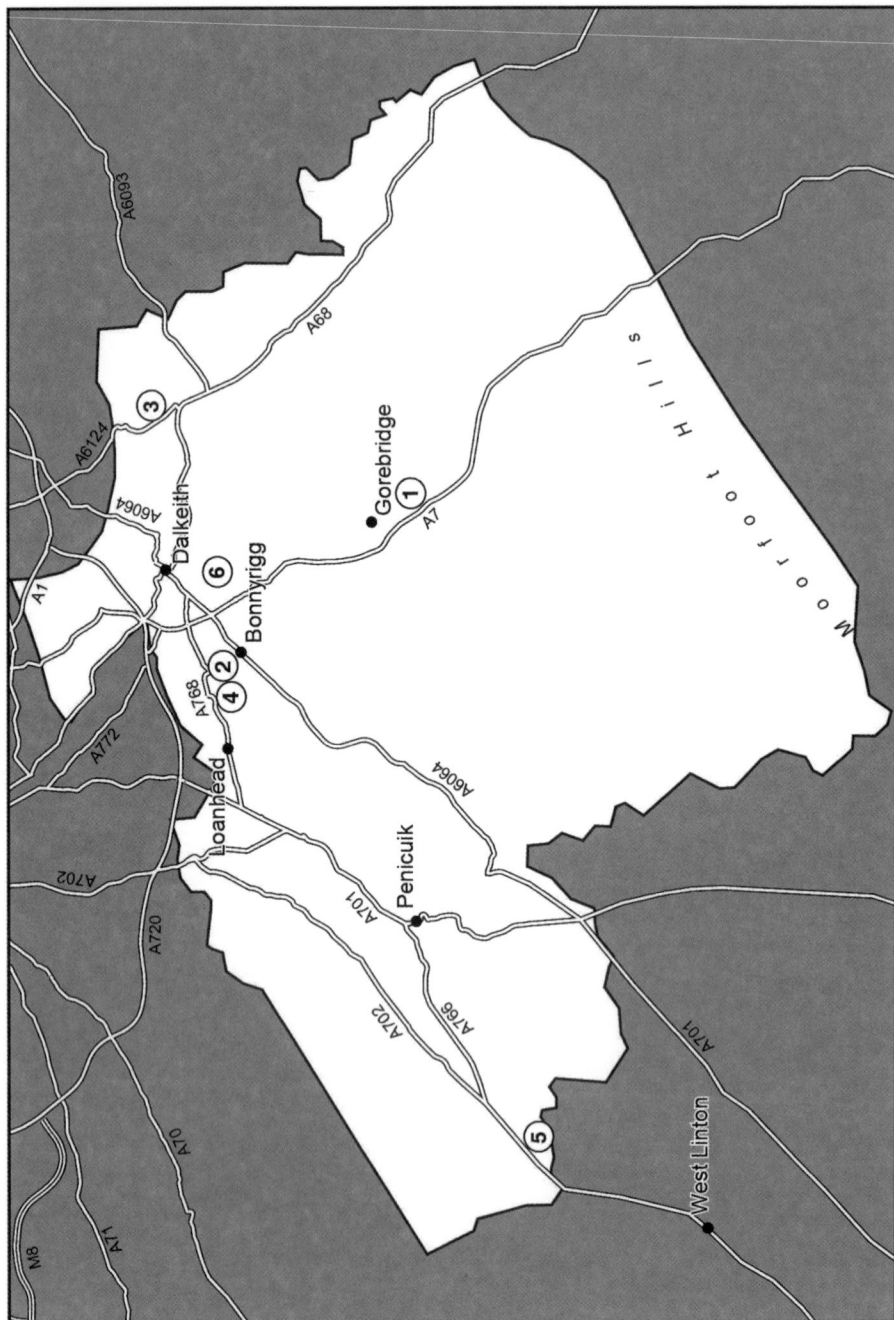

1 STANDPRETTY
Fuschie Bridge by Gorebridge EH23 4QG
Mrs Susan Adam   Tel: 01875 820 429
Email: susan.adam@akadamia.co.uk

A small tranquil cottage garden, set on high ground above Gorebridge. There are informal borders and island beds with a range of shrubs and herbaceous plants, vegetables grown in small raised beds, herbs and hens. Lovely local walks.

Directions: From A7 take Fuschie Bridge and Catcune turning (just beyond B6372 turn off). Go up hill, round bend, over railway bridge. Standpretty is 2ⁿᵈ house on left. Park beyond house on road.

Disabled Access: None

Opening Times:
Sunday 10 June 2:00pm - 5:00pm

Admission:
£3.00 Children Free

Charities: SSPCA receives 20%, The Woodland Trust receives 20%, the net remaining to SG Beneficiaries.

BROOMIEKNOWE GARDENS
Lasswade EH18 1LN
The Gardeners of Broomieknowe   Tel: 0131 663 8700
Email: ruthmehlsen@googlemail.com

Tucked away in the Broomieknowe conservation area of Lasswade are several charming gardens. Some are new to view, but all different in design yet complementary in style, witness to the skill and imagination of the owners. Many interesting trees and shrubs, with a variety of unusual herbaceous and bedding plants, brilliant colour, foliage and form. Lots of ideas and unusual garden features to interest the keen gardener.

Directions: Off B704 Broomieknowe between Lasswade and Bonnyrigg. Signposted. Lothian Region Transport Bus No. 31 to Cockpen (get off at Nazareth House Nursing Home).

Disabled Access: Partial

Opening Times:
Sunday 24 June 2:00pm - 5:30pm

Admission:
£4.00

Charities: Orbis (Flying Eye Hospital) receives 20%, Help For Heroes receives 20%, the net remaining to SG Beneficiaries.

COUSLAND SMIDDY AND VILLAGE GARDENS
Cousland EH22 2NX
Cousland Smiddy Trust & The Gardeners of Cousland

Cousland Village near Dalkeith is home to the oldest working smiddy in Scotland which has been in continuous use since 1703. The Cousland Smiddy Trust, established in 1989, now runs the Smiddy preserving it for future generations. There are 13 organic allotments in the garden grounds behind the Smiddy, which are let to local villagers, some of whom will be on hand to answer questions. Some of the village gardens will be open along with the Smiddy and Smiths Cottage Museum. Demonstrations will be given by the Blacksmith.

Other Details: Soup and rolls as well as teas and coffees available.

Directions: Route: 3 miles east of Dalkeith on the A68 (Dalkeith bypass) or A6106 (old A68) then A6124 or 1.5 miles south of Whitecraig on A6124.

Disabled Access: Full

Opening Times:
Sunday 3 June 12:00pm - 5:00pm

Admission:
£5.00 Children under 16 Free

Charities: Cousland Smiddy Trust receives 20%, Cousland Village Hall Association receives 20%, the net remaining to SG Beneficiaries.

4 KEVOCK GARDEN
16 Kevock Road, Lasswade EH18 1HT
David and Stella Rankin   Tel: 0131 454 0660
Email: info@kevockgarden.co.uk   www.kevockgarden.co.uk

A wonderful compact hillside garden overlooking the North Esk Valley with rockeries and a pond with damp loving plants. Several mature specimen trees, azaleas, rhododendrons and unusual shrubs are infilled with a range of rare woodland plants. Kevock Garden which has featured in many magazine articles and at the 2011 Chelsea Flower Show is open in March for Snowdrops and in the summer for interesting perennials and shrubs.

Other Details: Interesting plant stall with a range of unusual plants. Soup and rolls in March. Teas at local nursing home in June.

Directions: Kevock Road lies to the south of A678 Loanhead/Lasswade Road.

Disabled Access: None

Opening Times:
Sunday 4 March 12:00pm - 3:00pm
Sat 16 June 2:00pm - 5:00pm
Sun 17 June 2:00pm - 5:00pm

Admission:
£4.00 Children Free

Charities: The Building for the Future of Nepal receives 40%, the net remaining to SG Beneficiaries.

5 NEWHALL
Carlops EH26 9LY
John and Tricia Kennedy Tel: 01968 660206
Email: tricia.kennedy@newhalls.co.uk

Traditional 18th century walled garden with huge herbaceous border, shrubberies, fruit and vegetables. Many unusual plants for sale. Stunning glen running along the North Esk river in process of restoration (stout shoes recommended). Large pond with evolving planting.   Young arboretum and collection of Rosa pimpinellifolia. As in "Good Gardens Guide 2010", "Scottish Field", "Gardens Monthly", "Scotland on Sunday".

Other Details: Light lunches and teas available for arranged visits if organised in advance.

Directions: On A702 Edinburgh/Biggar, a ¼ of a mile after Ninemileburn and a mile before Carlops. Follow signs.

Disabled Access: Partial

Opening Times:
Sunday 22 July 2:00pm - 5:00pm
Also by arrangement 1 May - 31 August

Admission:
£4.00

Charities: L'Arche receives 40%, the net remaining to SG Beneficiaries.

6 THE OLD SUN INN
Newbattle, Dalkeith EH22 3LH
Mr and Mrs James Lochhead Tel: 0131 663 2648
Email: randjlochhead@uwclub.net

An interesting small half acre garden of island and raised beds containing a collection of species lilies, rock plants and some unusual bulbs. There are also two small interconnecting ponds and a conservatory.

Directions: B703 (Newtongrange) from Eskbank Toll. Garden is immediately opposite Newbattle Abbey College entrance. First bus 95 & 95X to Eskbank Toll only. Parking at Newbattle Abbey College.

Disabled Access: Partial

Opening Times:
Saturday 9 June 2:00pm - 5:00pm
Also by arrangement 1 June - 31 July

Admission:
£3.00 Children Free

Charities: All proceeds to SG Beneficiaries

MORAY & NAIRN

Scotland's Gardens 2012 Guidebook is sponsored by **INVESTEC WEALTH & INVESTMENT**

District Organiser

Mr and Mrs David Carter	The Old Granary, Letterfourie, Buckie AB56 5JP

Area Organiser

Mrs Lorraine Dingwall	Bents Green, 10 Pilmuir Road West, Forres IV36 2HL
Mrs Annie Stewart	33 Albert Street, Nairn IV12 4HF

Treasurer

Mr Michael Barnett	Drumdelnies, Nairn IV12 5NT

Gardens open on a specific date

Brodie Castle, Brodie, Forres	Saturday 14 April	10:30am - 4:30pm
Brodie Castle, Brodie, Forres	Sunday 15 April	10:30am - 4:30pm
42 Fife Street, Keith, Banffshire	Sunday 17 June	10:00am - 4:00pm
Bents Green, 10 Pilmuir Road West, Forres	Sunday 17 June	12:00pm - 5:00pm
Castleview, Auchindoun, Dufftown	Sunday 17 June	2:00pm - 5:00pm
Cuddy's Well, Clephanton, Inverness	Saturday 23 June	12:30pm - 9:00pm
Cuddy's Well, Clephanton, Inverness	Sunday 24 June	12:30pm - 9:00pm
Gordonstoun, Duffus, near Elgin	Sunday 24 June	2:00pm - 4:30pm
42 Fife Street, Keith, Banffshire	Saturday 21 July	10:00am - 4:00pm
Mill Road Allotments, Mill Road, Nairn	Sunday 22 July	12:00pm - 5:00pm

Gardens open by arrangement

When organising a visit to a garden open by arrangement, please enquire if there are facilities and catering available.

Bents Green, 10 Pilmuir Road West, Forres	1 June - 31 August	01309 674634
Carestown Steading, Deskford, Buckie	On request.	01542 841134
Cuddy's Well, Clephanton, Inverness	1 June - 31 July	01667 493639

Key to symbols

New in 2012	Homemade teas	B&B Accommodation
Teas	Dogs on a lead allowed	Plant stall
Cream teas	Wheelchair access	Scottish Snowdrop Festival

Garden locations

1 42 FIFE STREET
Keith, Banffshire AB55 5EG
Mr Robert Bean

A small town garden which has been cultivated over the last five years to create a wonderful colourful oasis in an urban setting. Still a work in progress, the garden encourages a variety of birds which act as pest control agents.

Other Details: Biscuits with teas.

Directions: Entering Keith from the A96 from the west follow the sign for Dufftown. Turn off Regent Street into Fife Street on B9014.

Disabled Access: Full

Opening Times:
Sunday 17 June 10:00am - 4:00pm
Saturday 21 July 10:00am - 4:00pm

Admission:
£3.00

Charities: All proceeds to SG Beneficiaries

2 BENTS GREEN
10 Pilmuir Road West, Forres IV36 2HL
Mrs Lorraine Dingwall   Tel: 01309 674634
Email: fixandig@aol.com   www.simplesite.com/hosta

Plantsman's small town garden with over three hundred cultivars of hostas, an extensive collection of hardy geraniums together with many other unusual plants. Managed entirely without the use of artificial fertilizers or chemicals, the owner encourages hedgehogs, toads and wild birds to control slugs.

Directions: From Tesco roundabout at Forres continue along Nairn Road. Take first left onto Ramflat Road, then right at the bottom, then first left onto Pilmuir Road West.

Disabled Access: None

Opening Times:
Sunday 17 June 12:00pm - 5:00pm
Also by arrangement 1 June - 31 August

Admission:
£4.00

Charities: Macmillan Nurses receives 40%, the net remaining to SG Beneficiaries.

3 BRODIE CASTLE
Brodie, Forres IV36 2TE
Shona Ferguson   Tel: 0844 493 2156
Email: sferguson@nts.org.uk   www.nts.org.uk

Brodie Castle's Daffodil Tea Event: The garden team will lead guided walks in support of Scotland's Gardens. In springtime the grounds are carpeted with the daffodils for which the castle is rightly famous. Bred by Ian Brodie, these daffodils are internationally significant. Some are found nowhere else in the world but the castle grounds! There is also a shrubbery garden with rhododendrons and a good tree collection, plus wildflowers. Contact property for further information.

Other Details: NCCPG Collection: Narcissus. Self-catering accommodation available. Special daffodil teas served on lawn. Tearoom in castle serves full baking and savoury selections.

Directions: Off A96 4½ miles west of Forres and 24 miles east of Inverness

Disabled Access: Partial

Opening Times:
Saturday 14 April 10:30am - 4:30pm
Sunday 15 April 10:30am - 4:30pm

Admission:
£3.00

Charities: Donation to SG Beneficiaries

4 CARESTOWN STEADING
Deskford, Buckie AB56 5TR
Rora Paglieri Tel: 01542 841134
Email: rora403@btinternet.com   www.carestownsteading.com

The Garden History Society in Scotland paid this garden the best compliment in describing it as "Garden history in the making". It was started in 1990 and has received press, TV and web accolades ever since. Every year a new addition is made, the latest: the epitome of the modern vegetable plot which is proving very successful: four year rotation, raised beds, seeping irrigation. Trees and shrubs are maturing, the maze is growing, the ducks are reproducing in the three ponds and the atmosphere is as happy as ever. The "pearl" of the garden, the courtyard with knot beds and topiary is now fully mature.

Directions: East of B9018 Cullen/Keith (Cullen 3 miles, Keith 9½ miles). Follow SG signs towards Milton and Carestown.

Disabled Access: None

Opening Times:
By arrangement on request

Admission:
£4.00

Charities: All proceeds to SG Beneficiaries

5 CASTLEVIEW
Auchindoun, Dufftown AB55 4DY
Mr and Mrs Ian Sharp   Tel: 01340 820 941
Email: ian@castleviewdufftown.co.uk

A small secluded riverside garden, created on three levels from scrub land by two enthusiastic beginners in 2005. The garden consists of two interconnected ponds, one formal, one natural and an abundance of herbaceous plants and shrubs. There are several sitting areas where you can admire the garden from many view points.

Directions: From Dufftown on the A920, travel approx. three miles towards Huntly. Drive until a small cluster of houses is reached, garden on the left approx. 20 yards off the main road.

Disabled Access: None

Opening Times:
Sunday 17 June 2:00pm - 5:00pm

Admission:
£3.00

Charities: Cat Protection League receives 40%, the net remaining to SG Beneficiaries.

6 CUDDY'S WELL
Clephanton, Inverness IV2 7QS
Jim and Jacque Smith   Tel: 01667 493639
Email: jimjacq1@btinternet.com

A relatively young family-friendly garden (started in 2006) designed to blend in with the surrounding rural woodland setting and to provide colour and interest throughout the year. There are colourful mixed herbaceous borders enclosing lawns, with ponds, rockeries and a herb garden to provide interest. A raised terrace contains productive rotational vegetable plots, a fruit garden and a well-stocked polytunnel.

Other Details: Children welcome.

Directions: From the A96 Inverness-Nairn road take the B9090 road south towards Cawdor. Clephanton is 1 mile up the hill. Cuddy's Well is the last house on the left going towards Cawdor.

Disabled Access: Partial

Opening Times:
Sat 23 June 12:30pm - 9:00pm
Sun 24 June 12:30pm - 9:00pm
Also by arrangement 1 June - 31 July

Admission:
£3.00 Children Free

Charities: Maggies Highland receives 20%, Raigmore Renal Unit receives 20%, the net remaining to SG Beneficiaries.

7 GORDONSTOUN
Duffus, near Elgin IV30 5RF
The Headmaster, Gordonstoun School   Tel: 01343 837837
Email: lambies@gordonstoun.org.uk   www.gordonstoun.org.uk

Gardens: Good formal herbaceous borders around lawns, terrace and orchard
School Grounds: Gordonstoun House (Georgian House of 1775/6 incorporating earlier 17th century house built for 1st Marquis of Huntly) and school chapel - both open. Unique circle of former farm buildings known as the Round Square. Scenic lake.

Directions: Entrance off B9012, 4 miles from Elgin at Duffus Village.

Disabled Access: Full

Opening Times:
Sunday 24 June 2:00pm - 4:30pm

Admission:
£4.00 Children £2.00

Charities: All proceeds to SG Beneficiaries

8 MILL ROAD ALLOTMENTS
Mill Road, Nairn IV12 5NJ
Nairn Allotment Society   Tel: 01667 454785
www.nairnallotments.org

A new allotment site of 30 plots laid out in an attractive community design beside the old parish church and graveyard.

Directions: The site is on the east side of Mill Road, beside the River Nairn. From Nairn High Street turn left onto Church Street which becomes Mill Road.

Disabled Access: Full

Opening Times:
Sunday 22 July 12:00pm - 5:00pm

Admission:
£3.00 including teas.

Charities: Highland Hospice receives 20%, Nairn Allotment Society receives 20%, the net remaining to SG Beneficiaries.

PEEBLESSHIRE

Scotland's Gardens 2012 Guidebook is sponsored by **INVESTEC WEALTH & INVESTMENT**

District Organiser

Mrs Mary Carrel	14 Leeburn View, Cardrona, Peebles EH45 9LS

Area Organisers

Mr J Bracken	Gowan Lea, Croft Road, West Linton EH46 7DZ
Mr Graham Buchanan-Dunlop	The Potting Shed, Broughton Place, Broughton ML12 6HJ
Ms R Hume	Llolans, Broughton ML12 6HJ
Mrs R Parrott	An Sparr, Medwyn Road, West Linton EH46 7HA
Mr K St C Cunningham	Hallmanor, Peebles, Tweeddale EH45 9JN
Mr Brian Taylor	5 Fawnburn Crescent, Cardrona EH45

Treasurer

Mr J Birchall	The Old Manse, Drumelzier, Biggar ML12 6JD

Gardens open on a specific date

Traquair, Traquair House, Innerleithen, Peeblesshire	Saturday 25 February	11:00am	-	4:00pm
Traquair, Traquair House, Innerleithen, Peeblesshire	Sunday 26 February	11:00am	-	4:00pm
Kailzie Gardens, Peebles	Sunday 4 March	2:00pm	-	5:00pm
Haystoun, Peebles	Sunday 27 May	1:30pm	-	5:00pm
Stobo Japanese Water Garden, Home Farm, Stobo	Sunday 3 June	1:30pm	-	5:00pm
West Linton Village Gardens, West Linton	Sunday 17 June	2:00pm	-	5:00pm
Glen House, Glen Estate, Innerleithen	Sunday 1 July	1:30pm	-	5:00pm
8 Halmyre Mains, West Linton	Sunday 29 July	2:00pm	-	5:00pm
Broughton Place Farmhouse, Broughton, Biggar	Sunday 5 August	2:00pm	-	5:30pm
Dawyck Botanic Garden, Stobo	Sunday 7 October	10:00am	-	5:00pm

Gardens open regularly

Dawyck Botanic Garden, Stobo	February & November	10:00am -	4:00pm
	March & October	10:00pm -	5:00pm
	April - September	10:00am -	6:00pm
Kailzie Gardens, Peebles	All Year	11:00am -	5:00pm
Traquair, Traquair House, Innerleithen, Peeblesshire	6 April - 30 September	11:00am -	5:00pm
	1 - 31 October	11:00am -	4:00pm
	1 - 30 November, weekends	11:00am -	3:00pm

Key to symbols

New in 2012	Homemade teas	Accommodation
Teas	Dogs on a lead allowed	Plant stall
Cream teas	Wheelchair access	Scottish Snowdrop Festival

**For updates and information,
visit our website
WWW.SCOTLANDSGARDENS.ORG**

Garden locations

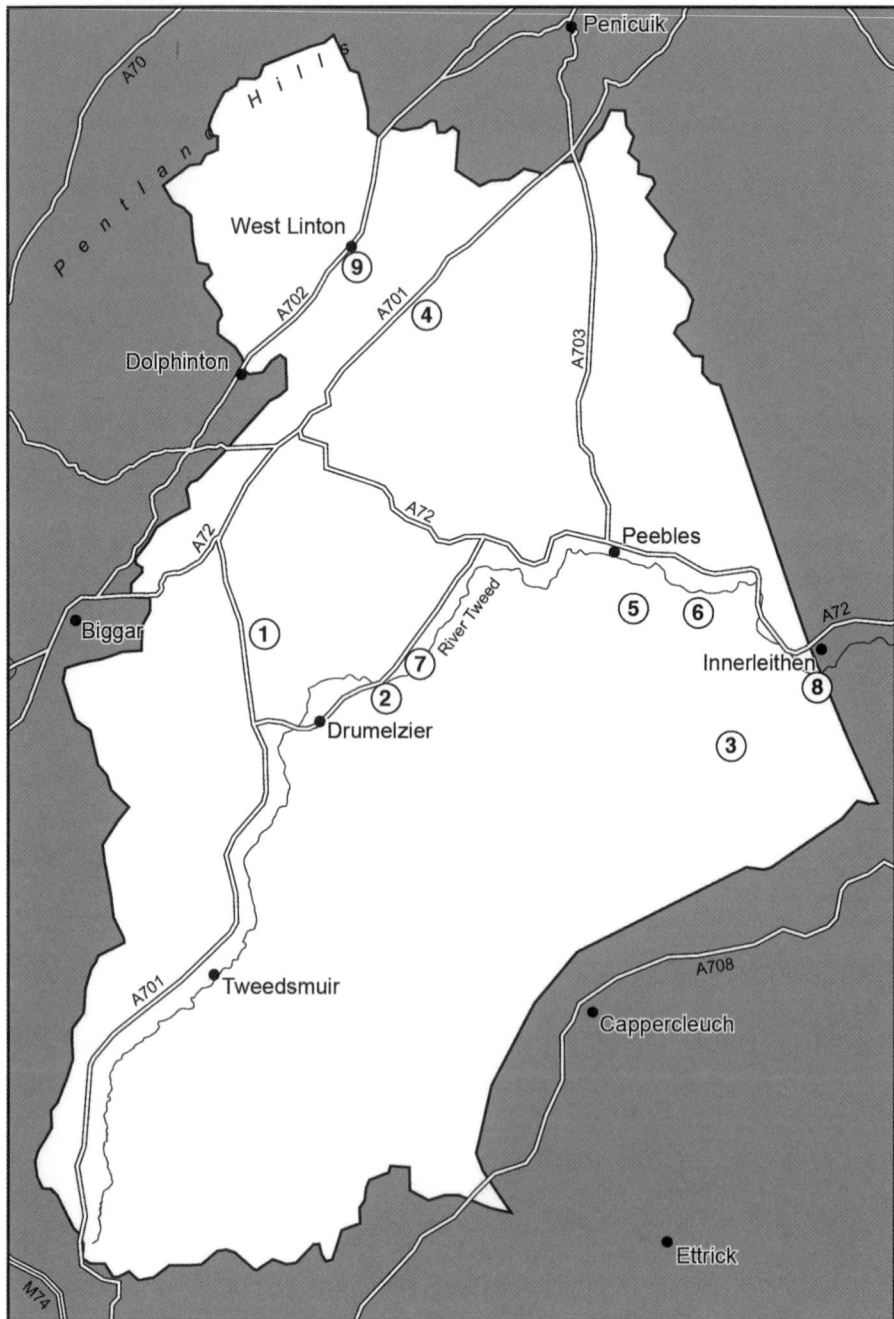

1 BROUGHTON PLACE FARMHOUSE
Broughton, Biggar ML12 6HJ
Mr and Mrs P Elliott

Walled kitchen garden with herbaceous borders and fruit trees. Shrubbery, rockery and peat garden; interesting and unusual plants with superb views to the Tweeddale hills and up Kilbucho Valley. The farm lies on the John Buchan Way with easy access to one of the finest heather valleys in the Borders. Ducks and hens to entertain young visitors.

Other Details: Cream teas in former cow byre. Some of the unusual plants may be for sale.

Directions: Off A701, turn up hill, as signed to Broughton Place.

Disabled Access: None

Opening Times:
Sunday 5 August 2:00pm - 5:30pm

Admission:
£4.00 Children under 15 Free

Charities: Tools for Self Reliance receives 40%, the net remaining to SG Beneficiaries.

2 DAWYCK BOTANIC GARDEN
Stobo EH45 9JU
Royal Botanic Gardens Edinburgh Tel: 01721 760 254
www.rbge.org.uk/dawyck

Stunning collection of rare trees and shrubs. With over 300 years of tree planting Dawyck is a world famous arboretum with mature specimens of Chinese conifers, Japanese maples, Brewer's spruce, the unique Dawyck beech and Sequoiadendrons from North America which are over 45 metres tall. Bold herbaceous plantings run along the burn. Range of trails and walks. Fabulous autumn colours.
Autumn Magic Guided Walks at 11.30am and 2:00pm - £3.50 (Please book with Dawyck Botanics).

Directions: 8 miles south west of Peebles on B712.

Disabled Access: Partial

Opening Times:
Sunday 7 October 10:00am - 5:00pm for Scotland's Gardens.
Feb. & Nov. 10:00am - 4:00pm
Mar. & Oct. 10:00pm - 5:00pm
Apr. - Sep. 10:00am - 6:00pm

Admission:
£5.50 Concessions £4.50
Family £11.00 Guided Walks £3.50

Charities: Donation to SG Beneficiaries

3 GLEN HOUSE
Glen House, Glen Estate, Innerleithen EH44 6PX
The Tennant Family Tel: 01896 830210
Email: info@glenhouse.com www.glenhouse.com

Surrounding the outstanding Scots Baronial mansion designed by David Bryce in the mid-19th century, Glen House gardens are laid out on a series of shallow terraces overhanging the glen itself, which offers one of the loveliest 'designed landscapes' in the Borders. The garden itself expands from the formal courtyard through a yew colonnade, and contains a fine range of trees, long herbaceous border, pool garden with pergola and newly established rose walk, all arranged within the curve of slopes sheltering the house.

Directions: Follow B709 out of Innerleithen for approx. 2.5 miles. Right turn at signpost for Glen Estate.

Disabled Access: None

Opening Times:
Sunday 1 July 1:30pm - 5:00pm

Admission:
£4.00 Children under 12 Free

Charities: Global Cool Foundation receives 40%, the net remaining to SG Beneficiaries.

4 HALMYRE MAINS
8 Halmyre Mains, West Linton EH46 7BX
Joyce Andrews and Mike Madden   Tel: 07774 609 547
Email: romanno@btinternet.com

Half-acre organic garden, formal beds, wildlife zone with large pond, vegetable plot, greenhouse, keder house and polytunnel, 25ft pergola to large composting area.

Directions: From North: Take A701 (Moffat) from Leadburn Junction for 5 miles. Turn left at Newlands Hall Sign.
From South: One mile north of Romanno Bridge on A701, 500 yds past junction to West Linton turn right at Newlands Hall sign.

Disabled Access: Full

Opening Times:
Sunday 29 July 2:00pm -
5:00pm

Admission:
£3.00

Charities: Newlands and Kirkurd Senior Citizens Lunch Fund receives 40%, the net remaining to SG Beneficiaries.

5 HAYSTOUN
Peebles EH45 9JG
Mrs David Coltman

A 16th century house (not open) has a charming walled garden with an ancient yew tree, herbaceous beds and vegetable garden. There is a wonderful burnside walk, created since 1980, with azaleas, rhododendrons and primulas leading to a small ornamental loch (cleared in 1990), with stunning views up Glensax valley.

Directions: Cross River Tweed in Peebles to south bank and follow garden open sign for approx 1 mile.

Disabled Access: Partial

Opening Times:
Sunday 27 May 1:30pm -
5:00pm

Admission:
£4.00

Charities: St Columba's Hospice receives 40%, the net remaining to SG Beneficiaries.

6 KAILZIE GARDENS
Peebles EH45 9HT
Lady Buchan-Hepburn   Tel: 01721 720007
Email: angela.buchanhepburn@btinternet.com   www.kailziegardens.com

Semi-formal walled garden with shrubs & herbaceous borders, rose garden, well stocked Victorian green-houses, a new chicken village, including rare poultry breeds. Woodland & burnside walks amongst spring bulbs, rhododendrons & azaleas. The garden is set among fine old trees including an old larch planted in 1724. Osprey watch with live C.C.T.V. recordings of Ospreys nesting in the recently extended nature centre. Kailzie has been featured on Landward & the Beechgrove Garden.

Other Details: Children (5 - 12) admission: 1 Jan - 1 Apr £1.00
Children (5 - 12) and Concession admissions: 2 Apr - 31 Oct £3.00. Under 5s free. Apply for group rates.

Directions: On B7062 2½ miles east of Peebles.

Disabled Access: Partial

Opening Times:
Sunday 4 March 2:00pm -
5:00pm for Scotland's Gardens
All Year 11:00am - 5:00pm or dusk. See website for details

Admission:
1 Jan - 1 Apr £2.50
2 Apr - 27 May £3.50
28 May - 31 Oct £4.00.
See "Other Details" for concession admissions.

Charities: Erskine Hospital receives 40%, the net remaining to SG Beneficiaries.

STOBO JAPANESE WATER GARDEN
Home Farm, Stobo EH45 8NX
Hugh & Charles Seymour   Tel: 01721 760245
Email: hugh.seymour@btinternet.com

Disabled Access: Partial

Garden was originally laid out 100 years ago and features magnificent trees and shrubs, Japanese artifacts, such as lanterns, a tea house and oriental style bridges. A spendid waterfall cascades from the lake at one end. The water divides into two burns which are crossed in several placed by stepping stones and bridges.

Opening Times:
Sunday 3 June 1:30pm - 5:00pm

Admission:
£4.50 Children Free

Other Details: This opening will coincide with a sale of second hand gardening books and a sculpture exhibition by local artists. (Find a baboon nestling in the bamboo....!) **Please wear sensible shoes.**

Charities: Eastgate Theatre, Peebles receives 40%, the net remaining to SG Beneficiaries.

Directions: 7 miles west of Peebles on the B712. 1½ miles from Dawyck Botanical Garden and keep following yellow arrows to car park.

TRAQUAIR
Traquair House, Innerleithen, Peeblesshire EH44 6PW
Traquair Charitable Trust   Tel: 01896 830323
Email: catherine@traquair.co.uk   www.traquair.co.uk

Disabled Access: Partial

The woodlands and grounds of Traquair House have a spectacular showing of snowdrops and will be open for the first time this year. Traquair is Scotland's oldest inhabited house and the grounds and gardens are an eighteenth century-designed landscape.

Opening Times:
Sat. 25 February 11:00am - 4:00pm for Scotland's Gardens
Sunday 26 February 11:00am - 4:00pm for Scotland's Gardens
6 Apr - 30 Sep 11:00am - 5:00pm
1 - 31 Oct. 11:00am - 4:00pm
1 - 30 November, weekends only 11:00am - 3:00pm

Other Details: The 1745 Cottage Restaurant will be open for light lunches and afternoon teas.

Admission:
£4.00, Concessions £3.00.

Directions: Traquair House is on the B708 1½ miles from Innerleithen and is well signposted.

Charities: Traquair Charitable Trust receives 40%, the net remaining to SG Beneficiaries.

WEST LINTON VILLAGE GARDENS
West Linton EH46 7EL
West Linton Village Gardeners

Disabled Access: Partial

Five gardens, one of which recently featured on the Beechgrove Garden. Of the five gardens, four are medium/large gardens of varying styles containing specimen mature trees, roses, collection of hostas, interesting features and herbaceous borders packed with traditional and more unusual varieties. In contrast the fifth is an eco-friendly garden growing fruit and vegetables using some novel techniques.

Opening Times:
Sunday 17 June 2:00pm - 5:00pm

Admission:
£4.00

Directions: A701 or A702 and follow signs.

Charities: Macmillan Nurses receives 40%, the net remaining to SG Beneficiaries.

PERTH & KINROSS

Scotland's Gardens 2012 Guidebook is sponsored by **INVESTEC WEALTH & INVESTMENT**

District Organisers

Mrs J Landale	Clathic House, By Crieff PH7 4JY
Mrs D Nichol	Rossie House, Forgandenny PH2 9EH

Area Organisers

Mrs C Arbuthnott	The Old Manse, Caputh PH1 4JQ
Mrs C Dunphie	Wester Cloquhat, Bridge of Cally, Perthshire PH10 7JP
Miss Henrietta Harland	Easter Carmichael Cottage, Forgandenny Road, Bridge of Earn PH2 9EZ
Mrs T Holcroft	Glenbeich, Lochearnhead FK19 8PZ
Mrs M Innes	Kilspindie Manse, Kilspindie PH2 7RX
Lady Lavinia Macdonald Lockhart	Thornton Hill, Fossoway, Kinross KY13 7PB
Miss Judy Norwell	Dura Den, 20 Pitcullen Terrace, Perth PH2 7EG
Miss Bumble Ogilvy Wedderburn	Garden Cottage, Lude, Blair Atholl PH18 5TR

Treasurer

Mr Cosmo Fairbairn	Alleybank, Bridge of Earn PH2 9EZ

Gardens open on a specific date

Megginch Castle, Errol	Sunday 15 April	2:00pm - 5:00pm
Branklyn, 116 Dundee Road, Perth	Sunday 6 May	10:00am - 4:00pm
Briglands House, Rumbling Bridge	Sunday 6 May	2:00pm - 5:00pm
Glendoick, by Perth	Sunday 6 May	2:00pm - 5:00pm
Fingask Castle, Rait	Sunday 13 May	2:00pm - 5:00pm
Glendoick, by Perth	Sunday 13 May	2:00pm - 5:00pm
Pitcurran House, Abernethy	Sunday 13 May	2:00pm - 6:00pm
Acres of Keillour, Methven	Saturday 26 May	10:00am - 5:00pm
Delvine, Spittalfield	Sunday 3 June	1:00pm - 5:00pm
Blair Castle Gardens, Blair Atholl	Saturday 16 June	9:30am - 5:30pm
Explorers Garden, Pitlochry	Saturday 16 June	10:00am - 5:00pm
Glenearn, Bridge of Earn	Sunday 17 June	2:00pm - 5:00pm
Bradystone House, Murthly	Sunday 1 July	2:00pm - 5:00pm
Wester Cloquhat , Bridge of Cally	Sunday 8 July	2:00pm - 5:00pm
Achnacloich, Balhomais, by Aberfeldy	Saturday 14 July	10:30am - 4:00pm
Croftcat Lodge, Grandtully	Saturday 14 July	10:30am - 4:00pm
Drummond Castle Gardens, Crieff	Sunday 5 August	1:00pm - 5:00pm

Gardens open regularly

Ardvorlich, Lochearnhead	22 April - 27 May	9:00am	-	Dusk
Blair Castle Gardens, Blair Atholl	21 January - 25 March	10:00am	-	4:00pm
	26 March - 26 October	9:30am	-	5:30pm
	3 November - 16 November	10:00am	-	4:00pm
Bolfracks, Aberfeldy	1 April - 31 October	10:00am	-	6:00pm
Braco Castle, Braco	1 February - 31 October	10:00am	-	5:00pm
Cloan, by Auchterarder	30 July - 5 August	1:30pm	-	5:00pm
Cluny House, Aberfeldy	1 January - 15 March and			
	1 November - 31 December	10:00am	-	4:00pm
	16 March - 31 October	10:00am	-	6:00pm
Dowhill, Cleish	1 May - 31 May Tues & Thurs	10:00am	-	4:00pm
Drummond Castle Gardens, Crieff	1 May - 31 October	1:00pm	-	6:00pm
Easter Meikle Fardle, Meikleour	16 April - End August			
	Mons & Fris	11:00am	-	5:30pm
Fingask Castle, Rait	4 February - 18 March	12:00pm	-	5:00pm
Glendoick, by Perth	1 April - 31 May Sats & Suns	2:00pm	-	5:00pm
	Mons- Fris	10:00am	-	4:00pm
Lands of Loyal Hotel, Loyal Road, Alyth, Blairgowrie	All Year	Dawn	-	Dusk

Gardens open by arrangement

When organising a visit to a garden open by arrangement, please enquire if there are facilities and catering available.

Briglands House, Rumbling Bridge	On request.	01877 840205
Croftcat Lodge, Grandtully	1 April - 31 October	01887 840288
Easter Meikle Fardle, Meikleour	On request.	01738 710330
Parkhead House, Burghmuir Road, Perth	1 May - 30 September	01738 625983

Key to symbols

🌳	New in 2012	☕	Homemade teas	B&B	Accommodation
☕	Teas	🐕	Dogs on a lead allowed	🌷	Plant stall
☕	Cream teas	♿	Wheelchair access	🌱	Scottish Snowdrop Festival

Garden locations

ACHNACLOICH (JOINT OPENING WITH CROFTCAT)
Balhomais, by Aberfeldy PH15 2JE
Mr and Mrs D Lee

Garden of one and a half acres set in a very scenic part of Perthshire consisting of an interesting and colourful mix of trees, shrubs and perennials.

Directions: From Weem, 1½ miles west on B846.

Disabled Access: None

Opening Times:
Saturday 14 July 10:30am - 4:00pm

Admission:
£4.00 - includes entrance to Croftcat

Charities: Dogs for the Blind receives 40%, the net remaining to SG Beneficiaries.

ACRES OF KEILLOUR
Methven PH1 3RA
Anthea & Stuart Pawley
Email: antheapawley258@btinternet.com

Garden made from neglected 1 acre during the last 18 years, with views over the Gask Ridge to the Ochils. Mature woodland area with pond. Varied collection of plants including primulas and meconopsis.

Other Details: Homemade teas from 2.30 to 5.00pm

Directions: Either 2 or 3 miles west of Methven on A85 turn north signposted Keillour. At T-junctions take road north signposted Buchanty. Acres of Keillour is first house on right after ¼ mile

Disabled Access: Partial

Opening Times:
Saturday 26 May 10:00am - 5:00pm

Admission:
£4.00

Charities: St. Ninian's Cathedral, Perth receives 40%, the net remaining to SG Beneficiaries.

ARDVORLICH
Lochearnhead FK19 8QE
Mr and Mrs Sandy Stewart

Beautiful hill garden featuring over 300 different species and hybrid rhododendrons, grown in a glorious setting of oaks and birches on either side of the Ardvorlich Burn. Quite steep in places. Boots advisable.

Directions: On South Loch Earn Road 3 miles from Lochearnhead, 5 miles from St Fillans.

Disabled Access: None

Opening Times:
22 April - 27 May 9:00am - Dusk

Admission:
£3.50

Charities: The Ghurka Welfare Trust receives 40%, the net remaining to SG Beneficiaries.

4 BLAIR CASTLE GARDENS

Blair Atholl PH18 5TL
Blair Charitable Trust   Tel: 01796 481207
Email: office@blair-castle.co.uk   www.blair-castle.co.uk

Blair Castle stands as the focal point in a designed landscape of some 2,500 acres within a large and traditional estate. Hercules Garden is a walled enclosure of about 9 acres recently restored to its original 18th Century form with landscaped ponds, a Chinese bridge, plantings, vegetables and an orchard of more than one hundred fruit trees. The glory of this garden in summer, the herbaceous borders which run along the 275m south facing wall. A delightful sculpture trail incorporates contemporary and 18th century sculpture as well as 8 new works, letter-carving on stone from the Memorial Arts Charity's Art and Memory Collection. Diana's Grove is a magnificent stand of tall trees including Grand Fir, Douglas Fir, Larch and Wellingtonia in just two acres.

In February, enjoy the seasonal delight of snowdrops in a walk around the grounds. A gentle meandering route passes through the Hercules Garden and weaves along to St Brides Kirk. The walk also includes access to two new paths (only open to the public at snowdrop time).

Other Details: . Free Access to the Castle's Tullibardine Restaurant.

Directions: Off A9, follow signs to Blair Castle, Blair Atholl.

Disabled Access: None

Opening Times:
Saturday 16 June 9:30am - 5:30pm
21 January - 25 March 10:00am - 4:00pm for Snowdrop Festival
26 March - 26 October 9:30am - 5:30pm
3 November - 16 November 10:00am - 4:00pm

Admission:
Adults/Seniors/Students £5.25
Children £2.40

Charities: Donation to SG Beneficiaries

5 BOLFRACKS

Aberfeldy PH15 2EX
The Douglas Hutchison Trust   Tel: 01887 820344
Email: athel@bolfracks.com   www.bolfracks.com

Special 3 acre garden with wonderful views overlooking the Tay Valley. Burn garden with rhododendrons, azaleas, primulas, meconopsis in woodland garden setting. Walled garden with shrubs, herbaceous borders, rose rooms with old fashioned roses. Rose and clematis walk. Paeony beds underplanted with tulips and Japanese anemone. Great selection of bulbs in Spring and good Autumn colour. Slippery paths in wet weather.

Other Details: Refreshments for groups by prior arrangement.

Directions: 2 miles west of Aberfeldy on A827. White gates and Lodge on left. Brown tourist signs.

Disabled Access: None

Opening Times:
1 April - 31 October 10:00am - 6:00pm

Admission:
£4.50 Children under 16 Free

Charities: Donation to SG Beneficiaries

BRACO CASTLE
Braco FK15 9LA
Mr & Mrs M van Ballegooijen Tel: 01786 880437

&

A 19th century landscaped garden comprising woodland and meadow walks with a fine show of spring flowering bulbs, many mature specimen trees and shrubs, with considerable new planting. The partly walled garden is approached on a rhododendron and tree-lined path and features an ornamental pond, extensive hedging and lawns with shrub and herbaceous borders. The planting is enhanced by spectacular views over the castle park to the Ochils. Good autumn colour.

Other Details: Catering facilities are not available.

Directions: 1 to 1½ mile drive from gates at north end of Braco Village, just west of bridge on A822.

Disabled Access: Partial

Opening Times:
1 February - 31 October
10:00am - 5:00pm

Admission:
£3.50

Charities: The Woodland Trust receives 40%, the net remaining to SG Beneficiaries.

BRADYSTONE HOUSE
Murthly PH1 4EW
Mr and Mrs James Lumsden

& ☕ ❧

True cottage courtyard garden converted 16 years ago from derelict farm steadings. Ponds, free roaming ducks and hens and many interesting shrubs and ornamental trees.

Other Details: Other stalls.

Directions: From south/north follow A9 to Bankfoot, then sign to Murthly. At crossroads in Murthly take private road to Bradystone.

Disabled Access: Full

Opening Times:
Sunday 1 July 2:00pm - 5:00pm

Admission:
£4.50 Children Free

Charities: The Caputh and Clunie Churches and the Village Hall receives 40%, the net remaining to SG Beneficiaries.

BRANKLYN
116 Dundee Road, Perth PH2 7BB
The National Trust for Scotland   Tel: 0844 493 2193
Email: smcnamara@nts.org.uk   www.nts.org.uk

& ☕

This attractive garden in Perth was once described as "the finest two acres of private garden in the country". It contains an outstanding collection of plants particularly rhododendrons, alpine, herbaceous and peat-loving plants, which attract gardeners and botanists from all over the world

Other Details: Four NCCPG collections: Cassiope, Lilium, Meconopsis (Himalayan poppy) and Rhododendron. Homemade scones served on patio - weather permitting.

Directions: On A85 Perth/Dundee road.

Disabled Access: Partial

Opening Times:
Sunday 6 May 10:00am - 4:00pm

Admission:
£5.00, Concessions £4.00, Family Ticket £14.00 (N.B. Correct prices on going to print).

Charities: Donation to SG Beneficiaries

BRIGLANDS HOUSE
Rumbling Bridge KY13 0PS
Mrs Briony Multon Tel: 01877 840205
Email: briony@briglands.com

Rhododendron and other spring shrubs, bulbs and walled garden, rock garden, woodland garden.

Other Details: Specialist alpine plant sale.

Directions: Half way between Crook of Devon and Powmill. Signposted off A977.

Disabled Access: Partial

Opening Times:
Sunday 6 May 2:00pm - 5:00pm
Also by arrangement on request

Admission:
£4.00, Children Free

Charities: Fossoway School Millunium Walk Fund receives 40%, the net remaining to SG Beneficiaries.

CLOAN
by Auchterarder PH3 1PP
Mr and Mrs Richard Haldane Tel: 01764 662299

Garden and policies extending to roughly seven acres, dating from the 1850s. Castle with magnificent views of the Grampian mountains, ancient trees, walled garden with herbaceous and flowering shrub borders, wild garden laid out as an arboretum, water garden and delightful woodland walks.

Directions: South out of Auchterarder (Abbey Road) then follow yellow signs.

Disabled Access: Partial

Opening Times:
30 July - 5 August 1:30pm - 5:00pm

Admission:
£3.00 Children Free

Charities: St. Margaret's Cottage Hospital, Auchterarder receives 40%, the net remaining to SG Beneficiaries.

CLUNY HOUSE
Aberfeldy PH15 2JT
Mr J and Mrs W Mattingley Tel: 01887 820795
Email: wmattingley@btinternet.com www.clunyhousegardens.com

A wonderful, wild woodland garden overlooking the scenic Strathtay valley. Experience the grandeur of one of Britain's widest trees, the complex leaf variation of the Japanese maple, the beauty of the American trillium or the diversity of Asiatic primulas. A good display of snowdrops. Cluny's red squirrels are usually very easily seen. A treasure not to be missed.

Other Details: Admission for other dates is free, but donations for squirrel food welcome. Seeds available for sale.

Directions: 3½ miles from Aberfeldy on Weem to Strathtay Road

Disabled Access: Partial

Opening Times:
1 January - 15 March and 1 November - 31 December 10:00am - 4:00pm
16 March - 31 October 10:00am - 6:00pm

Admission:
Snowdrop Festival: £4.00 Children £1.00
16 March - 31 October £5.00 Children £1.00

Charities: Donation to SG Beneficiaries

CROFTCAT LODGE
Grandtully PH15 2QS
Margaret and Iain Gimblett   Tel: 01887 840288
Email: gimblettsmill@aol.com

   ⎈ ⛽ 🐴

An odd shaped 1 acre with a small walled garden with mirror pond. An Autumn/ Spring garden, small alpine terraces, rose terrace, heathers, azaleas, clipped beehive laurels, a growing clematis collection and a Japanese garden being made this winter. Wonderful views and a garden for all seasons. The garden has mainly gravel and grass paths.

Other Details: Opening in conjunction with Achnacloich on 14 July. Teas available on 14 July only.

Directions: From A9 take A827 signed Aberfeldy. Through Grandtully village and 1 mile from traffic lights on bridge turn left by cream house set back from road. Croftcat is on left 300 yards up lane.

Disabled Access: Partial

Opening Times:
Saturday 14 July 10:30am - 4:00pm
Also by arrangement 1 April - 31 October 10:00am - 5:00pm

Admission:
£4.00 - includes entrance to Achnacloich on 14 July

Charities: Mary's Meals receives 40%, the net remaining to SG Beneficiaries.

DELVINE
Spittalfield PH1 4LD
Mr and Mrs David Gemmell

   ⎈ ⛽ 🐴

The gardens at Delvine are situated on Inchtuthill (the island that floods), an old Roman Legionary fortress abandoned 85 AD in a wild and secluded setting. A new arboretum and water project is taking shape below the existing gardens with wonderful views. The area is surrounded by particularly fine and very old trees.

Directions: On A984, 7 miles east of Dunkeld, 4 miles south west of Blairgowrie.

Disabled Access: Partial

Opening Times:
Sunday 3 June 1:00pm - 5:00pm

Admission:
£5.00 Children £0.50

Charities: Army Benevolent Fund receives 40%, the net remaining to SG Beneficiaries.

DOWHILL
Cleish KY4 0HZ
Mr and Mrs Colin Maitland Dougall

   🐴

A garden set off by the background of Benarty Hill and magnificent old trees. Lovely woodland walks to the ruins of Dowhill Castle. Nine linked ponds. Blue poppies and primulas together with temptingly placed seats make the garden a wonderful place for a picnic in fine weather.

Directions: ¾ mile off M90, exit 5, towards Crook of Devon on the B9097, in the trees.

Disabled Access: None

Opening Times:
1 May - 31 May Every Tuesday and Thursday 10:00am - 4:00pm

Admission:
£4.00

Charities: Motor Neurone Disease receives 40%, the net remaining to SG Beneficiaries.

15 DRUMMOND CASTLE GARDENS
Crieff PH7 4HZ
Grimsthorpe & Drummond Castle Trust Ltd
www.drummondcastlegardens.co.uk

The Gardens of Drummond Castle were originally laid out in 1630 by John Drummond, second Earl of Perth. In 1830 the Parterre was changed to an Italian style. One of the most interesting features is the multi-faceted sundial designed by John Mylne, Master Mason to Charles I. The formal garden is said to be one of the finest in Europe and is the largest of its type in Scotland.

Other Details: Raffle, stalls, entertainments and pipe band on 5 August.

Directions: Entrance 2 miles south of Crieff on Muthill road (A822).

Disabled Access: Partial

Opening Times:
Sunday 5 August 1:00pm - 5:00pm for Scotland's Gardens
1 May - 31 October 1:00pm - 6:00pm

Admission:
£4.00 OAPs £3.00 Children £2.00

Charities: British Limbless Ex-Servicemen's Association receives 40% on 5 August opening, the net remaining to SG Beneficiaries.

16 EASTER MEIKLE FARDLE
Meikleour PH2 6EF
Rear Admiral and Mrs John Mackenzie Tel: 01738 710330

A delightful old-fashioned 2 acre garden. Herbaceous borders backed by soft sandstone walls or beech hedges. Small enclosed garden with raised beds. There is also a maturing water garden and walks through maturing woodland.

Other Details: Homemade lunches and light refreshments available on request.

Directions: Take A984 Dunkeld to Coupar Angus 1½ miles, from Spittalfield towards Meikleour, third house on left after turning to Lethendy.

Disabled Access: Partial

Opening Times:
16 April - End of August, Mondays and Fridays 11:00am - 5:30pm
Also by arrangement: large groups welcome

Admission:
£4.00

Charities: Arthritis Research UK receives 40%, the net remaining to SG Beneficiaries.

17 EXPLORERS GARDEN
Pitlochry PH16 5DR
Pitlochry Festival Theatre
www.explorersgarden.com

This six acre woodland garden, now seven years old, is maturing nicely. More and more visitors are coming to see the wonders this four star VisitScotland attraction reveals - art and architecture, wildlife and birds, exotic plants, peat and rock gardens, extraordinary landscaping and magnificent views. Try the guided tours that reveal the stories of the Scottish Plant Hunters who risked their lives travelling the globe in search of new plants and trees. In this garden, which is divided into different parts of the world, you will see the plants they collected for cultivation, commerce and conservation.

Directions: A9 to Pitlochry town, follow signs to Pitlochry Festival Theatre.

Disabled Access: Partial

Opening Times:
Saturday 16 June 10:00am - 5:00pm

Admission:
£4.00 Guided Tour £5.00 (includes entry)

Charities: Acting for Others receives 40%, the net remaining to SG Beneficiaries.

8 FINGASK CASTLE

Rait PH2 7SA
Mr and Mrs Andrew Murray Threipland Tel: 01821 670777
Email: andrew@fingaskcastle.com www.fingaskcastle.com

The magical grounds of Fingask Castle are testament to both the present owner and his ancestors' eccentricity and architectural scavenging. Explore the grounds and discover statues, gargoyles, gravestones, bamboo forest, large collection of topiary and much, much more.

Other Details: Homemade teas on 13 May only.

Directions: Halfway between Perth and Dundee. From A90 follow signs to Rait until small crossroad, turn right and follow signs to Fingask.

Disabled Access: Full

Opening Times:
Sunday 13 May 2:00pm - 5:00pm
4 February - 18 March 12:00pm - 5:00pm

Admission:
February/March: £3.00 Children Free
13 May: £4.00 Children Free

Charities: All Saints Church, Glencarse and Fingask Follies receive 40%, the net remaining to SG Beneficiaries.

9 GLENDOICK

by Perth PH2 7NS
Peter, Patricia, Kenneth and Jane Cox Tel: 01738 860 205
Email: orders@glendoick.com www.glendoick.com

Glendoick was included in the Independent on Sunday's survey of Europe's Top 50 gardens, and boasts a unique collection of plants collected by three generations of the Cox family from their plant-hunting expeditions in China and the Himalayas. One of the world's finest collections of Rhododendron, Meconopsis, Kalmia and many other plants are displayed in the woodland walled and house gardens. Many of the rhododendron azalea species and hybrids have been introduced from the wild or bred by the Cox family and the gardens boast a huge range of plants from as far afield as Chile, Tasmania and Tibet. Three new waterfall viewing platforms have been built in the woodland gardens. You can also take a glimpse into the fascinating world of hybridising in the walled garden where you'll find new and as yet unnamed hybrids from the Glendoick breeding programme trial beds.

Peter and Kenneth Cox have written numerous rhododendron and plant hunting books. Kenneth Cox's book "Scotland for Gardeners" describes 500 of Scotland's finest gardens.

Though the gardens are open all of April and May, Scotland's Gardens open Sundays in May are the only time that the nursery areas at Glendoick are open to visitors and you will find members of the Cox family available in the gardens to answer questions. Glendoick Garden Centre, UK Garden Centre of the Year 2009-10 has a fine new shop which opened in 2011. It boasts a huge range of Glendoick plants as well as an award winning cafe and food hall. Open 7 days. Free display garden.

Other Details: NCCPG National Plant Collection: Rhododendron x 4. Tickets at garden centre except Scotland's Gardens open days when they will be at garden entrance. Teas at Garden Centre Cafe.

Directions: Follow brown signs to Glendoick Garden Centre off A90 Perth - Dundee road. Gardens are ½ mile behind Garden Centre. Please drive up and park at gardens (free parking).

Disabled Access: Full

Opening Times:
Sunday 6 May 2:00pm - 5:00pm for Scotland's Gardens
Sunday 13 May 2:00pm - 5:00pm for Scotland's Gardens
1 April - 31 May (Monday - Friday) 10:00am - 4:00pm
1 April - 31 May (Saturdays & Sundays) 2:00pm - 5:00pm

Admission:
£4.00 (£5.00 inc. guidebook)
School Children Free.

Charities: Donation to SG Beneficiaries

20 GLENEARN
Bridge of Earn PH2 9HL
Mr and Mrs Hans-Jurgen Queisser

This beautifully maintained garden sits at the foot of the Ochil Hills and has wonderful views of the Tay Estuary and the Ochils to the south. Lovely walks around the loch and up to the south facing sloped walled garden with sweet peas, roses, fruit trees and herbaceous borders.

Other Details: Tea is served in the impressive restored fortified 17th century Tower House, Ecclesiamagirdle, which nestles beside the Loch.

Directions: Exit 9 from M90 into Bridge of Earn. Take B935 (Forgandenny Road) for 1 mile, left to Pitkeathly Wells then ¾ mile to Glenearn gates on right.

Disabled Access: None

Opening Times:
Sunday 17 June 2:00pm - 5:00pm

Admission:
£4.00

Charities: Rachael House, Kinross receives 40%, the net remaining to SG Beneficiaries.

21 LANDS OF LOYAL HOTEL
Loyal Road, Alyth, Blairgowrie PH11 8JQ
Verity Webster Tel: 01828 633151
Email: info@landsofloyal.com www.landsofloyal.com

The main garden faces south overlooking the Vale of Strathmore and the town of Alyth with its three golf courses. Wide herbaceous borders provide lots of colour and interest all year round. In summer the walls are draped with spectacular roses.

Other Details: Plants for sale all year round from the polytunnel and kitchen garden. Food served all day. Fully licensed facilities.

Directions: From Alyth Market Square, follow official VisitScotland signage.

Disabled Access: Partial

Opening Times:
Open All Year Dawn - Dusk

Admission:
By Donation.

Charities: Help for Heroes receives 40%, the net remaining to SG Beneficiaries.

22 MEGGINCH CASTLE
Errol PH2 7SW
Mr Giles Herdman & The Hon. Mrs Drummond-Herdman of Megginch

15th century turreted castle (not open) with Gothic stable yard and pagoda dovecote. 19th century formal front garden, topiary and ancient yews. Splendid array of daffodils and rhododendrons. Double walled kitchen garden and orchard.

Directions: Approach from Dundee only, directly off A90, on south side of carriageway ½ mile on left after Errol flyover, between lodge gatehouses. 7 miles from Perth, 8 miles from Dundee.

Disabled Access: Full

Opening Times:
Sunday 15 April 2:00pm - 5:00pm

Admission:
£4.00 Children Free

Charities: All Saints Church, Glencarse receives 40%, the net remaining to SG Beneficiaries.

PARKHEAD HOUSE

Parkhead Gardens, Burghmuir Road, Perth PH1 1JF
Mr & Mrs M.S. Tinson   Tel: 01738 625983
Email: maddy.tinson@gmail.com

Parkhead is an old farmhouse sited within an acre of beautiful gardens. Mature trees include an outstanding 300 year old Spanish Chestnut. This hidden gem is a garden for all seasons. Gentle terracing and meandering paths lead you past a large variety of unusual and interesting plants and shrubs, including a collection of the increasingly scarce Minefield Lilies, originally developed by Dr Christopher North at the Scottish Horticultural Research Institute, Dundee.

Other Details: Application pending for NCCPG Minefield Lilies. Plant stall open when plants available. Homemade teas by prior arrangement.

Directions: Parkhead Gardens is a small lane off the west end of Burghmuir Road in Perth. More detailed directions on request.

Disabled Access: Partial

Opening Times:
By arrangement 1 May - 30 September

Admission:
£3.50

Charities: All proceeds to SG Beneficiaries

PITCURRAN HOUSE

Abernethy PH2 9LH
The Hon Ranald & Mrs Noel-Paton

Seven year old garden with many interesting and unusual plants. Behind the house semi-hardy euphorbia mellifera, melianthus major and sophora davidii grow happily amongst cistus and hebes. The garden also includes many ericaceous shrubs, meconopsis, paeonies, primulas and smilacina racemosa. A rose pergola is covered in Blush Noisette, Felicite Perpetue and Paul's Himalayan Musk. A large west facing hydrangea border brightens up the late summer.

Other Details: Good plant stall.

Directions: SE of Perth. From M90 (exit 9) take A912 towards Glenfarg, left at roundabout onto A913 to Abernethy. Pitcurran House is at far eastern end of village.

Disabled Access: Partial

Opening Times:
Sunday 13 May 2:00pm - 6:00pm

Admission:
£4.00   Children Free

Charities: Juvenile Diabetes Research Foundation (JDRF) receives 40%, the net remaining to SG Beneficiaries.

WESTER CLOQUHAT

Bridge of Cally PH10 7JP
Brigadier and Mrs Christopher Dunphie

Terraced garden enlarged in 2001 to include a water garden. Lawns, mixed borders with a wide range of shrubs, roses and herbaceous plants. Splendid situation with fine view down to the River Ericht.

Directions: Turn off A93 just north of Bridge of Cally and follow signs for ½ mile.

Disabled Access: None

Opening Times:
Sunday 8 July 2:00pm - 5:00pm

Admission:
£5.00

Charities: ABF - The Soldiers' Charity receives 40%, the net remaining to SG Beneficiaries.

RENFREWSHIRE

Scotland's Gardens 2012 Guidebook is sponsored by **INVESTEC WEALTH & INVESTMENT**

District Organisers

Mrs Rosemary Leslie	High Mathernock Farm, Auchentiber Road, Kilmacolm PA13 4SP Tel: 01505 874032
Mrs Alexandra MacMillan	Langside Farm, Kilmacolm PA13 4SA Tel: 01475 540423

Area Organisers

Mrs Helen Hunter	2 Bay Street, Fairlie, KA29 0AL
Mrs B McLean	49 Middlepenny Road, Langbank PA14 6XE
Mr J A Wardrop OBE DL	St Kevins, Victoria Road, Paisley PA2 9PT

Treasurer

Mrs Jean Gillan	Bogriggs Cottage, Carlung, West Kilbride KA23 9PS

Gardens open on a specific date

Ardgowan, Inverkip	Sunday 19 February	2:00pm	-	5:00pm
Carruth, Bridge of Weir	Sunday 20 May	2:00pm	-	5:00pm
Hill Cottage, Spey Road, Inverkip	Sunday 20 May	2:00pm	-	5:00pm
Sma' Shot Cottages Heritage Centre, Paisley	Sunday 24 June	12:00pm	-	4:00pm
Hill Cottage, Spey Road, Inverkip	Sunday 22 July	2:00pm	-	5:00pm
Barshaw Park Walled Garden, Paisley	Sunday 19 August	2:00pm	-	5:00pm
Knowes End, Auchans Road, Houston	Sunday 26 August	1:00pm	-	4:00pm
Quarriers Village Gardens	Sunday 2 September	2:00pm	-	5:00pm

Gardens open by arrangement

When organising a visit to a garden open by arrangement, please enquire if there are facilities and catering available

31 Kings Road, Elderslie, Johnstone	On request.	01505 320480

Plant Sale

SG Plant Sale at St Fillan's Episcopal Church, Kilmalcolm	Saturday 15 September	10:00am - 1:00pm

Key to symbols

New in 2012	Homemade teas	Accommodation
Teas	Dogs on a lead allowed	Plant stall
Cream teas	Wheelchair access	Scottish Snowdrop Festival

Garden locations

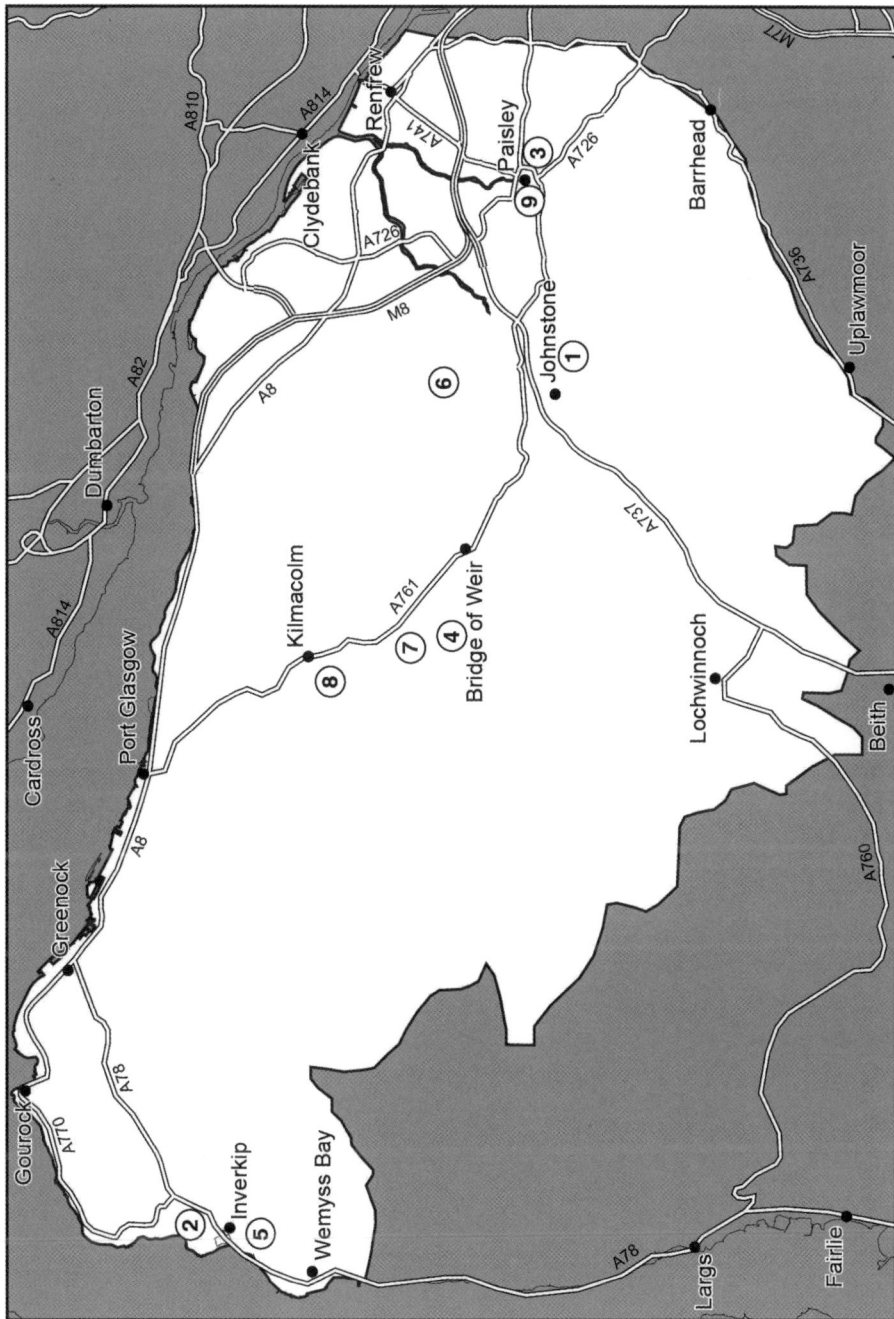

1 **31 KINGS ROAD**
Elderslie, Johnstone PA5 9LY
John and Muriel Gibb   Tel: 01505 320480

Delightful small suburban garden. Variety of trees, shrubs and herbaceous plants. At its most colourful in April/May with camellia, small rhododendrons and daffodils and June/July with foxgloves, clematis and magnolia. Worth a visit.

Directions: Kings Road is just beyond junction of Beith Road and Main Road on eastern edge of Johnstone. Turn off Main Road onto Kings Road just past traffic lights, heading to Elderslie.

Disabled Access: Full

Opening Times:
By arrangement on request

Admission:
£3.50 Children Free

Charities: Children 1st receives 40%, the net remaining to SG Beneficiaries.

2 **ARDGOWAN**
Inverkip PA16 0DW
Lady Shaw Stewart   Tel: 01475 521656/226
Email: info@ardgowan.co.uk

Woodland walks carpeted with snowdrops. Strong waterproof footwear advised as some paths may be wet/muddy depending on the weather.

Other Details: Snowdrop plant stall. Wheelchair access not advisable in wet weather.

Directions: Inverkip 1½ miles. Glasgow/Largs buses to and from Inverkip Village. Entrance at roundabout or via Marina.

Disabled Access: Partial

Opening Times:
Sunday 19 February 2:00pm - 5:00pm for Snowdrop Festival

Admission:
£2.00

Charities: Ardgowan Hospice receives 40%, the net remaining to SG Beneficiaries.

3 **BARSHAW PARK WALLED GARDEN**
Paisley PA1 1UG
Environmental Services Department, Renfrewshire Council

Walled garden displaying a varied selection of plants, some of which are suitable for the blind to smell and feel. These include a colourful layout of summer bedding plants, herbaceous borders, mixed shrub borders and rose beds.

Directions: From Paisley town centre along the Glasgow road (A737) pass Barshaw Park and take first left into Oldhall Road and then first left again into walled garden car park. Pedestrian visitors can also approach from Barshaw Park by mid gate in Glasgow Road.

Disabled Access: Full

Opening Times:
Sunday 19 August 2:00pm - 5:00pm

Admission:
By donation

Charities: Erskine Hospital receives 40%, the net remaining to SG Beneficiaries.

❹ CARRUTH
Bridge of Weir PA11 3SG
Mr and Mrs Charles Maclean

Over 20 acres of long established rhododendrons, woodland with good bluebells and lawn gardens in lovely landscaped setting. Young arboretum.

Other Details: Large plant stall with a wide selection of interesting locally grown plants.

Directions: Access from B786 Kilmacolm/Lochwinnoch road or from Bridge of Weir via Torr Road.

Disabled Access: Partial

Opening Times:
Sunday 20 May 2:00pm - 5:00pm

Admission:
£3.50

Charities: Marie Curie Cancer Care receives 40%, the net remaining to SG Beneficiaries.

❺ HILL COTTAGE
Spey Road, Inverkip PA16 0DA
Steve and Rona Saurin

Originally part of Ardgowan Estate the grounds have been developed over the past 30 years. The garden of almost 1 acre has woodland and open countryside on two sides and is screened by mature trees. There are three distinct areas. Cottage style planting provides colour throughout the summer. Formal front gardens are bordered by mature trees with mostly spring flowering shrubs & a large pond. There is a wide selection of herbaceous plants, specimen trees & shrubs attracting birds & wild life. Public footpath to adjacent woodland.

Other Details: Plant sale 20 May only. Teas 22 July only.

Directions: Take slip road (signed Hill Farm) approximately third of a mile past Inverkip Marina on A78 Greenock/Largs road. Left into Spey Road, go to top of hill and continue. Garden is on right 100 yards past Kinloss Place.

Disabled Access: None

Opening Times:
Sunday 20 May 2:00pm - 5:00pm
Sunday 22 July 2:00pm - 5:00pm

Admission:
£3.00

Charities: Teenage Cancer Trust Scotland receives 40%, the net remaining to SG Beneficiaries.

❻ KNOWES END
Auchans Road, Houston PA6 7EF
Liz and Phil Cotton   Tel: 01505 320667

The garden has been created from a barn conversion building works. The challenge has been to recycle and re-use as much as possible. Thus there are stone walls, slate, cobble, brick and gravel paths and rockeries built on slopes of debris. It is a garden with wildlife in mind with a pond, wildflower meadow, trees and hedges. We have created a meditative walk including a labyrinth and each year the vegetable/fruit garden is becoming more productive.

Other Details: Children's Treasure Hunt. Fairtrade stall and teas.

Directions: From Glasgow: M8 take J29, 4th exit at roundabout signed Erskine, Bishopton, Inchinnan (A726). Continue until B790 turn left (Bridge of Weir). Take Moss Rd on left with road closed sign until road block, turn right onto Auchans Rd. The Knowes is first house on left. **From Linwood:** take Craig Rd, turn right onto Auchans Rd (by river). Pass Auchans Farm on left, the Knowes is on right after ¼ mile.

Disabled Access: Partial

Opening Times:
Sunday 26 August 1:00pm - 4:00pm

Admission:
£3.00

Charities: Rainbow Turtle receives 20%, Habitat for Humanity receives 20%, the net remaining to SG Beneficiaries.

7 QUARRIERS VILLAGE GARDENS
PA11 3SQ
The Gardeners of Quarriers Village
www.petersrailway.com

Three adjacent gardens all different in character:
11 Craigends Avenue: Raised borders of herbaceous plants and vegetable plot.
13 Craigends Avenue: Well stocked informal family garden with vegetable plot and miniature steam railway.
17 Craigends Avenue: Three "rooms" with borders and vegetable plot. Water feature and hanging baskets.

Other Details: Train rides at 13 Craigends Avenue, by donation. Teas available by donation.

Directions: Access to Quarriers Village either from Bridge of Weir via Torr Road or from A761 Bridge of Weir - Kilmacolm Road. Craigends Avenue is off Torr Road and will be signposted on the day.

Disabled Access: Full

Opening Times:
Sunday 2 September 2:00pm - 5:00pm

Admission:
£4.00 Children Free

Charities: Macmillan Cancer Support receives 20%, Quarriers receives 20%, the net remaining to SG Beneficiaries.

8 SG PLANT SALE AT ST FILLAN'S EPISCOPAL CHURCH
Moss Road, Kilmacolm PA13 4LX
SG Renfrewshire & St Fillan's Episcopal Church

A wide variety of interesting and good locally grown plants and shrubs.

Other Details: Small charge for teas.

Directions: Turn off A761 Port Glasgow-Bridge of Weir Road in centre of Kilmacolm into Moss Road.

Disabled Access: Full

Opening Times:
Saturday 15 September 10:00am - 1:00pm

Admission:
Free but donations welcome

Charities: St Fillan's Episcopal Church receives 40%, the net remaining to SG Beneficiaries.

9 SMA' SHOT COTTAGES HERITAGE CENTRE
11/17 George Place, Paisley PA1 2HZ
Old Paisley Society
www.smashot.co.uk

Small enclosed courtyard garden. Enjoy the 19th century weaver's garden designed to celebrate the 21st anniversary of Sma' Shot Cottages. All plants are true to the period. Assistance in the creation of the garden was provided by the "Beechgrove Garden". Visitors may also see the rare "Paisley Gem" (Dianthus) and the new "Viola Sma' Shot Cottages" bred by local gardener, Hugh Boyd.

Other Details: Light refreshments.

Directions: Off New Street in Paisley Town Centre.

Disabled Access: Full

Opening Times:
Sunday 24 June 12:00pm - 4:00pm

Admission:
£2.00

Charities: Old Paisley Society receives 40%, the net remaining to SG Beneficiaries.

ROSS, CROMARTY, SKYE & INVERNESS

Scotland's Gardens 2012 Guidebook is sponsored by **INVESTEC WEALTH & INVESTMENT**

District Organiser

Lady Lister-Kaye   House of Aigas, Beauly IV4 7AD

Treasurer

Mrs Sheila Kerr   Lilac Cottage, Struy, By Beauly IV4 7JU

Gardens open on a specific date

Dundonnell House, Dundonnell, Little Loch Broom	Thursday 12 April	2:00pm - 5:00pm
House of Gruinard, Laide	Wednesday 23 May	2:00pm - 5:00pm
Inverewe, Poolewe, Achnasheen, Ross-shire	Wednesday 23 May	10:00am - 5:00pm
Sailean Cottage, 83 Aird Bernisdale, Skeabost Bridge	Saturday 26 May	10:30am - 4:00pm
Sailean Cottage, 83 Aird Bernisdale, Skeabost Bridge	Sunday 27 May	10:30am - 4:00pm
Dundonnell House, Dundonnell, Little Loch Broom	Thursday 31 May	2:00pm - 5:00pm
Inverewe, Poolewe, Achnasheen	Wednesday 6 June	10:00am - 5:00pm
Field House, Belladrum, Beauly	Sunday 10 June	2:00pm - 5:00pm
Novar, Evanton	Sunday 10 June	2:30pm - 5:00pm
House of Aigas and Field Centre, by Beauly	Sunday 24 June	2:00pm - 5:00pm
House of Gruinard, Laide	Wednesday 4 July	2:00pm - 5:00pm
House of Aigas and Field Centre, by Beauly	Sunday 22 July	2:00pm - 5:00pm
Hugh Miller's Museum & Birthplace Cottage, Cromarty	Tuesday 24 July	1:00pm - 5:00pm
Woodview, Highfield, Muir of Ord	Sunday 5 August	2:00pm - 5:00pm
Cardon, Balnafoich, Farr	Sunday 12 August	1:00pm - 5:00pm
Dundonnell House, Dundonnell, Little Loch Broom	Thursday 16 August	2:00pm - 5:00pm
Dundonnell House, Dundonnell, Little Loch Broom	Thursday 20 September	2:00pm - 5:00pm

Gardens open regularly

Abriachan Garden Nursery, Loch Ness Side	1 February - 30 November	9:00am - 7:00pm
Applecross Walled Garden, Strathcarron	15 March - 31 October	11:00am - 8:30pm
Attadale, Strathcarron	1 April - 13 October	10:00am - 5:30pm
Balmeanach House, Struan, Isle of Skye	2 May - 31 October Wednesdays & Saturdays	10:30am - 3:30pm
Clan Donald Skye, Armadale, Isle of Skye	1 January - 31 March	Dawn - Dusk
	1 April - 31 October	9:30am - 5:30pm
	1 November - 31 December	Dawn - Dusk
Dunvegan Castle and Gardens, Isle of Skye	1 April - 15 October	10:00am - 5:30pm

Leathad Ard, Upper Carloway, Isle of Lewis	1 June - 30 August ex Fris & Suns also not open Wed 1 August	1:45pm - 6:00pm
Leckmelm Shrubbery & Arboretum, By Ullapool	1 April - 31 October	10:00am - 6:00pm
The Lookout, Kilmuir	April - September Sundays & Tuesdays	11:00am - 4:00pm

Gardens open by arrangement

When organising a visit to a garden open by arrangement, please enquire if there are facilities and catering available.

Brackla Wood, Culbokie, Dingwall	1 - 29 July	01349 877765
Coiltie Garden, Divach, Drumnadrochit	June, July & second two weeks of October	01456 450219
Dundonnell House, Dundonnell, Little Loch Broom	On request	07789 390028
Dunvegan Castle and Gardens, Isle of Skye	16 October - 31 March weekdays only	01470 521206
House of Aigas and Field Centre, by Beauly	April - October	01463 782443
Novar, Evanton	On request Groups: minimum of 8 people	01349 831062
Sailean Cottage, 83 Aird Bernisdale, Skeabost Bridge	On request	01470 532353
The Lookout, Kilmuir	April - October	01463 731489

Key to symbols

🌳	New in 2012	☕	Homemade teas	B&B	Accommodation
☕	Teas	🐕	Dogs on a lead allowed	🌷	Plant stall
☕	Cream teas	♿	Wheelchair access	🌱	Scottish Snowdrop Festival

OPEN FOR GARDEN TOURS

2012 GARDEN TOURS

For information on the Scotland's Gardens Tours to Galloway & Northern Ireland and Badenoch & Strathspey please refer to page 13

Garden locations

1 ABRIACHAN GARDEN NURSERY
Loch Ness Side IV3 6LA
Mr and Mrs Davidson Tel: 01463 861232
Email: info@lochnessgarden.com www.lochnessgarden.com

An outstanding garden. Over 4 acres of exciting plantings, with winding paths through native woodlands. Seasonal highlights - snowdrops, hellebores, primulas, meconopsis, hardy geraniums and colour-themed summer beds. Views over Loch Ness. New path to pond through the Bluebell Wood.

Other Details: Working retail nursery. The garden will close at 5:00pm during the winter months. Tea/Coffee machine.

Directions: On A82 Inverness/Drumnadrochit road, approximately 8 miles south of Inverness.

Disabled Access: None

Opening Times:
1 February - 30 November
9:00am - 7:00pm

Admission:
£2.00

Charities: Highland Hospice receives 40%, the net remaining to SG Beneficiaries.

2 APPLECROSS WALLED GARDEN
Strathcarron IV54 8ND
Applecross Organics Tel: 01520 744440

Walled garden of 1.25 acres in spectacular surroundings. Derelict for 50 years but lovingly restored since 2001. Lots of herbaceous borders, fruit trees and raised vegetable beds. We try to have an interesting plant table in this wonderful peaceful setting.

Other Details: Restaurant open all day.

Directions: Take the spectacular Bealach na Ba hill road after Kishorn. At the T-junction in Applecross, turn right for half a mile. Entrance to Applecross House is immediately in front of you.

Disabled Access: None

Opening Times:
15 March - 31 October 11:00am - 8:30pm

Admission:
By Donation

Charities: Donation to SG Beneficiaries

3 ATTADALE
Strathcarron IV54 8YX
Mr and Mrs Ewen Macpherson Tel: 01520 722603
Email: info@attadalegardens.com www.attadalegardens.com

The Gulf Stream and surrounding hills and rocky cliffs create a microclimate for 20 acres of outstanding water gardens, old rhododendrons, unusual trees and fern collection in a geodesic dome, new sunken fern garden developed on site of early 19th century drain. Japanese garden. Sculpture collection. Giant sundial.

Other Details: DIY teas in tearoom with history of garden.

Directions: On A890 between Strathcarron and south Strome.

Disabled Access: Partial

Opening Times:
1 April - 13 October 10:00am - 5:30pm

Admission:
£6.00 Concessions £4.00
Children £1.00 Wheelchair users Free

Charities: Donation to SG Beneficiaries

BALMEANACH HOUSE
Struan, Isle of Skye IV56 8FH
Mrs Arlene Macphie Tel: 01470 572320
Email: info@skye-holiday.com www.skye-holiday.com

🅗 💐 B&B

Disabled Access: None

A garden with herbaceous border, bedding and a small azalea/rhododendron walk. To make this garden, one third of an acre of croft land was fenced in during the late 1980s and there is a woodland dell with fairies, three ponds and a small shrubbery.

Opening Times:
2 May - 31 October
Wednesdays & Saturdays
10:30am - 3:30pm

Other Details: Plant stall at Plants n' Stuff, Atholl Service Station. Teas at Waterside Cafe, Atholl Service Station.

Admission:
£3.00

Directions: A87 to Sligachan, turn left, Balmeanach is 5 miles north of Struan and 5 miles south of Dunvegan

Charities: SSPCA receives 40%, the net remaining to SG Beneficiaries.

BRACKLA WOOD
Culbokie, Dingwall IV7 8GY
Susan and Ian Dudgeon Tel: 01349 877765
Email: smdbrackla@aol.com

♿ 🅗 💐

Disabled Access: Partial

Mature 1 acre plot consisting of woodland, wildlife features, ponds, mixed borders, kitchen garden, rockery and a mini-orchard. Spring bulbs and hellebores, rhododendron, wisteria and roses followed by crocosmia, clematis and deciduous trees provide continuous colour and interest throughout the season. Chance of seeing red squirrels.

Opening Times:
By arrangement 1 - 29 July

Admission:
£4.00 includes teas and home baking.

Other Details: . Assistance is required for wheelchair access. Catering by arrangement for groups of up to 50.

Charities: MacMillan Nurses receives 40%, the net remaining to SG Beneficiaries.

Directions: From North: Take A9 and turn off to Culbokie. At far end of the village, turn right after the playing fields signposted "Munlochy". A mile up the road, turn right into "No Through Road" signposted "Upper Braefindon" **From South:** Take A9 and turn off to Munlochy. At the far end of the village, turn right and then sharp left up road signposted "Culbokie" and "Killen". After about 4½ miles turn left onto road signposted "Upper Braefindon" Brackla Wood is first house on left.

CARDON
Balnafoich, Farr IV2 6XG
Caroline Smith Tel: 01808 521389
Email: csmith@kitchens01.fsnet.co.uk

♿ 🅗 💐

Disabled Access: Full

Set in approximately 5 acres of woodlands. Feature pond and lawn area. Rockeries, wild woodland areas, cottage style planting.

Opening Times:
Sunday 12 August 1:00pm - 5:00pm

Directions: From Inverness: head south, turn right to Daviot (7 miles) and head to Balnafoich. Cardon 3½ miles. From Inverness Academy: take B861. 4½ miles take left to Daviot and Garden is 400 yards on left.

Admission:
£3.00 Children Free

Charities: Local Charities receives 40%, the net remaining to SG Beneficiaries.

7 CLAN DONALD SKYE
Armadale, Isle of Skye IV45 8RS
Clan Donald Lands Trust Tel: 01471 844305
Email: office@clandonald.com www.clandonald.com

The 40 acres of exotic trees, shrubs and flowers are remarkable for their beauty. The warm climate allows the sheltered gardens to flourish. When the Clan Donald Lands Trust took over, the gardens were overgrown and neglected. Several years of hard pruning, rebuilding and planting around the centrepiece of Armadale Castle has resulted in 40 acres of fascinating woodland gardens and lawns that provide a tranquil place to sit or walk. Leading off from the formal gardens visitors can enjoy woodland walks and nature trails, with beautiful views of the Sound of Sleat. A new children's adventure playground was added to the gardens in 2011.

Other Details: 3 retail outlets, 1 gardening. Coffee, tea and homebaking. Lunches, evening meals, alcoholic beverages at The Stable Restaurant.

Directions: From Skye Bridge: Head north on A87 and turn left just before Broadford onto A 851 signposted Armadale 15 miles. From Armadale Pier: ¼ mile north on A851 to car park.

Disabled Access: Full

Opening Times:
1 Jan - 31 Mar & 1 Nov - 31 Dec
Dawn - Dusk
1 April - 31 October 9:30am - 5:30pm

Admission:
£6.95 Conc/Children £4.95
Under 5 Free Families £20.00
Free Admission Jan - Mar &
Nov - Dec.

Charities: Donation to SG
Beneficiaries

8 COILTIE GARDEN
Divach, Drumnadrochit IV63 6XW
Gillian and David Nelson Tel: 01456 450219

A garden made over the past 35 years from a long neglected Victorian garden, now being somewhat reorganised to suit ageing gardeners. Many unusual trees, shrubs, herbaceous borders, roses, all set in beautiful hill scenery with a fine view of 100ft Divach Falls.

Directions: Take turning to Divach off A82 in Drumnadrochit village. Proceed two miles uphill, passing Falls. 150m beyond Divach Lodge.

Disabled Access: Full

Opening Times:
By arrangement June, July &
second two weeks of October.

Admission:
£3.00 Children Free

Charities: Amnesty
International receives 40%,
the net remaining to SG
Beneficiaries.

9 DUNDONNELL HOUSE
Dundonnell, Little Loch Broom, Wester Ross IV23 2QW
Dundonnell Estates Tel: 07789 390028

Camellias, magnolias and bulbs in spring, rhododendrons and laburnum walk in this ancient walled garden. Exciting planting in new borders gives all year colour centred around one of the oldest yew trees in Scotland. Midsummer roses, restored Edwardian glasshouse, riverside walk, arboretum - in the valley below the peaks of An Teallach.

Other Details: Homemade teas at house 31 May. Other days at Maggie's Tearoom 4 miles towards Little Loch Broom.

Directions: Off A835 at Braemore on to A832. After 11 miles, take Badralloch turn for half a mile.

Disabled Access: None

Opening Times:
Thurs 12 Apr 2:00pm - 5:00pm
Thurs 31 May 2:00pm - 5:00pm
Thurs 16 Aug 2:00pm - 5:00pm
Thurs 20 Sep 2:00pm - 5:00pm
Also by arrangement on request

Admission:
£3.50, Children Free

Charities: Red Squirrel Surviva
Trust receives 40% on 2
days, The Stroke Association
receives 40% on 2 days, the net
remaining to SG Beneficiaries.

DUNVEGAN CASTLE AND GARDENS
Isle of Skye IV55 8WF
Hugh Macleod of Macleod Tel: 01470 521206
Email: info@dunvegancastle.com www.dunvegancastle.com

Dunvegan Castle's 5 acres of formal gardens began life in the 18thC. The gardens are a hidden oasis featuring an eclectic mix of plants, woodland glades, pools fed by waterfalls and streams. There is a water garden with ornate bridges and islands, elegant formal round garden featuring a boxwood parterre as its centrepiece, a walled garden and what was formerly the castle's vegetable garden, now a diverse range of plants, flowers and features. A considerable amount of replanting and landscaping has taken place over the last 30 years to restore the gardens to their former glory and provide a legacy which future generations can enjoy.

Other Details: Clan exhibition, gift shops, MacLeod Tables cafe. Award winning seal boat trips on Loch Dunvegan. Wine and light refreshments.

Directions: 1 mile from Dunvegan Village, 23 miles west of Portree.

Disabled Access: Partial

Opening Times:
1 April - 15 October 10:00am - 5:30pm
Also by arrangement 16 October - 31 March Weekdays. Closed Christmas & New Year.

Admission:
Garden: £7.50 Conc. £6.00
Child 5 - 15 £4.00
Castle & Garden: £9.50 Conc. £7.00 Child 5 - 15 £5.00

Charities: Donation to SG Beneficiaries

FIELD HOUSE
Belladrum, Beauly IV4 4BA
Mr & Mrs D Paterson
www.dougthegarden.co.uk

Informal country garden in one acre site. Mixed borders with some unusual plants - a plantsman's garden.

Directions: 4 miles from Beauly on A833 Beauly to Drumnadrochit road, then follow signs to Belladrum.

Disabled Access: None

Opening Times:
Sunday 10 June 2:00pm - 5:00pm

Admission:
£4.00

Charities: Highland Hospice receives 40%, the net remaining to SG Beneficiaries.

HOUSE OF AIGAS AND FIELD CENTRE
by Beauly IV4 7AD
Sir John and Lady Lister-Kaye Tel: 01463 782443
Email: sheila@aigas.co.uk

Aigas has a woodland walk overlooking the Beauly River with a collection of named Victorian specimen trees now being restored and extended with a garden of rockeries, herbaceous borders and shrubberies. Guided walks on nature trails.

Other Details: Teas in House 24 June and 22 July. Lunch/tea available on request for 'By arrangement' openings.

Directions: 4½ miles from Beauly on A831 Cannich/Glen Affric road.

Disabled Access: Partial

Opening Times:
Sunday 24 June 2:00pm - 5:00pm
Sunday 22 July 2:00pm - 5:00pm
By arrangement April - October for groups

Admission:
£3.00 Children Free

Charities: Highland Hospice (Aird branch) receives 40%, the net remaining to SG Beneficiaries.

13 HOUSE OF GRUINARD
Laide IV22 2NQ
The Hon Mrs A G Maclay   Tel: 01445 731235

Superb hidden and unexpected garden developed in sympathy with stunning west coast estuary location. Wide variety of interesting herbaceous and shrub borders with water garden and extended wild planting.

Other Details: Homemade Teas 23 May only.

Directions: On A832, 12 miles north of Inverewe and 9 miles south of Dundonnell.

Disabled Access: None

Opening Times:
Wednesday 23 May 2:00pm - 5:00pm
Wednesday 4 July 2:00pm - 5:00pm

Admission:
£3.50 Children under 16 Free

Charities: Macmillan Nurses receives 40%, the net remaining to SG Beneficiaries.

14 HUGH MILLER'S MUSEUM & BIRTHPLACE COTTAGE
Church Street, Cromarty, IV11 8XA
The National Trust for Scotland   Tel: 0844 493 2158
Email: apowersjones@nts.org.uk   www.nts.org.uk

Garden of Wonders, created in 2008, with its theme of natural history, features fossils, exotic ferns, ornamental letter-cutting and a 'mystery' stone. Lydia Garden, a new garden completed in 2010. Walk around the crescent shaped sandstone path of fragrant climbing roses, herbs and wild plant areas.

Directions: By road via Kessock Bridge and A832 to Cromarty. 22 miles north east of Inverness.

Disabled Access: None

Opening Times:
Tuesday 24 July 1:00pm - 5:00pm

Admission:
Museum £5.50 Concessions £4.50 Family Ticket £15.00
Prices correct at time of going to print.

Charities: Donation to SG Beneficiaries

15 INVEREWE
Poolewe, Achnasheen, Ross-shire. IV22 2LG
The National Trust for Scotland   Tel: 0844 493 2225
Email: inverewe@nts.org.uk   www.nts.org.uk

Magnificent 54 acre Highland garden, surrounded by mountains, moorland and sea-loch. Created by Osgood Mackenzie in the late 19th century, it now includes a wealth of exotic plants from Australian tree ferns to Chinese rhododendrons to South African bulbs.
The Head Gardener's Walk on 23 May will focus on Woodland Gardening. Meet at Visitor Centre 2:00pm.
The Walk led by the First Gardener on 6 June will view some of the National Collection planting. Meet at Visitor Centre 2:00pm.

Directions: Signposted on A832 by Poolewe, 6 miles NE of Gairloch.

Disabled Access: Full

Opening Times:
Wednesday 23 May 10:00am - 5:00pm
Wednesday 6 June 10:00am - 5:00pm

Admission:
£8.50 Concessions £5.50
N.B. These prices are correct at time of going to print.

Charities: Donation to SG Beneficiaries

16 LEATHAD ARD

Upper Carloway, Isle of Lewis HS2 9AQ
Rowena and Stuart Oakley Tel: 01851 643204
Email: oakley1a@clara.co.uk www.whereveriam.org/leathadard

¾ acre sloping garden with stunning views over East Loch Roag. It has evolved along with the shelter hedges that divide the garden into a number of areas. With shelter and raised beds the different conditions created permit a wide variety of plants to be grown. Beds include herbaceous borders, cutting borders, bog gardens, grass garden, exposed beds, patio and vegetable and fruit patches, some of which are grown to show. A full tour by Stuart takes about 2 hours.

Directions: A858 Shawbost, Carloway is first right at village opposite football pitch. First house on right. The Westside circular bus ex Stornoway to road end, ask for the Carloway football pitch.

Disabled Access: None

Opening Times:
1 June - 30 August ex Fridays & Sundays. Also not open Wednesday 1 August. 1:45pm - 6:00pm

Admission:
Donations welcome. Recommended minimum donation: £3.00

Charities: Red Cross receives 40%, the net remaining to SG Beneficiaries.

17 LECKMELM SHRUBBERY & ARBORETUM

By Ullapool IV23 2RH
Mr and Mrs Peter Troughton

The restored 12 acre arboretum, planted in the 1880s, is full of splendid and rare trees including two "Champions", specie rhododendrons, azaleas and shrubs. Warmed by the Gulf Stream, this tranquil woodland garden has alpines, palms and bamboos along winding paths which lead down to the sea.

Directions: Situated by the shore of Loch Broom 3 miles south of Ullapool on the A835 Inverness/Ullapool road. Parking in walled garden.

Disabled Access: None

Opening Times:
1 April - 31 October 10:00am - 6:00pm

Admission:
£3.00 Children under 16 Free.

Charities: Donation to SG Beneficiaries and Local Charities.

18 NOVAR

Evanton IV16 9XL
Mr and Mrs Ronald Munro Ferguson Tel: 01349 831062

Water gardens with recent restoration and new planting, especially rhododendrons and azaleas. Large, five acre walled garden with formal 18th century oval pond (restored).

Other Details: Raffle/tombola

Directions: Off B817 between Evanton and junction with A836, turn west up Novar Drive.

Disabled Access: Partial

Opening Times:
Sunday 10 June 2:30pm - 5:00pm
Also by arrangement for groups of a minimum of 8 people

Admission:
£5.00 Children Free

Charities: Diabetes Charities receives 40%, the net remaining to SG Beneficiaries.

19 SAILEAN COTTAGE
83 Aird Bernisdale, Skeabost Bridge, Isle of Skye IV51 9NU
Mrs Ann Galbraith Tel:01470 532353
Email: annasdair@hotmail.com

Our 7 acre croft has chickens, geese, a small trout farm, a riverside walk, archaeological features, a polytunnel, vegetable garden, fruit trees, areas of woodland, a wildflower meadow, and a manageable garden surrounding the house.

Other Details: Tea, coffee, home baking.

Directions: From Portree, take A850 towards Dunvegan. At Bernisdale, turn right into Aird Bernisdale. Sailean Cottage is first on left. Park in lay-by as parking at the house is congested.

Disabled Access: None

Opening Times:
Saturday 26 May 10:30am - 4:00pm
Sunday 27 May 10:30am - 4:00pm
Also by arrangement on request

Admission:
£5.00

Charities: Brain Tumour UK receives 20%, MacMillan Nurses receives 20%, the net remaining to SG Beneficiaries.

20 THE LOOKOUT
Kilmuir IV1 3ZG
Mr & Mrs David & Penny Veitch Tel: 01463 731489
Email: david@veitch.biz

A ¾ acre elevated coastal garden with incredible views over the Moray Firth which is only for the sure-footed. This award winning garden is created out of a rock base with shallow pockets of ground, planted to its advantage to encourage all aspects of wildlife. There is a small sheltered courtyard, raised bed vegetable area, pretty cottage garden, scree and rock garden, rose arbour, rhododendrons, flowering shrubs, bamboos, trees and lily pond with waterside plants.

Other Details: Studio: Exhibition of landscape pictures for sale.

Directions: From Inverness take North Kessock left turn from A9 and 3ʳᵈ left at roundabout to go on underpass then sharp left onto Kilmuir road.
From Tore, take slip road for North Kessock and immediately right for Kilmuir. Follow signs for Kilmuir (3 miles) until you reach the shore. The Lookout is near far end of village with a large palm tree on the grass in front.

Disabled Access: None

Opening Times:
April - September, Sundays & Tuesdays 11:00am - 4:00pm
Also by arrangement April - October

Admission:
£3.00

Charities: Alzheimer Scotland receives 40%, the net remaining to SG Beneficiaries.

21 WOODVIEW
Highfield, Muir of Ord IV6 7UL
Miss Lynda Macleod Tel: 01463 871928
Email: lynwoodview@yahoo.co.uk

Award winning well-stocked mature garden of approximately third acre, containing many unusual trees. It comprises various "rooms" Italian inspired with sculptured trees. Pergola clad with golden hop, overlooking water feature. Chinese room very calm and relaxing with acers. Formal borders of twilight. Large exotic border. Abundance of colour from spring to autumn. Pond with waterside plants. Raised vegetable beds. Greenhouse. New borders and features ongoing every year. Special lawn sculptured chair. Garden of the Year 2010.

Other Details: Wonderful home baking.

Directions: Follow signs to Ord Distillery on the A832 Muir of Ord to Marybank. House opposite Clashwood Forest Walk. Parking in Clashwood.

Disabled Access: None

Opening Times:
Sunday 5 August 2:00pm - 5:00pm

Admission:
£4.00 Children Free

Charities: Highland Hospice receives 40%, the net remaining to SG Beneficiaries.

ROXBURGHSHIRE

Scotland's Gardens 2012 Guidebook is sponsored by INVESTEC WEALTH & INVESTMENT

District Organiser

Mrs Sally Yonge   Newtonlees, Kelso TD5 7SZ

Area Organiser

Mrs Clare Leeming   Loanend, Earlston, Berwickshire TD4 6BD

Treasurer

Mr Peter Jeary   Kalemouth House, Eckford, Kelso TD5 8LE

Gardens open on a specific date

Corbet Tower, Morebattle, Nr Kelso	Saturday 7 July	2:00pm	5:30pm
Yetholm Village Gardens, Town Yetholm	Sunday 15 July	2:00pm	5:30pm
Newcastleton Village Gardens: Floral Festival	Saturday 21 July	10:00am	5:00pm
Newcastleton Village Gardens: Gardens	Saturday 21 July	2:00pm	5:00pm
West Leas, Bonchester Bridge	Sunday 19 August	2:00pm	5:00pm

Gardens open regularly

Floors Castle, Kelso	6 April - 9 April and 1 May - 28 October	10:30am	5:00pm
Monteviot, Jedburgh	1 April - 31 October	12:00pm	4:00pm

Key to symbols

🌳	New in 2012	HP	Homemade teas	B&B	Accommodation
☕	Teas	🐕	Dogs on a lead allowed	🌷	Plant stall
CP	Cream teas	♿	Wheelchair access	🌱	Scottish Snowdrop Festival

Garden locations

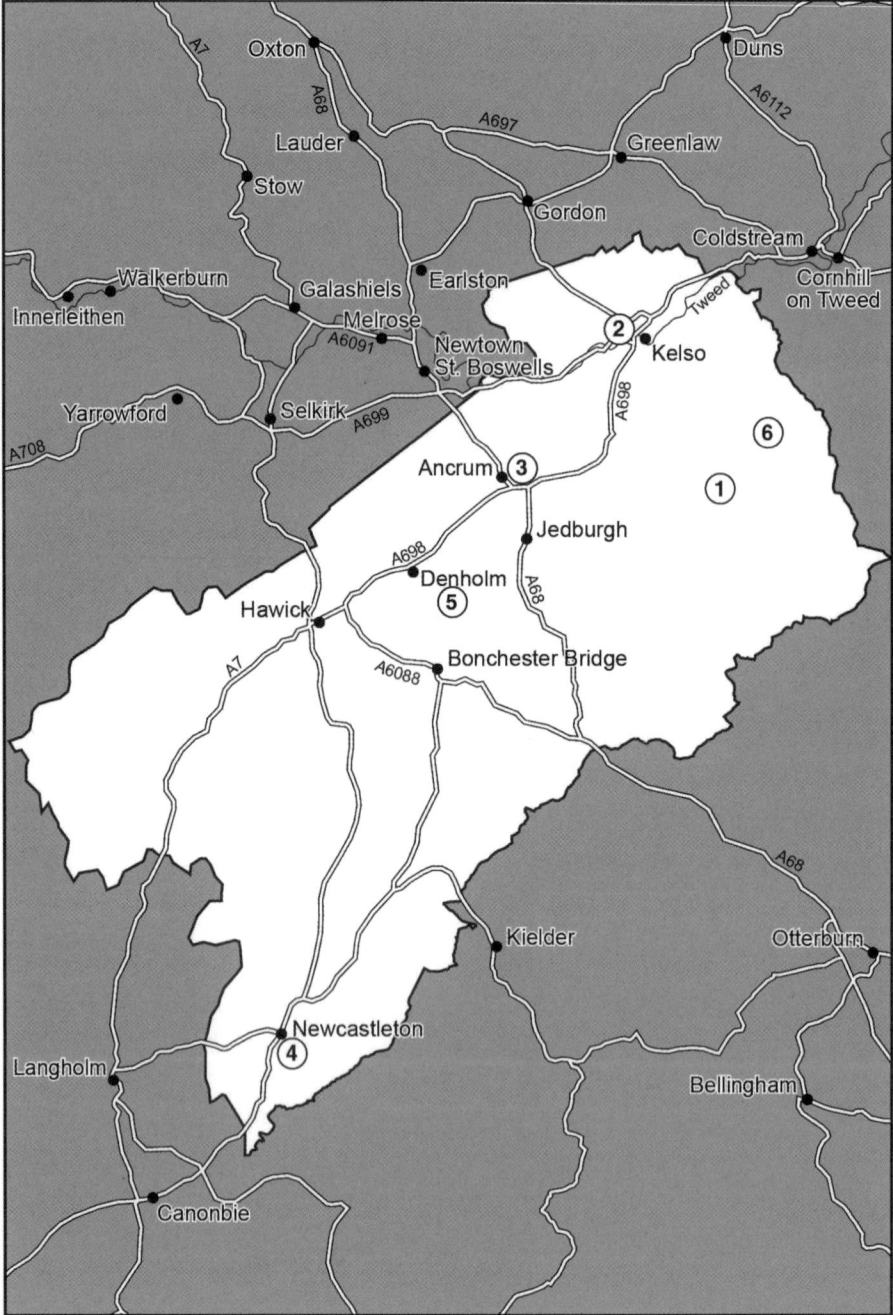

CORBET TOWER
Morebattle, Nr Kelso TD5 8AQ
Simon and Bridget Fraser

Scottish Victorian garden set in parklands in the foothills of the Cheviots. The garden includes a formal box parterred rose garden with old fashioned roses, a well stocked traditional walled vegetable and cutting garden, lawns with medieval peel tower and an attractive woodland walk.

Other Details: Homemade cakes and preserves, Ann Fraser cards.

Directions: From A68 north of Jedburgh take A698 for Kelso. At Kalemouth follow B6401 to Morebattle then road marked Hownam to Corbet Tower.

Disabled Access: Partial

Opening Times:
Saturday 7 July 2:00pm - 5:30pm

Admission:
£4.00

Charities: Talking Newspaper Association UK receives 40%, the net remaining to SG Beneficiaries.

FLOORS CASTLE
Kelso TD5 7SF
The Duke of Roxburghe Tel: 01573 223333
www.floorscastle.com

The largest inhabited house in Scotland enjoys glorious views across parkland, the River Tweed and the Cheviot Hills. Woodland garden, riverside and woodland walks, formal French style Millennium Parterre and the traditional walled garden. The walled garden contains colourful herbaceous borders, vinery and peach house, and in keeping with the tradition the kitchen garden still supplies vegetables and soft fruit for the castle.

Other Details: Floors Castle, gift shop, Terrace Cafe and Courtyard Restaurant. Terrace Cafe open all year round serving morning coffee, delicious lunches and afternoon teas.

Directions: Floors Castle can be reached by following the A6089 from Edinburgh; the B6397 from Earlston or the A698 from Coldstream. Go through Kelso, up Roxburgh Street to the Golden Gates.

Disabled Access: Partial

Opening Times:
6 April - 9 April and 1 May - 28 October 10:30am - 5:00pm

Admission:
Gardens: £4.00 OAPs £3.50
Children £1.50
House & Gardens: £8.00 OAPs £7.00 Children £4.00

Charities: Donation to SG Beneficiaries

MONTEVIOT
Jedburgh TD8 6UQ
Marquis & Marchioness of Lothian Tel: 01835 830380
www.monteviot.com

Series of differing gardens including herb garden, rose garden, water garden linked by bridges, and river garden with herbaceous shrub borders. Dene garden featuring ponds and bridges and planted with a variety of foliage plants.

Directions: Turn off A68, 3 miles north of Jedburgh B6400.

Disabled Access: Partial

Opening Times:
1 April - 31 October 12:00pm - 4:00pm

Admission:
£3.50

Charities: Donation to SG Beneficiaries

NEWCASTLETON VILLAGE GARDENS & FLORAL FESTIVAL
Newcastleton TD9 0QS
The Gardeners of Newcastleton Village

Newcastleton is a small Borders village with a variety of 'hidden' gardens. The village won "Best Village in Scotland" in 2010 and achieved silver gilt in "Britain in Bloom" in 2011. The gardens will be open in conjunction with the 'Floral Festival' and visitors are encouraged to come for the whole day to experience the full programme of events which includes horticultural activities, live music, scarecrow competitions, bric-a-brac stalls and refreshments.

Other Details: Ample free parking, public toilets. Excellent eating establishments within the village.

Directions: On B6357 approximately 10 miles from Canonbie (A7)

Disabled Access: Partial

Opening Times:
Saturday 21 July
Festival: 10:00am - 5:00pm
Gardens: 2:00pm - 5:00pm

Admission:
£4.00

Charities: Friends of the Park receives 20%, Newcastleton Floral Group receives 20%, the net remaining to SG Beneficiaries.

WEST LEAS
Bonchester Bridge TD9 8TD
Mr and Mrs Robert Laidlaw   Tel: 01450 860711
Email: ann.laidlaw@btconnect.com

The visitor to West Leas can share in the exciting and dramatic project on a grand scale still in the making. At its core a passion for plants allied to a love and understanding of the land in which they are set. Collections of perennials and shrubs, many in temporary holding quarters, lighten up the landscape to magical effect. New landscaped water features, bog garden and extensive new shrub and herbaceous planting. A recently planted orchard, with underplantings of spring bulbs demonstrates that the productive garden can be highly ornamental.

Directions: Signposted off the Jedburgh/Bonchester Bridge Road.

Disabled Access: Partial

Opening Times:
Sunday 19 August 2:00pm - 5:00pm

Admission:
£4.00.

Charities: Macmillan Cancer Relief, Borders Appeal receives 40%, the net remaining to SG Beneficiaries.

YETHOLM VILLAGE GARDENS
Town Yetholm TD5 8RL
The Gardeners of Yetholm Village

The village of Town Yetholm is situated at the north end of the Pennine Way and lies close to the Bowmont Water in the dramatic setting of the foothills of the Cheviots. A variety of gardens with their own unique features have joined the Yetholm Village Gardens Open Day this year.

Gardens open will include: Copsewood, Almond Cottage, 5 Yew Tree Lane, Rosebank, The Old Manse, The Hall House, Thirlestane, Hazeldean, Hillview, 3 Morebattle Road, 2 Grafton Court and Grafton House. In addition "The Yew Tree Allotments" running along the High Street will open again this year in turn providing an ever popular feature.

Yetholm Village Gardens Open Day offers visitors the chance to walk through several delightful gardens planted in a variety of styles and reflecting many distinctive horticultural interests. From newly established, developing and secret gardens to old and established gardens there is something here to interest everyone.

The short walking distance between the majority of the gardens provides the added advantage of being able to enjoy the magnificence of the surrounding landscape to include "Staerough" and "The Curr" which straddle both the Bowmont and Halterburn Valleys where evidence of ancient settlements remain.

Tickets will be sold in the Wauchope Hall. Ample parking available along the High Street.

Other Details: Plant and garden produce, home baking, bric-a-brac, craft and book stalls. "Music Ensemble" in one of the gardens during the afternoon. "Poetry Readings" at The Old Manse. Homemade cream teas served in the Youth Hall.

Directions: South of Kelso in the Borders take the B6352 to Yetholm Village.

Disabled Access: Partial

Opening Times:
Sunday 15 July 2:00pm - 5:30pm

Admission:
£4.00(includes all gardens)
Children under 10 Free.

Charities: Riding for the Disabled Association, Borders Group receives 40%, the net remaining to SG Beneficiaries.

STIRLINGSHIRE

Scotland's Gardens 2012 Guidebook is sponsored by **INVESTEC WEALTH & INVESTMENT**

District Organiser

Carola Campbell	Kilbryde Castle, Dunblane FK15 9NF

Area Organisers

Gillie Drapper	Kilewnan Cottage, Fintry, By Glasgow G63 0YH
Maurie Jessett	The Walled Garden, Doune FK16 6HJ
Pippa Maclean	Quarter, Denny FK8 6QZ
Iain Morrison	Clifford House, Balkerach Street, Doune FK16 6DE
Philip Penfold	Craigend House, Auchenbowie FK7 9QW
Douglas Ramsay	2 Slamannan Road, Falkirk FK1 5LG
Mandy Readman	Hutchison Farm, Auchinlay Road, Dunblane FK15 9JS
Lesley Stein	2 Southfield Crescent, Stirling FK8 2JQ

Treasurer

John McIntyre	18 Scott Brae, Kippen FK8 3DL

Gardens open on a specific date

West Plean House, Denny Road, By Stirling	Sunday 26 February	1:00pm	-	4:00pm
Kilbryde Castle, Dunblane	Sunday 4 March	1:00pm	-	4:00pm
The Linns, Sheriffmuir, Dunblane	Sunday 11 March	10:00am	-	4:00pm
Milseybank, Bridge of Allan	Sunday 8 April	1:00pm	-	5:00pm
West Plean House, Denny Road, By Stirling	Sunday 15 April	2:00pm	-	5:00pm
The Pass House, Kilmahog, Callander	Sunday 29 April	2:00pm	-	5:00pm
Southwood & 1 Laurelhill Place, Stirling	Sunday 6 May	1:00pm	-	5:00pm
Auchmar, Drymen	Sunday 13 May	2:00pm	-	5:00pm
Kilbryde Castle, Dunblane	Sunday 20 May	2:00pm	-	5:00pm
Thornhill Village, The Gardens of Thornhill	Sunday 27 May	1:00pm	-	6:00pm
Lanrick, Doune	Saturday 2 June	2:00pm	-	5:00pm
Burnbrae, Killearn	Sunday 3 June	1:00pm	-	5:00pm
Bridge of Allan Gardens, Bridge of Allan	Sunday 10 June	2:00pm	-	5:00pm
Kilbryde Castle, Dunblane	Sunday 10 June	2:00pm	-	5:00pm
Duntreath Castle, Blanefield	Saturday 16 June	10:00am	-	6:00pm
Duntreath Castle, Blanefield	Sunday 17 June	10:00am	-	6:00pm
Park House, Blair Drummond	Sunday 24 June	1:00pm	-	5:00pm
Doune Village, Doune Village Gardens	Sunday 1 July	2:00pm	-	5:00pm

Settie, Kippen	Sunday 8 July	2:00pm	- 5:00pm
Gean House , Tullibody Road, Alloa	Tuesday 31 July	2:00pm	- 5:00pm
Thorntree, Arnprior	Sunday 12 August	2:00pm	- 5:00pm
Rowberrow, 18 Castle Road, Dollar	Sunday 19 August	2:00pm	- 5:00pm
Avonmuir House, Muiravonside, by Linlithgow	Sunday 2 September	2:00pm	- 5:00pm
Gargunnock House, Gargunnock	Sunday 23 September	2:00pm	- 5:00pm

Gardens open regularly

Gargunnock House, Gargunnock	4 February - 18 March	11:00am	- 3:30pm
	Mid April - Mid June Weds	2:00pm	- 5:00pm

Gardens open by arrangement

When organising a visit to a garden open by arrangement, please enquire if there are facilities and catering available.

Arndean, By Dollar	Mid May - Mid June	01259 743525
Camallt, Fintry	1st April - Mid May	01360 860034
Culbuie, Buchlyvie	1 May - 31 October	01360 850232 & 07967 161214
Gargunnock House, Gargunnock	On request	01786 860392
Kilbryde Castle, Dunblane	On request	01786 824897
Milseybank, Bridge of Allan	On request	01786 833866
Thorntree, Arnprior	On request	01786 870710

Plant sales

Gargunnock House, Gargunnock	Sunday 23 September	2:00pm	- 5:00pm

Key to symbols

New in 2012	Homemade teas	Accommodation
Teas	Dogs on a lead allowed	Plant stall
Cream teas	Wheelchair access	Scottish Snowdrop Festival

Plant sale and garden opening at Gargunnock House on Sunday 23 September.

A wonderful opportunity to purchase a wide selection of azaleas and rhododendrons as well as other plants.

See entry on page 260.

OPEN FOR PLANT SALES

Garden locations

ARNDEAN

By Dollar FK14 7NH
Johnny and Katie Stewart   Tel: 01259 743525
Email: johnny@arndean.co.uk

This is a beautiful mature garden extending to 15 acres including the woodland walk. There is a formal herbaceous part, a small vegetable garden and orchard. In addition there are flowering shrubs, abundant and striking rhododendrons and azaleas and many fine specimen trees. Tree house for children.

Directions: Arndean is well sign posted off A977

Disabled Access: Full

Opening Times:
By arrangement Mid May - Mid June

Admission:
£5.00 Children Free

Charities: Scots Guards Colonel's Fund receives 40%, the net remaining to SG Beneficiaries.

AUCHMAR

Drymen G63 0AG
The Duke & Duchess of Montrose

Designed by the late Mary, Duchess of Montrose in 1935. This 5½ acre garden presents a fine show of bluebells, azaleas and rhododendrons amongst mature specimen trees. Deep glen and waterfall with woodland walks. Renovated walled garden with shrubs and herbaceous borders and recent bridge extension to a new area of the garden. Spectacular view of Loch Lomond.

Directions: From Erskine Bridge: A811 to Drymen. From Stirling: A811 to Drymen. From Glasgow: A809 to Drymen. From Drymen: 2½ miles on B837

Disabled Access: None

Opening Times:
Sunday 13 May 2:00pm - 5:00pm

Admission:
£4.00 Children Free

Charities: The Preshal Trust receives 40%, the net remaining to SG Beneficiaries.

AVONMUIR HOUSE

Muiravonside, by Linlithgow EH49 6LN
Mark and Jan Strudwick

The house and gardens are the old Manse of Muiravonside built about 1795. There is a walled garden with fruiting trees and a north and a south facing border. The gardens then lead through shrubs and young trees towards an old ruin with a walk along the burnside back towards the house.

Other Details: Produce stall. The Linlithgow Union Canal Society will run short canal trips every half hour between 2:00pm - 4.30pm.

Directions: Junction 4 M9. A803 to Linlithgow turn right signed Whitecross. In Whitecross first right past small football ground and just before bridge over Union Canal turn right, to Muiravonside Kirk and Cemetery and immediately right into field.

Disabled Access: Partial

Opening Times:
Sunday 2 September 2:00pm - 5:00pm

Admission:
£4.00 Children Free

Charities: Combat Stress receives 40%, the net remaining to SG Beneficiaries.

4 BRIDGE OF ALLAN GARDENS
Bridge of Allan FK9
The Bridge of Allan Gardeners
Email: annshaw@mac.com

Some delightful and interesting gardens in Bridge of Allan including:
Plaka, 5 Pendreich Road FK9 4LY (Malcolm and Ann Shaw) ½ acre of semi-terraced gardens divided into outdoor rooms with wild spaces. In addition, there are rhododendrons, perennials and interesting stone and other features.
Kilmun Cottage, 1b Pendreich Road FK9 4PZ (Frances Fielding) Designed and beautifully landscaped by the owner within the last four years, this third of an acre garden on a slope has much variety. A terraced garden with an attractive rockery and pond, raised beds with herbaceous plants including a fine Fothergilla major, vegetable plot with three handsome espalier apple trees and a potential fruit garden with blueberry and other bushes leading to a wild area.
Garvia, 10 Fishers Green FK9 4PU (Garth and Sylvia Broomfield). ½ acre of semi-terraced gardens divided into outdoor rooms with wild spaces. In addition, there are rhododendrons, perennials and interesting stone and other features.
Maps and tickets available at all gardens.

Other Details: Teas at St Saviour's Church Hall.

Directions: Signposted from village.

Disabled Access: None

Opening Times:
Sunday 10 June 1:00pm - 5:00pm

Admission:
£5.00 Children Free

Charities: St Saviour's Church receives 30%, Strathcarron Hospice receives 10%, the net remaining to SG Beneficiaries.

5 BURNBRAE
Killearn G63 9NB
Mrs Russell Bruce

Well designed garden with eye catching layout. Excellent sweeping lawn. Well stocked and interesting herbaceous borders. Varied shrubs. Magnificent backdrop of mature and specimen trees including spectacular red chestnut. Glen with burn available for agile. Burnbrae is a typical 1930s house (not open) designed by Hislop.

Directions: From Stirling: A875 through Killearn, turn 3rd right after the Co-op. From Glasgow: 2nd on left after Drumbeg Loan and mini roundabout.

Disabled Access: Full

Opening Times:
Sunday 3 June 2:00pm - 5:00pm

Admission:
£4.00 Children Free

Charities: Crossroads Care Attendant Scheme receives 40%, the net remaining to SG Beneficiaries.

CAMALLT

Fintry G63 0XH
William Acton and Rebecca East   Tel: 01360 860034
Email: enquiries@camallt.com

Eight acre garden previously open for its old and interesting daffodil cultivars dating from 1600 which carpet the woodland beside waterfalls and burn, at their best during April and early May. These are followed by bluebells, rhododendrons and azaleas. Herbaceous terraced gardens under continued progression of change meet lawns which run down to the Endrick Water. Other features include ponds and bog garden still under development.

Directions: From Fintry village B822 to Lennoxtown, approx 1 mile then turn left to Denny on B818, Camallt entrance on right.

Disabled Access: None

Opening Times:
By arrangement 1st April - Mid May

Admission:
£3.50 Children Free

Charities: Strathcarron Hospice receives 40%, the net remaining to SG Beneficiaries.

CULBUIE

Buchlyvie FK8 3NY
Ian & Avril Galloway   Tel: 01360 850232 & 07967 161214

Spring collection of rhododendrons, azaleas, narcissi, bluebells, primulas and meconopsis. Woodland walk with new planting. Early summer magnolias, cornus and viburnums. Colourful perennial borders. Wild flower meadow. Good autumn colour. Lots of interest throughout this 5 acre garden with splendid views to Ben Lomond and surrounding hills.

Directions: Take A811 to Buchlyvie, turn up Culbowie Road and Culbuie is almost at the top of the hill on the right.

Disabled Access: None

Opening Times:
By arrangement 1 May - 31 October : Groups Welcome

Admission:
£4.00 Children Free

Charities: The Preshal Trust receives 40%, the net remaining to SG Beneficiaries.

DOUNE VILLAGE

Doune Village Gardens FK16 6DE
Iain Morrison   Tel: 01786 841007
Email: Mor990@aol.com

An opening of several newly established gardens and others which have previously been opened but updated by their owners, including a Castle Hill garden with many different species of conifers.

Other Details: Plant stall at Kilmadock Development Trust garden. Other stalls. Teas at Doune Bowling Club.

Directions: Doune stands at junction of A820 from Dunblane and A84 Stirling to Callander main road.

Disabled Access: Partial

Opening Times:
Sunday 1 July 2:00pm - 5:00pm

Admission:
£5.00 Children Free

Charities: Scottish Firemens' Benevolent Fund receives 40%, the net remaining to SG Beneficiaries.

9 DUNTREATH CASTLE
Blanefield G63 9AJ
Sir Archibald & Lady Edmonstone Tel: 01360 770215
Email: juliet@edmonstone.com www.duntreathcastle.co.uk

Duntreath Garden Show: This is the first of its kind in Scotland. A two day garden bonanza - a horticultural spectacular with lots to see and do for all ages. Refer to pages 16 and 17 for full details.

Other Details: Many stalls and attractions. Refreshments, food stalls etc.

Directions: A81 north of Glasgow between Blanefield and Killearn

Disabled Access: Full

Opening Times:
Saturday 16 June 10:00am - 6:00pm
Sunday 17 June 10:00am - 6:00pm

Admission:
Refer to pages xxxxx for full details.

Charities: Scotland's Gardens, Canine Partners, Erskine Hospital, Artlink Central, S.A.F.A.S Rotary, Camphill Village Trust and others

10 GARGUNNOCK HOUSE
Gargunnock FK8 3AZ
By kind permission of the Gargunnock Trustees Tel: 01786 860392
Email: william.campbellwj@btinternet.com

Five acres of mature gardens, woodland walks, walled garden and 18th century Doocot. Snowdrops in February/March, daffodils in April/May. Glorious display of azaleas and rhododendron in May/June. Wonderful trees and shrubs, glorious autumn colour. Garden featured in articles in 'The Scotsman' and 'Scottish Field'. Good plant sales always. Guided tours can be arranged for Parties. September plant sale will include a wonderful selection of azaleas and rhododenrons.

Other Details: February/March: Snowdrops for sale.
23 September: Major plant sale
Homemade teas at Gargunnock House on 23 September only.

Directions: On A811 5 miles west of Stirling.

Disabled Access: Full

Opening Times:
Sun 23 Sept 2:00pm - 5:00pm
4 Feb - 18 Mar 11:00am - 3:30pm
Mid April - mid June Weds 2:00 - 5:00pm
Also by arrangement on request

Admission:
23 September: £4.00
Other Dates: £3.00

Charities: Children's Hospice Association receives 20%, Gargunnock Community Centre receives 20%, the net remaining to SG Beneficiaries.

11 GEAN HOUSE
Tullibody Road, Alloa FK10 2EL
Ceteris (Scotland)
Email: ebowie@geanhouse.co.uk www.geanhouse.co.uk

Gean House is an early 20th century Arts & Crafts style mansion. On arrival the sweeping driveway from the main road takes you through beautiful parkland lined with trees to the mansion set on top of the hill facing North East. The gardens surrounding the house were originally 40 acres and included a Japanese garden in the woods. All that remains now are seven acres on the southern and eastern aspects of the house.

Other Details: Cream teas in Gean House

Directions: Gean House is located on the Tullibody Road, Alloa.

Disabled Access: None

Opening Times:
Tuesday 31 July 2:00pm - 5:00pm

Admission:
£4.00 Children Free

Charities: Scottish Society for Autism receives 40%, the net remaining to SG Beneficiaries.

KILBRYDE CASTLE

Dunblane FK15 9NF
Sir James & Lady Campbell & Jack Fletcher Tel: 01786 824897
Email: kilbryde1@aol.com www.kilbrydecastle.com

The Kilbryde Castle gardens cover some 12 acres and are situated above the Ardoch Burn and below the castle. The gardens are split into three parts: formal, woodland and wild. Huge drifts of snowdrops are in the wild garden during March. Natural planting (azaleas, rhododendrons, camellias and magnolias) in the woodland garden. There are glorious spring bulbs and autumn colour.

Other Details: Plant Stall by Carol Seymour. Light refreshments on 8 May.

Directions: Three miles from Dunblane and Doune, off the A820 between Dunblane and Doune. On Scotland's Gardens days signposted from A820.

Disabled Access: Partial

Opening Times:
Sunday 4 March 1:00pm -
4:00pm for Snowdrop Festival
Sunday 20 May 2:00pm -
5:00pm
Sunday 10 June 2:00pm -
5:00pm
Also open by arrangement on request

Admission:
£4.00 Children Free

Charities: Leighton Library receives 40%, the net remaining to SG Beneficiaries.

LANRICK

Doune FK16 6HJ
Alistair & Penny Dickson and Maurie Jessett Tel: 01786 841684/842280
Email: maurie.jessett@hotmail.co.uk www.lanrick.co.uk

Mature policies with lovely woodland walks along the River Teith; a rural oasis where you can enjoy the peace and tranquillity of Scotland. Magnificent ponticums. Many interesting sights and features in the grounds. The Walled Garden (2 acres) is the original walled garden of Lanrick Castle (now demolished) but now a substantial work in progress. Planting began four years ago with ornamental shrubs, climbing roses, and many varieties of espalier fruit trees. Many interesting sights and features.

Other Details: Teas in Indian Tent on site of original Castle.

Directions: Turn off the A84 at Doune onto the B8032 and after about a mile the entrance is on the right.

Disabled Access: Full

Opening Times:
Saturday 2 June 2:00pm -
5:00pm

Admission:
£4.00 Children Free

Charities: The Sandpiper Trust receives 40%, the net remaining to SG Beneficiaries.

MILSEYBANK

Bridge of Allan FK9 4NB
Murray and Sheila Airth Tel: 01786 833866
Email: smairth@hotmail.com

Wonderful and interesting sloping garden with outstanding views, terraced for ease of access. Woodland with bluebells, rhododendrons, magnolias and camellias.

Directions: Situated on A9, 1 mile from junction 11, M9 and ¼ mile from Bridge of Allan. Milseybank is at top of lane at Lecropt Nursery 250 yards from Bridge of Allan train station.

Disabled Access: Full

Opening Times:
Sunday 8 April 1:00pm -
5:00pm
Also by arrangement on request

Admission:
£4.00 Children Free

Charities: Strathcarron Hospice receives 40%, the net remaining to SG Beneficiaries.

15 PARK HOUSE

Blair Drummond FK9 4UP
Jamie and Sue Muir   Tel: 01786 841799
Email: jamie@blairdrummond.com

Mature three acre garden with herbaceous borders, lawns, vegetable and wild gardens. Extensive woodland walks (under restoration) lead to Camphill Blair Drummond.

Other Details: Teas at Camphill Blair Drummond. Full wheelchair access provided grass is not too wet.

Directions: Six miles NW of Stirling on A84. One mile after Safari Park entrance turn right at sign to caravan park. Continue up hill (speed bumps), left at grass triangle and Park House is behind the hedge.

Disabled Access: Full

Opening Times:
Sunday 24 June 1:00pm - 5:00pm

Admission:
£5.00 Children Free

Charities: Camphill Village Trust receives 40%, the net remaining to SG Beneficiaries.

16 ROWBERROW

18 Castle Road, Dollar FK14 7BE
Bill and Rosemary Jarvis
Email: rjarvis1000@hotmail.com

On the way up to Castle Campbell overlooking Dollar Glen, this colourful garden has several mixed shrub and herbaceous borders, a wildlife pond, two rockeries, alpine troughs, fruit and vegetable gardens, and a mini-orchard. The owner is a plantaholic and likes to collect unusual specimens. Rowberrow was featured on Beechgrove Garden in summer 2011. The Hillfoot Harmony Barbershop singers will entertain you.

Other Details: Transport may be available from the golf club if specially needed. Sandwiches, scones, cakes and biscuits by Hillfoot Harmony Barbershop Singers.

Directions: Pass along the burn side in Dollar, turn right at T junction follow signs for Castle Campbell and Dollar Glen. Park at bottom of Castle Road or in Quarry car park just up from house.

Disabled Access: None

Opening Times:
Sunday 19 August 2:00pm - 5:00pm

Admission:
£4.00 Children Free

Charities: Hillfoot Harmony Barbershop Singers receives 40%, the net remaining to SG Beneficiaries.

17 SETTIE

Kippen FK8 3HN
James and Jane Hutchison   Tel: 01786 870428
Email: plantitdesign@aol.com   www.james-hutchison.com

A one and a half acre country garden located to the south west of Kippen on an exposed site benefitting from wonderful views of the Trossachs. Settie is gaelic for a windy spot and the Hutchisons have divided this garden up into a series of rooms divided by tall random rubble sandstone walls. As a landscape gardener James has used this challenging site as an opportunity to demonstrate what can be done in either a country garden or an enclosed urban space.

Other Details: Homemade teas in the barn.

Directions: Take the Fintry Road out of Kippen and take the 2nd on the right. Settie is approximately a third of a mile west of the outskirts of Kippen.

Disabled Access: None

Opening Times:
Sunday 8 July 2:00pm - 5:00pm

Admission:
£4.00   Children Free

Charities: Bob Savage Memorial Fund receives 40%, the net remaining to SG Beneficiaries.

SOUTHWOOD AND 1 LAUREL HILL PLACE
2 Southfield Crescent, Stirling FK8 2JQ
John & Lesley Stein and Richard & Rachel Nunn
Email: lesley@john-stein.co.uk

Disabled Access: Full

Southwood: Victorian walled garden with long double herbaceous borders within beech hedges, fine azaleas and rhododendrons, interesting varieties of shrubs and fully planted Dutch wall. Paeony bed on mound. Interesting specimen trees: Camperdown Elm, Himalayan Birch, Handkerchief tree, Cutleaf Beech, as well as good variety of fruit trees. Asparagus and vegetables area. Southwood was featured on the 'Beechgrove Garden' in June 2011.
1 Laurelhill Place: is a well laid out charming town garden with interesting shrubs and plants to the rear of the house, uncovered ponds and lots of animals.
Other Gardens: in addition there will be a number of other gardens opening.

Other Details: Home-baking and produce, bottle stall and many others

Directions: From city centre signed from Carlton Bingo at Allan Park. From south signed from St Ninian's Road. From west and north, signed from Drummond Place and Dunbarton Road.

Opening Times:
Sunday 6 May 1:00pm -
5:00pm

Admission:
£5.00 Children Free

Charities: Strathcarron Hospice receives 40%, the net remaining to SG Beneficiaries.

THE LINNS
Sheriffmuir, Dunblane FK15 0LP
Drs Evelyn and Lewis Stevens   Tel: 01786 822295
Email: evelyn@thelinns.org.uk

Disabled Access: None

A specialist collection of snowdrops. Open by arrangement on a first come first served basis as parking is limited.

Other Details: Snowdrop plants probably for sale.

Directions: Sheriffmuir by Dunblane, telephone for additional directions.

Opening Times:
Sunday 11 March 10:00am -
4:00pm

Admission:
£4.00 Children Free

Charities: Sophie North Charitable Trust receives 40%, the net remaining to SG Beneficiaries.

THE PASS HOUSE
Kilmahog, Callander FK17 8HD
Dr and Mrs D Carfrae
Email: carfraede@hotmail.com

Disabled Access: None

Well planted medium sized garden with steep banks down to swift river. Garden paths not steep. Camellias, rhododendrons, azaleas, alpines and shrubs. The Scotland's Gardens plaque awarded for 25 years of opening is on display.

Directions: 2 miles from Callander on A84 to Lochearnhead.

Opening Times:
Sunday 29 April 2:00pm -
5:00pm

Admission:
£4.00 Children Free

Charities: Crossroads receives 40%, the net remaining to SG Beneficiaries.

21 THORNHILL VILLAGE
The Gardens of Thornhill FK8 3QD
The Gardeners of Thornhill   Tel: 01786 841007
Email: Mor990@aol.com

Wester Corsehill FK8 3QD (Alyn Younie) A delightful garden, approached by a beech hedged driveway, created over the last twenty years when the house was built with extensive well stocked borders, lawns, vegetable garden and woodland.
Boghal FK8 3QD (Sir John and Lady MacMillan) Large farmhouse garden with borders flowing elegantly round from gable to gable of the house, nicely laid out shrub, perennial and woodland areas with fruit and vegetables.
24 Main Street FK8 3PN (Mrs Fiona MacDougall) This stunning village garden has densely planted double perennial borders, a mini potager, water feature and fruit trees, climbers over two arches.
57 Main Street FK8 3PJ (Mrs Margo Ritchie) Filled with colourful rhododendrons and azaleas this long narrow garden stretches from the Main Street down to the Common Grazing. Lots of interesting things to see.
Little Norrieston FK8 3QE (Tobin and Sue Duke) Delightful ecological garden. RHS plants for pollenators. Colours are important. Special planting for birds, bees and insects, trying to create a natural habitat. Pollen and nectar filled plants. Insect friendly, evolving garden.

Other Details: Various stalls at Norrieston Church Hall. The Rusty Strings will perform there at 4:00pm.

Directions: From A84 Stirling to Doune Road turn west on A873 towards Aberfoyle. On A811 signed from Kippen roundabout.

Disabled Access: Partial

Opening Times:
Sunday 27 May 1:00pm -
6:00pm

Admission:
£5.00 Children Free

Charities: Strathcarron Hospice receives 40%, the net remaining to SG Beneficiaries.

22 THORNTREE
Arnprior FK8 3EY
Mark and Carol Seymour   Tel: 01786 870710
Email: info@thorntreebarn.co.uk   www.thorntreebarn.co.uk

Charming country garden with flower beds around courtyard. Apple walk, fern garden and Saltire garden. Lovely views from Ben Lomond to Ben Ledi. Robin Morris a local bee keeper, will be available to answer your questions on bee keeping on 12 August and will have an inspection hive on display.

Directions: A811. In Arnprior take Fintry Road, Thorntree is second on right.

Disabled Access: Full

Opening Times:
Sunday 12 August 2:00pm -
5:00pm
Also by arrangement on request

Admission:
£4.00 Children Free

Charities: Riding for the Disabled receives 40%, the net remaining to SG Beneficiaries.

WEST PLEAN HOUSE
Denny Road, By Stirling FK7 8HA
Tony and Moira Stewart   Tel: 01786 812208
Email: moira@westpleanhouse.com   www.westpleanhouse.com

Woodland walks with snowdrops in February. Daffodil walk in April. Well established garden including site of iron age homestead and panoramic views over seven counties. Woodlands with mature rhododendrons, specimen trees, extensive lawns, shrubs and walled garden with variety of vegetables. Includes woodland walk with planting of azaleas and rhododendrons.

Directions: Leave all routes at Junction 9 roundabout where M9/M80 converge. Take A872 for Denny, go less than mile, turn left at house sign and immediately after lodge cottage. Carry on up drive.

Disabled Access: Full

Opening Times:
Sunday 26 February 1:00pm - 4:00pm
Sunday 15 April 2:00pm - 5:00pm

Admission:
February: £3.50 Children Free
April: £5.00 Children Free

Charities: Scottish Motor Neurone Disease Association receives 40%, the net remaining to SG Beneficiaries.

OPEN FOR DUNTREATH GARDEN SHOW

DUNTREATH CASTLE

A two day garden bonanza with lots to see and do and suitable for all ages.

See pages 16 and 17 for full details.

WIGTOWNSHIRE

Scotland's Gardens 2012 Guidebook is sponsored by **INVESTEC WEALTH & INVESTMENT**

District Organiser

Mrs Francis Brewis   Ardwell House, Stranraer DG9 9LY

Area Organisers

Mrs V Woseley Brinton   Chlenry, Castle Kennedy, Stranraer DG9 8SL
Mrs Andrew Gladstone   Craichlaw, Kirkcowan, Newton Stewart DG8 0DQ

Treasurer

Mr George Fleming   Ardgour, Stoneykirk, Stranraer DG9 9DL

Gardens open on a specific date

Kirkdale, Carsluith, Newton Stewart	Sunday 12 February	1:00pm	-	4:00pm
Dunskey Garden and Maze	Saturday 18 February	10.00am	-	4:00pm
Logan Botanic Garden, Port Logan, By Stranraer	Sunday 6 May	10:00am	-	5:00pm
Claymoddie Garden, Whithorn, Newton Stewart	Sunday 13 May	2:00pm	-	5:00pm
Glenwhan Gardens, Dunragit	Saturday 9 June	10:00am	-	5:00pm

Gardens open regularly

Ardwell House Gardens, Ardwell, Stranraer	1 April - 30 September	10:00am	-	5:00pm
Castle Kennedy & Gardens, Stranraer	4 February - 30 October	10:00am	-	5:00pm
Dunskey Garden and Maze	Easter - October Daily	10.00am	-	5.00pm
Claymoddie Garden, Whithorn, Newton Stewart	1 April - 30 September Fridays, Saturdays & Sundays	2:00pm	-	5:00pm
Glenwhan Gardens, Dunragit	1 April - 31 October	10:00am	-	5:00pm
Logan Botanic Garden, Port Logan, By Stranraer	1 March - 31 October	10:00am	-	5:00pm

Gardens open by arrangement

When organising a visit to a garden open by arrangement, please enquire if there are facilities and catering available

Castle Kennedy & Gardens, Stranraer	November - December	01581 400225
Claymoddie Garden, Whithorn, Newton Stewart	On request.	01988 500422
Craichlaw, Kirkcowan, Newton Stewart	On request.	01671 830208
Dunskey Garden and Maze	November - March	01776 810905

Key to symbols

New in 2012	**H** Homemade teas	**B&B** Accommodation
Teas	Dogs on a lead allowed	Plant stall
C Cream teas	Wheelchair access	Scottish Snowdrop Festival

SCOTTISH SNOWDROP FESTIVAL

Scotland's Gardens season starts with the popular Snowdrop Openings.

We are very keen to add more Snowdrop Gardens in 2013 so please let us know if you would like to share your snowdrops with us next year.

All our Snowdrop Gardens are listed on page 49

Garden locations

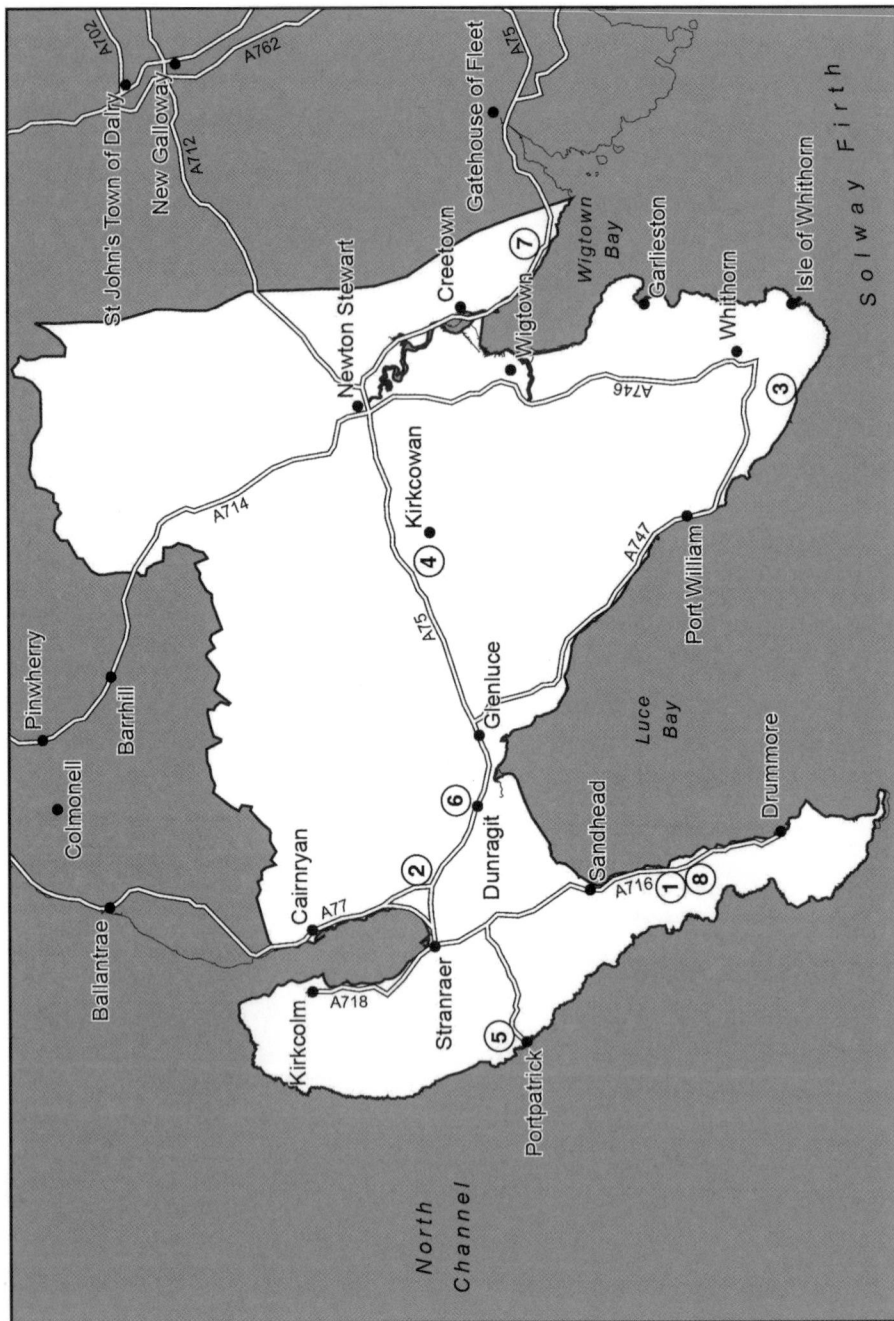

ARDWELL HOUSE GARDENS
Ardwell, Stranraer DG9 9LY
Mr and Mrs Francis Brewis

Daffodils, spring flowers, rhododendrons, flowering shrubs, coloured foliage and rock plants. Moist garden at smaller pond and a walk around larger ponds with views over Luce Bay. Collection Box. House not open.

Other Details: Self-pick fruit in season. Picnic site on shore.

Directions: A716 towards Mull of Galloway. Stranraer 10 miles.

Disabled Access: None

Opening Times:
1 April - 30 September
10:00am - 5:00pm

Admission:
£3.00, Concessions £2.00, Children under 14 Free.

Charities: Donation to SG Beneficiaries

CASTLE KENNEDY & GARDENS
Stranraer DG9 8RT
The Earl and Countess of Stair   Tel: 01581 400225

These famous 75 acre gardens of landscaped terraces and avenues are located on an isthmus surrounded by 2 large natural lochs. At one end the ruined Castle Kennedy overlooks a stunning herbaceous walled garden with Lochinch Castle at the other. Over 300 years of planting has created an impressive collection of rare trees, rhododendrons and exotic shrubs featuring many spectacular Champion Trees (tallest or largest of their type) with 6 British Champions, 11 Scottish and 25 for Dumfries & Galloway. Snowdrop walks, daffodils, spring flowers, rhododendrons and magnolia displays, tree trails and herbaceous borders make this a 'must visit' garden throughout the year.

Other Details: Charming tearoom serving homemade teas and light lunches.

Directions: On A75 5 miles east of Stranraer.

Disabled Access: Partial

Opening Times:
4 Feb - 31 Mar 10:00am - 5:00pm for Snowdrop Festival
1 Apr - 30 Oct 10:00am - 5:00pm
Also by arrangement Nov - Dec

Admission:
£5.00 Conc £3.00 Children £1.50 Disabled Free Families £11.00(2 adults & 3 Children).

Charities: Scots Guards Colonels Fund for Injured Soldiers and their Families receives 40%, the net remaining to SG Beneficiaries.

CLAYMODDIE GARDEN
Whithorn, Newton Stewart DG8 8LX
Mr and Mrs Robin Nicholson   Tel: 01988 500422

This romantic garden, developed over the last 40 years, with its backdrop of mature trees was designed by the owner, an enthusiastic plantsman. Imaginative hard and soft landscaping provides a wide range of settings, both shady a sunny, for a mass of meticulously placed plants, both old favourites and exotic species, all helped by the proximity of the Gulf Stream. Running through the lower part of the garden is the burn which feeds the pond, all newly planted. There are changes in levels, but most of the garden is accessible to wheelchairs.

Other Details: All plants in the nursery shop are propagated from the garden. Teas available on Sunday 13 May only.

Directions: Claymoddie is off the A746, 2 miles south of Whithorn.

Disabled Access: Partial

Opening Times:
Sunday 13 May 2:00pm - 5:00pm
1 April - 30 September - Fridays, Saturdays & Sundays 2:00pm - 5:00pm
Also open by arrangement.

Admission:
£3.00 Children under 14 Free

Charities: Macmillan Cancer Support receives 40%, the net remaining to SG Beneficiaries.

CRAICHLAW
Kirkcowan, Newton Stewart DG8 0DQ
Mr and Mrs A Gladstone   Tel: 01671 830208

Formal garden with herbaceous borders around the house. Set in extensive grounds with lawns, lochs and woodland. A path around the main loch leads to a water garden returning past an orchard of old Scottish apple varieties.

Directions: Signposted off A75, 8 miles west of Newton Stewart, and B733 one mile west of Kirkcowan.

Disabled Access: Partial

Opening Times:
By arrangement on request

Admission:
£4.00 Concessions £3.00
Children under 14 Free

Charities: Donation to SG Beneficiaries

DUNSKEY GARDEN AND MAZE
Portpatrick, Stranraer DG9 8TJ
Mr & Mrs Edward Orr Ewing   Tel:01776 810905
Email: garden@dunskey.com   www.dunskey.com

From the swathes of snowdrops in late winter through the tapestry of flowers and the warm glowing colours of autumn, there is always something to see in these relaxed gardens. Plant enthusiasts will be fascinated by the wide range of flora. The working Mackenzie and Moncur glasshouses in the 17th century walled garden house exotic plants and fruit. There is a simple tree spotting game through the woodland gardens past the lochs. The maze, probably the first planted in southwest Scotland is fun for all the family.

Other Details: There are no facilities available November - March. Dogs are allowed on the walks but not allowed in the walled garden, shaded dog parking. Disabled loos and mobility scooter. Plants for sale all raised at Dunskey. NCCPG collection of Clianthus and Sutherlandia. Seasons Tearoom for light lunches and teas.

Directions: 1 mile from Portpatrick on B738 off A77.

Disabled Access: Partial

Opening Times:
Sat 18 February 10:00am - 4:00pm for Scotland's Gardens
19, 25 & 26 February 10:00am - 4:00pm
Easter - October daily 10:00am - 5:00pm
Also by arrangement on request

Admission:
February: £3.60 Children 50p
Other dates: £4.60 Concession
£4.00 Children over 14 £2.00

Charities: On 18 Feb all proceeds to SG Beneficiaries.

GLENWHAN GARDENS
Dunragit, By Stranraer DG9 8PH
Mr and Mrs W Knott

Glenwhan Garden has been described as one of the best newly created gardens in recent times. 25 years ago there was nothing but bracken, gorse and willows but careful planting has created a 12 acre garden filled with glorious collections of plants from around the world. There is colour in all seasons and the winding paths, well placed seats, sculptures and water all add to the tranquil atmosphere. There is a 17 acre moorland wildflower walk, the chance to see red squirrels and magnificent views over Luce Bay, the Mull of Galloway and the Isle of Man.

Other Details: No dogs allowed in the garden but dog walk available. Shop. Tea room.

Directions: 7 miles east of Stranraer, 1 mile off A75 at Dunragit (follow signs).

Disabled Access: None

Opening Times:
Saturday 9 June 10:00am - 5:00pm
1 April - 31 October 10:00am - 5:00pm

Admission:
£4.50 Children £1.50 Family £10.00 Concessions £3.50
Season Ticket £15.00.

Charities: World Wildlife Fund receives 40%, the net remaining to SG Beneficiaries.

KIRKDALE
Carsluith, Newton Stewart DG8 7EA
Mr & Mrs Neil Hannay

Fabulous woodland snowdrop walks around historic 18th century property. A chance to view the only working water driven sawmill in South of Scotland and nature trail.

Directions: On A75 six miles west of Gatehouse of Fleet. Signposted Cairnholy Chambered Cairn.

Disabled Access: Partial

Opening Times:
Sunday 12 February 1:00pm - 4:00pm for Snowdrop Festival

Admission:
£3.00 Children Free

Charities: Homestart, Wigtownshire receives 40%, the net remaining to SG Beneficiaries.

LOGAN BOTANIC GARDEN
Port Logan, By Stranraer DG9 9ND
The Royal Botanic Gardens Edinburgh
www.rbge.org.uk

At the south western tip of Scotland lies Logan which is unrivalled as the country's most exotic garden. With a mild climate washed by the Gulf Stream, a remarkable collection of bizarre and beautiful plants, especially from the southern hemisphere, flourish out of doors. Enjoy the colourful walled garden with its magnificent tree ferns, palms and borders along with the contrasting woodland garden with its unworldly gunnera bog. Explore the Discovery Centre or take an audio tour.

Other Details: Home baking, Botanic shop, discovery centre, guided tours.

Directions: 10 miles south of Stranraer on A716 then 2½ miles from Ardwell village.

Disabled Access: Partial

Opening Times:
Sunday 6 May 10:00am - 5:00pm
1 March - 31 October 10:00am - 5:00pm

Admission:
£4.00 Concessions £3.50
Children £1.00 Family £9.00

Charities: Royal Botanic Garden, Edinburgh receives 40%, the net remaining to SG Beneficiaries.

GARDENS INDEX

1 Burnside Cottages, Sundrum	105	Attadale	242
1 Standpretty	209	Auchmacoy	76
2 Houstoun Gardens	149	Auchmar	257
5 Rubislaw Den North	75	Avonmuir House	257
8 Laggary Park	134	Baitlaws	198
9 Braid Farm Road	150	Balcaskie (in conjunction with Kellie Castle)	162
10 Pilton Drive North	149	Balmeanach House	243
15 Linkshouse (in conjunction with Fernbank)	120	Balmerino Abbey	162
20 Smithycroft	198	Barguillean's "Angus Garden"	97
23 Don Street	75	Barham	162
31 Kings Road	236	Barr Village Gardens	105
42 Fife Street	213	Barshaw Park Walled Garden	236
45 Northfield Crescent	150	Benmore Botanic Garden	97
61 Fountainhall Road	150	Bents Green	213
101 Greenbank Crescent	149	Biggar Park	198
123 Waterfoot Row	174	Birch Garden	120
Aberarder (Joint opening with Ardverikie)	204	Birkhill Castle	163
Abriachan Garden Nursery	242	Blair Castle Gardens	226
Achnacloich	95	Blair House (in conjuntion with Oakleigh Bank)	191
Achnacloich (Joint opening with Croftcat)	225	Blairwood House	76
Acres of Keillour	225	Blebo Craigs Village Gardens	163
Airlie Castle	87	Bolfracks	226
Alford Village Gardens	75	Borgue Parish Gardens	191
Amat	114	Bowerhouse	141
An Cala	95	Brackla Wood	243
Anton's Hill and Walled Garden	111	Braco Castle	227
Applecross Walled Garden	242	Bradystone House	227
Ardchapel and Seven The Birches	134	Branklyn	227
Ardchattan Priory	95	Brechin Castle	87
Ard-Daraich	204	Bridge of Allan Gardens	258
Ardgowan	236	Briglands House	228
Ardkinglas Woodland Garden	96	Brodick Castle & Country Park	178
Ardlussa House Garden	96	Brodie Castle	213
Ardmaddy Castle	96	Broomieknowe Gardens	209
Ardtornish	204	Broughton House Garden	191
Arduaine	97	Broughton Place Farmhouse	219
Ardverikie (Joint opening with Aberarder)	205	Bruckhills Croft	76
Ardvorlich	225	Bughtrig	111
Ardwell House Gardens	269	Burnbrae	258
Arndean	257	Burravoe	120

Cally Gardens	192	Dalfruin	88
Camallt	259	Dalswinton House	128
Cambo House	163	Danevale Park	193
Canna House Walled Garden	205	Dawyck Botanic Garden	219
Caol Ruadh	98	Dean Gardens and Belgrave Crescent	151
Caprington Castle	106	Delvine	229
Cardon	243	Dippoolbank Cottage	200
Carestown Steading	214	Dirleton Village	141
Carmichael Mill	199	Dougarie	178
Carnell	106	Douneside House	183
Carolside	157	Doune Village	259
Carruth	237	Dowhill	229
Castle Fraser	77	Drim na Vullin	99
Castle Kennedy & Gardens	269	Dr Neil's Garden	151
Castleview	214	Druimneil House	99
Ceres Village Gardens	164	Drum Castle	183
Claddagh	174	Drumlithie Village	184
Clan Donald Skye	244	Drummond Castle Gardens	230
Claymoddie Garden	269	Drumpark	128
Cleghorn	199	Dundonnell House	244
Cloan	228	Dunecht House Gardens	77
Cluny House	228	Dunninald	88
Coiltie Garden	244	Dunskey Garden and Maze	270
Conaglen	205	Duntreath Castle	260
Corbet Tower	251	Dunvegan Castle and Gardens	245
Corsock House	192	Earlshall Castle	165
Cortachy Castle	87	Easter Meikle Fardle	230
Cousland Smiddy and Village Gardens	209	Ecclesgreig Castle	184
Cowhill Tower	128	Edzell Village & Castle	88
Craichlaw	270	Esslemont	78
Crail: Small Gardens in the Burgh	164	Explorers Garden	230
Crarae Garden	98	Fairwinds	100
Crathes Castle	183	Falkland Palace and Garden	165
Crathes Castle Events	181	Falkland's Small Gardens	165
Crinan Hotel Garden	98	Fernbank (in conjuction with 15 Linkshouse)	121
Croftcat Lodge	229	Field House	245
Crofts	192	Fife Diamond Garden Festival	166
Crossburn	174	Findrack	184
Cruickshank Botanic Gardens	77	Fingask Castle	231
Cruisdale	121	Finzean House	185
Cuddy's Well	214	Flagstone Village Gardens	114
Culbuie	259	Floors Castle	251
Culross Palace	164	Fyvie Castle	78
Culter Allers	199	Gagie House	89
Culzean	106	Gallery	89
Dal an Eas and Dalnaneun	99	Gardens of West Kilbride and Seamill	107

Gargunnock House	260	Kellie Castle (in conjunction with Balcaskie)	167
Gean House	260	Kevock Garden	210
Geilston Garden	134	Kew Terrace Secret Gardens	175
Gerdi	121	Kilarden	135
Gifford Village	141	Kilbryde Castle	261
Glassmount House	166	Kildrummy Castle Gardens	80
Glenarn	135	Kilsyth Gardens	175
Glenarn Plant Sale	135	Kincardine	186
Glenbervie House	185	Kinghorn Village Gardens	168
Glendoick	231	Kinlochlaich House Gardens	100
Glenearn	232	Kirkdale	271
Glen House	219	Kirkside of Lochty	89
Glenkindie House	78	Kirkton House	90
Glenkyllachy Lodge	206	Knock Cottage	101
Glensone Walled Garden	193	Knowes End	237
Glenwhan Gardens	270	Lands of Loyal Hotel	232
Gordonstoun	215	Langwell	115
Grandhome	79	Lanrick	261
Greenbank Garden	175	Largs Open Gardens	107
Greenhead Farmhouse	167	Laundry Cottage	80
Greenridge	79	Lawton House	90
Greywalls	142	Lea Gardens	123
Grovehill House	129	Leathad Ard	247
Halmyre Mains	220	Leckmelm Shrubbery & Arboretum	247
Harmony Garden (Joint with Priorwood Gardens)	157	Leith Hall	81
Hatton Castle	79	Lennel Bank	111
Haystoun	220	Letham Village	90
Highlands	122	Linn Botanic Gardens	136
Hill Cottage	237	Logan Botanic Garden	271
Hillockhead	80	Malleny Garden	152
Hill of Tarvit Plant Sale and Autumn Fair	167	Mansefield	81
Holla	122	Megginch Castle	232
Holmes Farm	107	Merchiston Cottage	152
Holmlea	122	Mill of Benholm Project	186
House of Aigas and Field Centre	245	Mill Road Allotments	215
House of Gruinard	246	Milltown Community Gardens	186
House of Tongue	114	Milseybank	261
Hugh Miller's Museum & Birthplace Cottage	246	Milton House	136
Humbie Dean	142	Monteviot	251
Hunter's Tryst	151	Montrose and Hillside Gardens	91
Inchmarlo House Garden	185	Moray Place & Bank Gardens	152
Inveraray Castle Gardens	100	National Records of Scotland	153
Inveresk Village	142	Newcastleton Village Gardens & Floral Festival	252
Inverewe	246	Newhall	210
Inwood	143	New Lanark Roof Garden	200
Kailzie Gardens	220	Newliston	153

Newtonairds Lodge	129	Stratholm	102
Nonavaar	123	Sundrum	176
Norby	123	Tayfield (In Conjunction with Willowhill)	170
Novar	247	Tayport Gardens	170
Oakbank	101	Teasses Gardens	170
Oakleigh Bank (with Blair House)	193	The Burn House & The Burn Garden House	187
Old Inzievar House	168	The Castle & Gardens of Mey	116
Parkhead	136	The Garth	130
Parkhead House	233	The Kilmichael Hotel	179
Park House	262	The Linns	263
Pentland Firth Gardens	115	The Lookout	248
Pilmuir House	143	The Old Mill	130
Pitcurran House	233	The Old Playground	124
Pitmedden Garden	81	The Old Sun Inn	210
Pitmuies Gardens	91	The Pass House	263
Pitscurry Project	82	The Scots Mining Company House	200
Ploughman's Hall	82	The Shore Villages	102
Portrack House	129	The Shrubbery	91
Priorwood Gardens (Joint with Harmony Garden)	157	The Tower	171
Quarriers Village Gardens	238	The Waterhouse Gardens at Stockarton	194
Ralia Lodge and Milton Lodge	206	Thornhill Village	264
Redcroft	153	Thorntree	264
Rocheid Garden	154	Threave Garden	195
Ross Priory	137	Tillypronie	82
Rowberrow	262	Toam	124
Sailean Cottage	248	Traquair	221
Settie	262	Tyninghame House	144
SG Hill House Plant Sale	137	U.R.G.E.	125
SG Plant Sale at St Fillan's Episcopal Church	238	Wellbutts	201
SG Spring Plant Sale at St Andrews Botanic Garden	168	Wester Cloquhat	233
Shangri-La	124	Westfield Lodge	83
Shepherd House	143	Westhall Castle	83
Skeldon	108	West Leas	252
Sma' Shot Cottages Heritage Centre	238	West Linton Village Gardens	221
Southwick House	194	West Plean House	265
Southwood and 1 laurel hill place	263	Willowhill (in Conjunction with Tayfield)	171
Springpark House	115	Winton House	145
Stenton Village	144	Woodview	248
St Mary's Road and Fernie Gardens	169	Wormistoune House	171
St. Monans Village Gardens	169	Yetholm Village Gardens	253
Stobo Japanese Water Garden	221		
Stobshiel House	144		
Stockarton	194		
Strabane	178		
Strachur House Flower & Woodland Gardens	101		
Strathmiglo Village Gardens	169		

INDEX OF ADVERTISERS

Alastair Sawdays	31
Bennybeg Plant Centre	40
Blair Castle, Atholl Estates	36
Bonhams	37
Brightwater Holidays	Back cover, 13
British Plant Nursery Guide	41
Castle of Mey	35
Cheshire's Gardens	29
Chest, Heart & Stroke Scotland	45
Corney & Barrow (Scotland) Ltd	25
Damhead Nursery	47
David Welch Winter Gardens	48
Dobbies Garden Centres	27
Duntreath Castle Garden Show	16, 17
Erskine Garden Centre	39
Gardening Scotland 2012	28
Gardens Etc.	30
Garden Solutions	44
Houses for Hens	44
Inchmarlo	38
Investec	6
James Byatt, Garden & Estate Cartographer	36
Jamesfield Garden Centre	40
Lycetts	Inside front cover
Macallan	Inside back cover
Munro Greenhouses	45
Nairn Brown	33
National Gardens Scheme	30
National Trust for Scotland	26, 43
New Hopetoun Gardens	40
Open Gardens Australia	32
Perennial	12
Plant Heritage	35
Quercus Garden Plants	41
Royal Botanic Garden Edinburgh	34, 46
Terra Firma Gardens	42
The Garden Conservancy	32
The Nomads Tent	42
Turcan Connell	24
Woodbury Estate	48

OUR GUIDE FOR 2013

ORDER NOW
and your copy will be posted
to you on publication in December 2012.

Send order to:

Scotland's Gardens, 42a North Castle Street, Edinburgh EH2 3BN

Please send me _____ copy / copies of **Our Guide for 2013**,

price £7.25, to include postage and packing, as soon as it is available.

I enclose a cheque / postal order made payable to Scotland's Gardens.

Name   _____

Address   _____

             _____

Postcode   _____

Copies of Our Guide for 2013 may also be purchased on our website:
www.scotlandsgardens.org

NOTES

WOULD YOU LIKE TO OPEN YOUR GARDEN FOR CHARITY?

If you would
like information on how
to open your garden for charity
please write to us
at the address below,
call 0131 226 3714
or email info@scotlandsgardens.org

We welcome gardens large and small and also groups of gardens.

To: Scotland's Gardens, 42a North Castle Street, Edinburgh EH2 3BN

Please send me more information about opening my garden for charity.

Name

Address

Postcode   Tel

Email

NOTES